Ramism in William Perkins' Theology

Donald K. McKim

Ramism in
William Perkins' Theology

WIPF & STOCK · Eugene, Oregon

Wipf and Stock Publishers
199 W 8th Ave, Suite 3
Eugene, OR 97401

Ramism in William Perkins' Theology
By McKim, Donald K.
Copyright©1987 by McKim, Donald K.
ISBN 13: 978-1-4982-8512-4
Publication date 3/19/2017
Previously published by Peter Lang Publishing, 1987

Dedicated to the memory of Ford Lewis Battles:
Doctor Ecclesiae
Scholar, Teacher, Churchman and Friend

TABLE OF CONTENTS

Preface ... ix
Introduction ... 1

Part I **WILLIAM PERKINS**

Chapter I. Life and Work of William Perkins ... 5

    A. Life of Perkins ... 5
    B. Perkins and English Puritanism ... 8
    C. Perkins and Calvinism ... 11
    D. Perkins' Influence ... 12

Part II **PETER RAMUS**

Chapter II. Life and Work of Peter Ramus ... 15

    A. Life of Ramus ... 15
    B. Reform of Education ... 17
    C. Reform of Logic ... 19
    D. Ramus' Logic ... 21
        1. Nature of Dialectic ... 22
        2. Art of Dialectic ... 22
        3. Use of Dialectic ... 24
        4. Revisions ... 24
    E. Ramus and Method ... 25
    F. Ramus and Rhetoric ... 33
    G. Ramus and the Art of Memory ... 33

Part III **RAMISM**

Chapter III. Transmission of Ramism in Great Britain ... 37

    A. Roland MacIlmaine ... 37
    B. Scotland ... 39
    C. Controversies ... 39
    D. English Logics ... 40
    E. Oxford ... 42
    F. Cambridge ... 43

Part IV **RAMISM IN WILLIAM PERKINS**

Chapter IV. Ramism in Perkins' Earliest Works ... 51

    A. Polemical Works ... 51
    B. Theological Works ... 59

Chapter V. Ramism in Perkins' Exegetical Works 69

    A. Biblical Commentaries 69
    B. The Arte of Prophecying 80

Chapter VI. Ramism in Perkins' Later Works 93

    A. Theological Works 93
    B. Cases of Conscience 96
    C. Polemical Works 103
    D. Works on Christian Life, Ministry, and Vocation 108
    E. Summary 116

Part V. **SIGNIFICANCE OF RAMISM IN WILLIAM PERKINS**

Chapter VII. Importance of Perkins' Use of Ramism 119

    A. Perkins' Legacy through his Students 119
    B. Theology and Ethics 121
    C. Educational Tool 122
    D. Plain Style Preaching 126
    E. Art of Memory 128
    F. Biblical Interpretation 129
    G. Philosophical Implications 130

Appendices

    A. A Short History of Logic 137
    B. A Short History of the Art of Memory 147
    C. The Spread of Ramism 148
    D. Chronology of Perkins' Works 149

Notes 151

Bibliography 235

PREFACE

I was first introduced to Peter Ramus through the doctoral dissertation of my former teacher at Westminster College, New Wilmington, Pennsylvania, Dr. Jack B. Rogers. In *Scripture in the Westminister Confession*, Rogers pointed to the impact of the Ramist logic on the framers of the Westminster Confession of Faith. His contention was that this was an important background influence to be understood when examining that document's doctrine of Scripture.

I was introduced to William Perkins through my study of English Puritanism with Dr. Robert S. Paul at Pittsburgh Theological Seminary. There and in my doctoral research at the Seminary and the University of Pittsburgh I was able to work on both Ramus and Perkins.

The facilities of the Barbour Library at Pittsburgh Seminary and the Hillman Library at the University of Pittsburgh were excellent resources. The Henry E. Huntington Library in San Marino, California permitted me to use its marvelous collection of sources for a period of time. To the staffs of these institutions I am grateful.

My gratitude also extends to the parishioners of Friendship Presbyterian Parish, Slippery Rock, Pennsylvania. The people of the West Liberty, Wolf Creek and Bethel churches for which I had been Stated Supply Pastor were indulgent of the demands of my time and cared for me as a student and pastor for some ten years as research and writing progressed on this and other projects.

I thank my parents Keith and Mary McKim for years of nurture and encouragement. They have guided and helped me in countless ways.

Dr. Jack Rogers has been a teacher, colleague and friend beyond compare. He introduced me to the joys of scholarship and has continued to honor the worth of my work in many supportive ways. Our relationship has been one of the deepest delights of my life.

I would like to thank too those who particularly helped this work on its way. Dr. Robert S. Paul of Austin Presbyterian Theological Seminary has been a respected teacher and friend. Dr. Paul's knowledge and affection for the study of Puritanism has been contagious and a real motivation for me. His insights have always been most welcomed and never ceased to be fruitful avenues for research. Dr. Richard H. Wilmer, Jr. supported me in every way. His careful concern was matched only by his graciousness as a person and his grasp of the history of the Elizabethan period. Dr. Hugh F. Kearney was a stimulating teacher. Our conversations gave me much to work on and contemplate. Dr. Charles B. Partee offered helpful suggestions and has become a valued friend.

My wife LindaJo and our sons Stephen and Karl have been joys. They provide loving support so crucial to work and to life itself. My debts to them are great indeed.

My thanks extend to the University of Dubuque Theological Seminary and Dean Arlo D. Duba for many forms of aid and for a grant to help make publication possible. Mr. Thomas Smith gave careful attention to many details. Mr. Richard Shaffer provided significant help in readying the figures for publication.

This study is offered to the memory of Dr. Ford Lewis Battles. Dr. Battles was a distinguished scholar, teacher and churchman. But even more, he was a man of compassion and concern for his students. Dr. Battles supported my endeavors wholeheartedly throughout my seminary years and on through my work on this project. He was an important resource for me in many ways until he died in November, 1979. Dr. Battles' death left us all greatly saddened. But his life challenged us to use the gifts we've been given and to carry out the concerns he embodied. It is to this task that the following labor is dedicated.

ABBREVIATIONS

General Works

CR	*Corpus Reformatorum*, eds. C.G. Bretschneider and H.E. Bindseil (Hale, 1834-1860)
DNB	*Dictionary of National Biography*, eds. Leslie Stephen and Sydney Lee
EP	Patrick Collinson, *The Elizabethan Puritan Movement*
GFPM	Robert Kingdon, *Geneva and the Consolidation of the French Protestant Movement*
HP	Frederick Copleston, *A History of Philosophy* (9 vols.)
IO	Christopher Hill, *Intellectual Origins of the English Revolution*
"Introduction"	Walter J. Ong, "Introduction" to Ramus, *Scholae liberales artes* (1970)
L&R	Wilbur S. Howell, *Logic and Rhetoric in England 1500-1700*
L&T	Ian Breward, "The Life and Theology of William Perkins 1558-1602," Diss. University of Manchester, 1963
NEM	Perry Miller, *The New England Mind The Seventeenth Century*
ODC	*Oxford Dictionary of the Christian Church*, eds. F.L. Cross and E.A. Livingstone, 2nd ed. (1974)
RAMUS	Walter J. Ong, *Ramus, Method and the Decay of Dialogue*
RTI	Walter J. Ong, *Ramus and Talon Inventory*
STC	*A Short-Title Catalogue of Books Printed in England, Scotland, and Ireland 1475-1640*, compiled by Alfred W. Pollard and G.R. Redgrave
WAT	Lee W. Gibbs, *William Ames Technometry*
WORK	*The Work of William Perkins*, ed. Ian Breward, Courtenay Library of Reformation Classics
WORKS	*The Workes of that Famous and Worthy Minister of Christ in the Vniuersitie of Cambridge*, Mr. William Perkins, 3 vols. (1616-1618)

Ramus' Works

Arist. anim.	*Aristotelicae animadversiones* (1543)

Commentariorum	*Commentariorum de religione Christiana, libri quatuor* (1576)
Dial. A. Talaei pr. ill.	*Dialecticae libri duo, Audomari Talaei praelectionibus illustrati* (1569)
Dial. inst.	*Dialecticae institutiones* (1543)
Dialectici comm. tres.	*Dialectici commentarii tres authore* (Audomaro Taleo editi (1546)
Dunn, ed.	*The Logike of Peter Ramus*, trans. Roland MacIlmaine, ed. Catherine M. Dunn
Pro phil. disc.	*Pro Philosophica Parisiensis Academiae Disciplini* in *Scholae in liberales artes* (1569)
Sch. dial.	*Scholae Dialecticae* in *Scholae in liberales artes* (1569)
Sch. in lib. arts	*Scholae in liberales artes* (1569)

INTRODUCTION

The importance of the French philosopher Pierre de la Ramee (1515-1572; Peter Ramus) for sixteenth and seventeenth century English and American Puritanism was established in the 1930's.[1] Perry Miller perceived that the logic of Ramus was joined with the theologies of Augustine and John Calvin to form a basis for Puritan intellectual endeavors. According to Miller, the philosophy of Ramus gave Puritanism a mighty concern for logic. It forged Puritan views of nature. It fashioned Puritan choices in literary styles. And it explains Puritan views of the knowledge process or epistemology.[2]

A reawakening of interest in the work of Ramus was sparked by the writings of Walter J. Ong in the 1950's. His two major works, *Ramus, Method, and the Decay of Dialogue* and *Ramus and Talon Inventory* along with numerous articles are said to have "revolutionized Ramist studies."[3] Ong located Ramus in the intellectual tradition of international humanism. He described Ramus as

> a man of the sixteenth century, and he is eminently a man concerned with language, and the traditional arts of expression, grammar, rhetoric, and logic. As the first and only professor of eloquence and philosophy at what was later to be called the Collège de France, he was a kind of humanist-scholastic who stood on the middle ground between linguistics & metaphysics.[4]

Ong's catalogue of editions of Ramus' works evidence how widely spread the thought of Ramus was distributed. Some 750 separately published editions of single or collected works by Ramus or his associate Amdomarus Talaeus (ca. 1510-1562; Omer Talon) were found. Some 1100 separate printings of individual works were located, most having been done between 1550 and 1650.[5]

The works of Miller and other writing about the same time, also highlighted the thought of one of the most influential English Purtians, William Perkins (1558-1602).[6] Perkins, described by William Haller as "a man of brilliant intellect and potent speech," played a significant part in the development of the Puritan movement in and around Cambridge at the end of the sixteenth century.[7] Perkins was a Fellow of Christ's College of the University of Cambridge and gained the respect of a large number of students through his teaching. Many of his students went on to become leaders in the Puritan effort to reform the Church of England spiritually in the seventeenth century.[8] Perkins as a preacher attracted crowds after his direct association with the University was over. His collected works circulated widely in England and America after his death.

But while the connection between Ramus and the Puritans is well known and while Perkins is widely known as a leading Puritan theologian, there is not a complete study of the influence of Peter Ramus on William Perkins. Keith L. Sprunger has clearly demonstrated how Ramus stood behind the work of William Ames (1576-1633), a pupil of Perkins' and called the "learned doctor" of Puritanism.[9] But no one has thoroughly examined the works of Perkins to see to what extent they are influenced by the philosophy and logic of Ramus. It is the purpose of this study to do that.

There have been various fleeting references to the influence of Ramus on Perkins. But none of these are based on a thorough analysis. Miller said: "We can hardly doubt he [Perkins] was a disciple of Ramus."[10] Miller found confirmation of this hypothesis in that Perkins was at Cambridge University in the 1590's when Ramism was prominent there. Also, he said, Perkins' vocabulary and the internal evidence of Perkins' work on preaching, *The Art of Prophecying,* leads to the belief that "certainly, if Perkins was not wholly guided by Ramus, he must have been strongly influenced" by Ramus.[11]

When Perkins' *Art of Prophecying* was examined by Wilbur Samuel Howell in Logic and Rhetoric in England, 1500-1700, a work which dealt extensively with the spread of Ramism in England, Howell concluded that Perkins "derives his doctrine from sources closer to Ciceronian rhetoric and scholastic logic than to the logic and rhetoric of Ramus."[12] Howell pointed out that Perkins had not listed Ramus as one of the sources from which his work on preaching was drawn. The structure of the work, however, led Howell to say that Perkins "must be regarded as a traditionalist in respect to most of his subject matter, and as a Ramist only in respect to method of presentation and to a few points of doctrine." Thus Perkins, according to Howell, was "not a thoroughgoing disciple of that master" (Ramus).[13]

Other scholars accepted Howell's conclusion. They judged the Ramism in Perkins from Howell's comments on *The Art of Prophecying*. For example, H.C. Porter in this study of the Cambridge Puritans, cited Howell and said: "It would appear that the importance of the influence of the language and method of Peter Ramus on the Cambridge Puritans can be exaggerated."[14] Ian Breward, author of a thorough description of Perkins' theological thought as well as editor of an abridge edition of some of Perkins' works, echoed Howell's language about Ramus and Perkins, Breward wrote:

> He was by no means a slavish disciple of Ramus, only occasionally using ramist terms....Perkins made use of ramist methods to present his material when he thought it would serve his purpose....The influence of Ramus on Perkins can be described as important, though its main impact was on Perkins' methods of presentation, rather than on the content of his thought.[15]

Ong listed Perkins as a "Semi-Ramist."[16] Sprunger, while classifying him with other Ramist teachers at Cambridge, also referred to him as "at least half a Ramist."[17]

The thesis of the following work is that Perkins' allegiance to Ramus was more widespread and deeper than has been realized. Perkins' use of Ramism was not limited to only one work or to a few. This study shows that Perkins used the methods of Ramus to order nearly all his published works. His debt to the Ramist philosophy was substantial and real. As this study indicates, Ramism was attractive to Perkins (and other Puritans) for a number of reasons. It was not simply a good method to use for the preparation of a sermon and nothing else. Perkins found Ramist teachings applicable to many areas of his theological enterprise. Ramism served him on a number of fronts. This study of his works shows that while at times his treatises were written elaborately, with many definitions and divisions -- these in themselves were part of a large Ramist plan for the organization and presentation of discourses (both oral and written). Individual components in Perkins' works fit together systematically to form a discourse constructed according to the method advocated by Ramus. John G. Rechtien pointed to this but did not elaborate when he wrote that "like his other treatises, Perkins' *Art of Prophecying* exemplifies prose written according to Ramist method."[18] The following study now makes it possible to see how thoroughly Perkins used Ramist method. The finding is that Perkins' use of Ramism was thorough indeed.

The study proceeds as follows. Part I describes William Perkins in terms of his life and work. While Perkins himself did not like the term "Puritan," his zeal for reform of the Church of England and his association with those of like concern make this a proper designation for him.[19] Perkins' urge for renewal, however, never led him to separate from the established Church or to advocate publicly a specific form of church government. Perkins' relationship to the Puritan movement is discussed as well as his theological adherence to the emerging Calvinism of that time. This part concludes with a description of Perkins' influence as a theologian and preacher both in England and in New England.

Part II presents the life and work of Peter Ramus. Ramus' goals for the reform of education and logic are outlined here. To set these reforms in a wider context, an Appendix is provided to trace the historical development of the study of logic prior to Ramus. Ramus is seen reacting against the technical and linguistic study of logic advocated by scholastic logicians who styled themselves "Aristotelians." His sympathies were much stronger with the reforms of logic advocated by Humanists such as Lorenzo Valla and Rudolph Agricola. Ramus built on their work to develop his own approach to logic. This part focuses on the major components of Ramus' reform of logic. The prime elements in this approach were the nature, art, and use of dialectic (logic). They expressed themselves in logical discourse by "method." Method became the dominant feature in the Ramist reform. Developments in method prior to Ramus as well as his own teachings on the subject are discussed in this part of the study. The relationship of Ramus to rhetoric, the counterpart of logic according to the ancients, is explored. This part of the study concludes with an exposition of the teachings of Ramus on the art of memory. An Appendix is provided to give additional background on the history of this topic. As is later shown, the art of memory was an important bridge between Ramus and William Perkins.

In Part III, the transmission of Ramism into Great Britain is examined. An Appendix notes the spread of Ramism on the European continent. Primary emphasis here, however, is on how the teachings of Ramus reached and radiated through Scotland and England. Logical textbooks written prior to the influx of Ramism are described. Particular attention is given to the reception of the Ramist philosophy at the two English universities, Oxford and Cambridge. Cambridge was where the strongon the history of this topic. As is later shown, the art of memory was an important bridge between Ramus and William Perkins.

In Part III, the transmission of Ramism into Great Britain is examined. An Appendix notes the spread of Ramism on the European continent. Primary emphasis here, however, is on how the teachings of Ramus reached and radiated through Scotland and England. Logical textbooks written prior to the influx of Ramism are described. Particular attention is given to the reception of the Ramist philosophy at the two English universities, Oxford and Cambridge. Cambridge was where the stronger tradition of Ramism developed. A major portion of this part is therefore devoted to a description of the significant Cambridge Ramists prior to or contemporaneous with William Perkins' residency at the University.

At this point it is possible to deal with the specific question of the influence of Ramism in Perkins' works. Part IV is thus divided into three chapters which trace Perkins' works chronologically. The grouping of his works in each of these chapters reflect the broad area of interest which he held. His earliest works (chapter IV) were polemical (against astrologers chiefly) and theological in the sense reflected by a catechism and a work of systematic theology *(A Golden Chaine)*. A major portion of Perkins' pieces were expositions of Scripture in the form of Biblical commentaries and exegetical works. These are discussed in chapter V along with an analysis of *The Arte of Prophecying* in which Perkins dealt with hermeneutics as well as with method for preaching. Chapter VI focuses on the various topics of Perkins' later works--theology, cases of conscience, polemics, and works on Christian vocation and ministry. The approach taken has been chronological throughout insofar so that is possible.

Part V of this study purposes some areas of significance for which the Ramist philosophy served Perkins. Initially it is noted that the effects of Perkins' Ramism were transmitted through his students. Of particular importance here was William Ames who developed the implications of Ramism more explicitly than Perkins his teacher. Further importance of Ramism for Perkins and the Puritans was in that it helped them preserve a unity of theology and ethics. Ramism also functioned as a powerful educational tool. It contributed to the development of plain style preaching. It had something to say abou the art of memory as well as serving as a framework for Biblical interpretation. All of these are examined in chapter VII and final remarks are made about the philosophical implications of Ramism for the Puritans.

This study analyzes each of Perkins' treatises. It provides some historical framework for their investigation by setting their contexts as to specific issues or controversies which caused Perkins to address a certain subject. Yet the study does not give a complete description of Perkins' theology. It does not provide a detailed outline of the contents of his works. The focus is specifically on "Ramism in William Perkins." A description of the theological method Perkins used for his treatises is presented. In nearly every instance, Perkins dealt with his subject by using the logical method of Ramus as his controling framework. This methodology stand in direct contrast to that of other theological contemporaries of Perkins. These were Protestants who more closely followed the practices of medieval scholastic logicians.

The overall structure of Perkins' treatises is presented and appendices provided so that visual structure of his method becomes clear. To see Perkins' writings in this light is to see that there was a definite plan and procedure at work in the construction of his pieces. Without an awareness of the Ramist format, one would have no conception of how Perkins' divisions were made and how the constituent parts of his works fit together. With no knowledge of Ramism, Perkins' *Works* would seem to be only so many partitions of a subject made for no apparent reasons. The only purpose would seem to be to dissect his topic. But seeing these pieces as drawn according to Ramist method uncovers an overarching plan. Individual divisions fit together to form a finished whole. A visual symmetry becomes apparent. It is elucidated as the branches of the Ramist chart are unfolded. What before were perceived as apparently meaningless divisions are now realized to be part of a larger scheme. The findings of this study indicate that Perkins' vocabulary, emphases, and method show him to have done his theological work with the philosophy of Peter Ramus firmly in mind and freely used.

The theme of this study has made it impossible to deal directly with related aspects of interest which the reading of Perkins raises. His views of society, family, ethics, or science and witches cannot be commented on fully. Nor has it been possible to speak fully of the social and political implications of his use of Ramism.[20] A full survey of Perkins' teachings *vis-á-vis* those of other Ramist Puritans has had to be neglected as well. All this is work for future times.

Instead, this study provides a discussion of the Ramist elements in Perkins' *Works*. This has been set within the story of Perkins' place in the Elizabeth Puritan movement, the teachings of Ramus and the spread of Ramism in Great Britain during the sixteenth and seventeenth centuries. The wide-reaching implications of Ramism for Perkins' theological work have been explained. These have been identified and synthesized in a way not done before. Now too, Perkins' works (as well as a number of other Ramist works) are almost completely diagrammed as Ramist charts or "analyses." The structure of Perkins' pieces are for the first time available at a glance.

Much more is left to be done in Ramist studies, in Puritan studies, and in the interaction between the two. But now further work can be done with this additional knowledge and documentation; that William Perkins, whose leadership was so much respected by his contemporary Puritan and Ramist colleagues and students, was himself fully a Ramist Puritan.

PART I

WILLIAM PERKINS

Chapter I. LIFE AND WORK OF WILLIAM PERKINS

A. *Life of Perkins*

Few details are known about the life of William Perkins. Thomas Fuller gave a basic picture in his *The Holy State and the Profane State* (1642) and *Abel Redivivus* (1651). But beyond this, very little else has survived.

Perkins was born in 1558 to Thomas and Anna Perkins. His family was apparently "on the borderline of the gentry."[1] They lived in the village of Marston Jabbet, Warwickshire and were members of the parish of Bulkington. Since no parish registers exist, it is impossible to trace the family ancestry further.

In June, 1577 Perkins entered Christ's College, Cambridge as a pensioner. This seems to suggest that there was enough money in the family to send at least one son to the University.[2] At Christ's College he secured the services of Laurence Chaderton as his tutor. Chaderton was a Reader in Logic at the time and was a well-known figure in the Elizabethan Puritan movement. He lived to be over one-hundred years of age and has been described as "the pope of Cambridge puritanism."[3] Perkins' early association with Chaderton is some cause for suspecting that his family may have had Puritan sympathies.

Perkins completed his Bachelor of Arts degree in 1581. He stayed on at Christ's College and completed his Master of Arts degree in 1584. Between these years, Perkins evidently underwent a religious experience of significant importance. Benjamin Brook in *The Lives of the Puritans* recounted the story that

> while Mr. Perkins was a young man and a scholar at Cambridge, he was much devoted to drunkenness. As he was walking in the skirts of the town, he heard a woman say to a child that was forward and peevish, 'Hold your tongue, or I will give you to drunken Perkins yonder.' Finding himself become a by-word among the people, his conscience smote him and he became so deeply impressed, that it was the first step towards his conversion.[4]

This story is probably apocryphal. It does not appear in the writings of Samual Clarke or Fuller both of whom would most likely have repeated it if it were known to them. The judgment of Fuller was that when Perkins was at the university:

> quickly the wild fire of his youth began to break out....It is not certain whether his own disposition, or the bad company of others betrayed him to these extravancies. Sure it is that he took such wild liberties to himself as cost him many a sigh in his reduced age. Probably divine providence permitted him to run himself with the prodigal son out of breath, that so he might be the better enabled experimentally to reprove others of their vanity, effectually sympathising with their said condition, and be the better skilled how to counsel and comfort them on their repentance.[5]

Only a faint trace of autobiography exists in Perkins' published writings. In *A Resolution to the Country-Man* (1585), Perkins remarked concerning astrology:

> I haue long studied this Art, and was neuer quiet vntil I had
> seene all the secrets of the same: but at the length, it please God
> to lay before me the profanenes of it, nay, I dare boldy say,
> Idolatrie, although it be couered with faire and golden shewes.⁶

Fuller wrote: "There goeth an uncontrolled tradition, that Perkins, when a young scholar, was a great studier of magic, occasioned perchance by his skill in mathematics."⁷ But nine years later, Fuller wrote that

> when first a graduate, he was much addicted to the study of
> natural magic, digging so deep in nature's mine, to know the
> hidden causes and sacred qualities of things, that some conceived
> be bordered on hell itself in his curiosity.⁸

Ian Breward has suggested that since Perkins' first works dealt with astrology, he was perhaps reacting strongly against his former activities.⁹

The intellectual transformation in Perkins was accompanied by a new activity as well. Perkins began to preach to the prisoners in the Cambridge jail. He gained permission to gather the inmates together and began weekly preaching services. These services also attracted outsiders for an audience. Perkins began to acquire a reputation as an earnest and effective preacher. He also administered pastoral care to the prisoners. According to one account, when a young man was in despair as he approached the scaffold from which he would hang:

> whereupon Master Perkins laboured to cheer up his spirits, and
> finding him in an agony, and distress of mind, he said unto
> him. What man? What is the matter with thee? Art thou afraid
> of death?
>
> Ah no (said the prisoner, shaking his head) but of a
> worser thing.
>
> Sayest thou so (said Master Perkins) come down again
> man, and thou shalt see what God's grace will do to strengthen
> thee; Whereupon the prisoner coming down, Master Perkins
> took him by the hand, and made him kneel down with himself
> at the ladder foot....when that blessed man of God made such
> an effectual prayer in confession of sins....as made the prisoner
> burst out into abundance of tears; and Master Perkins finding
> that he had brought him low enough, even to hell gates, he pro-
> ceeded to the second part of his prayer, and therein to show in
> the Lord Jesus....stretching forth his blessed hand of mer-
> cy....which he did so sweetly press with such heavenly art....as
> made him break into new showers of tears for joy of the inward
> consolation which he found....who (the prayer being ended) rose
> from his knees cheerfully, and went up the ladder again so com-
> forted, and took his death with such patience, and alarcity, as if
> he actually was himself delivered from the hell which he feared
> before, and heaven opened for the receiving of his soul.¹⁰

Perkins' skill in preaching led to his appointment as a lecturer (preacher) at Great St. Andrew's Church parish, Cambridge. He began this work near the end of 1584 and continued until his death in 1602. At St. Andrew's he preached to large audiences composed of university personnel, townspeople and country folks as well.¹¹

Perkins had also been elected a Fellow of Christ's College in 1584. His parish position was worth only f 10 per year which came as a gift from the Dean and chapter of Ely. The remainder of his income was from "the free contributions of his congregation, aided by gifts from gentlemen in the neighborhood, of whom Mr. Wendy of Haslingfield was chief."[12]

A description of Perkins' preaching comes from Fuller:

> His sermons were not so plain but that the piously learned did admire them, nor so learned but that the plain did understand them. What was said of Socrates, 'that he first humbled the towering speculations of philosophers into practice and morality'; so our Perkins brought the schools into the pulpit and, unshelling their controversies out of their hard schoolterms, made thereof plain and wholesome meat for his people....An excellent surgeon he was at jointing of a broken soul, and at stating of a doubtful conscience....He would pronounce the word *damn* with such an emphasis, as left a doleful echo in his auditors' ears a good while after; and when cathecist of Christ-College, in expounding the Commandments, applied them so home, able almost to make his hearers' hearts fall down, and hairs to stand upright. But in his older age he altered his voice, and remitted much of his former rigidness; often professing that to preach mercy was that proper office of the ministers of the Gospel.[13]

Perkins' preaching ministry evidently appealed to both "town and gown." Fuller described it as "a burning and shining light, the sparks whereof did fly abroad into all the corners of the kingdom."[14] His sermons were delivered in a language and style which captivated the attention of his hearers. His attraction for a wide range of his audience led Fuller to write:

> But this may be said of Master Perkins, that as Physicians order Infusions to be made, by steeping ingredients in them, and taking them out againe, so that all their strength and virtue remains, yet none of the Bulke or Masse is visible therein, he in like manner did distill, and soake much deep Scholarship into his preaching, yet so insensibly as nothing but familiar expressions did appear. In a word his Church consisting of the University and Town, the Scholar could heare no learneder, the Townsmen plain Sermons.[15]

The example of Perkins was such that it was as if "he lived sermons, and as his Preaching was a comment of his Text, so his Practice was a comment on his preaching," according to Fuller.[16]

Perkins' intellectual endeavors were aided by his ability to read books very quickly. It was said he read "so speedily that one would think he read nothing; so accurately, one would think he read all."[17] His collected works were published by J. Legate as early as 1603. Over forty treatises made up this edition.[18] After Perkins' death, others brought out their own editions of his works even though these editions were unauthorized by his wife's executors.[19] During his life, Perkins did not make much money from his published writings.[20] When Perkins died on October 22, 1602, he left an estate of f 402 16s 4d.[21]

Perkins was a Fellow of Christ's College from 1584 till 1595 when he forfeited this position to marry Timothye Cradocke of Grantchester.[22] They were married on July 2, 1595. On July 5th, Samuel Ward a former student of Perkins' wrote in his diary: "....Good Lord, graunt that now after Mr. Pirkins departure ther follow no ruyne to the colledg, seyng that some of the fellows begin to use such pollicy without any care of the future good of the colledg."[23] Seven children were born to Perkins and his wife, three of whom died in childhood.

Near the end of his life Perkins was afflicted with the stone. It was from this he died.

In great pain on his death bed he cried out for mercy and forgiveness and "hearing his Friend praying for a mitigation of his paines, said, 'Pray not for an ease of my Torment, but for an increase of my Patience.'"[24] His funeral was held at Christ's College and he was buried in St. Andrew's Church. Perkins' best friend Dr. James Montagu preached the funeral sermon from Joshua 1:2 -- "Moses my servant is dead." The preacher paid high tribute to Perkins' learing, piety, labors, and usefulness.[25] Ward's diary records his feeling on the day of Perkins' death:

> Consider the great blow given unto the gospell of Christ by the death of Mr. Perkins, who by his doctrine and life did much good to the youth of the university, of whome he was had in great reverence, and who likewise did exceeding much good by his advice and direction to many Ministers in the Country, who did resort unto him from everywhere. His Life was most unblameable and upright, he was very sparing in censuring any man, very wise and discreet in his carriage, very humble and meek. In his sickness being in great extremity by reason of the stone, he was quiet and patient, and when it was motioned unto him as he was putting out his hand, what he wanted, he answered, 'Nothing but mercy.' On Wednesday, the 2nd of October, when I was with him, he willed me to pray for him. God knows his death is likely to be an irrecoverable loss and a great judgment to the university, seeing there is none to supply his place....[26]

B. Perkins and English Puritanism

William Perkins stood as a leader in the Elizabethan Puritan movement. Yet his position in that movement must be accurately gauged. The Puritan party in England arose in part before Perkins came to prominence. It was led by men like Thomas Cartwright, Walter Travers and John Field who advocated a spiritual reformation of the English Church as well as a reform of the Church's government.[27] These leaders were convinced that a "presbyterian" form of church government was the system divinely taught in the New Testament and the system that should be instituted in the Church of England.[28] William Perkins was associated with these men in the desire to see a spiritual reformation of the Church. But Perkins did not openly advocate a presbyterial form of church government. He maintained silence on this point. In this sense, Perkins must be seen as representing a different kind of Puritan leadership than these orders.[29]

Also, it is important to realize that the persistent identification of men like Perkins with the Church of England in effect helped pave the way for attempts to establish a different form of church government. When frequent attempts by Puritans to influence Parliament toward Presbyterianism failed, some Presbyterians proposed to institute their own form of church government. But internal disputes, the death of key leaders, and other causes made this effort unsuccessful. Others who had reformist sympathies, separated from the national church to form their own chruches. These were the Separatists.

William Perkins was neither a "Presbyterian" nor a "Separatist." But by identifying with neither of these parties, Perkins represented a "non-separating Puritanism" which focused more strongly on matters of spiritual reform than on ecclesiastical polities. When those who shared similar aims to Perkins but who also had strong opinions about the need for reform of church government became frustrated with attempts to gain their goals through constitutional channels, they took their own courses of action. In this Perkins did not follow them.

It was William Perkins who became a dominant voice in the "Puritanism" which emerged in the last years of Elizabeth's reign. He along with such men as Richard Rogers, Henry Smith, Laurence Chaderton, Richard Greenham and others showed a strong interest in "purifying" the established Church. But in their writings, teaching, preaching and personal examples they were not concerned so much with the outward forms of the Church as much as with the inward spiritual well-being of those who made up the Church. These men were mostly uninterested in matters of church government. But they were zealously concerned about the renewal of the Church's life. Thomas Full indicated this about Perkins when he wrote of him that:

> Mr. Perkins, whatsoever, his judgement was in point of Church discipline, never publicly medled with it in his preaching; and, being pressed by others about the lawfulness of subscription, he declined to manifest his opinion therein, glad to enjoy his own quiet, and to leave others to the liberty of their own consciences.[30]

Peter Heylyn called Perkins "a professed Presbyterian." Daniel Neal described him as a "Puritan nonconformist." But neither of these labels can be derived from his published writings.[31]

Neal's description was drawn from the fact that Perkins was twice before the authorities because of matters related to the Church. On January 13, 1587 Perkins preached a sermon in the chapel of Christ's College. Allegedly he said that kneeling to receive the Communion was superstitious and antichristian. He was charged with preaching that to administer the elements of Communion to oneself instead of receiving them from the hands of others who received them from the presiding minister was also superstitious and antichristian as was the turning of one's face toward the east.[32] For these statements Perkins was summoned to appear before John Copcot of Trinity College who was the Vice-Chancellor. He did so on the 19th of January and was cleared of these charges after he had asked to know his accusers.[33] But Perkins was ordered to read "a paper in the college chapel qualifying some and denying others of the opinions imputed to him and professing that he had not sought to disquiet the congregation, although admitting that he might have spoken at a more convenient time.[34] Breward's assessment from examining the official minutes of the trial are revealing:

> Perkins managed to clear himself of all charges, but the official minutes of the trial suggest an inner struggle between his convictions about obedience to conscience and his belief that the authorities ordained by God had power to enact laws for the good order of the church. He denied having rejected kneeling to receive the elements, but he can scarcely have blamed his hearers from drawing that conclusion when he suggested that sitting was more convenient, 'because Christ he sat, the Pope he kneeleth. And in things indifferent we must go as far as we can from idolatry' -- a position which he supported by adducing the authority of Jewel, Calvin and Bucer. In addition he urged that existing practice was unseemly. 'I beseech you, how can we altogether clear ourselves, which sitting before, fall down of our knees, and having received it, rise up again, and so do in like manner unto the wine?' Further evidence about his uneasiness over the Book of Common Prayer appeared in his reply about the minister serving himself with the elements of bread and wine. He argued that in a college chapel 'it was better to receive from another, because we are thirteen ministers, and by this means the minister not only receiveth the sacrament, but also

receiveth an approbation from his brother that he is a worthy receiver.' Nor did his final reply suggest that he saw any need to modify his position. 'This I marvel at, why the cross standeth still in the window, and why we turn ourselves toward the end of the chapel at the end of the first and second lesson.' Despite such frank expression of puritan uneasiness, he was obviously chastened by being called to account and was discharged because he agreed with the authorities that he might have spoken at a more convenient time.[35]

The only other recorded difficulty with the authorities that Perkins faced came in 1591. Perkins appeared in the Star Chamber as a witness for the prosecution in the trial of Puritan ministers. He was examined about a "conference" or "synod" he had attended in 1589 at St. John's College, Cambridge at which various matters concerning the Presbyterian movement had been discussed.[36] Perkins, when asked if there had been meetings to debate how the discipline might be advanced replied that "he does not know that any minister did at any time meet at any place to the purpose to conclude, debate or order how the said discipline might be advanced or practised." But he did agree that at this meeting there was discussion on "whether the rules and method of the said book of discipline called *Disciplina Ecclesia* etc. were agreeable to the word of God or not."[37]

Perkins appears to be cooperative with the authorities in what he told them. Yet in answer to the eleventh interrogatory when he was asked to disclose who had been Moderator at the meetings, "he [taketh himself not bound to expresse]ᴸ-dareth not to tell for ye reasons before rebred."[38]

This suggests that Perkins drew a line beyond which he would not go while he still tried to be faithful to his duty "to answer the magistrate." Perkins would confess his own part, tell what he knew about defendants, but "he refused to involve others not then accused whom he knew to be as innocent as himself -- notably his old tutor Laurence Chaderton."[39]

Perkins regarded himself as a loyal member of the Church of England. But he did not write at all on church government. He did not mention elders, deacons, church courts, or bishops. He regarded the church as a

> companie of God's people called by the doctrine of the Prophets and Apostles vnto the state of saluation....this our Church of England (through Gods mercie) doth maintaine, beleeue, and professe this Doctrine of the Prophets and Apostles: for the proofe hereof, let him that doubeth haue recourse to *our English confession,* and to a book intituled, *the Articles of Religion established in the Church of England;* in which are set downe the foundations of Christian Religion, allowed and held by all Euangelicall Churches.[40]

Perkins had no patience with separating sects. He wrote: "Our Church doubtlesse is Gods corne field, and we are the corne-heap of God: and those *Brownists* and *Sectaries* are blind and besotted, who cannot see that the Church of *England* is a goodly heape of Gods corne..."[41] Perkins viewed these separatists as undermining the authority of the magistrate. He wrote:

> In all things which concerne the authority of the Magistrate, and belong vnto him by the rule of Gods word, we must attempt to do whatsoeuer we do by leaue. And by this wee see what vnaduised courses they take, that beeing priuate men in this our Church, wil notwithstanding tak vpon them to plant churches without the leaue of the magistrate beeing a Christian Prince.[42]

Perkins believed that "among vs, til we separate from Christ, none should seuer themselues from our Church, ministerie, and seruice of God."⁴³ Perkins viewed his whole life's labor as his being able "to cast my mite into the treasurie of the Church of England."⁴⁴

Perkins rejected the term "puritan" when it referred to those who taught it was possible to obtain complete sanctification or to live without sin in this life. He saw it as a "vile term" when applied to the godly.⁴⁵ But as the term "Puritan" is used now, in light of Perkins' historical context and relationship with other "puritans," William Perkins can justly be called a "Puritan." His supreme goal was to work for the well-being of the Church of England. He did so by providing preaching and teaching designed to fortify the faithful and to bring others to an experience of God's grace. His concerns were those of other Puritans, some of whom were prepared to take different and more radial approaches (especially in regard to questions of church governmen). Perkins cared about the Church's inadequate ministers, about worship services which obscured the simplicity of the Christian Gospel and about sermons which reflected the preacher's learning rather than the majesty of the Spirit of God.⁴⁶ He lamented the lack of reformation near the end of Elizabeth's reign when he said: "We are not now that which wee haue beene twentie or thirtie yeares agoe. For now we see the world abounds with Atheists, Epicures, Libertines, Worldlings, Newters, that are of no religion..."⁴⁷ Perkins' "Puritanism" must not be mistaken for Presbyterianism. His acquaintances included Cartwright, Field, and Travers. But his friends were also James Montagu (later Bishop of Winchester), George Downame, and William Bedell -- later Irish Bishops. All in all, Perkins had "far more in common with Chaderton, Greenham or Richard Rogers than with convinced "presbyterians" such as Travers or Cartwright, who had the greatest difficulty fitting into the Elizabethan Church."⁴⁸

C. Perkins and Calvinism

If Perkins' views of church government need careful distinguishing, so also do his theological viewpoints. In a Preface to a work on predestination, Perkins wrote that he wished to "cleare the truth, that is (as they call it) the Caluinists doctrine."⁴⁹ Perkins has been called an "unswerving follower" of Calvin; a "thorough Calvinist." Insofar as the doctrine Perkins taught (particularly predestination) represented the "Calvinism" which opposed "Arminianism" at the Synod of Dort in the seventeenth century, this description is true.⁵⁰ Yet it needs elucidation.

To be truer to Perkins and his own historical context, other influences besides Calvin's must be noted. A study of Perkins works shows that he certainly honored and respected Calvin. He referred to him as "Master Caluin of blessed memory" and "that worthie instrument of the Gospel."⁵¹ Perkins cited Calvin's *Institutes* as well as his Biblical commentaries.⁵² But Geneva was not the only center or Reformation to influence sixteenth century English Protestants. Zurich, Heidelberg, and Leiden were significant too.⁵³ Thus Perkins also quoted other reformers extensively. He referred to Martyr, Beza, Zanchius, Olevianus, Tossanus, Junius, and Marloratus.⁵⁴ Breward has pointed out that "the parallels which can be drawn between Perkins' *Armilla Aurea* and *Exposition of the Creed* and *The Summe of Christianity* by Ursinus make it certain that Perkins used this work quite extensively."⁵⁵ Calvin's works were not the only ones with which Perkins was familiar.

Perkins also used Lutheran writers in support of his positions. He recognized the broad areas of agreement between his tradition and the Lutherans. So he cited Luther, Melanchthon, Strigel, Chemnitius, Hemmingsen, Illyricus, and Hyperius.⁵⁶ But he also criticized the Lutherans on their views of Christology, the Sacraments, and Predestination.⁵⁷

Besides these sources, Perkins also drew on the writings of Tyndale, Bradford, Hooper and Latimer.⁵⁸ Breward sees these works as standing behind Perkins' emphasis on "pastorally sensitive piety."⁵⁹ According to Breward, John Bradford (a disciple of Martin Bucer) was "the first English reformer whose writings were strongly marked by an experimental emphasis."⁶⁰ In one work, Perkins claimed to be carrying on the tradition of Bradford.⁶¹ But in comparing the works of the two men, Breward sees that Perkins' "own conversion experience has been refracted throught second generation reformed theology as well as throught a tradition of English practical piety.[62]

Therefore, it is not helpful to label too easily Perkins' theological positions. Various strands were weaved together in his thought. He drew widely on the theological works of continental Protestants as well as fellow-Englishmen. Perkins' theological heritage included Calvin *and others*. Before Perkins can be positioned theologically at any one point, it is imperative to study his teaching on the particular issue at hand. His doctrine on a specific topic may owe more to one Reformer than to another. His view of the nature of Scripture, for example, may be closer to Calvin's while his speculations into the nature and order of the divine decrees in predestination may bear more resemblance to the teachings of someone else. In this sense, Perkins drew on the developing "Reformed" tradition in formulating his theological viewpoints. He was not a "slavish disciple" to any one figure for the substance of his theology. As Breward rightly remarks: "If the term 'calvinist' is to be used, it must be given such a broad connotation that it is better to replace the term by "reformed."[63]

D. Perkins' Influence

On the basis of editions of his works published outside Britain, it is safe to say that William Perkins was "the first theologian of the reformed Church of England to achieve an international reputation."[64] Within England, only the works of Henry Smith were circulated more.[65]

Perkins' impact came throught his preaching, his students, and his writings. He was a well-known preacher in a town which numbered then perhaps five-thousand.[66] If it is true that "changes in the content of the sermons in the college chapels probably had a greater influence on attitude formation than changes in the content of reading lists in the classrooms," Perkins had a powerful platform from which to press his preaching through being able both to preach and to teach at Christ's College.[67] As Lecturer at Great St. Andrew's Church, only across the street from the main gate of Christ's College, Perkins' preaching was available to an even wider audience.[68]

The original charter of Christ's College (1505) provided for some sixty perons to live on the "foundation" of the College. These were one Master, twelve fellows, and forty-seven scholars.[69] The Fellows were elected for an indefinite period of time and were required to conduct divine service and preach as well as to conduct exercises and lectures.[70] Paying students (pensioners and fellow commoners) were given the services of tutors. These tutors acted as "guides to learing as well as guardians of finances, morals, and manners."[71] The relations between students and tutor were personal, the pupils often residing in the tutor's own rooms.[72] The 1570 Cambridge Statutes said that "tutors shall teach their pupils diligently, shall correct them in proportion to their faults, and shall not allow them to wander idly in the town.[73] As Fellow and Tutor, William Perkins not only taught by word, but also by exemplary living. The testimonies of his students show that he molded the thought and lives of these young men not only by what he said, but also by how he lived. His Cambridge students spread his fame in many places.[74]

Contemporary scholars of Puritanism (particularly in America) have directed attention to the importance of Perkins.[75] He has been called "the principal architect of Elizabethan Puritanism";[76] "the Puritan theologian of Tudor times";[77] "the most important Puritan writer";[78] "the prince of puritan theologians";[79] "the ideal Puritan clergyman of the quietist years";[80] and "the most famous of all Puritan divines."[81] For some forty years after his death in 1602, Perkins is said to have been "the dominant influence in Puritan thought."[82] Thirty years after he died, Archbishop Laud's visitors to areas with "puritan" leanings found "Perkin's books commoner than the Prayer Book in Puritan districts."[83] In New England, "your typical Plymouth Colony library comprised a large and a small Bible, Ainsworth's translation of the Psalms, and the works of William ('Painful') Perkins, a favorite theologian," according to Samuel Morison.[84] Perkins' *Arte of Prophecying* is said to have been found "on nearly every book-list in early New England."[85] Perkins affected New

England in the seventeenth century through his pupil William Ames and directly by his writings themselves. As Perry Miller has said, "Anyone who reads the writings of early New Englanders learns that Perkins was indeed a towering figure in their eyes."[86]

PART II

PETER RAMUS

Chapter II. LIFE AND WORK OF PETER RAMUS

A. *Life of Ramus*

Pierre de la Ramée (Petrus Ramus in Latin; Peter Ramus in English) was born in the village of Cuth (or Cut) in the Vermandois region of Picardy, France in 1515.[1] His ancestors had once been nobility. But in 1468 they lost their holdings in the wars of Charles the Bold. Ramus' grandfather was a charcoal burner and his father a farmer. When he was eight, Ramus became the servant of a wealthy student at the College of Navarre, Paris.[2] He had little time to study for himself but after several interruptions took his Master of Arts degree from the University of Paris at age twenty-one.[3]

Ramus then began his teaching career. First he lectured in Philosophy at the Collège du Mans. Then he taught at the Collège de l'Ave Maria. There be began a friendship with his close colleague Audomarus Talaeus (Omer Talon; 1510?-1562). In 1543 Ramus published two works which stemmed from his lectures: *Dialecticae partitiones (The Structure of Dialectic,* or, *Dialecticae institutiones, Training in Dialectic* which was the second edition also published in 1543) and *Aristotelicae animadversiones (Remarks on Aristotle)*. These provided the basic frameworks and structures on which Ramus' later theories were built.[4]

Due to the vehemence with which Ramus attacked Aristotle and the University curriculum as confused and disorganized, Ramus' colleagues prosecuted him before a civil magistrate. He was charged with seeking to destroy the foundations of religion and philosophy.[5] Before the Paris Parliament could hear the case, however, Ramus' accusers appealed directly to King Francis I. Five university professors were appointed to hear the case. After two days of unproductive discussion, Ramus' representatives resigned from the Commission and he did not replace them. On March 1, 1543/4 a royal decree prohibited Ramus' books throughout France. It ordered him not to teach or write publicly on Philosophy without the King's permission.[6]

Ramus was undeterred. He next took up the teaching of classical authors and mathematics since the prohibition related only to Philosophy (including logic or "dialectic"). He also began his association with Talon. In 1545 they both moved to the Collège de Prèsles and by December Ramus had become its principal.[7] Ramus smuggled into print another edition of his *Training in Dialectic* under the title *Dialectici commentarii tres authore Audomaro Talaeo (Three Commentaries on Dialectic Published under the Authorship of Omer Talon,* 1546). This became one of the most important editions of this work. Here Ramus first gave his logic its final forms and also treated method as a separate subject for the first time.[8] Ramus published a Latin version of Euclid's *Elements of Geometry* titled *Euclides* (1545) and assisted Talon with his *Institutions Oratoriae (Training in Oratory,* 1545). This work eventually became *Talon's Rhetorica* (1548).[9] Ramus' own lectures on Rhetoric drew enthusiastic crowds.[10]

In 1547 Ramus published a commentary on the eight books of Cicero's *Orator* under the title *Brutinae quaestiones (Brutus' Problems)*.[11] Ramus dedicated this work to the new King, Henry II. Charles de Guise (1525-1574), Cardinal of Lorraine and a former schoolmate of Ramus', interceded with the King and the ban against Ramus' philosophical work was lifted.[12] By 1551 Ramus had become Regius Professor of Eloquence and Philosophy at the institution later known as the College de France. He subsequently became Dean.[13] This position was supported by a royal grant. It gave Ramus a good platform from which to teach and write. He established a reputation as a leading orator of his day.[14] Ramus managed to enjoy wide-ranging influence. He gained important privileges by maintaining his favored position at the Court.

Ramus' career was marked by many quarrels within the University during the years

1551-1562. During this time he also continued at working to develop his thought. The death of Talon in 1562 left him greatly saddened. The same year Ramus converted to Protestantism though he was suspected of harboring secret Protestant sympathies years before.[15] This intensified the hostility of his enemies. Ramus was forced to leave the University when the civil wars of religion broke out in France.[16] He receive permission from King Charles IX to withdraw safely from Paris to Fontainebleau. There he studied geometry and astronomy in the royal library.[17] Ramus returned to Paris and resumed his teaching and writing when peace was achieved in March, 1563.

In 1566 when Ramus was Dean of the Regius Professors, he protested to the Paris Parliament and the Privy Council about the appointment of Jacques Charpentier to the Regius Chair of Mathematics.[18] He charged Charpentier, a lecturer in arts and doctor of medicine, with incompetence and unprofessional conduct. In 1554 Charpentier had attacked Ramus' *Training in Dialectic*. He charged Ramus with being unaware of what Aristotle had truly meant by "dialectic." He also attacked Ramus' handling of "method."[19]

Further civil wars in France broke out in September, 1567. Again Ramus was compelled to leave Paris. He took refuge with Protestants. Later he denied any participation with their army in the Battle of St. Denys.[20] Ramus began teaching again in March, 1568. But soon he saw that further outbreaks of fighting were inevitable. He obtained royal permission to visit German and Swiss universities and act as a kind of "royal commissioner" of French culture.[21] Ramus used the opportunity to stop in Strasbourg, Bern, Zurich, Heidelberg and Geneva where he lectured on mathematics as well as on Cicero, Quintilian, and Plato.

A trail of controversy followed Ramus nearly everywhere on these travels.[22] Student enthusiasm was inflamed and professional colleagues grew angry. Ramus provoked the ire of Thomas Erastus (1524-1583), a physician who also wrote on theology, as well as other local theologians when he spoke in Heidelberg.[23] In Basel, he quarreled with Simon Sulzer among others. While in Geneva, local pastors begged the City Council in May, 1570 to allow Ramus to lecture in order to "help the university's reputation." But by the end of the month, the same pastors were formally reproving Ramus for his teaching methods. Ramus immediately ceased to lecture. Angry students protested on his behalf by posting verses of praise to Ramus and condemnation of his detractors.[24]

When Ramus was in Strasbourg he visited his former teacher Johannes Sturm (1507-1589).[25] In Basel Ramus spent more than a year writing and studying theology while he superintended the publication of his books.[26] Ramus first participated in a Protestant Communion service while in Heidelberg in 1570.[27] But despite his controversial experiences, there was one city where Ramus maintained friendships with prominent leaders and where his influence was particularly felt. This was Zürich, the city of Zwingli.

Heinrich Bullinger (1504-1575) was Zwingli's successor as chief pastor of the city. He and other pastors were very impressed with Ramus' intellectual abilities. Ramus responded to this attention. He adopted a modified form of the Zwinglian theology as his own.[28] Ramus' loyalty to this position led him to urge the church of Zurich to break with the church of Basel over the question of eucharistic theology in 1569. In 1571 Ramus tried to influence Bullinger to reject the actions of the La Rochelle national Synod of France.[29] Ramus criticized this Synod for putting too much power in pastors' hands in disciplinary cases; for voting to damn as heretics those who mixed ecclesiastical affairs with civil and political ones; and for attacking those who refused to accept the word "substance" as a valid description for what happened in the sacrament of the Lord's Supper.[30]

Ramus' letter to Bullinger was counteracted by that of Theodore Beza (1519-1605). Beza was Moderator of the Synod and wrote what amounted to a small book to Bullinger to explain the Synod's position fully. This letter also included blasts at Ramus for stirring up controversy and criticisms of his teachings. Beza claimed Ramus could never lecture on any noble ancient writer without subjecting that writer's ignorance to an outrageous attacke.[31]

Ramus managed to influence a provisional synod meeting at Lumignyen-Brie in March, 1572. That body agreed to increased lay participation in decision making in the Church in a way so that "the advice of some would weight more than others, according to geometrical proportions."[32] Ramus' program was not completely adopted. But enough was passed to satisfy him.

Yet the concessions of the provisional synod were a short-lived victory for Ramus. In early May, 1572, the next National Synod of the Reformed Church met at the Protestant stronghold of Nîmes. This gathering was apparently called to deal with the vocal protests of Ramus and his allies. Beza again played a central role in the deliberations. Papers on both sides of the battle for structural reform of the Church were presented. But the Nîmes Synod rejected all the reforms offered by saying:

> none of these shall be received among us, because they have no Foundation in the Word of God, and are of very dangerous consequences unto the Church, as the whole hath been verified and made appear in the presence of this Synod.[33]

Further retaliation followed. The memoirs of the Lumigny Synod were to be razed and its members warned not to enact any "canons on their own." They were further warned to abide by the Synod's discipline from then on. Individual reformers Ramus, Jean Morély, Hugues Sureau, and Bergeron were to have individual notices of the Synod's decisions and were to be summoned to the Colloquy of Beauvoisin. There the Colloquy would

> remonstrate to them for their offenses, but....deal gently and sweetly with them: And in case upon their appearance they should reject their Admonitions, they shall be proceeded against as Rebels and Schismaticks, according to the Canons of our Discipline.[34]

Beza and his colleagues had won the victory. The Synod reported to the Syndics and Council of Geneva that Beza had warded off the greatest internal threat ever mounted in the French Reformed Church at one of her Synods.[35]

Ramus returned to Paris in 1570 after his tour of the European universities. His espousal of Protestantism endangered his position in the Collège de Presles and his Regius Professorship. He alternately maintained and lost his lecturing position due to the French political situation. King Charles IX ordered the assassinations of French Protestant political leaders on August 23, 1572. Massacres quickly spread throught France. Known Protestants and Protestant syampathizers were killed.[36] The prominence of Ramus made him a particularly deisred target for the mob in search of victims in Paris. On August 26th, after one group of would-be assassins were mollified by bribes, a second gang broke into Ramus' apartments and found him praying. He was shot and stabbed immediately. His body was thrown out an upper-story window and further mutilated by fanatics below. Then it was thrown into the Siene.[37]

B. Reform of Education

Ramus' life was spent in teaching and writing. His primary passion, however, was educational reform.[38] His published writings covered a wide field of interests: dialectic, rhetoric, grammar (Latin, Greek, French), Aristotelian physics and metaphysics (which he derided), arithmetic, algebra, and geometry. He also did some Latin translations from Greek, some classical commentaries (a few dealing with legal and military sciences), as well as letters, academic orations, remonstrances, prefaces and one systematization of basic Christian doctrine published after his death. Ramus wrote about six works by himself and thirteen more with his associate Talon. Some eight-hundred editions of the works of the two men are known. If counted separately, works appearing in various collected editions total over eleven-hundred. Approximately four-hundred fifty of these are editions of works on logic and rhetoric.[39]

Ramus' work had its impact in its thrust to reorganize and reform dialectic. The reorganization of rhetoric the counterpart of dialectic (logic) was also associated with this reform. Ramus was educated at the University of Paris at a time when the scientific and highly structured logic of the Middle Ages was being eclipsed. The humanist movement was making its mark during Ramus' lifetime.[40] A new humanist curriculum challenged the established arts course for the power to shape and direct the education of the new generation. Humanism itself was not a particular philosophical system. Rather, it was a whole cultural and educational approach to that area of studies known as the "humanities" (*studia humanitatis*).[41]

The *studia humanitatis* of the Renaissance was in contention with the prevailing teaching programs of the schools. It differed from these programs in its emphases. Erasmus (1469-1536) and other humanists stressed the subjects of the "humanities": grammar, rhetoric, history, poetry, and moral philosophy. These were learned in conjunction with references to classical texts and with attention given to the practical results of such studies.[42] The established "scholastic philosophy" on the other hand, gave most attention to formal disciplines which related less directly to the actual conduct of human affairs. The grammar taught by the scholastics was highly philosophical and theoretical in nature. Minimal study of rhetoric was in the scholastic curriculum. For the scholastics, logic was the "art of arts" in that it directed the operation of the intellect which in turn directed the other arts.[43] Natural philosophy was also taught by the scholastics in terms of what might be called today physics, chemistry, meteorology, astronomy, biology, and faculty psychology. The scholastics also showed some concern for metaphysics and highly formalized ethics.[44]

The approach of humanists and scholastics to the educational process differed markedly. But the two movements did not so much "battle" each other as "interact" with each other in the sixteenth century.[45] The break between the two approaches was definite. But the break was not clean. That is, the humanists themselves were post-medieval persons who operated within the frameworks of normal, post-medieval thought. This past could not be negated and the whole scholastic medieval experience could not be completely shed or forgotten. In their attitute toward language, for example, humanists extended rather than negated medieval scholastic concerns. The scholastic desire for exactitude and precisions rested in its dependence on written sources and documents. Humanist expanded on this rather than rejecting it out of hand. They took up the concern to see that even literary styles was fixed and controlled by prescribed forms which were responsive to the immediacy of human experience. In this sense the humanists' watchword: "*Ad fontes!*" ("back to the sources!") and the desire to return to classical antiquity was not carried through with complete consistency. For while they identified strongly with the Ciceronian orator and sought to revive the ancient eloquence by making rhetoric the all-encompassing discipline, humanists nevertheless had to depend on written or literary sources for their knowledge of the past in a way that the ancients did not.[46] The humanists therefore had to restore and receover lost or mangled classical texts. In the ancient world, however, knowledge came predominantly through oral forms by discourse and the spoken word.[47]

The reforms Ramus tried to enact stemmed from this interaction of scholasticism and humanistic ideals. They began with the incident of Ramus' Master of Arts thesis in 1536. Some biographers painted the picture of Ramus valiantly defending the following thesis against a learned assembly of academic antagonists: *Quaecumque ab Aristotele dicta essent, commentitia esse* ("*All that Aristotle taught is 'artificial.'*") On this, see below). By defending this thesis, Ramus would have risked the immediate scorn and contempt of the scholars. But the incident symbolizes Ramus' concern for reform. He wished to jettison the scholastic accretions to Aristotle. He sought to simplify the whole approach to the arts curriculum. To put his criticism of the accepted Aristotle so boldly as in this thesis would have signaled Ramus' dramatic departure from the traditional approach to studies.

It is now known that Ramus would have had his degree before he would make any oral presentation or defend any thesis. The exercise was called the *inceptio*. It was the first activity for a new Master of Arts recipient. It was literally a "commencement" and a required formality. With his new degree the candidate moved from "bachelor" or apprentice teacher into the former profession. The first order of the day was to display what the candidate was now permitted to do: to teach.[48]

A surer source for the origins of Ramus' educational reforms comes from his own writings. Ramus made no reference to a commencement thesis. Instead he said that it was "after my regular three and a half years of scholastic philosophy, mostly the *Organon* of Aristotle's logical works, terminating with the conferring of my master's degree, I began to consider how I should put the logical arts to use."[49] Ramus found that his scholastic training in the arts "had left me no better off in history, antiquity, rhetoric, or poetry" as he began the chore of formulating lectures for his classes.[50] Thus Ramus went back to the study of rhetoric. His aim became "to put the logical books of the *Organon* to the service of erudition."[51]

C. Reforms of Logic

Ramus wished to subject the study of the liberal arts to the rules of logic. This included all subjects in the curriculum from philosophy through the humanities. To do this, Ramus needed a "logic" that could be taught quickly and grasped easily by young students. Ramus had memorized bits and pieces of the Aristotelian logical system while a student. But no attention was given to the inter-relatedness of the elements. Nothing was taught about the over-arching connections among the subjects, let alone their practical application for the lives of students. Ramus told how he found the logic he needed:

> For implementing my program, I discovered (1) the distribution of dialectic in Cicero and (2) in Quintilian. (3) I found that Rudolph Agricola was the only one who had envisioned a dialectic fitted to humanistic aims [*usum humanitatis*], but that Agricola explained only a part of the art.
> At this point, I finally hit on (4) Galen, whom I found commending to (5) Hippocrates not (6) Aristotle but (7) Plato, whose dialogues I then read avidly, getting from his Socratic dealogues the equation that to discourse [*disserere*] is the same as to use one's reason [*ratione uti*], and hence that the distribution of dialectic which I had come across applied to the whole mental apparatus [*logica*]. (8) Thereupon, I began to think that Aristotle's authority was a deception.
> Nevertheless, I am grateful to Galen, more grateful to Plato, and most grateful of all to Aristotle, for from his *Posterior Analytics* I learned about the matter and form of an art.[52]

Several lines and roots of Ramus' thought are exposed in this account. Ramus was obviously concerned with justifying his whole enterprise in light of its grounding in classical antiquity. Yet Ramus also picked and chose what elements from that past to adopt. He found the simplest definition for "dialectic" (in practice used synonymously with the term "logic") in Plato's dialogues rather than in Aristotle's *Organon*. The simplest divisions or distributions of dialectic were in Cicero and Quintilian.[53] The distinction that Aristotle made which Ramus found beneficial was that between "matter" and "form."

Ramus said he discovered the "Socratic method" from Plato. He described this method as the withdrawal "from the senses and from human testimony to calm of mind and freedom of judgment" (*aequitas animi et libertas iudicii*).[54] This "freedom of judgment" or "judgment" was the second half of dialectic. Agricola, said Ramus, had not developed this part of logic. Socrates *had* developed it, according to Ramus. With this "calm examination of the thing known" (logic itself), Ramus claimed to be able to determine "the final and general end of *logica*" (*summus et generalissimus finis*) which was "expressed by its definition, *ars bene disserendi*" (the "art of discoursing well"). This in turn was just as general as the use of one's reason (*uti ratione*) to Ramus. He stated: "My definition I could find nowhere in the *Organon*."[55]

Ramus' definition of logic as *ars bene disserendi* was actually part of the medieval rhetorical heritage. It had its roots in the classical past with Cicero and with St. Augustine.[56] But Ramus had found a definition which would allow him to apply "logic" to all the arts. In the most general way, to "discourse" was to use one's reason. One could apply one's reason to any form of discourse -- history, poetry -- any of the liberal arts. The humanist program for dealing with subjects and their practical application to human life could be advanced. Once the application of "logic" was made theoretically, it remained only to find the best method of reasoning, or arranging, or ordering discourses. It was this concern with "method" which became a hallmark of Ramus' reform of logic and practically a synonym for his name itself.[57]

These applications from classical sources opened the door for Ramus to launch his reforms. They enabled him to put every subject under the feet of his "logic" and "method." All discourse -- from curriculum subjects to scientific writings, orations, personal letters, and even poetry -- could now be conceived and ordered according to logical "method." For Aristotle, "dialectic" was a logic which dealt with and ended with probabilities. These probabilities were used in debate or hypothetical discussion. "Scientific" logic for Aristotle, was of the type used for reasoning in mathematics, for instance geometry. But for Ramus, these "logics" were one in the same. Summarized, his account read:

> Finding no division of logic in the Organon, I called to mind [*commemini*] the division of dialectic into invention and judgment. With this in mind, I went back to the *Organon* and found the chaos fall into order -- a great light had dawned on me.[58]

To bring order out of *Organon*, Aristotle's separate logical treatises collected by his followers, was no easy task. But Ramus concluded that Aristotle himself was actually a lover of the Socratic method of "calm judgment." Ramus believed he had been deceived by "false scholastic opinions" (*falsa scholasticae opinionis*). Ramus asked: "....would you believe how happy I was at finding this out, how moved, how carried off my feet?....I can only thank God in the name of Galen, Plato, and Aristotle who gave these men to me to save me from the waves of tempests."[59]

In what then does Ramus' alleged "anti-Aristotelianism" consist? There is a definite historical problem with his supposed thesis: *Quaecumque ab Aristotele dicta essent, commentitia esse*. Biographers who have accepted the authenticity of the thesis have often translated it as: "all that Aristotle has said is false";[60] or "a lie"[61]; or "forged."[62] The forgery notion has some small connection with Ramus himself. In his *Remarks on Aristotle* Ramus made the comment that Aristotle's reputation could only be cleared if it could be shown that the writings accepted as his really were not his.[63] However, it has been pointed out that Ramus never connected this forgery theory with a direct use of the term *commentitia*. The term *commentitius* and its cognate verb *comminiscor* are derived from the Latin term *men*. Terms related to "memory" such as *meminisse, memoria* stem from this word rather than terms dealing directly with truth or falsehood per se. *Mens* is also related in a particular sense to the term "mind" or to the intellectual faculties. The *com-* prefix, suggesting a grouping together, gives *comminiscor* the meaning and connotation of "contrive," "devise", and "invent" in the sense of letting one's mind run inventively and irresponsibly. The notion of "fabrication" catches this sense as one might say, "I made it all up" or "I fabricated the story." Here "artificial," "fabricated," or "contrived" is the primary sense and "forged" or "false" is secondary.[64] If this interpretation is valid, as it appears to be, Ramus was attacking the detailed Aristotelian logical system as being too unduly complicated and useless from a practical point of view. Other direct usages of *commentitia* by Ramus bear this out.[65]

A final note about Ramus' use of *commentitia* is that he connected these "fabrications" with the mnemonic constructs used by Aristotelians to classify the moods of the syllogism.[66] Ramus rejected this schema because it was "external" (*externis*) or "arbitrary," not because it was untrue. Ramus wished to base memory on so-called "natural schemes."[67]

All in all, the following paraphrase may be offered for the statement *Quaecumque ab Aristotele dicta essent, commentitia esse*: "All the things that Aristotle has said are inconsistent because they are poorly systematized and can be called to mind only by the use of arbitrary mnemonic devices."[68]

Ramus saw his task, then as one of revising and adapting Aristotle's work on logic and rhetoric.[69] He would remove the errors that accumulated through the centuries. These had been perpetuated by Aristotle's followers -- the Aristotelians.[70] Aristotle himself, according to Ramus, had "enriched dialectic by employing it in discursive fashion." But these works, Ramus lamented, have been lost. By "discursive fashion" Ramus meant informal usage. That is, to use dialectic for something such as a political speech rather than exclusively for logical or mathematical purposes in a highly technical way is "discursive fashion."[71] Yet Aristotle did not use dialectic for oratorical purposes. For according to Ramus, while Aristotle gave impetus to dialectic for use in practical fields, his elaborate theoretical treatment of logic actually hindered this development of a "true exercise" or *usus* of logic.[72] In this sense, the case of Aristotle and the Aristotelians are one (*quonia Aristotelis, Aristoteleorumque causa una*). Therefore, Ramus opposed them all.[73] He wanted to state what others had done in a briefer and more practical way.[74] He wished to recover the true dialectic of the pre-Aristotelian philosophers -- Prometheus, Zeno the Eleatic, Socrates, Hippocrates and Plat. The dialectic of these men according to Ramus was of "nature," *i.e.* "natural."[75] Among these ancients it was Plato who was the "prince of dialecticians" to Ramus.[76]

D. Ramus' Logic

Ramus developed his dialectical and educational reforms in the context of continuing interaction between the regnant scholasticism and the developing humanist alternative approaches to knowledge.[77] Ramus found a dialectic fitted for the humanist agenda of subjecting all liberal arts subjects to the rules of a "simplified" logic in the work of Rudolph Agricola (Roelof Huusman; 1444-1485). The major divisions of dialectic were "invention" and judgment." These served to "discover" and "dispose" arguments. They did so by drawing on the "topical" or "commonplaces" tradition developed by the ancient rhetoricians. Rhetoric itself was to serve only as a means for ornamentation and delivery of what logic had produced. This logic was not to be separated into a logic of science and a logic of opinion. To Ramus there should be only one logic for both. "Method" was the key for organizing all that logic discovered. Thus the logician and rhetorician were equipped to give full expression to human thought.[78] The system of the arts Ramus envisioned corresponded to the

> two universal and general gifts given to man by nature, reason
> and speech. The first is the concern of dialectic, the latter of
> grammar and rhetoric. Dialectic seeks to establish the all-round
> strength of the human reason in the discovering and disposing of
> matter. Grammar seeks the purity of speech in words and syntax
> to speak or write well. Rhetoric demonstrates how to ornament
> an oration with tropes and figures and the dignity of proper
> delivery.[79]

Ramus' first exposition of his "one logic" was in his *The Structure of Dialectic* (*Dialecticae partitiones*) of 1543. The second edition of this work, *Training in Dialectic* (*Dialecticae institutiones*) also published in 1543 did not differ dignificantly from the first edition.

In the *Training in Dialectic*, Ramus divided dialectic into three parts. These were the nature (*natura*), art or teaching (*doctrina; ars*), and exercise (*exercitatio*) of dialectic. Ramus' definition of dialectic was "the ability to discourse" or "the power of discoursing."[80] To Ramus discoursing was essentially "conversing" or "disputing" or even "using one's reason."[81] Thus dialectic could serve as discerner, or discriminator or "decision-maker" (*disceptatrix; iudex*) in making the division between truth and falsehood.[82]

1) Nature of Dialectic

For Ramus the "nature" of dialectics meant its origins or birth. He used the terms *natura dialecticae* (the origin of dialectic) and *naturalis dialectica* (natural dialectic) synonymously. They referred to an innate dialectic which Ramus believed all humans had at birth. In the manner of Plato, Ramus referred to this as "aptitude, reason, mind, the image of God, the light rivaling the eternal light."[83] The true art of dialectic could be developed by "imitation and study of natural dialectic."[84]

2) Art of Dialectic

Natural dialectic was opposed in Ramus' mind to the art of doctrine of dialectic. Eventually Ramus was to define dialectic as "the art of discoursing well."[85] One might be able to use natural dialectc. But one could not discourse as "well" as if formal training in the "art of dialectic" had been undergone. The goal of each art and its study was so that one might do the art "well" (*bene*). In this Ramus stood with the humanists who understood bene to mean "in a particular fashion" or "effectively." The scholastics, on the other hand, often looked to dialectic to provide technical correctness (*recte*). Hugh of St. Victor for example had defined dialectics as teaching "the rules of correct disputing." Rhetoric taught "the rules of correct speaking."[86]

Ramus usually opened his various textbooks that expounded the different arts by defining the art in terms of its end or purpose. Thus geometry was the "art of measuring well" (*Geometria est ars bene metiendi*).[87] Theology was the "art of living well" (*Theologia est doctrina bene vivendi*) etc.[88] The art itself or even obtaining knowledge about the art was not the sole goal for Ramus. He combined this search for knowledge of the art with a quest for the practical application of this knowledge (*bene*). Knowledge and action proceeded together simultaneously in Ramus' program. Knowledge of the object, the "art," was coupled with the insights produced when the art was effectively subjected to the methods of logic. Ramus spelled these methods out.

For Ramus the "art of dialectic" was related to "natural dialectic" as a picture or portrait is related to the person who is painted.[69] An art is a picture of reality. It is a picture in the same way a map is a picture of a certain terrain. The arts were tables or charts of things (*Artes....rerum tanquam tabulae*).[90] In the 1543 *Training in Dialectic* Ramus provided the first of his many charts of the arts. This one was "The Summa of the Art of Dialectic."[91] It turned out to be the blueprint for the rest of Ramus' reform. It laid out the art of dialectic which to Ramus "seeks to be not only an art, but the queen or indeed the goddess of the arts."[92]

Ramus followed Agricola in dividing the art of dialectic into two parts: invention (*inventio*) and judgment (*iudicium*). Invention had the function of arranging individual concepts or arguments by which discourses were constructed. Judgment served to put these arguments together. Ramus considered all discourse as involved with the resolving of questions explicitly formulated such as: "Are humans dialectical?" The purpose of invention was to seek out the links or "middle terms" that would join the two parts of a question, the subject (minor part) and predicate (major part). Ramus proposed a list of fourteen "arguments" or topics (loci) where all possible middle terms of arguments could be found in his *Training in Dialectic*. His *Remarks on Aristotle* that year indicated he wanted nothing to do with Aristotle's "categories." He preferred this topical orientation instead.[93] The rejection of categories was expanded in Ramus' French *Dialectique* of 1555. There he called the *loci* themselves "arguments" rather than the traditional "seats of arguments." The 1543 arguments were divided into two branches, "first" and "derived." The first were: causes, effects, subjects, adjuncts, disagreeings; the derived were: genus, form, name, notations, conjugates, testimonies, contraries, distributions, and definitions.[94]

Ramus defined judgment as "the doctrine of collocating (or assembling) what invention was found, and of judging by this collocation concerning the matter under consideration." This teaching of judgment was for Ramus the same thing as memory training.[95]

In later works, Ramus made a subtle shift in his concept of judgment. This was to the use of the term *dispositio* or "arrangement" for *iudicium*.[96] Ramus began the second book of his *Dialectique* (1555) with the definition of judgment as: "the second part of logic, which shows the ways and means of judging well by means of certain rules of arrangement."[97] By explaining judgement this way, Ramus gave the impression that it was a very simple natural operation. It was merely a matter of matching or comparing statements with each other.[98]

According to Ramus, judgment proceeded by three steps. He called these the first, second, and third judgment in this *Training in Dialectic*.[99] In turn he built these steps on the works of the Stoics, Prometheus, and Plato.[100] The first was generally related to the syllogism (including induction, example, and enthymeme). The second was concerned with the linking together of arguments (which became Ramist "method"). The third judgment was related to religion.

The first step of judgment was defined by Ramus as a step in which "one argument is attached firmly and fixedly to a question so that the question itself is thereby recognized as true or false."[101] He called this arrangement syllogism. The argument found by invention was thus compared with one or the other terms of the question posed. Ramus divided syllogism into simple (*simplex*; categorical) and composite (*coniunctus*; all the rest). These were further subdivided into three types of simple syllogisms. Ramus borrowed from Agricola and Cicero for his terms. He named the first part (major premise) the *propositio*. The second part (minor premise) was the *assumptio*. The conclusion was the *complexio*.[102]

In this initial logic, the *Training in Dialectic* (1543) Ramus gave no attention to "propositions." He did treat them, however, in his *Dialectique* (1555) and its Latin adaptation *Dialecticae libri duo, Audomari Talaei praelectionibus illustrati* (1556.) In these Ramus treated the proposition (Fr.--*enonciation*; Latin--*enuntiatio*) as the "arrangement by means of which something is stated of something else."[103] The parts of the proposition were subject (antecedent) and predicate (consequent). Ramus tested whether or not a proposition was truly scientific by subjecting it to the three laws of Aristotle: the laws of truth, justice, and wisdom.[104]

The second step in judgment was defined by Ramus as that which "provides the collocation and arrangement of many and various arguments cohering to one another and linked as by an unbroken chain so as to lead to one determined end."[105] This step in judgment was to be the starting point for his description of "method" developed more thoroughly in later editions. For Ramus, the "gluing" of things together and their "juncture" involved first defining the final end in view, bringing forth the most general *genera*, and finally filling in the "parts" of the *genera*. This process went on all the way down to the most minute of the individual parts.[106] This step in judgment proceeded for the most part by definition and division.[107] These two (definition and division) actually underlay all discourse for Ramus. To him, a sentence was thought of as having emerged from the sentence before it, either by defining something which was there or by dividing something there.[108] This was clearly seen when Ramus wrote that "the principles of the arts are definitions and divisions; outside of these, nothing."[109] For him, demonstration also meant definition.[110] Syllogisms were helpful here, not primarily because as in scholastic logic they cinched the question of truth. Instead the function of the syllogism was to solve doubts when questions arose in matters of definition and division. The syllogism was not so much an argument in itself as a way of arranging an argument.[111]

The third judgment of Ramus was that by which all humans might be freed from the shadows of the cave (Plato's cave) and all things subjected to the divine light of God.[112] This gave his *Training in Dialectic* a Platonic flavor. It was also a slap at the Aristotelians who had no such doctrine as this in Aristotle's *Organon*.[113] Ramus taught that the mind moved to God by realizing that of the three parts of philosophy (dialectic, physics, and ethics), only dialectic can serve as a sure guide. Through grammar and rhetoric one moved until one came to dialectic. Dialectic rules over all other arts and their organization. And when one reached the point of seeing how all the arts were organized, one had gotten a clear look at how these exist in the mind of God.[114] Ramus himself had not yet clearly "methodized" all the arts. But he looked forward to doing exactly that. In this he could once and for all eliminate the *commentitia* -- the poor systematizations and inconsistencies of the Aristotelian system. This pursuit of an ascent to the mind of God clearly showed the Platonic movement of Ramus' thought. However, this third judgment dropped out of the later editions of Ramus' logic. But it does give a clear picture of how Ramus viewed the enterprise in which he was engaging. His logic would indeed be able to "unlock the secrets of the universe" if he actually could deal with any subject or art in a way congruent with the Divine mind.

3) Use of Dialectic

The third part of dialectic after its nature and art was its exercise (*exercitatio*) or use (*usus*). An art in itself had no "life", according to Ramus. It was merely a "portrait" or a "chart of things," as he said.[115] The function of exercise or use was to draw out these precepts of the art in a way that would "shape and express in examples the force contained within the precepts."[116]

There were three forms which use could take. The first was interpretation (*interpretatio*). It was concerned with reading in all arts and thinkers. The first question to ask was: "What is the question?" When this was determined, one next asked: "What is the argument?"[117] The goal of interpretation was to disentangle or "unweave" (*retexere*) the various strands or threads of argument that ran throughout the discourse. This was a value of the syllogism. It could help with this task. Ramus used the term *retexere* as a translation of the Greek *analuein* which was usually rendered into Latin as *resolvere*. This means there is an equivalence between "to unweave" and the English "to analyze."[118] Analyzation is the process of breaking down or unweaving various strands. The goal for Ramus was to reduce all discourse into its simplest components. This "analysis" produced the true meaning of the discourse. To Ramus, Cicero's oration *For Milo*, for example, was only one "dialectical ratiocination: It is permissible to kill a criminal."[119] Ramus wrote:

> When you have cut out from the parts of the continuous discourse the many syllogisms therein, take away all the amplifications, and, after making brief headings to note the arguments used, form into one syllogism the sum total of the discourse, this sum total being ordinarily self-evident, although it may be swelled to undue proportions by accumulation of ornaments.[120]

Ramus did not deal much with writing and speaking, the other two form of interpretation at this point. The procedures for each of these activities was to be subject to the same precepts as interpretation.[121] As Ramism developed, interpretation began to be called simply "analysis." On the other hand, written or spoken compositions were referred to as "genesis" or synthesis." This genesis was analysis in reverse. It was weaving what later could be unweaved. When both processes went on, "imitation" occurred. To Ramus, imitation was the basic rule for all use. The best ancient guide for imitation was Cicero.[122]

4) Revisions

Ramus' logic evoked criticism. His 1543 work was attacked by a Benedictine monk Joachim Perion and by Antonio de Gouveia (c. 1505-1565). In 1554 Ramus was attacked by his enemy Charpentier. He charged that Ramus should deal only with the art of dialectic and not comment at all on the nature and exercise of dialectic. Further, he criticized Ramus' division of dialectic into invention and judgment since these did not give any clear direction as to what method to use in framing logical arguments.[123]

Ramus thus frequently revised his logic. His French *Dialectique* (1555) aside from being (apparently) the first dialectic printed in French, was also his first to eliminate discussion of nature and art of dialectic. Dialectic was left as a two-part art: *Les parties de Dialectique sont deux, Invention et Jugement*.[124] The form of this work was discursive. There was no ordering of materials. There was not even division into books or chapters.

The final Latin form of Ramus' work was published in 1556 as *Dialecticae libri duo, Audomari Talaei praelectionibus illustrati*.[125] Further revisions in the text, however, were made through the years. The 1569 edition divided the two books Invention and Judgment into 33 and 19 chapters. This became the final complete edition published in Ramus' lifetime. During the next one-hundred years, this Dialectic underwent some 250 printings.[126]

Ramus defined invention as "the part of dialectic concerned with finding arguments" in both the 1569 and 1572 editions of the Dialectic.[127] Judgment or disposition, however, was quite different from his 1543 treatment. The "third judgment" was omitted (though Ramus had once described this as the only true dialectic).[128] His discussions of definition and division which had formerly been treated as parts of the second step of judgment were now placed in the opening section of the first part of dialectic.[129] The first judgment or syllogism and the second judgment were combined before 1572 in a second part of judgment termed "judgment of syllogism and of method." The first part of judgment was then called judgment of enunciation.[130]

In the final 1572 revision of his work, Ramus redid his treatment of judgment. The two parts of judgment were then cast as axiomatic and dianoetic respectively. Ramus defined the second part of dialectic this way:

> So far the first part of the art of dialectic has been in invention;
> the second part follows in judgment. Judgment is the part of
> logic concerning the arrangement of arguments for judging well;
> for everything is judged by a certain rule of arrangement, so
> that this part of logic is indifferently called judgment or arrangement. Judgment is either judgment of enunciation, or judgment
> of syllogism and method.[131]

E. Ramus and Method

Ramus' development of "method" became his most important and influential contribution to communication theory.[132] To the Greeks, *methodus* with its root meaning of "following after" or "way through," connoted a pursuit of knowledge or investigation.[133] This pursuit took place in the arena of logical procedure. The followers of Socrates, however, combined this perception with that of dialogue or the dialectical procedure.[134] In rhetoric, the Greeks used *methodus* to describe a way of recognizing an argument or developing a theme. *Methodus* came to have a practical side to its usage because of its association with the medical tradition. A routine of efficiency concerned both with a proper way to approach and talk about a medical problem as well as a proper way to heal a patient was developed and thus described.[135]

In the Middle Ages, curriculum organization and pedagogical procedures grew alongside concerns for scientific investigation. In the Latin translations of Aristotle's *Topics* by Boethius, *methodus* took on the meaning (along with other things) of a curriculum subject. It was, in a word, a "short cut to knowledge."[136] It too was called an art (*ars*). In its briefest form "method" was a compendium.[137] Teachers in all university faculties was well as doctors of medicine, law, and theology constantly looked for orderly arrangements throught which they could teach their subject matter to students.

The scholastic logicians, however, did not devote any special attention to method as such.[138] Nor did the humanist dialecticians Valla, Agricola, or Vives develop it.[139] It was

Ramus who expanded method most fully. He was apparently spurred by the work of Sturm his teacher at Paris. Sturm was the first to devote space to a discussion of method within a logical or dialectical treatise.[140] Sturm had brought the topical logic of Agricola to Paris. Sturm drew from the Hellenic rhetorician Hermogenes (ca. 161 A.D.) and the medical man Galen (129-c. 199) in developing his thoughts on method. By introducing discussion of method into a dialectical manual (*The Structure of Dialectic in Two Books* -- Paris, 1539) Sturm shifted the arena for method to develop for rhetoric to logic.

One year after Ramus made his first mention of method (in the 1546 edition of his Dialectic published under Talon's name)[141] Phillip Melanchthon (1497-1560) published his *Questions in Dialectic* (*Erotemata dialectices*).[142] Melanchthon's earlier works on dialectics had not treatment of method.[143] His *Questions in Dialectic* included a separate section on *De methodo* at the end of Book I.

Melanchthon looked to John the Damascene (c. 675-c.749) and Peter Lombard (1095-1160) for theological method. But for dialectical method, in general Melanchthon looked to Aristotle. To him Aristotle alone was the true "master of method" (*artifex methodi*). This was a phrase later used to describe Melanchthon himself. Aristotle was to be commended because he did not digress from his subjects and explained each in an orderly fashion.[144] The educational aspect of method was very strong in Melanchthon. He was trained as a humanist and his definition of dialectic stressed the instructive side to the art.[145]

Book I of Melanchton's work dealt with the predicables and predicaments, definitions, and divisions. Book II was on propositions. Book III discussed argumentation and induction while Book IV spoke of the places and fallacies. The organizational pattern from Aristotle's *Organon* was plain. Melanchthon called his first three books "judicative dialectic." Book IV he named "inventive dialectic." This preserved the humanistic divisions of Cicero and Agricola -- invention and judgment. But it reversed their priority. It was also a work cast in an Aristotelian framework.

Melanchthon's treatment of method at the end of Book I thus associated method with the "judicative" part of dialectic. This was what Ramus was also to do. But Melanchthon's discussion was set within the framework of predicables, predicaments, definitions and divisions -- those elements which, if they corresponded to anything in Ramus, corresponded to his "arguments" which were handled in invention, not judgment.

Melanchthon echoed Agricola's conception of topical logic in his discussion of method. Melanchthon wrote:

> The Greeks thus define this term: Method (*methodus*) is an acquired habit establishing a way by means of reason. That is to say, method is a habit, that is, a science (*scientia*) or an art (*ars*), which makes a pathway (*via*) by means of a certain consideration (*certa ratione*); that is, which finds and opens a way through impenetrable and overgrown places (*loca*), throught the confusion of things, and pulls out and ranges in order the things (*res*) pertaining to the matter proposed.[146]

For Agricola the goal was to identify arguments and then to put them in their "places" (*topoi*). Once securely located there, they were available for use. Melanchthon operated similarly with his "method." He perceived method as being the process one went through in using these arguments once they were removed from the Agricolan places. In brief, method for Melanchthon was "a straight or direct way or order of investigating and explaining either simple questions or propositions."[147]

Whether a subject was being investigated or taught, Melanchthon's method was to deal with it by asking these questions in this order:

> 1) what does the word signify? 2) does the thing signified exist?
> 3) what is the thing? 4) what are its parts? 5) what are its
> causes? 7) what are its effects? 8) what things are 'adjacent' to

it? and finally 10) what things are repugnant to it?[148]

These were questions derived from Aristotle's *Posterior Analytics* where Aristotle had posed four questions. Melanchthon said these four reduced "chiefly" (*praecipue*) to four of his own ten: Does the thing exist? What is it? Of what kind is it? Why is it? Ramus had reproached Aristotle's *Posterior Analytics* in favor of his own "arguments." But there was still a strong correspondence between Ramus' arguments and these questions of Melanchthon's. In a later period, some sought a compromise between the logic of Melanchthon and the logic of Ramus. These people were called "Philippo-Ramists."[149]

Ramus was attacked by Gouveia for confusing what Ramus called second judgment in his *Training in Dialectic* (1543) with "the order in teaching the arts which the Greeks call method."[150] Ramus first treated method separately in 1546. His remarks were placed at the end of the second book that dealt with disposition which was the seond part of the art of dialectic. Ramus' only source of reference at this point was a vague reference to Plato at the end of his discourse.

Ramus divided method into two parts: the method of teaching and the method of prudence. Of the method of teaching he wrote that it was:

> the arrangement of various things brought down from universal
> and general principles to the underlying singular parts, by which
> arrangement the whole matter can be more easily taught and ap-
> prehended. In such method, this alone has to be prescribed: that
> in teaching the general and universal explanations precede, such
> as the definition and a kind of general summary; after which
> follows the special explanation by distribution of the parts; last
> of all comes the definition of the singular parts and clarification
> by means of suitable examples.[151]

This method operated in all discourse according to Ramus. It made no difference whether the discourse was connected with the arts or not.

Ramus said the method of prudence was to be used for teaching those "who do not want to be taught." It was also to be used when the physical or emotional aspects involved were working against the speaker. In these cases, the speaker may have to disguise "the summary of the matter, its definition, and the distribution of its parts."[152] Of the two methods, Ramus clearly preferred the method of teaching rather than the method of prudence. Ramus gave credit to Plato for developing the method of teaching.

Further attacks on Ramus' position led him to further revisions. The 1553 edition of his *Remarks on Aristotle* was radically revised when Ramus dealt with books IX and X which treated Aristotle's *Posterior Analytics*. In 1556 these books were reworded again. In 1557 the section from Book IX on method was separately published. Its title was *Quod sit unica doctrinae instituendae methodus*. This work has only recently been translated into English with the title: *That there is but one Method of Establishing a Science.*[153]

This work attempted to show that all arts or sciences have only one method throught which they are developed and taught. At the start, one begins with what is by its nature better known. Then one moves on to what is better known to us. The movement is from cause to effects; from the universal to the specific. Ramus acknowledged (with Aristotle) that the arts and sciences are discovered in the opposite way -- by moving from what is better known to us and proceeding to what by its nature is better known. But this inductive procedure Ramus would not dignify by calling it "method." He was concerned he said with only one method. This was the method to be followed for developing and teaching all arts and sciences.[154]

According to Ramus this was the method taught by Aristotle, Galen, and Plato. Aristotle appeared to teach two methods in his *Physics*: the method of discovery and of organization and exposition. But Ramus pointed out that in the text of this work, Aristotle said there was only one method. This, Ramus claimed, was the true method. Greek commentators on Aristotle asserted that Aristotle's "method of discovery" was not really a method at all. The commentators claimed it was only a useful subsidiary technique which was sometimes valuable. This interpretation Ramus accepted. To Ramus, "it is on a movement from causes to effects, and from the general to the specific, that Aristotle erected this whole philosophy."[155]

Ramus argued that the Greek commentators on Aristotle had taught there were two scientific methods; analysis and genesis. Analysis was the true method; genesis the inverse or "method of discovery." for Ramus the commentators on Aristotle taught two methods "one of descent, the other of ascent; one in one direction, the other in the opposite direction." "Analysis," said Ramus, "descends from what is most complex and composite to what is simple; genesis, on the other hand, arrives at the composite from the simple."[156] Ramus charged the commentators of Aristotle with not knowing how to use logic. Ramus believed genesis was not a method. It was rather the introductory study prior to true method. The commentators on Aristotle thought sciences were discovered by analysis and arranged and taught by the method of genesis. Ramus claimed the reverse was true. Genesis was merely in the discovery of the sciences. Analysis was used for their arrangement and teaching. Ramus wrote:

> These foolish men offer the true rule of method under the name of analysis. But they wrongly assign it to the discovery of the arts, this using an inappropriate example. And they oppose to it [*analysis*] a false, contrary rule under the name of genesis (arrangement). In short, they create a false and unreliable example of a false rule.[157]

These mistakes had led Aristotelian commentators to arrange Aristotle's logical works, the *Organon*, in a wrong and confusing order. Ramus said the correct order would be: *Categories, Topics, On Interpretation, Prior Analytics, Posterior Analytics, Refutations*. In this order, the first two works dealt with discover, the next three with arrangement, and the final work with the errors in each.[158] The remainder of *That There is but One Method...* was devoted to establishing the fact that both Galen and Plato as well as Aristotle himself worked by the one true method.

This work provided the clearest demonstration of Ramus' teachings on method. Ramus did not cease to adjust his teachings on method with this 1557 work. But here his basic principles came through clearly. This work has been said to be "the dead center of the axis on which Ramism turns." For "Ramism is dialectic, dialectic is method, and this is the theoretical underpinning of method."[159]

The 1569 edition of the *Dialectic* reflected Ramus' expanded teachings on method:

> Method is disposition by which, out of many homogeneous enunciations, each known by means of a judgment proper to itself [*i.e.* the way an axiom is known, without dependence on syllogisms] or by the jugment of syllogism, that enunciation is placed first which is first in the absolute order of knowledge, that next which is next, and so on: and thus there is and unbroken progression from universals to singulars. By this one and only way one proceeds from antecedents entirely and absolutely known to the declaration of unknown consequents. This is the only method that Aristotle teaches."[160]

Ramus reiterated his concern to move from the general to the special, from the "universals to singulars." This was the only way, he argued, to progress from the known "antecedents" to the unknown "consequents." The prime illustration of method for Ramus was again the arts:

> The chief examples of method are in the arts. Here, although all the rules are general and universal, nevertheless there are grades among them, insofar as the more general a rule is, the more it precedes. Those things which are most general in position and first in order which are first in luminosity and knowledge; the subalterns follow, because they are next clearest; and thus those things are put down first which are by nature better known (*natura notiora*), the less known are put below, and finally the most special are set up. Thus the most general definition will be first, distribution next, and, if this latter is manifold, division into integral parts comes first, then division into species. The parts and species are then treated respectively in this same order in which they are divided. If this means that a long explanation intervenes, then when taking up the next part or species, the whole structure is to be knit back together by means of some transition. This will refresh the auditors and amuse them. However, in order to present things more informally, some familiar example should be used.[161]

Ramus was convinced that his method and logic could be applied with success to all discourses. He wrote: "But Method is used not only in the matter of arts and curricular subjects (*artium et doctrinarum*), but in every matter which we wish to teach easily and clearly."[162]

Finally, Ramus produced an even more elaborated method in his *Dialectic* of 1572. There he wrote:

> Method is the intelligence order (*dianoia*) of various homogeneous axioms ranged one before the other according to the clarity of their nature, whereby the agreement of all with one another is judged and the whole committed to memory. As in the axiom one considers truth and falsity, and in the syllogism consequence or lack of consequence, so in method one sees to it that what is of itself clearer (*per se clarius*) precedes, and what is more obscure follows, and that the order and confusion in everything is judged. Thus among homogeneous axioms that is put first which is first in absolute signification (*absoluta notatione*), that second which is second, that third which is third, and so on. Thus method proceeds without interruption from univerals to singulars. By this one and only way one proceeds from antecedents entirely and absolutely more known to the clarification (*ad....declarandum*) of unknown consequents. And Aristotle teaches this one and only method.[163]

By this time too, Ramus' two-fold division of method into the method of teaching and method of prudence begun in 1546 (and maintained in the 1555 *Dialectique*) was modified. There was only one "method" but this Ramus divided into two separate uses. One use was for the arts such as mathematics, grammar, and dialectics where "certainly" is possible. The orther use was for such people as poets, historians, and others whose goal was persuading an audience to draw certain "probable" conclusions.

Some important final shifts were evident in Ramus' last treatment of method. For one thing, he used the term *dianoia* for *dispositio*. Jacob Schegk and others charged Ramus himself with being "unmethodical" and that method was not as easy as Ramus made it out to be. They said that method was no less difficult than the sciences themselves. Ramus' change to *dianoia* gave a stronger impression that now to him, method involved more thought or "intelligibility" than before when judgment was seen more as natural "arrangement."[164]

Further, In the 1572 *Dialectic* there was a stronger emphasis on the "clarity" of method. Previously Ramus appealed to that which was in itself better known (*per se notius*). This was what the scientific logic was interested in as well. But now Ramus cast his method in terms of proceeding from what was "of itself clearer" (*per se clarius*). Ramus did not develop this in much detail. But there seemed to be a rhetorical and pedagogical purpose in mind. How would one scientifically prove, for example, that the definition of a subject -- which is the first step in expounding an art -- was actually "of itself more known" than the partitions or divisions of the subject which were the next step in the Ramist agenda? That proof in and of itself was hard to clinch. By saying, however, that the definition and the whole method process was "of itself clearer," Ramus was in effect saying: This process and method is the one that works best. It is the best way to proceed with teaching. There was a practicality in view here. Ramus found this to be the method which functioned best rhetorically and pedagogically. Ramus' language here posed a subtle danger. For it was now easy to assume that a Ramist presentation moved from that which was "clearer" of itself of "in the nature of things" and was thereby "more known." If this impression was given, the distinction between *per se notius* and *per se clarius* would be lost. A blur of this distinction could lead to a confident assurance that one could indeed discern with clarity, propositions which are objectively real and built into the very fabric of the universe itself. In "method," the logician was merely arranging these propositions or classifying them in the most "intelligible order" (*dianoia*).[165]

A third shift in focus in the 1572 decription of method was in Ramus' new use of the term *axioma*. Ramus wrote: "An axiom is the arrangement of an argument with another argument, whereby something is judged to be or not to be. In Latin it is called a thing enunciated, an enunciation, a thing pronounced, a pronouncement, or as assertion."[166] Previously Ramus named his first part of judgment "enunciation" (*enuntiatio*; see above note 131). This dealt with the combining of terms to form true propositions. The second part of judgment was dianoetic or deduction. It concerned the combing of propositions. Deduction was divided into two parts: syllogistic, that dealt with the strict or scientific sense of logical deduction; and method, that was for the correct ordering of propositions to form a discourse.[167] By now styling *enuntiatio* as *axioma* (axiom), Ramus suggested that any statement might become the starting point for scientific demonstration which was the term "axiom" usually meant. Any statement could simply be stated as an axiom. It did not need to appeal either to induction or deduction to establish its truth. In the normal dialectic process, by the power of the natural reason, certain combinations of terms are self-evidently true according to Ramus. He wrote: "It [the proposition or now axiom] is tru when the consequent is truly ioned with the antecedent, or truly separated from the same: as here it is truly ioned: all men are synners: and here truly separated: no man is iust" (MacIlmaine translation).[168] Ideally, according to Ramus, these self-evident axioms could be laid out in sequence to lead finally to a conclusion. There was no need to appeal to either deduction or induction to come to the truth.

Ramus argued that it was only when dealing with propositions that were doubtful that the deductive process needed to be used. Syllogistic reasoning, the first branch of deduction, sought to clarify doubtful propositions by deriving them from self-evident axioms. The syllogism was useful because of its "constancy" and the fact that it could prevent all judgments from being made purely on an emotional or "irrational" basis. But Ramus urged the syllogism be used as little as possible. It was the axiom, not the syllogism that should be emphasized. Ramus declared: "From the nature itself or proposition and assumption is furnished abundant light, as though some gleam, for illuminating the complexion of art."[169] He meant that axioms appear to be true on sight. They do not need to be proved. They are self-evident. When axioms are joined together, discourses are made. Syllogisms should be kept within proper limits. For Ramus the syllogism only removed from "dubiety of a proposed question by the legitimately manifested truth of one of two dispositions."[170] Its only function was to serve as "the arrangement by means of which a question under examination is ordered along with the proof and brought to a necessary conclusion."[171] Even in the syllogism, the first premise is an axiom, the conclusion is an axiom and axiomaticall judgment," said Ramus. The arguments and the axioms, not the conclusions, were the basic certainties within the Ramean system. Syllogisms were based on axioms, not vice versa. As Ramus wrote: "For if the premisses in a syllogisme bee not sometimes certayne and so iudged by axiomaticall iudgement, and graunted; there will bee no end of making syllogismes."[172]

Thus Ramus' logic rested very heavily on self-evidencing axioms rather than on the syllogism and all its complexities. The highly technical development of syllogisms was a hallmark of the scholastic logic against which Ramus and the humanists protested. The elaborate machinery of scholastic logic with its figures, modes, and forms of syllogisms; its ways of establishing valid conclusions throught induction, enthymeme, example etc. was now vastly simplified by Ramus. The scholastics identified some forty-five illegitimate forms of the syllogism and only nineteen legitimate combinations of terms.[173] Students of the classical logic were expected to be able to cast their arguments in the legitimate molds and also to be able to analyze the fallacies of the forty-five illegitimate forms.[174] For Ramus the syllogism had just two modes -- simple and composite. The simple included the three modes of the scholastics; the composite was dichotomized into hypothetical and disjunctive.[175]

Since the ultimate goal of all dialectic for Ramus was discourse, the task of combining propositions -- whether self-evidencing axioms or the conclusions derived from syllogism -- was given to method. As described above, Ramus' teaching on method evolved through the several editions of his *Dialectic*. But significantly, this ultimate task of logic was not given to syllogistic. This represents a further importance difference between the logic of the scholastics which Ramus sought to simplify and his own logical theory. To the scholastics, reasoning proceeded from the intellect's grasp of one truth to the second truth, also intellectually grasped and done so by means of the first. One must move from proposition to proposition to come to truth and establish the previously uncertain.[176] The syllogism was the master instrument in this enterprise. It struck "downward" so to speak, through deduction. Each deduction was derived from the one that went before by means of the laws of logic. The "bottom line" was the conclusion that was secured "of necessity" if the laws of logic had been rightly obeyed.[177]

For Ramus the process was different. The goal of dialectic was discourse. This was achieved not through syllogistic but through method. Ramus did not see discourse as a series of syllogisms rightly joined through immutable laws of logic. Instead, discourse was a series of axioms. The "truth" of these axioms shone through by their very nature. They were "self-evident" by definition. Axioms could be perceived directly, immediately, once they were uncovered. Proper discourse was these axioms arranged in an orderly, intelligible arrangement or manner. To do this task, one followed proper "method." The proper method of discourse meant the same to Ramus as the method of teaching: "Method is the intelligible order of various homegeneous axioms ranged one before the other according to the clarity of their nature, whereby the agreement of all with one another is judged and the whole committed to memory."[178]

In Ramus' treatment of the method of discourse, there were four outstanding characteristics. Ramus used Aristotle's three laws -- *lex veritatis, lex justitiae, lex sapientiae*, the laws of truth, justice, and wisdom to say that discourse should be made up only of statements which were true, universal and necessary.[179] Those statements only true at certain times or places were ruled out. Secondly Ramus taught that all these statements should be homogeneous. They must all deal with the same subject matter. Thirdly, statements must follow the proper order. One began with the most general and proceeded to the more specific and "finally the examples, which are most particular, will be placed last."[180] Fourthly, these statements for Ramus were usually definitions or divisions of a subject. Most often these partitions were made by a dichotomy.[181]

This method of handling the divisions of an art made it possible to lay out a Ramist treatise in the form of a bracketed chart (see above note 91). A Ramist "analysis" (see above note 118) unwove the various strands of arguments to reduce discourse to its simplest components. To Ramus this reduction showed the true meaning of the discourse. Divisions or linaments on which the discourse was built were what stood. These could easily be diagrammed and their form exposed. What resulted was a bracketed outline which spread in a geometrical pattern of bifurciations. It resembled a "tree" with its "branches" spreading outward. It epitomized the humanist preference for topical over categorical logic in that it immediately displayed the *loci* ("places") from which the "arguments" were drawn. The chart showed how one division was subdivided, divided again and thoroughly "analyzed" down to its smallest unit or most particular member. The topic head or division was extended indefinitely and its individual components quantified. The movement in a Ramist piece was thus horizontal as opposed to vertical or downward like the thrust of the syllogism in scholastic logic.[182] The task of the logician in the Ramist scheme was classification. The job was to arrange everything (usually in pairs) under the proper heading or rubric. The progression was not toward the discovery of knowledge by discovering a truth derived from the proposition that went immediately before by using certain formal "laws" of logic. Rather one tried to unveil or uncover an "ideal form" in the sense of unweaving (analyzing) or laying bare the undisputed axioms of which true discourse was composed.[183]

"Logical analysis" was Ramus' basic way of operating dialectically upon a text. One reduced the text to its simpliest and most severe divisions. Once this was done, one could reverse the process. By "genesis" the parts could be reassembled to produce one's own discourse.[184] The spatial diagrams that resulted from Ramist method became prominent distinguishing features among those who followed Ramus. If a discourse could be outlined in the bracketed fashion, it was a sure sign that the Ramist method of composition had been employed. In fact,

> the term 'logical analysis' (*analysis logica*) or its equivalent "dialectical analysis" (*analysis dialectica*), when these terms first became current in the sixteenth century, is, at the very least, an all but certain hallmark of a Ramist work. Examination of most of the accessible texts points to the conclusion that 'logical analysis' is in the sixteenth and early seventeenth centuries a term so unmistakably partisan that no one but a professing Ramist or one intellectually described from a professing Ramist would use it.[185]

Since all discourse was a form of teaching for Ramus, the movement throughout his analyses was from general or generic to specific. Essentially, this was a genus/species relationship in which the starting point was the broadest definition and subsequent divisions were made from there. Even the syllogism was subservient to this process because in itself it too must first have its terms defined and then divided. The relationship of all such terms to each other was immediately visible with a look at the "logical analysis" of the work. Ramus rejected out of hand such Aristotelian categorical distinctions as "act," "potency," etc.[186]

Ramus made much use of the doctrine of "contraries" when he made his divisions. He believed ideas could be promptly distinguished if they were set against their opposites. Thus, what was good could be defined by saying what was evil etc.[187] Yet Ramus did not strictly follow his bi-partie or dichotomous division scheme at every point. He did not assume a contradiction to be involved with every distinction or division. Ramus' method as he defined it moved toward the arranging of ideas beginning with the most general and moving to the most specific. He did not invariably divide each part into two sub-parts. But it is true that later followers of Ramus engaged in this proclivity for dichotomization with a passion.[188]

An example of how the Ramist method worked with regard to an art is found in Ramus' treatment of grammar. The definition was his first concern: "Grammar is the doctrine of speaking well." This was the most general statement which could be made. Secondly grammar was divided into its constitutive "parts"; "The parts of grammar are two, etymology and syntax." This was the second most general statement to be made. Ramus next defined etymology. After that came all statements which belonged to etymology. Each was arranged in proper order from general to particular. With syntax, the same process was followed: definition, less general statements, then finally examples. In between each topic throughout the discourse being constructed, Ramus inserted "transitional statements." These told what the topic just discussed had been and what topic would follow. Be believed that "by means of these notes of transition the spirit is refreshed and simulated."[189] This was Ramist method in action.

F. Ramus and Rhetoric

Ramus' discussion of method came at the end of his logical textbook. With it in hand, he set about his reform of the arts curriculum. Ramus found that his fully developed logic overlapped traditional rhetoric at certain points. The scholastics had followed Cicero in dividing rhetoric into five parts. These were invention, arrangement, style, memory, and delivery.[190] The repetition of invention and arrangement with the same parts in dialectic was no problem for the scholastics. This was because they dealt both with the logic of "necessity" (dialectics) for scientific enterprises and the logic of "probabilities" for persuasion in popular orations.

But Ramus insisted there was only one logic for both logician and rhetorician; "so the art of knonwing, that is to say, dialetic or logic, is one and the same doctrine in respect to perceiving all things...."[191] Therefore Ramus dropped invention and arrangement (judgment) from rhetoric in his reforms. He made logic in the sole domain for these two processes. Memory as a separate component of rhetoric, Ramus disposed of completely. Ramus left only style and delivery as parts of his scheme of rhetoric. Style consisted of the use of tropes (metaphors etc.) and figures (alliteration). Rhetoric became in essence for Ramus only an art of ornamentation.[192]

It is paradoxical that the logic of Ramus is often referred to as a "rhetorical logic." By this it is meant that Ramus' reforms which so much simplified the study of logic were far less formal, technical, and highly structured than the scholastic-Aristotelian logic. The paradox lies in the fact that Ramus consciously tried to divorce logic and rhetoric from each other as formal disciplines. In the educational curriculum he devised, these were to be two separate subjects. Theoretically they were to operate in two distinct spheres. It was only in use or practice, that is, in actual oral discourse itself that the two necessarily were at work at the same time.[193]

G. Ramus and the Art of Memory

The fifth part of traditional rhetoric was memory. Ramus' system absorbed memory into "judgment" and dropped it altogether from rhetoric. Ramus believed that if one could only "judge" things properly, they would immediately be called to mind. If one followed the "natural" order demanded by logic or the proper "method," recall or memory would be not problem. One thing followed another self-evidently. There was thus no need to contrive artificial memory devices to facilitate the memory faculty.[194]

Ramus was led to this by the confidence he had in the dialectical process. To him dialectic was used to find the true order and relationships of concepts to each other. Whenever dialectic would be reapplied to the same subject, the same order and relationships would inevitably reappear. This was because dialectic was simply uncovering the order and relationships which intrinsically existed among the components of the art or discourse. Thus one never needed to fear forgetting. The method that led one initially to establish the order and relationships would serve as memory itself.

The views of Ramus on memory came in conflict with those of the Italian philosopher Giordano Bruno (1548-1600). Bruno was a Dominician friar who was accused of heresy in

1576. He fled his convent and spent the rest of his life wandering around Europe.[195] His several books on the art of memory revealed Bruno to have been profoundly affected by Renaissance textbooks on magic, particularly the *De Occulta Philosophia* of Henry Cornelius Agrippa. From it Bruno quoted incantations, lists of magic images of the stars and other occult procedures.[196] His first book on memory, *De umbris idearum* (*Shadow of Ideas*) was published in 1582. His *Triginata Sigilli* (*Thirty Seals*) was published in London when Bruno was in England in 1583.

Bruno's works on the occult arts of memory were connected with the Hermetic tradition.[197] This began from a literature written in Greek in the early centuries after Christ. The works carried the name "Hermes Trismegistus." They were concerned with astrology, alchemy, and other occult practices as well as certain philosophical issues. In the Renaissance certain manuscripts of these writings were translated in Italy by Marsilio Ficino (1433-1499) and these texts were preceived as Egyptian sources of Greek wisdom.[198] The Hermetic gnostic portrayed in these writings believed himself capable of reflecting the whole universe within his mind or memory. He believed the human mind itself was divine and therefore able to reflect the divine mind that stood behind the universe. Bruno sought to cultivate this world-reflecting magic memory as a technique for achieving the personality of a genuine *magus*. In Bruno, imagination became the sole power of knowledge.[199]

Bruno's books on memory used magical images and signs. These included the signs of the zodiac. In one work he introduced the art of memory with magical incantations uttered by a sorceress.[200] Bruno made extensive use of "memory wheels." In these he sought to combine features of the classical art of memory, featuring places and images, with Lullism a system that used moving figures and letters.[201] But these were framed in the context of the occult. The images used were not classical ones but magical ones. The wheels used were called "conjuring wheels."[202]

This approach to the art of memory developed by Bruno eventually came into conflict with the art of memory according to Ramus.[203] Ramus dropped memory as a part of rhetoric. But this did not mean he was uninterested in memorizing. Ramus believed that simply following the proper method would lead one unerringly from one point to another. There was no need for artificial memory devices of the classical or occult sort. Ramus' logic with its heavy reliance on the topical tradition was actually a system of memory in itself.[204] In a real sense, Ramus made the problem of method also the problem of memory.[205] Ramus wrote this in reaction to the classical art of memory:

> The art of memory (says Quintilian) consists entirely in division and composition. If we seek then an art which will divide and compose things, we shall find the art of memory. Such a doctrine is expounded in our dialectical precepts...and method....For the true art of memory is one and the same as dialectics.[206]

While Ramus rejected the classical *loci* and *imagines*, he did maintain certain elements of the old traditions. He like Aristotle and Aquinas stressed proper order. But he objected to the use of artificial mnemonic devices. He rejected the "laying out external and fictitious signs and representations." Ramus' dialectic sought to lay bare "the order found within things themselves." To Ramus this gave "the truest possible representations" of reality.[207] Ramus saw this as suited for memory in a way no other system could match. The Ramist diagrams with their spatial structures facilitated memorizing as well. There was now no need to use the imagination. No vivid images were needed to stimulate the imagination. Now the "natural" stimulus for memory was something far different. Not the emotionally exciting memory image, but the abstract order of dialectical analysis was what triggered the memory for Ramus.[208]

As such, Ramus and the system of memory advocated by Bruno stood at opposite poles. Bruno sought a vivid use of the imagination to enhance occult memory. It was for him a "magico-religious technique." Ramus on the other hand, sought a simplified teaching method. He found it in the natural dialectical order by which an art is arranged. Once proper method was followed, the art of memory "naturally" followed.[209]

PART III

RAMISM

Chapter III. TRANSMISSION OF RAMISM IN GREAT BRITAIN

A. Roland MacIlmaine

The first editions of Ramus' *Dialectic* to be published in England were printed in London in 1574.[1] Roland MacIlmaine (or M'Kilwein), a young Scot, brought out a Latin verions of Ramus' *Dialecticae Libri Duo* and also and English translation entitled *The Logike of the most Excellent Philosopher F. Ramus Martyr, Newly translated, and in diuers places corrected, after the mynde of the Author*.[2] Not much is known of MacIlmaine. It is known that he graduated with his Bachelor of Arts degree in 1569 from St. Mary's College of the University of St. Andrews. He received his Master's degree in 1570.[3] MacIlmaine produced a second Latin edition of Ramus' logic at London (Thomas Vautrollier, printer) in 1576 and two later editions in Frankfort, Germany in 1579 and 1580. In 1581 MacIlmaine published his second edition of the English translation.[4]

MacIlmaine made some changes in Ramus' work. These consisted chiefly of simplifying and shortening some of the analyses and discussions in his English translation. At some point, additional subdivisions were added.[5] At other points, MacIlmaine omitted many of Ramus' classical illustrations and replaced them with Scriptural quotations.[6] This, along with the fact that he brought out editions in both Latin and English, showed MacIlmain's concern to bring Ramus to the general as well as the learned English public.

In the "Introduction" to the English translation, MacIlmaine commended Ramism as being able to serve the preacher, scientist, lawyer, orator, mathematician and other writers, teachers, and learners, very well. MacIlmaine claimed Ramus had taken "that only perfecte methode which Plato and Aristotle dyd knowe obserued by many noble wryters" and "raysed" it as it were "from deathe." It is now "set before our eyes that his perfecte methode maye be accommodate to all artes & sciences."[7] In short, Ramism was a system of communication which was adaptable for any and all occasions.

MacIlmaine gave examples of how various professionals could use the Ramist system to meet their needs. Of particular interest here is his description of how a minister could use Ramus for framing a sermon:

> If thou be a deuine this methode willethe thee that in place of
> the definition, thou sett forthe shortly the somme of the text,
> whiche thou hast taken in hand to interprete; next to parte thy
> text into a fewe heads that the auditor may the better retaine the
> sayinges: Thirdly to intreate of euery heade in his owne place
> with the ten places of inuention, shewing them the causes, the
> effectes, the adionts and the circumstances: to bring in thy com-
> parisons with the rest of artificiall places: and last to make thy
> matter playne and manifest with familiar examples & authorities
> out of the worde of God: to sett before the auditor (as euery
> heade shall geue the occasion) the horrible and sharpe punyshing
> of disobedience, and the joyfull promises appartayning to the
> obedient and godlie.[8]

These prescriptions by MacIlmaine followed fully from Ramus' natural method. MacIlmaine summarized this method:

> The forme and methode which is kept in this arte, comaundethe
> that the thing which is absolutely most cleare, be placed first:

and secondly that which is next cleare, & so forthe whith the rest. And therefore it continually procedethe from the generall to the speciall and singular. The definition as most generall is first placed, next folowethe the diuision, first into the partes, and next into the formes and kyndes. Euery parte and forme is defined in his owne place, and made manifest by examples of auncient Authors, and last the members are limited and ioined togeather with short transitions for the recreation of the Reader.'

Here MacIlmaine promised the Ramist method to be an effective communicative vehicle. He outlined this method as a four-step process. First, MacIlmaine believed hearers would remember the preacher's message much better if it were set forth in Ramist fashion with the main heads of the sermon organized homogeneously. The heads would then be explicated in turn. Secondly, by presenting the discourse in a "general to particular" flow, the preacher would end with "familiar examples & authorities out of the worde of God." These final, specific examples and testimonies helped the hearer not only to remember, but also permitted the preacher to express effectively the rewards and punishments he wished the people to associate with this doctrine. He was seeking to influence their behavior. Thus methodologically, after the Doctrine of each head was explained, the application or "use" for Christian living was preached.[10]

MacIlmaine did not stress how the method would be successful for the audience in the last two steps of his explanation of Ramist method. Instead he spoke of the ease and efficiency this method provided the preacher. The first aid was that Ramus' system permitted the preacher to condense his text. This was instead of defining it fully. One might expect from this, therefore, the Ramist preacher to be less concerned with detailed etymologies of the individual words of a text than with the meaning of the whole text itself. It was 'the somme of the text,'' that MacIlmaine interpreting Ramus urged the preacher to set before the congregation.

Then finally, in mentioning Ramus' ten topics, MacIlmaine called them into service as a help for the preacher in presenting the argument of the text. They served as a way to "dispose" that argument.[11] For the divine as well as the lawyer, the physician and all artisians, the Ramist system would "work" according to MacIlmaine. He tried to show how by using Ramus' three laws for invention (justice, veritie, and wisdome) and organizing by using Ramist method (moving from general to particular) one could present any subject easily, successfully, and efficiently.

A further significance of MacIlmaine's work was that he showed neglect, and even contempt, for Ramus' prudential method. The natural method of moving from general to particulars was primary for Ramus. He believed it could be used for presenting scientific discourse as well as for oratory and poetry. But he also recognized the prudential method (see above p. 27). The prudential method moved in the opposite direction -- from specifics to generals. It was to be used when the audience was unlearned or unread. The theory was that the speaker (or writer) could gain the immediate interest of this audience if the discourse began with a specific rather than a general incident or thrust.

MacIlmaine devoted a short final chapter to what he termed this "craftie and secrete methode."[12] He spoke of its chief purpose as being "to deceaue the auditor." One did this by introducing into the discourse "thinges appartaining nothing to the matter: but most chiefly see that in the begining thou inuerte thy order, and place some antecedentes after there consequentes." MacIlmaine termed this a "more imperfect forme of methode" since it inverted the natural order and was hence "preposterous and out of all good fashion and order."[13] Ramus himself had deprecated his method used by "poets, orators, and historians." He saw these people as seeking to "deceive" their audiences in that they sought to persuade them not on the basis of true logical thinking, but by appealing to their senses of pleasure and interest. But the result of what MacIlmaine did on this point was to give support to the view that Ramus had only proposed the natural method. This view of Ramus eventually became very influential in England.[14]

B. Scotland

MacIlmaine was a Scot. In the same year he produced his editions of Ramus, Andrew Melville (1545-1622) a distinguished Scots educator, became Principal of the University of Glasgow.[15] Under the leadership of Melville, the Universities of Glasgow, Aberdeen (1575), and St. Andrews (1578) for a while adopted university curriculum reforms based on Ramist teachings.[16] Melville lived on the continent between 1564 and 1573 where he listened to Ramus' lectures.[17] Within five years of becoming Principal at Glasgow, Melville was teaching "the Dialectic of Ramus."[18] Under the Nova Erectic of Glasgow University granted by James VI on July 13, 1577, Melville as Principal gained the leverage he needed to reform the courses of instruction and the system of teaching.[19] In 1583 Melville led the General Assembly of the Presbyterian Church in Scotland, its highest governing body, to condemn Aristotle.[20]

The Presbyterian Melville linked other theological and social concerns to the championing of Ramus. For example, his commitment to the Presbyterian system of church government minimized as much as possible the power of the Scottish aristocracy. Melville opposed the power of aristocrats in the church, except as they were judged "godly" by his standards. In September, 1593 he managed to have certain leaders of the nobility excommunicated from the church by the General Assembly.[21] By 1595 Melville's influence was such that his Ramism was the major influence in all but one of Scotland's universities.[22]

But church and state engaged in bitter battles in Scotland during the last twenty years of the sixteenth century. Melville's Ramism was perceived as part of a programmatic effort to extend "godliness" into all fields -- including logic. Thus the opponents of Melville could not pass by his Ramism, nor his Presbyterianism. To them this reform of logic was connected to a man bent on overturning the established order of King and aristocracy alike.[23] In 1597 Melville lost his rectorship at St. Andrews University when King James VI installed his own supporter George Glandstanes to the post of Vice-chancellor. Over the next ten years Melville's power declined. When James VI became James I of England in 1603, Melville's influence was at an end. In 1606 he was forced into exile. With him also went the dominance of Scottish Ramism in that land.[24]

C. Controversies

While Andrew Melville was introducing Ramism to Scottish universities in the last quarter of the sixteenth century and MacIlmaine's editions of Ramus were being prepared, the English universities were already being exposed to the Ramist philosophy. Before discussing the reception of Ramism at Oxford and Cambridge, the only English universities, brief mention may be made of several intellectual controversies involving Ramists and anti-Ramists from the years 1580-1621.

In 1580, Everard Digby (fl. 1590) wrote a book with the English title *Two Books on the Bipartite Method, in Refutation of the Unipartite Method of Peter Ramus, elucidating from the Best Authors a Plain, Easy, and Exact Way towards the Understanding of the Sciences.*[25] This work purposed against Ramus' "one method," that scientific discourses should be organized by two methods.[26] Digby's work was answered by one Franciscus Mildapettus Nevarrenus (Francis Mildapet) who published *An Admonition to Everard Digby, the Englishman, seeking the Preservation of the Unipartite Method of Peter Ramus, and the Rejection of Other Methods* (1587). Mildapet turned out to be a pseudonym for William Temple (1555-1627). Several more books were issued in the debate.[27] But from this controversy, Digby became known as a conservative philosopher and Temple as one of England's leading Ramistic logicians.[28]

A second controversy in the 1590's involved Gabriel Harvey (1545?-1630) and Thomas Nash (1567-1601). The volley of insults exchanged between these men did not concern specific points of the Ramist philosophy. Instead they were over the whole Ramist enterprise itself.

For example, Nash grieved that in Cambridge University the lamp of learning was flickering. Especially in the training of preachers, he charged, "those years which shoulde bee employed in *Aristotle* are expired in Epitomes."²⁹ Epitomes were favorite tools of the Ramists. Nash named Ramus himself as one of the culprits in trying to shortcut the true educational process and thus corrupting the arts. Nash was answered by Gabriel Harvey, also of Cambridge, who in his *Fovre Letters and certaine Sonnets* tried to vindicate Ramus. He claimed that Ramus along with Agricola, Melanchthon, and Vives had actually "notably reformed many absurdities" into which the corrupted Arts had already fallen.³⁰

The same issue, the legitimacy of epitomes, arose again in a debate between Richard Montagu (1577-1641) and John Selden (1584-1654) a jurist and Semitic scholar. The issue was whether tithes were required by divine or by ecclesiastical law. Selden, Oxford educated, argued in his *The History of Tithes* (1618) that they were required by ecclesiastical law. Montagu, a vigorous defender of the Church of England against the inroads of Puritanism and Catholicism, argued that the requirements stemmed from divine law. In their debate, Montagu attacked those who sought knowledge only with epitomes. Montagu wrote: "He that can carry an Epitome in his pocket,....imagineth mightily, that he knoweth much, and yet indeed is but an *ignaro*. In a day he is taught, but to little purpose, as much as others can learne in a whole yeere."³¹ According to Montagu, Ramus was one of those responsible for this habit of abridging important learned works. When Selden castigated those who distinguished between three or four kinds of tithes and disregarded the most simple, modern approach: "Tithes are best diuided into the first, and second Tithe," Montagu countered: "And why best?....Doubtlesse it is the *best*, which includeth all of that kinde: where the *membra diuidentia* be so full, that nothing is exorbitant, or without the verge of that diuision: else there is, sure there may be, a better diuision than that...."³²

These literary quarrels are but a measure of the controversy raised in England by the introduction of the Ramist system. In the period from 1573-1700 there were 33 editions of Ramus' *Dialectic* and 29 editions of the *Rhetoric* published in the British Isles.³³ While England produced few Ramists who wrote academic treatises on the system itself for the benefit of colleagues in university circles, there was nevertheless a significant impact of the Ramist philosophy on the universities and Enlgish educational systems.³⁴ Cambridge University was a seedbed for Ramism. The Ramism germinated there grew fruitfully in the Puritan movement within the English Church. As several scholars have pointed out, "most of the great English Puritans were followers of Ramus."³⁵ At times the Ramist system carried with its social and political implications that went far beyond intellectual debates about Aristotelianism, method, and epitomes.³⁶

D. English Logics

When MacIlmaine's editions of Ramus were published in 1574, England had already produced several important works on logic and rhetoric that bore outward resemblances to the systems Ramus had attacked in Europe previously. These logics represent English vernacular appropriations of the Continental scholastic traditions.³⁷

The earliest logical textbook written in English was by Thomas Wilson (1525?-1581). *The rule of Reason, conteinying the Arte of Logique, set forth in Englishe* was published in 1551 with reprints issued in 1552, 1553, 1563, 1567, and 1580.³⁸ In 1553 Wilson published *The Arte of Rhetorique* which was the first English treatment of rhetoric to be based on Cicero, Quintilian and the *ad Herennium*.³⁹

Wilson did not distinguish between logic and dialectic. He said that "they are bothe one."⁴⁰ He divided logic into two parts, invention and judgment. But he took up the treatment of invention after he spent about seventy-five pages treating judgment.⁴¹ By adopting the judgment/invention order, Wilson followed Agricola.

Basically, Wilson tried to render into English the main ideas and terms of Aristotle's *Organon* as these had been interpreted in the Renaissance. But while Wilson expounded the Aristotelian terminology: substance, accident, predicables or categories etc.,⁴² there were also strong indications of the further influence of Agricola's logical theory -- especially in Wilson's treatment of the *loci*.[43] Wilson did not acknowledge Agricola as his source. But he translated Agricola's twenty-four *loci* into English and gave a similar account of each. Wilson followed Agricola in defining a *locus* ("place") as a "mark" which "gives warning to our memory what we may speak probably."[44] Wilson repeated the same two uses for *loci* in inventing arguments that Agricola had propounded.[45] In illustrating the second of these uses, Wilson tried to adapt Agricola's question: "Should a philosopher marry?" to the troubled English religious situation. His question was: "Ought a priest to marry?"[46] Thus while this earliest of the English "scholastic" logicians expounded Aristotle, he seems also to have imbibed some of the spirit of the humanists' dialectical concerns. He was particularly indebted to Agricola.[47]

A second important English logician was John Seton. Seton was born around 1498 and was a Roman Catholic who left England after the death of Henry VIII. He died in Rome in 1567. His *Dialectica Ionnis Setoni* was initially published in 1545 and was a standard textbook in logic for many years.[48] The edited and annotated versions of this work by Peter Carter -- In *Johannis Setoni Dialecticam Annotationes* (1560's) and *Dialetica Ioannis Setoni Cantabrigiensis, annotationibus Petri Carteri* (1572) heightened its popularity.[49]

Seton followed the arrangement of Aristotle's *Organon*. But he too was influenced by Agricola. He was more scholastic than Wilson in treating the choices and arrangement of logical considerations. But on the other hand, Seton acknowledged his use of Agricola where Wilson had not. He cited Agricola not only in places where he agreed with him, but also at places where they diverged and where Seton modified the Dutch logician.[50] Three of the four books of Seton's work were on judgment. The reason for this was, he said, that Agricola had treated invention fully and sufficiently.[51] Seton like Wilson exactly reproduced Agricola's classification of the *loci* and used all of Agricola's terms and subdivisions. On the whole there was less of Agricola in Seton's work than in Wilson's. But what was there was mostly acknowledged. Seton used Agricola's classifications whereas Wilson also used his definitions, rationale, classifications and uses for *loci*. Still, Seton clearly used Agricolan terminology and concepts.[52]

The third major English logical manual was Peter Carter's commentary on Seton's *Dialectica*.[53] When it was published in 1563, there were no longer many editions of Agricola's *Invention* being produced.[54] In his annotations, Carter added his own theory of invention to that of Seton's. In Carter's section (which was twelve pages long compared to Seton's four), Carter's treatment of the topics leaned more towards the scholastic traditions of Boethius than to Agricola. Boethius conceived the topics as *maximae* or "rules of thumb." In Agricola each *loci* was logically analyzed and then illustrated from classical literature.[55] In the topics, Carter and Seton listed thirty-three *loci*.[56]

Seton's and Carter's logical textbook began with the definition: *Dialecticta est scientia probabiliter de quouis themate differendi*. Seton continued with further statements and definitions that elaborated this first sentence. After two pages, he moved on to a further explanation. The notes by Carter were in smaller type. He expounded Seton and also arranged Seton's material more schematically. Then he explained each word in Seton's statements by his own. This epitomized the scholastic approach to learning logic. The initial definition was subjected to minute dissection, word by word. Each new point was derived from that which went before.[57] Though the work of Ramus had been available since 1555, there was no mention or interaction by Carter with the French logician.[58] Ramus' definition of dialectic as the art of disputing well, his preference for invention over judgment as a pedagogical priority, his use of the three laws instead of the traditional predicables, and his simplified syllogism and method in place of the induction process were all ignored. Instead, Wilson, Seton, and Carter, while showing some influence of Agricola's humanist theory of invention, on the whole maintained medieval scholasticism's interpretation of Aristotle's *Organon* with its terminology of predicables, categories, predicaments etc.[59]

The final logic produced in England before the influence of Ramus was felt was Ralph Lever's (d. 1585) *The Arte of Reason, rightly termed, Witcraft*. It was published in London in 1573.⁶⁰ Lever was the younger brother of Thomas Lever the Marian exile. He did his undergraduate work at St. John's College, Cambridge and also took a Master's and Doctor's degree from that University. Lever's *Witcraft* was apparently written some twenty years before it was published. In the "Dedicatory Letter" Lever wrote that "Martine Bucer read ouer this arte, in his old days, and renevved in his age, the rules that he learned thereof in his youth."⁶¹ Bucer had been Regius Professor of Divinity at Cambridge from the fall of 1549 until his death at the end of February, 1551. During that same period, Lever was a Fellow of St. John's and completing his Master's degree. Thus it is likely Lever's work was written at this time.⁶²

Wilson in his *Rule of Reason* adapted English terms from Latin to use for logical vocabulary. He used terms such as predicables, predicaments, proposition etc. Lever chose another route. He believed the English language excelled other languages in that it was capable of developing new terms and "compouding" words to express ideas. For "logic" or "dialectic," Lever came up with "witcraft." For "rhetoric" he used "speechcrafte." He explained "witcraft" by saying that "Wit in oure mother toung is oft taken for reason: and crafte is the auncient English woorde, whereby wee haue vsed to expresse an Arte: whiche two wordes knit together in Witcrafte, doe signifie the Arte that teacheth witte and reason."⁶³ Other examples of Lever's vocabulary included: "storehouse" for "category"; "saying" for "proposition"; "saywhat" for "definition"; "reason by rule" for "deduction"; and "endsay" for "conclusion."⁶⁴

Lever's logical terminology did not endure in future English logical works. But his *Witcraft* did stand as the last major scholastic work on logic to be produced in England before the influx of Ramist logic. Lever followed Seton in dividing his work into four books. The first three were on judgment, the last on invention. He moved from the simplest to the most complex features of discourse when he wrote of words in Book I; propositions in Book II; inductive and deductive arguments in Book III; and places (*loci*) or topics in Book IV.⁶⁵ For Lever, Aristotle was the greatest logician and ultimate authority. He wrote: "In my three firste bookes, I onely folow Aristotle: both for manner, & also for order."⁶⁶ In his fourth book, Lever admitted to being independent of earlier writers on invention. But he did acknowledge the strength of Aristotle's treatment in the *Topics*.⁶⁷ For Lever the purpose of logic was to learn "the order of reasoning in doubtful matters, to speak forcefully on them for or *contra*." It also "teaches how to discover and disprove error."⁶⁸

E. Oxford

In both Oxford and Cambridge through medieval times, the *trivium* (grammar, rhetoric, and dialectic) occupied the key position at the center of the arts course. It was seen as teaching the basic skills needed for the student to speak well, handle language, and argue correctly. These skills were a necessary preliminary step to the rest of the curriculum. This was the *quadrivium* (arithmetic, astronomy, geometry, and music) as well as the threee philosophies: natural, moral, and metaphysics.⁶⁹ A study of the Statues of the universities over along period of time in the medieval era reveals a close conjunction in the texts used and the arts curriculum followed.⁷⁰

In the only English universities, Oxford and Cambridge, as in the universities of Europe until the 1520's, the main textbook for the teaching of logic was Peter of Spain's Summulae logicales. This work taught that dialectic was basically a study of language and how it is used, rather than of concepts and processes of thought. Falsehood could be detected by exposing a faulty linguistic formulation of a case.⁷¹

Humanist reaction to scholastic logic culminating with Ramus appears not to have been very strong at Oxford.⁷² It was at Cambridge where the logic of Ramus took more substantial hold.⁷³ This is not to say the works of Ramus were unknown at Oxford (see above, John Selden).⁷⁴ It means, though, that Ramus did not influence the logical and philosophical teachings at that University as he did at Cambridge.⁷⁵ While Ramus was read and discussed at Oxford, there is no evidence that his work began a recognizable school of thought there.[76]

Officially Oxford went on record with its Statute of 1586. This ordered that only the views of Aristotle or other authors *secundum Aristotelem* could be debated during the Lenten exercises in the school that year. Questions "disagreeing from the ancient and true philosophy" (*vera et antiqua philosophia*) were banned. This Statute was directed against scholastic subtleties which accumulated with the study of Aristotle. But it was also aimed against Ramus as well.[77]

John Case (d. 1600), called "the most important English Aristotelian of the renaissance period," attacked Ramus in the first book published by the Oxford University Press in 1585, *Speculum Moralium Quaestionum*. This was a commentary on Aristotle's *Ethics*.[78] It was dedicated to the Earl of Leicester, the University Chancellor and founder of the Press.[79] In Cases' treatise on logic *Summa veterum interpretum in universam dialecticam Aristotelis* (1580; 1584; 1592; 1598), he criticized Ramus on two points. First, he saw Ramus not as simplifying method in logic but as impoverishing the logical tradition because of the bitterness of Ramus' attack on ancient teachers. Secondly, Case objected to Ramus' classificatory logic that sought to replace the use of the traditional syllogism in logical demonstration. For Case dialectic "serves as the hand to the rest of the sciences, for it provides the manner of proving it all."[80] In this Case stood securely in the medieval logical tradition on the nature and function of dialectic. He acknowledged his main teachers from the past to have been Aquinas, Boethius, Lambert of Auxerre, Agostino Nifo and others.[81]

There is evidence of an awareness of Ramus by others who attended Oxford in the latter part of the sixteenth century. Richard Hooker in his *Of the Lawes of Ecclesiasticall Politie* which began publication in 1593 saw Aristotle as the one who came closer to true art and learning than anyone else. "Ramystry" to him was only "an Art which teachest the way of speedie discourse, and restrayneth the minde of man that it may not waxe our wise."[82] Later, Richard Mather who sojourned in Oxford for only a few month before identifying himself with the Puritan party in the church and emigrating to New England, was appointed to read Ramus by his tutor Dr. Thomas Worrall.[83] But by and large it must be said that the logic and philosophy of Ramus did not gain a significant, organized foothold in this university.

F. Cambridge

At Cambridge a strong succession of Ramist adherents arose. This tradition had important implications for the Church of England and particularly for the "Puritan party" within that church.

From 1560-1590 the largest part of the Bachelor of Arts course at Cambridge was devoted to the *trivium*. In 1570 University statutes prescribed: "He shall teach rhetoric the first year, dialectic the second and third. In the fourth year he should add philosophy."[84] On the whole, university statutes referred to the complete arts course as "dialectical." It was stated: "No one shall be admitted as scholar in any college unless he has reached fourteen, nor shall anyone be accepted into any college unless he has been instructed and prepared for the learing of dialectic."[85] Five lectureships established at Trinity College in 1560 were designated "dialectic lectureships" with the lecturers to teach elementary dialectics (one transcription of the statutes specifying from John Seton's manual; Porphyry; Aristotle; and Agricola.)[86] These all took place before the student's third (sophister) year. Examination of students' texts and courses of study indicate that by the time a student reached the university, rhetoric was already studied fully.[87] Dialectic was yet to be mastered as the key for higher education.

Recent studies have examined the logic textbooks used at Cambridge in the second half of the sixteenth century. Indications are that texts by the following authors were the most widely used at Cambridge in this period: Agricola, Melanchthon, Caesarius, Seton (Peter Carter's annotated edition) and Ramus. The text of Ramus' was evidently a later edition of his 1543 *Dialecticae institutiones*. Three reasons have been advanced to explain its popularity here: 1) It was simple. It was simpler than the logical manual of John Seton. 2) It represented an aggressive approach to the curriculum. Ramus wrote not only on logic but on many other subjects as well. 3) The work of Ramus was presented clearly and coherently. It was well-suited for the needs of those beginning their Arts course in that it equipped them with "the bare minimum" needed to carry out the required academic exercises.[88]

The earliest proponent of the Ramist logic at Cambridge was Laurence Chaderton (1536?-1640).[89] This influential figure began a Ramist tradition at Cambridge, particularly in Christ's College, and forged a strong link between the Ramist logic and Puritanism.[90]

Chaderton entered Christ's College in 1562. While there he became a convinced Protestant and pursued studies in Divinity. He was elected Fellow of the College and obtained the B.A. in 1567, his M.A. in 1571. From 1571-1584 Chaderton held various college and university offices.[91] Chaderton was most influential as a tutor. Among Chaderton's pupils at Christ College was William Perkins.[93]

Chaderton was a Fellow of Christ's from 1568 to 1577. He was a wide-ranging scholar but officially held the office of Reader in Logic in the public schools of the University. He could read French, Spanish, and Italian as well as Latin, Greek, and Hebrew. In the course of his teaching, Chaderton lectured on "the *Ars logica* of Peter Ramus" and "roused a great interest in that study through the University."[94] Chaderton himself never published anything on Ramus. But it is likely that fragments of his lectures survive in *The Sheapheardes Logike* by Abraham Fraunce.[95]

Chaderton had a long career and died in 1640.[96] He left his position at Christ's College in 1584 and became Master of Emmanuel College, a college "founded by a Puritan for Puritans" where he served for thirty-eight years until 1622.[97] Chaderton preached at St. Clement's Church, Cambridge for fifty years. When he finally gave up this lectureship, "forty clergymen begged him to continue, alleging that to him they owed their conversion."[98] Chaderton was active in theological controversies.[99] He played a major role in the development of the Puritan party. He pleaded for tolerance for Puritans before King James I at the Hampton Court Conference (1603-1604).[100] This "pope of Cambridge puritanism"[101] was said to have had "a plain but effectual way of Preaching."[102] At one point after having preached two hours, it is reported the congregation cried out: "For God's sake, sir, go on, we beg you, go on!" At this Chaderton preached for one hour more.[103]

Chaderton's Puritan sympathies led him to agree with Walter Travers that "universities ought to be the seed and the fry of the holy ministry throughout the realm."[104] For this purpose, Chaderton designed a two year program of study "for the training up and exercising of students in divinity, whereby they may be made fit and meet to discharge the duties belonging to that profession."[105] Chaderton's emphasis was on two types of training: Bible study and disputation. As he saw it, a broad base of learning through several fields of knowledge was crucial if students were to "search out by themselves the true sense and meaning" of the Bible. Hebrew and Greek were to be mastered. So also was rhetoric, for "it teacheth truly to discern proper speeches from those that are tropical [from a *trope*] and figurative." Next followed the study of logic. Then similar passages of Scripture were to be compared and consultation made of the ancient and modern commentators. Also important was a thorough acquaintance with Greek and Roman history. In disputation, which was the second means "for the attaining unto the...principal gifts of the ministry," the student needed to learn how to defend truth and confute error. For this Chaderton urged following "the usual practised in all universities."[106]

Chaderton himself, who was created a Bachelor of Divinity in 1578, is reported to have joined Lancelot Andrewes and three men who were later to become well-known Puritan preachers Ezekiel Culverwell, John Knewstub, and John Carter for weekly conferences where the meaning of a passage of Scripture was sought. These men divided the duties:

> One was for the original language; another's task was for the
> grammatical interpretation; another's for the logical analysis;
> another's for the true sense and meaning of the text; another

gathered the doctrines; and thus they carried on their several employments, till at last they went out like Apollos, eloquent men, and mighty in the scriptures.[107]

An example of how Chaderton himself approached Scripture and used the Ramist method for its exposition is found in the sermon attributed to him entitled: "A fruitfull sermon, upon the 3.4.5.6.7.&8. verses of the 12. Chapter of the Epistle of S. Paule to the Romans."[108] A Ramist chart complete with divisions and brackets introduces the sermon under the heading: "The parts and order of the Sermon." Briefly Chaderton argued that these six verses in Romans "contain a perpetuall law touchying the government of Christes Church" which is "eyther": "Generall" or "speciall." These were dichotomized. The "Generall" law "appertayning to all the members of the Churche," was "declared by two familiar Arguments." These were (in verse 3) a "contrarie vnto the law" found in the joining of "the same sentence with the Lawe" in verse 2; and the other as "a similitude" taken from "the naturall disposition of the bodie" (vs. 4,5). The special law of Church government belonged "only to publike perons" who were either "Prophetes" ("disposers of the worde and secrets of God") or "Officers." The prophets were either "Doctours" (v. 7) or "Pastours" (v. 8). The officers were divided into "deacons," "rulers" and "attenders on the poore."[109] In short, this sermon was basically one of the proof-texts in Romans 12 for a presbyterian or congregational system of church government.[110]

Chaderton's grounding in the Ramist logic was thus useful for him in presenting the case for his theological position. He quite simply divided the passage of Scripture into its proper parts, subdivided when appropriate and came out with a "logical analysis" in the form of a Ramist chart. This showed at a glance the main topics of his argument. In true Ramist fashion Chaderton moved from the most general head to the more specific (called here by Chaderton the "special"): The general law of church government pertained to all church members; the "special" only to "publike persons" either prophets or officers. The final divisions were then made.

Here then was a clear example of the way that the Ramist logician could "analyze" a portion of Scripture. On the other hand, Chaderton's sermon outline is but an early example of a long string of Puritan preachers who did their preaching and their theological writing by making use of Ramist principles.

The line of those influenced by Chaderton at Cambridge branches out almost like a Ramist chart itself. While Chaderton was expounding Ramist logic at Christ's College, Gabriel Harvey was a student there.[111] In later years in controversy with Thomas Nash, Harvey mentioned Chaderton's sermons. He described them as "methodicall," a fitting term for a Ramist pupil to use of his Ramist master at a time when the term "method" was almost "a confession of the author's awareness of Ramus."[112] However, Harvey did not mention Chaderton when he spoke of what drew him to Ramism. He connected his interest in Ramus to a reference he found to Ramus' *Ciceronianus* in a work entitled *Ciceronianus* by Johannes Sambucus. When Harvey purchased Ramus' *Ciceronianus* he read it twice in two days. This most likely occurred in 1569. Five years later, on April 23, 1574 Harvey was appointed Praelector in Rhetoric at Pembroke College, Cambridge (two months before MacIlmaine's Latin translation of Ramus was registered for publication). In his initial lecture course and in two inaugural lectures published as *Rhetor* and *Ciceronianus* (1577), Harvey presented the Ramist view of rhetoric.[113]

This meant that Harvey, following Ramus, restricted rhetoric to the development of style and delivery. Harvey urged his readers (and hearers) to disregard the numerous topics and *loci* drawn out of Aristotle by his disciples. Instead, exhorted Harvey, use Ramus' simple scheme and method. Classes of concepts and disciplines must be carefully distinguished or else confusion would result. Harvey went on to advocate a complete program based on Ramist methods for the studies of the whole *trivium* at Cambridge.[114]

While Harvey lectured in 1575 and 1576 on Ramist rhetoric and Chaderton on Ramist logic between 1571 and 1577, William Temple (1555-1627) was a student at King's College,

Cambridge. He was to become perhaps England's most well-known Ramist logician.[115] It is possible that he heard both Harvey and Chaderton. Temple had entered Cambridge in 1573 and became a Fellow (1576) and Bachelor of Arts (1577-1578 term). Temple stayed on at King's to become a tutor in logic. In the controversy with Everard Digby, Temple defended Ramus' "unipartite method."

In 1584 Temple published a Latin text of Ramus' *Dialecticae Libri Duo* and his own commentary on it. He added to this volume a disputation of his own on Porphyry's *Isagoge* and a rebuttal (under twenty-nine heads) to a letter of Johannes Piscator that had been an answer to Temple's earlier letter to him on Piscator's criticism of Ramus.[116] Temple dedicated this work to Sir Philip Sidney with the hope that "you may begin to love this discipline which was saved as from ruin by the genius of P. Ramus and quite splendidly elucidated by him...."[117] From 1572-1575 Sidney toured the continent. In Frankfurt he stayed at the home of Ramus' printer Andre Wechel. There he met a traveling companion of Ramus' Hubert Languet who also was visiting there.[118] Sidney apparently helped direct many of the Wechel's works into England.[119] Temple became Sidney's secretary as a result of this dedication and their meeting in 1585. Temple wrote a commentary on Sidney's *Defence of Poesie* entitled *Analysis tractationis de poesi contextae a nobilissimo viro Phillipo Signeio Equite Aurato*.[120]

William Temple also applied the Ramist logic to the Bible. In 1605 be published *A Logicall Analysis of Twentie Select Psalmes* in which he laid out his analysis of twenty Psalms in Ramist fashion.[121] Temple had become Provost of Trinity College, Dublin and dedicated this work to Prince Henry of Wales. In that dedication, which has been called "an essential document for understanding the effects of the Ramist system on English thinkers," Temple outlined some of the goals, methods, and results of the Ramist logical system.[122] The "art of loglike" enables one to contrive and frame a discourse and then "to discouer and lay foorth in the pure naturals not onely the seuerall members, but the particular structure and conformation of the same." When first one has "found and obserued the question," one next examines "the qualities of the proofes alleaged, and how iudiciously the illustration thereso is carried." This logic enables one to detect "whatsoeuer is base or fine" in the discourse and will in particular.

> shew whether the wit hath failed in the search of allegations: and whether error is liew of truth, inconsequence in steede of an vncensurable conclusion, disorder in place of methodicall proceeding hath been intertained.[123]

There was "no subject of what nature soeuer, falling within the reach of naturall reason, which by Logike the expresse image thereof cannot be disputed." This included "matters diuine and Theological." Indeed "in the handling and iudging of them also Loglike serueth for a singular light and helpe." Temple's work was a "Logicall Analysis (whereby it is stripped as it were of all outward habit, and laid foorth in the first and naturall lineaments)." Temple claimed his logic would give arguments for clearing a cause; direct one to what is "true and iustifiable," disclaiming what is inconsequential; and "marshall each thing in his proper ranke and place." This being done, the true meaning of the art and thus the true meaning of the Word of God (when the method was applied to Scripture) will be made plain and eminently useful according to Temple. The body of Temple's work was set out in a mixture of prose and brackets indicating the branches of the different "arguments."[124] Temple showed how Ramist logic could be used as a vehicle for Scriptural exegesis and how by "analysis" any portion of the Bible could be "logically resolved."

Temple was perhaps influential in introducing the Ramist philosophy to Anthony Wotton (1561?-1626).[125] Wotton was a student at King's College during the time Temple lectured there. He received his B.A. in 1583-1584 and his M.A. in 1587. In 1594 Wotton gained his Bachelor of Divinity degree and became the first professor of Theology at Gresham College (1596), a newly established college under Puritan control.[126] After two years Wotton became a Puritan lecturer, a position he held till his death.

Wotton prevailed upon his son Samuel Wotton to render a fresh translation of Ramus' Latin *Dialecticae Libri Duo*. This was published as *The Art of Logick* (London, 1626) under Anthony Wotton's name. This was some forty years after Wotton's initial exposure to Ramist logic. The set of Latin notes given by Wotton to his son to prepare him to translate and which appear in the books as the basis for the exposition of Ramus' doctrine were probably Anthony Wotton's notes from William Temple's lectures. The Scriptural examples that abound in the work were added by Samuel Wotton. This work was unusual in that it stated on its title page that the Ramist logic was basically scholastic logic reorganized.[127]

The influence of Chaderton was further felt through Abraham Fraunce (fl. 1587-1633). Fraunce mentioned Chaderton as one of the sources for his *The Sheapheardes Logike*. This work was not published and exists only in manuscript.[128] Fraunce obtained his B.A. in 1579-1580 at St. John's College where he must have been able to hear Chaderton still lecturing on Ramus. His education was paid for by his patron, Sir Philip Sidney. Fraunce dedicated his *The Sheapheardes Logike* to Sidney. Fraunce became a lawyer after he took his M.A. degree in 1583. In 1588 he published *The Lawiers Logike*. This was an explication of Ramus' philosophy adapted for lawyers by the use of many legal illustrations. This was the first time Ramus had been specifically interpreted for lawyers.[129]

Fraunce also retained examples drawn from Edmund Spenser's *The Shepheardes Calendar* that were included in his own *The Sheapheardes Logike*. Fraunce's literary flare abounded in his "Preface" where he defended Ramus against "the importance exclamations of a raging and fireyfaced Aristotelean" who hated Ramus' profaning of logic by making it so that "euery Cobler can cogge a Syllogisme, euery Carter crake of Propositions."[130] While Fraunce made additions to and at times disagreed with the texts of Ramus, he was still firmly committed to the Ramist enterprise. These variances, however, display the flexible nature of the Ramist system. As has been noted, some "discrepancies between one Ramist and another are always in evidence....and they are to be accepted only as a reminder that they can exist and flourish without thereby creating any serious divisions within Ramism as a movement."[131]

Along with William Temple, Cambridge University produced two other major commentators on Ramus' logic. These were George Downame (1565?-1634), Professor of Logic at Christ's College and Alexander Richardson of Queen's College. Downame was the son of the Bishop of Chester and graduated with his B.A. from Christ's College in 1585. This was one year after William Perkins had become a Fellow there and one year after Temple's publication and annotations on Ramus' *Dialecticae*.[132] Downame remained at Christ's as Professor of Logic and Fellow. It was said of him that "no man was then and there better skill'd in *Aristotle*, or a greater Follower of *Ramus*."[133]

Downame was Puritan in his sympathies and was involved in several theological disputes within the University.[134] In fact he was "so Puritan that he could only obtain an Irish bishopric, though he came of an episcopal family. In 1631, he was in trouble with Laud for publishing an attack on Arminianism."[135] Downame published his *Commentarius in Rami Dialecticam* in 1605 (and again in 1610 at Frankfurt). When it was later published in London in 1669, the text of Ramus' *Dialecticae* used fifty-four pages and Downame's commentary nearly five-hundred pages.[136]

Downame also published sermons and theological works along with his commentaries on Ramus. In these theological pieces Downame applied Ramist method to Scripture. Invention contained the places and homes of the arguments as Downame said, "whence the furniture of all oratory as well as abundance of reason is drawn forth."[137] By proper arrangement of arguments, a discourse becomes intelligible. To the Ramist Downame, Scriptural statements were self-evident axioms. They were "arguments" which bore certain relationships to each other. He wrote when expositing the first chapter of Luke: "....the former part of this Psalm, from the beginning therof to the end of my Text, is but one sentence or Axiome wherein there is relation of consequence...."[138] His whole exposition could thus be skeletonized in the Ramist fashion.[139] The same method was applied also when Downame preached on a single verse as in his sermon "The Christian Art of Thriving whereby a man may become rich to God, or a Sermon on Matt. 6:33" (London, 1620).[140]

Alexander Richardson (fl. 1587) of Queen's College received his Bachelor of Arts degree in 1583-1584 during the time Downame was at Christ's. He became a Master of Arts in 1587 and lectured at Queen's on a variety of subjects. Notes on these lectures were taken by hearers and were published in 1629 (and 1657) as *The Logicians School-Master*. Richardson lectured on Ramist logic. According to Samuel Thomson the London bookseller who published the second edition of *The Logicians School-Master*, "it was his Logick whereby, as by a Key, he opened the secrets of all other Arts and Sciences, to the admiration of all that heard him."[141] Richardson's method in commenting on the *Dialecticae* was to quote Ramus in Latin and then explain the text in "Latin-studded English," while also answering objections raised by critics.

Richardson's comments about the use of syllogisms in the Ramist system are particularly revealing. Ramus' goal was to reduce all discourse to its simples components. This meant he was not so much interested in intricate varieties of syllogisms as he was with arriving at axioms. Abraham Fraunce had written as a true Ramist: "The first, and almost the chief kinde of judgment is in axioms, yea, the very foundation of all other judgment."[142] But when one needed help in arriving at an axiom, syllogism could be used. Richardson followed Ramus in seeing syllogisms as tools to be used when a chain of thought was broken. Richardson wrote:

> Syllogisms serve but for the clearing of the truth of axioms, and then afterward we return again to the rule of an axiom to judge whether it be true or false, and this is all that is required for disposing arguments, *ergo*, method is *dispositio axiomatum* onely.[143]

Method amounted to judging axioms only. Richardson believed that all thinking is "the running about of our reason for the finding out of truth." When axioms are discovered and laid bare, "the sea is calm" as he said. When syllogistic judgment must be used, there is a troubled sea "full of storms, winds and tempests, for there our reason beats every corner to conclude that which is doubtful." The goal was to find the axioms and set them in proper order (method). Then, said Richardson, "our reason is quiet, being satisfied with the truth."[144]

Before leaving the line of Cambridge University Ramists, mention should be made of Dudley Fenner (1558?-1587). Fenner entered Peterhouse College, Cambridge in 1575. This means it is possible he might have heard the lectures given by Gabriel Harvey in the spring of that year which eventually became the *Rhetor*.[145] It has been speculated that Harvey inspired Fenner's idea to produce a work in which logic and rhetoric would be clearly distinguished as two separate arts, yet at the same time be bound in the same volume.[146] Both these arts were necessary if the art of communication was to be carried out well.

After Fenner left the University he stayed with English Calvinists in Antwerp for a while. He returned to England and had a brief and stormy career as a pastor in Kent. Fenner ended up in jail in the summer of 1584.[147] When released, Fenner succeeded his teacher Thomas Cartwright as chaplain to the English merchants living in Middleburg in the Netherlands. There he also became Paster of the Reformed church. While in the Netherlands, Fenner renounced his Anglican orders. In 1587 he died.

In 1584 *The Artes of Logike and Rethorike* was published in Middleburg by Richard Schilders. There was no author's name attached to this book.[148] The work on logic came from Ramus' *Dialecticae Libri Duo*. The corresponding work on rhetoric was drawn from Omer Talon's *Rhetoricae Libri Duo*. Here was the whole Ramist theory of communication brought together for the first time in the English language. Fenner argued that since "the common vse and practise of all men in generall, both in reasoning to the purpose, and in speaking with some grace and elegancie, hath sowen the seede of these artes, why should not all reape where all haue sowen?"[149] Fenner did not acknowledge openly that Ramus was the source of his works. But he defined himself against charges that he was unduly tampering with a received body of established truth.[150] It has been rightly said that "Fenner was working within the accepted body of Ramistic doctrine, and...the changes which his preface refers to and discusses are not unlike the minor changes made by most other good Ramists when they were seeking to promulgate their master's teachings."[151]

Fenner went beyond MacIlmaine's exposition of Ramus in recognizing more clearly that Ramist philosophy included both the natural and the prudential method.[152] Fenner said Ramist method analyzed "the best and perfectest" as well as "the worst & troublesomest" way to handle a matter. His initial definition of method was

> the iudgement of more axiomes, whereby many and diuers axiomes being framed according to the properties of an axiome perfectly or exactly iudged, are so ordered as that the easiest and most generall bee set downe first, the harder are lesse generall next, vntill the whole matter be so conueited, as all the parts may best agree with themselues, &c be best kept in memorie.[153]

This "perfect way" (Ramus' natural method) used for learned writing proceeded this way:

> the definition of that which is to be handled, must first be set downe, and then the diuision of the same into the members, &c the generall properties of the same, and then the diuers sortes of it, if there by any and so proceeding vntill by fit and apt passages or transitions, the whole be so farre handled, that it can be no more deuided.[154]

According to Fenner, "this Methode because it is so agreeable to reason, and easie to be practised, is for the most part followed of all writers or speakers." Fenner announced he would exemplify this proper method in his treatise on household government which was to follow.[155] But he also said that writers or speakers "may and doe according to their matter, time, place, persons, and all such circumstances, wisely alter, change, or hide the same." This method Fenner called "the hyding or concealing, or crypsis of Method." It was actually Ramus' prudential method which was geared to "unlearned" audiences. In this method Fenner said, writers and speakers

> leaue out the former orderly placing of definitions, Diuisions, and transitions, & do take in diuers repitions, declarations, making lightsome, enlargings, or amplifications, prouings of the thing, preuenting of obiections, out goeing from the matter, called digressions, as it shall make most fit for their purpose.[156]

The adaptation of Ramus and Talon by Fenner was the only one of his works that was not specifically theological in nature. In 1585 he published *The Sacred Doctrine of Divinitie Gathered out of the Word of God*. This was one of the very first ventures into systematic theology by an Elizabethan Englishman.[157]

Fenner's opening definition of Divinity was typically Ramist; "Divinitie is a doctrine of glorifying God, whereof there be two partes, Theologie and Religion."[158] Theology, pertaining to God, was divided into God's Kingdom and God's Honor. God's Kingdom was divided into "purpose" and "works." "Works" divided into "Creation" and "Government." Religion, pertaining to righteousness, was discussed by Fenner as parts including "piety" and "justice" and kinds which included "our own" and "another's (Christ's)." These were further divided, always by dichotomies.[159]

Certain characteristics of the Ramist philosophy and method stand out when applied to theology. The first division, corresponding to the initial partition after the definition, is more "theoretical" in nature. The second division is likely to be more "practical" or "useful." In Fenner's *Sacred Doctrine*, the first division ("Theology") concerned God. Fenner there discussed God's Kingdom, Honor, Purposes, Works, etc. In a logical sense, these subjects were the underpinnings for the second division. This was "Religion" and had to do in Fenner's treatise with "righteousness" or the individual's standing before God. When righteousness was divided, the first division was "theoretical" in the sense of discussing the constitutive "parts" of righteousness. The second division discussed the "kinds" and was divided into "our own" and "another's," thus being concerned with how righteousness expressed itself. The movement was from the abstract to the concrete; the theoretical to the practical; the general to the specific; the inward to the outward. In broadest terms, Fenner's discourse can be seen as dividing Divinity into two parts: "faith" and "works" (theory and practice). In all this, he and other Ramists were following the precepts of Ramist method. As Fenner traced the movements: from definition, to members with their general properties, to the general sorts. His axioms moved from "the easiest and most generall' to the "lesse general next" until "the whole be so farre handled, that it can be not more deuided."[160]

PART IV

RAMISM IN WILLIAM PERKINS

Chapter IV. RAMISM IN PERKINS' EARLIEST WORKS

The fact that William Perkins was a student of Laurence Chaderton's might lead one to suspect that Perkins would become a Ramist. Given the influence of tutors over their students at this time, the suspicion becomes all the more likely. Further, Perkins lived at a time when Ramist works -- translations, annotations, commentaries etc. were becoming available. Since Perkins was considered by many Puritans as their leading theological spokesman, the question of Ramist influence of Perkins is of more than passing interest. In order to come to a conclusion on this matter, attention and analysis must be made of Perkins' published works.[1]

A. *Polemical Works*

The very earliest of Perkins' published works appear to have been written with specific polemical intents in mind. The first of these appeared in 1584, the year Perkins became a Fellow of Christ's College, Cambridge. In that year a controversy arose over the art of memory. This dispute occurred between a follower of Giordano Bruno and a Ramist from Cambridge.

The opening volley in this contention came when the following work was printed in London by Thomas Vautrollier: *Alexandri Dicsoni Arelii de umbra rationis et iudicii siue de memoriae virtute prosopcoia.*[2] The title page gave the date as 1583.[3] Alexander Dickson (Dicson), a supporter of Mary, Queen of Scots, was a graduate of St. Andrews in Scotland and lived in England as a "gentleman" amidst company that included Robert Dudley, Earl of Leicester (and uncle of Sir Philip Sidney). Dickson's book was a book on the art of memory based on the theories of Bruno who had published his memory work some ten years before.[4]

A response to this work soon appeared under the title *Antidicsonus* (1584). The author signed himself "G.P. Cantabrigiensis." It seems certain that this "G.P." was William (Guglielmus) Perkins.[5] In this work and another little tract bound with it, G.P. of Cambridge explained why he rejected "the impious artificial memory of Dicson." This accompanying tract was entitled "Libellus in quo dilucide explicatur impia Dicsoni artificiosa."[6] Dickson, under the pseudonym "Heius Scepsius" defended himself in *Defensio pro Alexandro Dicsono*.[7] He was attacked again in 1584 by "G.P." in *Libellus de memoria verissimaque bene recordandi scientia...Admonitiuncula ad Alexandrum Dicsonum de artificiosae memoriae vanitate.*[8]

This literary battle pitted the artificial memory system of Bruno with its reliance on images and the occult against memory as conceived by Ramus where following the dialectical order naturally produced unfailing memory. Perkins defended the Ramist system. He called Dickson a "Scepsian" after a Greek rhetorician Metrodorus of Scepsis who used the zodiac as a basis for memory.[9]

Dickson's *De umbra rationis* followed Bruno's *De umbris idearum* (*Shadows*) very closely. Dickson used Bruno's terminology. The *umbra* or images stemmed from the shadows of the light of the divine mind which humans perceive only through its shadows, vestiges, and seals.[10] Memory was based on the sequence of the signs of the zodiac which are repeated. The whole was overlaid with Greek figures: Thamus, Theutates, Socrates, Mercurius (Hermes) in dialogue with each other and with figures from Egyptian mystery religions.[11] One theme in these dialogues was Dickson's view that

> the inner writing of the art of memory represents Egyptian profundity and spiritual insight, carries with it Egyptian regenerative experiences as described by Trismegistus, and is the antithesis of

> the beast-like manners, the Greek frivolity and superficiality, of
> those who have not had the Hermetic experience, have not
> achieved the gnosis, have not seen the vestiges of the divine in
> the *fabrica mundi*, have not become one with it by reflecting it
> within.[12]

Without thoroughly explicating all these terms, it is apparent that the Dickson/Brunian system was a complicated mix of ancient philosophical "wisdom" and lore, combined with mystical and occult overtones. As such, it had a religious character. At the bottom, the controversy between Brunian and Ramist memory as represented by Dickson and Perkins was religious in nature.[13]

Perkins viewed Dickson's artificial memory as an impious art that deserved to be anathematized. In his dedication of *Antidicsonus* to Thomas Moufet, an "illustrious philosopher and doctor of medicine" as Perkins called him, Perkins explained that there were two kinds of arts of memory. These were *una ex locis & umbris constans; alters, qua singula structa & collocata proponit, Logica dispositio* (one using places and "umbra"; the other using "logical dispostio"). This second system was taught by Ramus. This was the only true method of memory according to Perkins. All others are vain.[14]

Perkins saw Bruno whom he called "Nolanus" (from Nola, Italy) as the real force behind this debate. A year before Bruno had caused uproars in Oxford particularly with his clandestinely printed works including the *Triginta Sigilli*, the *Seals*, described as "an extremely obscure work on his magic art of memory." In this work he concluded by calling for "a new religion based on love, art, magic, and mathesis."[15] Perkins was aware of Dickson's connections with Bruno. But he did not refer directly to Bruno's works on memory. Instead Perkins directed his barrage against the disciple Dickson's *De umbra rationis*.[16]

Perkins claimed that Dickson's Latin style was obscure and did not smell of "Roman purity."[17] He said that to use celestial signs for the art of memory was absurd.[18] Perkins claimed that the sole discipline for memory should be logical disposition, as Ramus taught: *Dispositionem Logicam esse solam memoriae instruendae disciplinam docere sum cognatus.*[19] The soul of Dickson was blind and in error and knew nothing of the true and good (*verum & bonum*), said Perkins.[20] In logical disposition there is a natural power to remember. All other systems were false.

Throughout, Perkins referred to Ramus and often quoted him. He admonished Dickson to "open your ears" and hear the words of Ramus against him. He should "recognize the immense river" of Ramus' genius.[21] Perkins quoted from Ramus' *Scholae dialecticae* and the *Scholae rhetoricae*. These citations both extolled the far greater value of logical disposition over the art of memory that used places and images. Ramus said:

> Whatever of art may help the memory is the order and disposi-
> tion of things, the fixing in the soul of what is first, what is se-
> cond, what third. As to those places and images which are
> vulgarly spoken of they are inept and rightly derided by any
> master of arts. How many images would be needed to remember
> the Philippics of Demosthenes? Dialectical disposition alone is
> the doctrine of order; from it alone can memory seek aid and
> help.[22]

Following the *Antidicsonus*, Perkins went through the "*Ad Herennian*" rules quoted by Dickson and opposed them to the system of Ramus.[23] This work itself was arranged in the Ramist fashion. A Ramist chart stood at the beginning of the discourse. In this Perkins schematized the parts of artificial memory. This chart appears as follows:

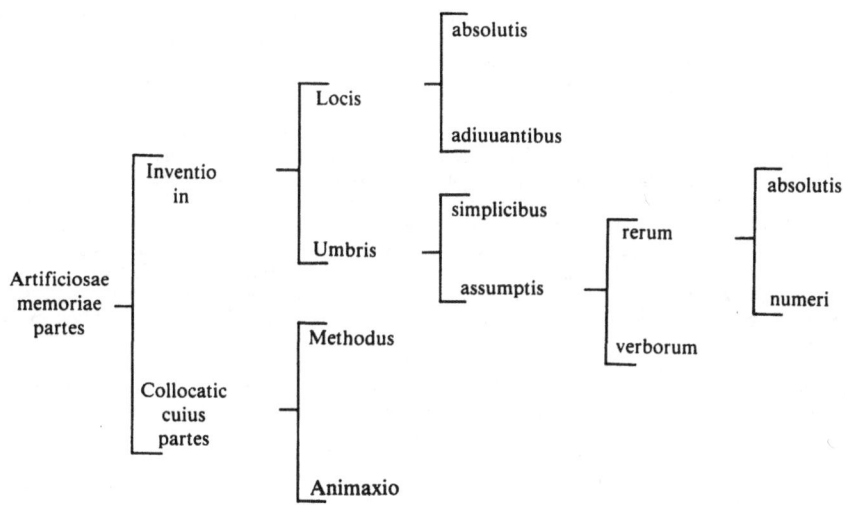

The two books were Invention and Arrangement.[24] Perkins' method was to expound the position of Dickson in nine chapters in the first book and three in the second. He countered each small chapter with "Opinion G.P." (*Censura G.P.*). The whole enterprise took only twelve pages.

As Perkins moved through his chapters, he displayed the order that a Ramist discourse would follow. Each major division in his Ramist chart was dealt with in one chapter. Book I, ch. 1 was the parts of artificial memory. Chapter 2 divided these into invention and arrangement. Perkins censured Dickson here for transgressing the laws of justice and wisdom with this division.[25] Then followed chapter 3 with the first division of invention (*locus*) and its divisions (*absoluis*; *adiuuantibus*). Chapter 4 (which had no counterpart on the chart) was a gathering of the characteristics of the *loci*. Chapter 5 discussed the second division of invention, "images" (*umbris*) and its two parts (*simplicibus*; *assumptis*) along with the divisions of assumptis (*rerum*; *verborum*). Chapter 6 (*absolutis*) was the first division of *rerum*. Chapter 7 was the second division of *rerum* (*numberi*). From there, Book II began with chapter 1 devoted to the first division of arrangement (*methodus*) and chapter 2 to the final division of arrangement (*animatio*). Chapter 3 discussed "the uses" (*De usu*).

In this short work with its chart, the path of a Ramist exposition is seen. Discussion moves through the divisions from general to particular. This was Ramus' precept for constructing a discourse (genesis). When "analyzing" a discourse to see if it follows Ramus, one should expect the piece to move in the same way. In following the path of this movement on a Ramist chart, there is an horizontal thrust as each division is dealt with in turn. The progress is from main division to main division first member; main division first member, first division; main division, first member, second division etc. Then comes main division second member; main division second member first division; main division, second member, second division etc. When all the divisions of the initial division are completed, the divisions of the second initial division are begun. This movement from general to particular meant that the more abstract truths were gradually being elucidated by division to concrete cases. The "unfolding" of a text or passage of discourse was a movement toward specificity.

The final branch of the diagram or final division made, represented what was most implicit in the original discourse. It gradually became clearer and clearer as the division process took place. In scholastic "logic," the goal was to prove "truth" by the proper joining of propositions according to certain pre-established "laws" of logic. In Ramism, "truth" was found by proper analyzing and dividing so that what was there implicitly already in a text would be laid open and made plain.

To return specifically to Perkins' *Libellus in quo dilucide*, Perkins faulted Dickson not only for breaking Ramus' laws of justice and wisdom, but also for his use of images for memory. A Ramist believed memory naturally followed if one kept in mind the mental Ramist chart where a discourse was logically disposed. Since the divisions of the subject were self-evidently plain in that they were composed of axioms, Ramist argued that the subject could not be conceived without these natural divisions suggestting themselves automatically to the mind. A tour of the mental map, the Ramist chart, was all that was needed when memory was called upon to reproduce the subject. Once a subject had been logically disposed in a proper manner (by Ramist method), its divisions were fixed and became indelibly imprinted in the memory.

Dickson's occult memory tradition urged the "antimating" of the memory by mental images that were also to stir the emotions. A striking, active, or unusual impression needed to be made on the memory so that the proper subject might be recalled.[26] Perkins argued that this system "failed" logically and was also at fault morally because it aroused impious passions by imprinting impure images in the mind.[27] The artificial memory system of Brunco/Dickson depended upon exciting the affections (*excitare affectus*) by arousing one's anger, hate, fears, lusts, etc.

Perkins cited Peter of Ravenna as an example of the evils of this artificial memory system. Peter of Ravenna urged the young to develop their lustful imaginations. He used the classical principle of trying to make memory images resemble people of one's acquaintance if possible. Thus Ravenna mentioned his girl friend, Juniper of Pistoia, whose image he found stimulated his memory since they were very dear to each other when they were young. Perkins found this method to be against all divine laws. He argued that this "worthless fellow" should not be excused for his stupidity and for trying to excite passions.[28]

In 1584 "G.P." also published *Libellus de memoria verissimaque bene recordandi scientia*. This work expounded on Ramist memory. It had numerous passages of poetry and prose that were "logically analyzed" so they could be easily memorized.[29]

Before this work Perkins gave a brief excursus or epistle capsulizing the history of the classical art of memory. He mentioned early practitioners of the art -- Simonides, Quintilian, Peter of Ravenna, Rosselius etc. Then he asked what it all amounted to. His answer was that there was nothing wholesome or even learned about it. Rather, Perkins said, it smelled of "some kind of barbarism and Dunsicality."[30] The word "Dunsicality" here brought to mind the epithet "Dunses" hurled by Protestant extremists against Roman Catholics. This word stimulated the burning of Dunsical manuscripts when Protestants cleared out monastic libraries.[31] To Perkins, then, this artificial art of memory was associated with the medieval order. As he had said, its proponents did not speak with a "Roman purity." Theirs was a system of an older era, one of barbarism and Dunsicality according to Perkins.

Next Perkins went on to give "Admonitions" to his opponent Dickson. These were more detailed than in the *Antidicsonus*. Particularly Perkins attacked the "astronomy" on which Dickson's memory system was built. He did this by questioning the astrological assumptions on which the system was built and thus trying to undermine it. Perkins based his argument here on a Ramist distinction. He claimed that it was wrong to use astronomy in memory because it was a "special art." Memory, on the other hand said Perkins, was part of dialectic/rhetoric and was a "general art."[32]

Perkins joined the issue of memory when he called on Dickson to compare his memory method with Ramist method. With Ramus, memory happened because it was an outgrowth of the natural order. Dickson's system was artificially contrived by the Greeks according to Perkins. In the Ramist system, Perkins argued, the *loci* are "true" in that generals have the highest place, subalterns the middle place, and specials the lowest place. This is the "natural order." But what of the *loci* in Dickson's system? Perkins asked if they were true or fictitious. According to Perkins, if Dickson said they were true, he would be a liar. If he said there were false, he had admitted his folly. In Ramist method there was clarity, said Perkins. The images to be remembered (which are the *loci*) are clear, distinct, and clearly divided. This was a sharp contrast to the "shadows" of the Brunian/Dicksonian system. As Perkins put it: "Hence the palm is given to the method over that broken and weak discipline of memory."³³

While this 1584 quarrel was confined specifically to the art of memory, it had overtones for other subjects. Both sides saw their methods as virtuous, moral, and religious. Each saw the other as impious, immoral, and irreligious. Dickson drew on the "wisdom" and "mystery" traditions, Egyptian in origin. Perkins drew his inspiration from Ramus who ultimately derived from the Greeks whom Dickson saw as "superficial." Thus culture and religion became involved in the fray. These topics were bound up with pure speculation about the merits of "artificial" or "natural" memory. Dickson aligned himself with the "art" of Metrodorus of Scepsis. Perkins supported the "method" of Peter Ramus.

Two of Perkins' later works illuminate further his thinking on memory and images. Perkins included a chapter on "Of Memorie in Preaching" in his *Prophetica sive de sacra et unica ratione concionandi tractatus* (1592) translated in 1606 as *The Arte of Prophecying*.³⁴ There he wrote:

> Artificiall memorie, which standeth vpon places and images, will very easily without labour teach how to commit sermons to the memorie: but it is not to be approoued. 1. The animation of the image, which is the key of memorie, is impoius, because it requireth absurd, insolent and prodigious cogitations, & those especially, which set an edge vpon and kindle the most corrupt affections of the flesh. 2. It dulleth the wit and memorie, because it requireth a threefold memorie for one: the first of the places: the second of the images: the third of the thing that is to bee declared.³⁵

Thus Perkins' critique of artificial memory followed the same lines as his earlier attack against Dickson. Artificial memory was both impious because it excited corrupt and carnal affections and it was intellectually inferior because it required the mind (and memory) to follow a three-step process.

Perkins' solution to the problem of memory in this work was to propose a literary structure founded on logic. He wrote:

> It is not therfore an vnprofitable aduice, if he that is to preach doe diligently imprint in his minde by the helpe of disposition either axiomaticall, or syllogisticall, or methodicall, the seuerall proofes and applications of the doctrines, the illustrations of the applications, and the order of them all: in the meane time nothing carefull for the words, Which (as *Horace* speaketh) *will not unwillingly follow the matter that is premeditated*.³⁶

Perkins believed once the Ramist outline was "imprinted" on the mind, following this mental map one could move through its various loci with no trouble whatsoever. The problem of memory would be solved. The structure of the discourse was the organizing principle in the speaker's mind. There was no need for elaborate images or rhetorical flourishes.³⁷ Perkins' divisions were reminiscent of Ramus' where his section on disposition was divided into the three parts of propositions, syllogisms, and method.³⁸

Perkins rejected the Bruno/Dickson artificial memory scheme because it was complex. But he also severely criticized it for its use of images. In *A Warning Against the Idolatry of the Last Times* (1601) Perkins struck out against "idols, that is, images that haue beene abused to idolatry."³⁹ Perkins wrote this tract against the practices of the Roman Catholic Church since he was convinced that "the remainders of Popery yet sticke in the mindes of many."⁴⁰ He tried to "declare and conuince the Church of Rome of manifest idolatry" which expressed itself in the worship of images. Perkins wished his readers "to put from us all manner of idols, and to sanctifie God in our hearts."⁴¹ The worship of idols throught images was a sin in the eyes of God according to Perkins. He wrote:

> The gentiles said that images erected were elements or letters to know God by: so say the Papists, that images are Lay-mens bookes. The wisest among the Gentiles vsed images and other ceremonies to procure the presence of Angles and celestiall powers, that by them they might attaine to the knowledge of God. The like doe the Papists with images of Angels and Saints.⁴²

But Perkins rejected this justification for the use of images in worship. To him, it was not permissible to

> binde the presence of God, his operation, grace, & his hearing of vs, to certaine things, places, signes to which hee hath not bound himselfe, either by commandement or promise...[and] we haue no like warrant, either by promise or commandment to tie Gods presence to an image or crucifixes.⁴³

Yet it was not external idolatry or the construction of visible images alone that Perkins rejected. Images within the mind were also prohibited according to him. For

> so soone as the minde frames vnto it selfe any forme of God (as when hee is popishly conceiued to be like an old man, sitting in heauen ina throne with a scepter in his hand) an idoll is set vp in the minde.⁴⁴

The only proper way to conceive God in the mind according to Perkins was to "conceiue in minde his properties and proper effects."⁴⁵ But internal idolatry wherein a visual, albeit it mental construct or image of God is established, is sin just as much as the erection of a golden calf. For Perkins, "a thing fained in the mind by imagination is an idoll."⁴⁶

Thus Perkins rejected artificial memory schemes. The occult memory systems of Bruno *et. al.* were wrong, sinfully wrong because they conjured up images and stirred carnal affections which did not have any place in the life of the Christian according to Perkins. On a deeper level, Perkins rejected the concept of the classical memory systems themselves where images were set up as keys to memory. To him, any image established in the imagination had the potentiality of becoming idolatrous. And, Perkins rejected artificial memory on the grounds that it involved too much. It asked a speaker to memorize the "places," images, and then finally the thing in itself. There was a short-cut to good memory, however, according to Perkins. This was the Ramist method. It worked because of the inherent truth of the natural dialectical order. It was thus an infallible system. It required one to memorize only the structure of a discourse itself. The rest would follow naturally. There was not need for other steps in the process. The Ramist system to Perkins, could not be perverted into idolatry. There were no images to imagine. There potential sources of idolatry were thus eliminated. There was not triggering of base affections to lead a person to sin. In short, according to Perkins, the Ramist system was superior in every way.⁴⁷

Perkins' reaction against astrology was closely related to his aversion to artificial memory system. He disdained all systems which appealed to images of the occult and zodiac. Perkins' nest three published works after the 1584 controversy were all 'concerned to some degree with this subject. *Foure Greate Lyers* (1585) showed the uselessness of consulting almanacs. It did so by placing the predictions of four almanacs side by side. *A Resolution to the Countrey-man* (1585) gave a theological as well as practical set of reasons for not using almanacs. *A Fruitfull Dialogue concerning the End of the World* (1587) also showed Perkins' familiarity with astrological literature. It sought to persuade its readers that the "things to come, belongeth to God alone, and none must be so bold as to chalenge this to himselfe." The prognostications of astrologers and the other "blind prophets" were to be rejected.[48]

The original *Short-Title Catalogue* gave no author for the work published in 1585 entitled *Foure Great Lyers, Striuing who shall win the siluer Whetstone*. There was also no author given for *A Resolution to the Country-man, prouing it utterly unlawfull to buye or use our yearly Prognosticiations. Written by W.P.* It is now realized that this "W.P." was William Perkins.[49]

In the *Foure Great Lyers*, the first twenty-one pages present in parallel columns the daily predictions of four professional astrologers. The initials given were "B," "F," "T," and "D" presumably standing for Buckminster, Frende (Forster), Twyne, and Digges (Dade). All of these predictions disagreed with each other. By showing this, Perkins like others before him, held the astrologers up for ridicule.[50]

In *A Resolution to the Country-man* Perkins attacked astrologers directly and forcefully. In the "Preface" he made an autobiographical reference when he said he had studied the art and found it to be nothing less than idolatry.[51] Here again, Perkins connected idolatry with astrology and the signs and images of the zodiac.

The practice and extent of astrology as well as its social and intellectual role and relation to religion in Tudor England has been well-discussed.[52] In Perkins' time, astrology was "less a separate discipline than an aspect of a generally accepted world picture."[53] It appealed to people as a way to "reduce the baffling diversity of human affairs to some sort of intelligible order," to provide " a coherent and comprehensive system of thought."[54] But for Perkins, as for many of his Protestant predecessors, all such systems of judicial astrology were vain, idolatrous, and were to hold no fascination for a Christian.[55] Perkins attacked the purchasers of prognostications for exercising immoderate care, distrust in God, and contempt for providence. His concern with a pure imagination surfaced again when he taunted, asking why people buy books of prognostications: "because the pictures and Characters which they make, delight thy minde?"[56] Perkins castigated astrology advocates for explaining phenomena by attributing explanations to the movements of celestial bodies when true Christians knew that all things moved according to the secret purpose of God. When an unlearned person read astrological predictions there was no "mention of the speciall prouidence, and hand of God in euery thing, but long discourses on the vertues of Planets, and signes." Perkins went so far as to suggest that "in a Christian Commonwealth, those onely books should be published for thine use, which might beat into thine head, and make thee euery houre and moment to thinke on the prouidence of God."[57] Those who consulted the "starres" for everything from the "cutting of thy haire, for the putting on of thy shooes, for taking a iourny two or three miles from thine house" should be made to realize something basic. Perkins said they should know that

> if thou be a Christian man, thou oughtest onely to be contented
> with knowing the times and ordinary seasons of the yeare: not
> regarding nor searching any secret and speciall Predictions, for
> which the Lord neuer gaue any many warrant, but in plaine
> words hath forbidden them.[58]

Perkins here was echoing the thought of John Calvin who had written:

> when unbelievers transfer the government of the universe from
> God to the stars, they fancy that their bliss or their misery
> depends upon the decrees and indications of the stars, not upon
> God's will; so it comes about that their fear is transferred from

him, toward whom alone they ought to direct it, to stars and comets. Let him, therefore, who would beware of this infidelity ever remember that there is no erratic power, or action, or motion in creatures, but that they are governed by God's secret plan in such a way that nothing happens except what is knowingly and willingly decreed by him.[59]

Thus the concern of Perkins that the imagination be kept free of images which were potentially idolatrous came to the fore in his *A Resolution* just as it had in *Antidicsonus*. This was coupled with a strong sense of God's providence and purposes as the true source of events in the world. Astrology was idolatrous because it erected images in the mind and attributed power to them. These images were looked to and in a sense worshipped as being able to prognosticate the future -- whether it be a weather forecast or personal fortunes. Perkins was an "inner iconoclast" in the sense that he wished to smash all images in the mind related to celestial astrology. These images were impious and turned the focus of one's attention away from God who rightly deserves all human praise and worship.[60]

The link between the themes of idolatry and imagination in *Antidicsonus* and *A Resolution* is strengthened when it is noticed how Perkins structured *A Resolution*. A Ramist chart appeared directly after the title page. This chart with four large brackets in the familiar Ramist style diagrammed the main heads of Perkins' discourse.[61] Perkins purpose in this work was to convince common people of the dangers of astrology. He wished to show them why it was wrong in this eyes (and he would say in God's eyes) for them to seek astrological advice. His chart shows his "Reasons" were divided into two branches: 1) Concerning the buyer; 2) Concerning the maker. Of the buyer there were two reasons why it was wrong; of the maker four reasons with the first of these being divided into three further branches. Throughout the work Perkins presented lists of features in the same bracketed form.[62]

This work makes it clear that Perkins perceived the Ramist method of analysis and presentation to be quite suitable for his task. It helped him in "proouing it vtterly vnlawful to buy or use our yeerely Prognostications" and "to perswade thee, not to spend thy money in buying any of them."[63] Perkins was involved in argumentation here. He was out to persuade his readers. To do this he presented his argument as simply as he could. He divided his work into two main parts as he told his readers: "My reason shall partly concerne thee, partly the Prognosticatour himselfe."[64] Then Perkins moved through his argument according to the chart he presented, adding further points to his main divisions as he went. True to the Ramist style, he moved through the places of his first division before he went on to the second. Even without the benefit of the initial chart, it would be clear that Perkins was using the Ramist method here. With the chart as further evidence, it seems a clear indictation that Perkins was consciously framing this discourse against astrology with Ramist method in mind.

Perkins next work was A *Frvitfvll Dialogve Concerning the End of the World*. This work contined to show the folly of the astrologers. But this piece was written in dialogue form. The discussion was between a "Christian" and a "Worldling." *A Fruitful Dialogue* was said to have been the "first fruits" of Perkins' labours, published in "a year of dearth" and written "against couetous hoarding vp of corne (amongst other sinnes)."[65] To console "Worldling" who was afraid the world was going to end the next year (in 1588), Perkins had "Christian" point to all the times in the past when prognosticators were wrong in predicting the world's end: 1584, May, 1583, 1460, and 1364.[66]

Several of the concerns mentioned above run throughout these early writings of William Perkins. He was concerned with the art of memory -- to promote the Ramist system over artificial systems. He opposed idolatry -- particularly as it showed itself in the artificial memory systems as well as in the astrological apparatus linked to these systems. In place of astrology, Perkins advocated faith in the providence of God. To aid in his efforts against prognosticators, he framed his *A Resolution to the Country-man* in Ramist fashion.

B. Theological Works

Perkins shifted from polemical works directed against astrology to more specifically theological topics with his 1586 work *A Treatise Tending vnto a Declaration, Whether a Man be in the Estate of Damnation, or in the Estate of Grace*. This was actually a book composed of eight smaller treatises.[67] The theme throughtout was whether "professours of Christ, in the day of grace, [may] preswade themselues that they are in the estate of grace."[68] Theologically, this was the question of whether or not a Christian can have assurance of salvation. This was an issue of continuing interest to Perkins throughout his career. He dealt with it in much more detail in 1597 with his *A Graine of Mustard-Seede*.[69] Another of Perkins' recurring concerns appeared in *A Treatise Tending unto a Declaration*. This was a polemic against the Roman Catholic Church. Perkins wrote quite frequently in opposition to its theology and practices. This was the theme of one of the short treatises here: "How a Reprobate may performe all the Religion of the Church of Rome."[70]

This tract began with the assertion: "A Reprobate may in truth be made partaker of all that is contained in the religion of the Church of Rome: and a Papist by his religion cannot goe beyond a Reprobate." Perkins proceeded by listing four arguments and then discussing them under the title: "The proofe of the argument." The "arguments" were set up as a syllogism though Perkins did not use that term. The first one reads: "He which may in truth bee made partaker of the chiefe points of the Popish Religion, may be made partaker of all: but a Reprobate may be made partaker of the chiefe points of the Popish Religion: therefore a Reprobate may be made partaker of all."[71]

Perkins' comment was that "The proposition is plaine...All the controuersie is of the assumption: wherefore I prooue it thus."[72] Perkins then went on to show how a reprobate might partake of "the chiefe points of the Popish Religion." This was the method he used with all four arguments: state that the proposition was "plaine" or "certaine" or "most true." Then he listed reasons for establishing his charge against Rome contained in what he termed the "assumption." In two of the arguments he said he would prove the assumption by "induction of particulars."[73]

In his decription of the terms of his syllogisms, Perkins followed Ramus. Ramus had adapted his terminology for the parts of the syllogism from Agricola and Cicero.[74] He called them *propositio* (major premise), *assumptio* (minor premise) and *complexio* (conclusion). Ramus had simplified the treatment of syllogisms as found in the traditional, scholastic logics. For him they only helped establish the truth of doubtful propositions. Syllogistic and Method were the two main parts of deduction which with axiomatics were the two main divisions of "judgement" in the Ramist system.[75] Syllogims and syllogistic reasoning served to clear up propositions that were doubtful by deriving them from axioms already self-evidently true.[76]

This was precisely what Perkins did with his "arguments." He admitted in each case that his first premise was always "plaine" or "certaine." In other words it was self-evident. His conclusion was secure, he needed only to show the truth of the middle member the *assumptio*, he said. In each case this *assumptio* was a statement about the Church of Rome and how its doctrine or practices were faulty. In his "proof," Perkins showed how the Roman Church was at fault. He had then proved his *assumptio*. In his eyes he had made his conclusion and the whole syllogism true. As Ramus had said."....in brief the art of the syllogism does not inform us of any other thing than that of resolving a stated question by the manifest truth of two well-arranged parts."[77] Once Perkins had proved his *assumptio*, the two "well-arranged parts" were not become "self-evident axioms" and the whole argument held true. When Perkins said he would prove the *assumptio* from an "induction of particulars," he collected exampled to validate his point. In the fourth argument, for example, he was proving that "the religion of the Church of Rome is quite contrarie to itselfe." To prove this he listed fifteen doctrines and instances where he alleged that the Papists say they believed one thing while actually they believed or practiced something else.[78] Once these instances became evident, Perkins confidently believed he had cleared up any doubts about the proposition that the Roman religion was self-contradictory. He thus had proved his point in his own eyes.

So once more, Perkins' works show traces of Ramus. His use of the syllogism for his description of its terms to how it was used are in line with Ramus' teachings. At one point in this little work Perkins referred to Aristotle as "the Prince of Philosophers." But this remark was made in reference to proving the Roman doctrine of Transubstantiation a "monster" as he cited Aristotle who said that "every magnitude hath his parts fited in some one place" -- in other words, Christ's body cannot be simultaneously in heaven and on earth in the Sacrament.[79] But Perkins showed no interest in using Aristotle's categories or causes or other terminology to enhance his arguments. Nor did Perkins use the syllogism itself as a tool to prove further the points he made as he set out to prove his *assumptio*. The syllogistic form merely provided a platform for Perkins to set forth examples as "induction of particulars" to lay bare the self-evidencing truth of what he was saying. These examples for Perkins carried the weight of the proof and thus the truth. Thus Perkins' "arguments" in this piece appear to owe more to Ramus than to Aristotle.

Two other small treatises in *A Treatise Tending Unto a Declaration* are set up in a similar form. In "Certaine Propositions Declaring How Farre a Man My Go in the Profession of the Gospell, and yet be a wicked man and a Reprobate," Perkins listed thirty-six numbered paragraphs.[80] These "propositions" were not set in the form of "arguments" but rather as theses or assertions. As such, Perkins did not try to prove them in a rigid or logical fashion. Instead they described what to Perkins was evident from the teachings of Scripture. As such, these propositions functioned more like axioms than anything else. The same might be said for the ten paragraphs (numbered) that form the brief piece "How a man should apply aright the Word of God to his owne soule."[81] The main parts were four ways in which the Law might be applied to a Christian to work humiliation and eleven ways the Gospel might be applied for comfort. Two more small tracts in the larger Treatise are cast in dialogue form. One is "A Dialogve of the State of a Christian Man, Gathered Here and There ovt of the Sweet and Savory Writings of Master Tindall and Master Bradford." The other was "A Dialogue containing the conflicts between Sathan and a Christian."[82]

There are, however, two remaining pieces in Perkins' Treatise that were written according to Ramist method. In these, Perkins took a particular topic and developed his exposition of it in Ramist fashion.

The first piece is "The estate of a Christian man in this life, which also sheweth how farre the Elect may goe beyond the Reprobate in Christianitie, and that by man degrees."[83] The subject of this work was faith. Perkins dealt with it in four discussions: What faith is; How God Works It; What degrees there be of faith; and the Fruits and benefits of faith.

Perkins began with a definition of faith as "a wonderful grace of God, by which the elect do apprehend and apply Christ and all his benefits vnto themselues particularly."[84] Sections of this work are numbered as are some of the other tracts in Perkins' *Treatise*. But examination shows that Perkins worked here with a definite pattern in mind. It was a Ramist pattern. He moved through his initial dichotomy of "What Faith Is": Power of Apprehending and applying Christ and the Wonderful Grace of God to his second question; "How God Works It." There again a dichotomy was made: "Prepares Heart by Humiliation" and "How Faith Springs." Each of these were divided into four heads with the third head ("sorrow for sin") in the first division having three parts to it. Perkins divided his third question: "What Degrees of Faith" into two members: "Least Measure" and "Greatest Measure." The "least measure" member had four parts with it and the fourth of its parts was divided into three further parts. From there Perkins divided the fourth question on the fruits and benefits of faith into three heads: Justification, Adoption, and Sanctification. Justifications was divided into outward and inward benefits with three and four further divisions respectively. Adoption was resolved into "benefits" with six divisions and "assurance" with two divisions. Sanctification had four parts with each of them divided into two, three, or four parts and several further subdivisions in some of them. In each instance where Perkins introduced a specifically theological term (such as justification, sanctification, or adoption) he defined the term first before making his further divisions.[85]

In "A Declaration of Certaine Spiritvall Desertions," Perkins dealt with the question of God's "desertions" of people. There are times in the lives of Christians, Perkins maintained, when God apparently "deserts" his creatures.[66] This desertion was dichotomized by Perkins into "Eternal" in the cases of reprobates or those God has chosen to forsake forever; or "Temporary" in the cases of God's elect who will ultimately be brought to salvation. Eternal desertion was split into two branches: the forsaking of God's creatures which happens in three ways; or God's particular desertion which was split into God's withholding of "temporal benefits" or "spiritual blessings" which included four particular instances.

After Perkins expounded this first major division of his subject, he moved on to a fuller discussion of the temporary desertions experienced by God's elect. These he divided into sorts, manners, kinds, ends, and uses with each of these further divided into two's, three's, or four's and some of those divisions subdivided again.[67] Perkins believed that God would never ultimately forsake the true Christian. But his work here showed what he believed God did in seeming to desert the Christian temporarily. Perkins' ultimate appeal was for the Christian to let this experience teach increased fear of God, to restore the spirit, draw one near to God, and cause one to search his or her "own ways."

These two pieces on faith and desertion were written with the practical questions Christians ask in Perkins' mind. His discussions atomized the doctrine of faith by discussing what it was, how it was formed, in what degrees it was found, and what its fruits and benefits were. Perkins followed the same pattern when he discussed God's "forsaking his creatures." He defined what the desertion was, how God worked it, of what sorts, manners, and kinds it was and finally to what ends and uses this "doctrine" might be put. To conduct both discussions, Perkins used a form or arrangement which can only be considered to have been influenced by Ramus' doctrine of method. He began with definitions, then divided the definition into its most general components and made further divisions and subdivisions into its most general components and made further divisions and subdivsions down to the most particular element, just as Ramus had advised. In many cases a tip-off to the fact that this method was being employed is the use of the "either/or" pattern. "Benefits" might be "either outward, or inward." God's blessings might be "either positiue or priuatiue."[68]

This "either/or" pattern was used when a topice was dichotomized. Yet the Ramist system was not one of dichotomization exclusively. After he divided his logic into invention and judgment, Ramus discussed his nonartisitc proofs under five headings rather than two. In arrangement he had three parts. In artistic proofs there were primary and derivative primary but these were divided into six and three parts respectively. More accurately, then, Ramus' system was not one of dichotomization but one in which ideas or terms were arranged by means of descending generalities.[69] This expression of his "one logic" could be used in any type of discourse -- learned as well as popular. But throughout, Ramus' goal was communication. As he wrote: "Now this method is not solely applicable to the material of the arts and doctrines, but to all things which we intend to teach easily and clearly."[70]

Perkins' frequent use of the "either/or" pattern should not obscure the fact that he did not always divide by two's. The treatises just cited show that there were often three, four, or more divisions in his discussion of a topic. While these latter divisions might appear in themselves to be only "listings" of certain points, they apparently represented to Perkins the essential ingredients that made up the more general heading of which they were parts. When one of his works is charted in the Ramist fashion, in moving toward the right through various branches, one moves from the most general to the most specific. Each head the farther one moves rightward represents a proportionately smaller part of the whole topic itself. This was how an "art" was "unfolded" in the Ramist mind: definition, division, division, division....When the subject was then represented visually in a diagram, the relationship of all these divisions became apparent at a glance. Hence it was presumably easier to "memorize" when in the mind's eye the relationships were so graphically displayed. In a sense the whole interior logic of the topic became immediately apparent. A reconstruction of the discourse again from the chart ("synthesis" instead of "analysis") would not be difficult. According to the Ramist view of memory, one could begin with the opening division and follow through to each further division in turn. At any point along the way, a valid statement could be made about the art by constructing it from following the interrelated "branches" of the Ramist "tree."

An example of how this system works can be seen from the chart of Perkins' "Estate of a True Christian." By moving through each division and taking a member one could say: "Faith has as one of its fruits, sanctification which includes repentance as a holy labor to cleanse the self of sin through good works which come from obedience to God's revealed Word." This statement was constructed through six divisions after the initial topic "faith." This statement is a chain made of the following links, each one connected to the next through the Ramist branch: faith, fruits (of faith), sanctification, repentance, holy labor to cleanse self of sin, good works, obedience to God's revealed Word. This was one of the most complex statements that could be made from the treatise according to the chart. There was only one more route through which one could pass and follow yet another division. Then one would have been through seven divisions after the initial topic "faith." One of the most simple statements made could be: "Faith is the power of apprehending and applying Christ." Other statements, varying in complexity, spring from how far to the right on the chart the reader or speaker chooses to go. The reverse order could be followed as well. Then one would move from specific to general. An example of this would be: "Reconciliation is one of the outward benefits of justification which is a fruit of faith." Thus the Ramist chart served as a tool for both "analysis" and "synthesis."

In "The Estate of a True Christian in This Life" and "A Declaration of Certaine Spiritual Desertions," Perkins took a theological topic and presented it in a way that indicates he was working with the Ramist doctrine of method in mind. Hence these works can be diagrammed in the Ramist fashion. In many cases Perkins made dichotomous divisions. But he did not follow this practice slavishly. When Perkins made a division, he supported it or justified it by citing a verse or verses of Scripture. At this level he did not enter into discussion about what was a "proper" interpretation of a Scripture verse. That was the work he did in his Biblical commentaries. When Perkins wrote on a theological topic systematically he used the verses as he himself interpreted them.

In some cases, Perkins used a word from a text to stand for a division made in his discourse. When he listed an "outward benefit" of justification, for instance, he mentioned reconciliation. His Scriptural support was II Corinthians 5:18 which reads (from the Geneva Bible that Perkins used): "And all things *are* of God, which hath reconciled vs vnto him self by Iesus Christ...."

More often, however, Perkins used a term (frequently a standard theological term) as a heading for his division. He then cited texts from which that term or theological doctrine was derived. This was in place of using a term actually found in the verse or text itself. For example, Perkins listed "Adoption" as a "benefit of faith." The verses he cited were John 1:12; Galatians 3:26; and Hebrews 2:11. These verses themselves did not contain the term "adoption" (though it is a term used in the Geneva Bible -- in Romans 8:15; Galatians 4:5; Ephesians 1:5 etc. to render the Greek *huiothesiû*.) But the verses Perkins cited did point in Perkins' mind to what he understood thelogically as the doctrine of adoption. Thus he perceived the term as a valid one to use. He would have considered his Scriptural support for the term as proper.

By adopting either or both of these methods for making divisions, Perkins apparently enabled himself to make as many or as few divisions as he wished. In some cases he could combine many texts into a few divisions. In other cases, even a few texts could be divided many ways. One instance where Perkins' theological understanding shaped fully his division was when he wrote of sanctification. Perkins said it occured "throughout the whole man." There his treatment was divided into three main parts: spirit, soule, and body. The first two of these were further divided into dichotomies and one manner of each divided again. Perkins cited I Thessalonians 5:23 as the basis for his initial three-fold division. This verse read: "....and I pray God that your whole spirit and soule and bodie, may be kept blameless vnto the comming of our Lord Iesus Christ." Thus Perkins' theological anthropology, based on this Scripture verse, was the warrant for the division of his discourse as he made it.

In a sense, Perkins returned to the dialogue form of discourse in 1588 when he wrote his *The Foundation of Christian Religion, Gathered into sixe Principles*. This was a catechism written for "ignorant people, that they may be fit to heare Sermons with profit, and to receiue the Lords Supper with comfort."[91]

Catechisms played an important role in spreading and consolidating the Protestant faith in the sixteenth and seventeenth centuries.[92] In England, many catechisms appeared between 1558 and 1660, often written by those committed to Puritan causes.[93] These usually sought not only to supplement or replace the brief catechism found in the Prayer Book but also to give the heads of households a means by which to acquaint their family and households thoroughly with the Christian faith. As Perkins himself wrote: "Gouernours of families must teach their children, and seruants, and their whole houshold, the doctrine of true religion, that they may know the true Good, and walk in al his waies in doing righteousnesse and iudgement."[94]

Perkins began his *Foundation* with a list of thirty-two errors that ignorant people professed. This ignorance in Perkins' eyes led to sin and "where sinne raignes, there the diuell rules: and where he rules men are in a damnable case."[95] To Perkins, true knowledge of the Christian faith was intimately connected to ethical behavior. Perkins was concerned to make plain the "true meaning" of the Apostles' Creed, the Ten Commandments, the Lord's Prayer etc. -- those facets of Christian teaching to which the common person would be exposed yet might not fully understand. Perkins' purpose was to expound the meaning of these elements so that the "unlearned" would be able to make what he called "right use" of them.[96] The common person could do this by "applying them [the words] inwardly to your hearts and consciences, and outwardly to your liues and conuersations."

The inner-relatedness of "faith" and "works" or the "understanding" and "ethical behavior" was a recurring concern throughout Perkins' works. Some of his treatises focused directly on complicated theological subjects. But in them, Perkins also made a "practical application" of his teaching. He wished to spell out specifically how a doctrine or theological point was to make an impact on the life and actions of his readers. In the same manner, when Perkins wrote of topics that had a particular moral, spiritual or ethical content, he based his arguments on specifically theological considerations.[97] But in a sense the theoretical consideration for this dual emphasis was set here in the "Epistle" to his 1588 Catechism. To Perkins, ignorance led to sin. Sin meant that people acted in accord with Satan and this meant their ultimate damnation. So Perkins wished to present a simple digest or catechism of the Christian faith so that sermons, sacraments, and other parts of worship would be more profitable to these people.[98]

Perkins' instructions were that people first learn the six principles he set forth. Then they could master his question/answer exposition of these six principles. Unlike some earlier catechisms, Perkins did not begin with expositions of the Apostles' Creed, the Ten Commandments, or the Lord's Prayer.[99] Instead he proceeded:

> What doest thou beleeue concerning God?
> What doest thou beleeue concerning man, and concerning thine owne selfe?
> What meanes is there for thee to escape this damnable estate?
> But how maist thou be made partaker of Christ and his benefits?
> What are the ordinarie or vsuall meanes for obtaining faith?
> What is the estate of all men after death?

In short, Perkins moved through the doctrines of God, sin, Christ, justification, faith, and judgment. In his expositions, Perkins ranged throughout these theological topics and took up many other facets of them. He dealt with the offices of Christ, law, good works, sacraments, prayer etc. These expositions as well as the principles themselves were buttressed by Scriptural references. Perkins' Catechism proved very popular and was widely used. It was translated into Latin, Dutch, German, Irish and Welsh. New Englanders translated it to use with local Native Americans.[100]

In 1590 Perkins published a Latin work entitled *Armilla aurea, id est, miranda series causarum et salutis & damnationis iuxta verbum Dei*. In the next two years this work was enlarged and published in 1592 in English as *A golden chaine, or the description of theologie, containing the order of the causes of saluation and damnation according to Gods word*.[101] Many topics of theology were discussed in this work. But major attention was given to the doctrine of predestination. All of the theological *loci* Perkins considered in this work dealt with the question of individual salvation. There were no discussion, for instance, of the doctrines of the Holy Spirit or the church.[102]

A prominent feature at the beginning of this work was a large foldout chart entitled: "A survey, or Table declaring the order of the causes of Saluation and Damnation, according to Gods word."[103] This presented in schematic form, a chart of salvation and reprobation with each "step" in the process clearly shown. Perkins did not follow Peter Lombard exactly, but there was a "broad similarity" in the arrangement of the doctrinal topics with which Perkins dealt and the medieval arrangements of Lombard's *Sentences*. In that standard theological work, Lombard had discussed: God's nature, name and properties; creation, angels, man, sin, free-will; Christ's incarnation, passion, merits, faith, hope, charity; and the sacraments, resurrection, and judgment.[104] Perkins, particularly in his early chapters, proceeded in a corresponding fashion.

A comparison of Perkins' chart with one by Beza in his *Summa Totius Christianismi, siva Descriptio et Distributio Causarum Salutis Electorum et Exitii Reproborum, ex Sacris Literis Collecta* (1555) reveals some similarities.[105] This raises the complicated question of Perkins' relationship to Beza and to the developing tradition of Reformed theological scholasticism.[106] This question cannot be considered fully here. But a few comments on the relation of Perkins' chart to Beza's can be made.[107]

Both charts followed similar schema. They began with God and moved "downward" through His decree. They then followed the paths to salvation or damnation through two symmetrical lines: on the one side the "elect," on the other the "reprobate." Beza's entire work was an exposition and explication of his schematized table. To summarize Beza's views,

> Predestination is seen as the structure or framework in which we can rightly view all theology; the beginning of theology is the eternal purpose, design or decree of God. In that design he as predestined those who will enjoy his favor in the one Mediator, Christ, and those who are reprobated and damned. Only at this point does Beza discuss the doctrine of creation; after creation comes the corruption of the whole human race by the spontaneous choice of Adam's own will. Beza finds the category of permission a useful one in describing the fall. After the fall, and according to the plan of God, there now are two parallel streams which run throughout history (metaphysics of history). Beza wants his doctrine to be one of 'equal ultimacy' -- the results of hardening are as much as work of God as the results of faith; eternal death is as much decreed by God as eternal life; there is not disjunction in the mode of decree and election and reprobation both redound to the glory of God. Everything is seen as the unravelling of God's decree.[108]

Beza set up a definite, logical order of God's decress: "God decreed to glorify himself through the salvation and perdition of men, then to create the world, then to permit the fall, and then to justify the elect and condemn the non-elect."[109] Beza was concerned with the relationship of predestination to the fall and the question of the *succession* of God's decrees. His system "furnished the *ordo decretorum* with a full-fledge supralapearian scheme: election and reprobation logically and theologically precede the decrees of creation and man's actual fall."[110]

To what extent did Perkins' chart follow this same theology? An initial difference between the two was that Perkins began his work with a description of the persons of the Godhead and their circumincession (the interpretation of the three Persons of the Trinity). Perkins' initial division was a Ramist division of theology into: God and His works.[111] Beza, however, began with a statement on the inscrutability of the divine will: "The ways of God omnipotent are completely inscrutable."[112] This was not connected to any fuller discussion of the doctrine of God. But Perkins did make this connection. Before he expounded "Gods workes, and his decree" (Chapter VI of *A Golden Chaine*), he discussed the "nature," "life," "glorie and blessednesse" and "persons" of the Godhead. He did this in successive chapters (II-V). This discussion was a foundation upon which Perkins' exposition of God's works and decree was built. This inner-relatedness of the persons of the Triune God with His works was captured when Perkins wrote: "The workes of God, are all those, which he doth out of himselfe, that is, out of his diuine essence. These are common to the Trinitie, the peculiar manner of working alwaies reserued to euery person."[113]

This point has significance. By relating the persons of the Trinity to the works of God, Perkins avoided subordinating Jesus Christ to the decree of God for salvation or damnation itself.[114] Perkins wrote that Christ is the "foundation" of election "from all eternitie."[115] To the question of "How can Christ bee subordinate vnto Gods election, seeing hee together with the Father decreed all things?" Perkins answered: "Christ as he is a mediatour, is not subordinate to the very decree it selfe of election, but to the execution thereof only."[116] In other words,

> although the Son incarnate as Mediator subordinates himself to the execution of the decree, the Son as eternal God having in himself the full essence of the Godhead stands prior to the decree. With the Father and the Spirit the Son is the God who sets forth the decree in eternity.[117]

That Perkins could preserve this understanding stemmed from his initial division of theology into God and His works. His discussion of Christ's role in predesination was backed by the full realization of Christ as an eternal member of the Godhead who fully participated in the predestination decree. Christ only "subordinated himself" in the execution of the decree in his office as Mediator. He was not, as Perkins pointed out, "subordinate to the very decree itselfe of election." Beza included a Christological discussion in the midst of his *Tabula*.[118] But Perkins made explicit the relationship of the Person of the Mediator to the decree and its execution. In a real sense, the ordering of salvation finds its origins and effects in Jesus Christ for Perkins.[119]

This does not imply that Beza bypassed or lessened the importance of Christ in the plan of salvation. But Beza's chart did not put forth any detailed account of how the person and work of Christ related to the whole plan of salvation. Perkins' diagram did this. The broad outlines of the two men are the same. Perkins, like Beza, moved from the love of God (to the elect in Christ) to effectual calling to justification and then sanctification before moving to God's final judgment and ultimate salvation or damnation. Both charts show the very "bottom line" to be the glory of God. But whereas in Beza's chart there is that "equal ultimacy," or symmetrical schema by which on one side there is the elect and on the other side the reprobate and there is nothing between them; in Perkins' chart, there is detail there concerning the work of Christ. In Beza there is nothing in the central pathway from the fall to judgment. In Perkins there is a decription of the mediatorial work of Christ for the elect. Perkins drew connecting lines between aspects of Christ's work of redemption and the path and progress of the Christian life. He described these lines as showing how "faith doth apprehend Christ and all his benefits, and applieth them to the person of euery beleeuer for his iustification and sanctification."[120] By doing this, Perkins related the specifically theological terms to the practical use of the individual Christian believer (a combination again of the "theory/practice" pattern). In the same way he lined out the connections between the theological terms he used and the various spiritual struggles a Christian combats: doubting of election, justification, concupiscence of the flesh etc. But central to Perkins' whole enterprise, all the way from God's decree through election, calling, justification etc. to the end was the relation of it all to the work of Jesus Christ. Christ was at the center of Perkins' predestinarian understanding.[121]

Though Perkins' diagram appeared to give an "equal ultimacy" to election and reprobation, his discussion in *A Golden Chaine* paid much more attention to the causes of salvation than damnation. A main theme for Perkins in this work as in others was the epistemological problem of salvation -- how would one know if he or she were among the elect or saved? Since anyone must be potentially regarded as possible being numbered among the elect, Perkins spent much more effort in laying out the way of salvation. The Holy Spirit applied a knowledge of Christ to persons whereby they become persuaded of the mercy of God toward them. They thus become a Christian, confirming the fact that they have been elected by God.[122] If the Holy Spirit has actually worked to cause faith to grow in a person's life, Perkins argued that people may inquire within themselves for signs of their election. The elect are known only to themselves and to God. They know themselves elect "not....from the first causes of Election, but rather from the last effects thereof....the testimonie of Gods spirit, and the works of Sanctification."[123] The so-called *syllogismus practicus* (practical syllogism) propounded by Beza was avoided here by Perkins.[124] He did not urge as Beza had that assurance of salvation could be logically deduced from external works. For Perkins, the work of assurance by the Holy Ghost took place in inner attitudes and affections. As he wrote: "for the holy Ghost draweth not reasons from the works, or worthines of man, but from Gods fauour & loue: & this kind of perswasion is farre different from that which Satan vseth."[125] When Perkins did urge his readers to examine the "effects of Sanctification," these were all in terms of attitudes, or strivings, or desires rather than actual "works" themselves.[126] Doing this, he said, was part of "the right applying of Predestination to the persons of men."[127]

Thus, while there are similarities between the charts of Beza and Perkins, there are also important differences as well. Perkins did append an excerpt from Beza's debate with the Lutheran Jakob Andreas (1528-1590) to his *Golden Chaine*.[128] Had he used Beza, he would have had to use a Continental edition since none of the English versions of the *Tabula* published during Perkins' lifetime included the table of causes.[129] Since Beza's works were widely distributed in the sixteenth century, this is entirely possible. Yet Perkins in his chart made more explicit the function of Jesus Christ in the order of salvation. Beza and Perkins agreed generally on the order of the decrees. But Perkins also analyzed the plan of salvation practically and pastorally. He spelled out the relation of the stages of Christ's work to the spiritual pilgrimmage of Christian believers. Perkins treated doctrines as they related to the question of the assurance of salvation.

Besides the opening diagram, there were other diagrams included in Perkins' *A Golden Chaine*. The first of these were printed before the opening chapter. It was an enlargement of the first statements Perkins made in chapter I: "Of the body of Scripture, and Theologie." There his text read: "The Bodie of Scripture is a doctrine sufficient to liue well. It comprehendeth many holy sciences, whereof one is principall, others are hand-maids or retainers. The principall science is *Theologie*.[130]

Perkins' chart is Ramist in form and expands on his statements by listing and defining the "hand-maiden" sciences that are part of the body of Holy Scripture. The division of the chart was Scripture divided into its principal and attendant sciences. Sciences related to Theology according to Perkins were: Ethiques, Oeconomickes, Politikes, Ecclesiasticall discipline, The Iewes Common-weale, Prophecie, and Academie.[131] *A Golden Chaine* was devoted only to the principal science, Theology.

Perkins' division of Theology into "God" and "His workes" was just the first of numerous divisions that extended throughout the treatise. Perkins' complete *Golden Chaine* could be laid out diagrammatically as a Ramist chart given enough size and space. Throughout, Perkins' use of dichotomies is prevalent. Perkins' divisions of "God" were: God's "nature" which "is either Simplenesse, or the Infinitenesse thereof." The "simplenesse" is "immutable and spirituall"; the "infinitenesse of God is two-fold: his Eternitie, and exceeding greatnesse."[132] God's "workes" were likewise initially divided into His "Decree" and the "execution of his decree" which in turn was dichotomized into "operation" and "operative permission."[133] So too, "predestination" which Perkins defined as "Gods decree, in as much as it concerneth man," was accomplished by two means: creation and fall.[134] The "parts" of predestination were two: "Election and Reprobation."[135] The degrees of executing the decree of election were two, as was the "declaration of Gods loue," "sanctification," "the parts of Christian warfare," "the profession of Christ in dangers," "blessednesse," and the "fruits" that come from blessedness among other topics.[136] Perkins takes up these many parts and other divisions with more than two members in turn as he followed his Ramist map.[137]

Other charts in this work include two that are similar to the "orders and causes of salvation" in the front of the work. These were views of the order of salvation and predestination held by the Church of Rome and certain "later Diuines in Germanie."[138] Like Perkins' own chart on salvation, these were to be read downward since they started with God and His decrees at the top.

Also of interest are two charts for the sacraments of Baptism and the Lord's Supper.[139] The Baptism chart, entitled "The Sacramentall Vnion of the parts of Baptisme" showed two Ramist-style charts adjoining. One moved through "externall baptisme." The other was of "inward baptism" and moved in the opposite direction. The charts were situated this way with the inscription running vertically between them reading: "The union of the signs and the thing signified."

In the same manner, the chart for the Lord's Supper was divided into "the sensible and externall actions" and "the spirituall & internall actions." The vertical inscription between these divisions read the same as the one for baptism. Each followed the same contrasting pattern in the chart by setting the "things sensible" across from "things spirituall." "Sensible" (external) actions of the minister were placed across from "spirituall" actions of God. The duties of the Christian receiver of the Sacrament were set facing the benefits received.

In Perkins' chapter on the Sacraments in the 1590 Latin edition, he provided a small chart for the "parts" (*partes*) of the Sacraments.[140] In the 1591 and later the English editions, this chart was omitted and the parts "divided" into prose. The 1591 English translation read:

> The partes of a Sacrament are, eyther the externall signes, or the thing signified, that is, the substance of the Sacrament.
> The externall signe is, either some prescript and sensible matter, or the externall action in the use of the same.
> The thinges signified in the Sacrament, are eyther Christ and his benefites, or the internal action that is about Christ.
> The internal action, is the action either of God, or of faith.
> The action of God is his offering, applying, and sealing up of Christ and his benefites in the heartes of the faithfull.
> The action of faith is the consideration, desire, apprehension, and receiving of Christ in the Sacrament.[141]

The significance of this point is that it indicates the basic interchangability of prose and charts in the mind of Perkins and other Ramists. The "either/or" pattern was prominent here and it is apparent how easy it was to translate the 1590 Latin chart into prose in 1591 when for some reason the chart itself was not included in the work. This translation followed the movement to be expected in synthesizing something Ramist from an "analysis." The only "irregularity" was in the last division where on the chart "faith" was given prior to "God" while in the English rendering, God's action was expounded first. But as the chart indicates, the object of both of these is Christ. In terms of Ramist doctrine, the better order would seem to be the 1591 English translation order. Movement there was from the action of God to the action of faith. Perhaps this variation was the reason the chart was omitted.

Perkins' use of Ramist method in *A Golden Chaine* is an example of how a Ramist theologian could present "art" or "science" in a "methodical" manner. A major focus of this work was the doctrine of predestination. But Perkins covered many other theological topics as well. Despite the complexity of his thought, Perkins constantly tried to simplify and specifically to apply his doctrines in a practical and pastoral way to his readers. This concern for simplicity and relevance to life were also aspects that Ramist method was designed to highlight.

Chapter V. RAMISM IN PERKINS' EXEGETICAL WORKS

A. Biblical Commentaries

William Perkins devoted much time to Biblical exegesis. Many of the works now known as his Biblical commentaries had their origins in the sermons he preached in Cambridge. He preached at times on whole books of the Bible through a series of sermons, at times on portions or chapters of books, and at times on one or several verses.[1] Perkins certainly saw one of his most basic tasks to be the interpretation of Scripture.

If the Ramist method was adequate for presenting systematic theology, Perkins also found it suited for doing Biblical exposition or exegesis. Perkins' citations of Scripture to buttress the divisions and headings he made in this theological works have been mentioned. In like manner, when Perkins exegeted Scripture, the theological terms reappear as being "properly" drawn from a passage or text.[2] Perkins preceived a mutual interdependence between systematic theology and Biblical exegesis. Each would have been incomplete without the other.

Perkins' Biblical commentaries had their roots in this sermons which were compiled and expanded. Some of this editorial work was done by him. After his death, others completed some of his work for publication. Many of his sermons and hence his commentaries contained repetitions. But this was no problem for Perkins. He saw repetition not only as useful but as Biblical.[3] Perkins had a high reputation for exegetical ability among his contemporaries. According to Ralph Cudworth (d. 1624), a Fellow of Emmanuel College and Perkins' friend, the ideal for a Biblical commentary was to collect doctrines and not just to paraphrase the Biblical text. A good commentary was to apply these doctrines with practical uses instead of merely pointing out the main heads of doctrine. Only experts, according to Cudworth needed only that "literal sense of the place, without making further use of application, or instruction." Most people needed the text "minced, and cut small unto them before they can receiue it."[4] Perkins won Cudworth's praise as an exemplary exegete. According to Cudworth, Perkins in his commentaries (particularly in Perkins' *Commentary on Galatians*) provided

> beside the meaning, he hath briefly drawne out such doctrines as
> naturally arise from the text; shewing withall, how they ought to
> be applied for confutation, correction, instruction, consolation.
> Which he hath done with such dexteritie, (artificially matching
> together two things, heretofore insociable, Breuitie, and
> Perspicuitie,) that the like (I take it) hath not beene performed
> heretofore by any Expositor upon this Epistle: which we may
> well call the key of the new Testament.[5]

Some forty years later, a bibliography for ministers listed Perkins as one of England's leading Scriptural commentators.[6]

Perkins' commentaries followed the Ramist pattern or method. Earlier commentators had most often exegeted their texts in a straightforward fashion, verse by verse.[7] Occasionally these commentators digressed into some discussion of doctrine.[8] Some Continental commentators such as Johannes Piscator had begun to employ "logical analysis" in the tradition of Ramus to the books of the Bible.[9] Others such as Francis Junius and L. Daneau did the same.[10] In addition, they frequently used their knowledge of rhetoric when they commented on Scripture. Often they very carefully analyzed various figures of speech in what might be termed "rhetorical exegesis."[11] They complemented this approach by their examinations of individual terms through word studies. This was frequently termed "grammatcial exegesis."[12]

In England, Dudley Fenner had published his small Ramist commentary on Philemon.[13] But in 1591 Richard Turnbull, sometimes Fellow of Corpus Christi College, Oxford and then minister in London used the Ramist logic to set forth "An Exposition of the Book of James." This was complete with "the Tables, Analysis, and resolution both of the whole Epistle, and euerie Chapter thereof: with the particular resolution of euerie singular place." Turnbull claimed this was the most ample exposition available and "also more orderly then by any heretofore." Turnbull further asserted that he was the first to use the logical method on Scripture: "in such a methode, as (to my knowledge) none hath laboured, eyther in this, or other like places of the Holy Scripture."[14] Turnbull hoped that by "hauing drawen first the generall Analysis, or resolution of the whole Epistle: then the particular of euery chapter, with the like prefixed before euery Lecture or sermon in this exposition," those who were but of "simple capacities, by the very tables, may see and search out, the very meaning of the holy Apostle."[15] Yet none of Perkins' English predecessors appear to have used the Ramist logical structure to the same extent he did for Biblical exposition.[16]

An examination of Perkins' Biblical commentaries shows that he approached the Scriptural books with the tools of the Ramist philosophy firmly in hand. Some of his Biblical expositions have Ramist charts at their beginnings with the whole Scriptural book already "methodized" or "analyzed" or "resolved" according to Ramist method.[17] Others were clearly written according to the method.

For Perkins, to analyze a Scriptural book or a passage according to the logic he knew was most natural. It was a duty of the Scriptural exegete. Perkins showed this quite plainly at one point when he commented on Revelation 1:19. He said: "Write the things which thou has seene, and the things which are, and the things which shall come hereafter." To Perkins the words of that commandment contained "the diuision of this whole booke....Thus then is the whole book distinguished. I. It containeth things touching the present estate of the Church in Iohns daies. II. It entreateth of things which concerne the future estate thereof from Iohns time, to the ende of the world."[18] Then Perkins wrote clearly of how he justified his approach to Scripture in this way.

> Hence oserue the lawfulnesse of the art of Logicke: for diuisions are lawfull, (else the holy Ghost would not here haue vsed them) and so by proportion are other arguments of reasoning: and therefore that art which giueth rules of direction for the right vse of these arguments, is lawfull and good. Those men then are farre deceiued, who account the arts of Logicke and Rhetoricke to be friuolous and vnlawfull, and in so saying, they condemne the practise of the holy Ghost in this place.[19]

Perkins not only believed the exegete needed to use the arts of logic and rhetoric, he also believed (as his commentaries repeatedly show) that the Bible itself contained the natural divisions which it was the exegete's job to uncover using the tools of logic and rhetoric at his disposal. In this sense Perkins perceived the task of the logician and the Scriptural exegete to be exactly as Ramus had said: to discover and dispose of matter.[20] The logician's job was to define, divide, and classify so that the thought of the discourse might become clear. To Perkins, the task of the Biblical exegete was precisely the same.

Perkins' sermons on the Book of Revelation were preached in 1595. But they were not gathered and published until after his death.[21] His preaching and commentary, however, did not extend beyond the third chapter of the book. Perkins did not entangle himself with figuring out mysterious imageries or interpreting the book "prophetically" to identify current events or persons as actors in the divine drama.[22]

Before Perkins begain his exposition, a "Generall Analysis of the Vision shewed to Iohn" was prefaced to the work.[23] Since this work did not reach printed form until Perkins was dead, it is possible that this Ramist chart was drawn by Thomas Pierson who was in charge of the revisions and enlarging of the work "after a more perfect Copie at the request of M. Perkins Exequutors."[24] The style of Perkins' exposition was to deal with each verse in turn. But it is clear throughout that he had his more "general analysis" in mind. Whether or not Perkins himself actually constructed the Ramist chart at the beginning of the work is of little consequence. Each verse as indicated by the chart was related to the larger whole. The exposition was the unfolding of these verses in relation to each other and to the overall plan of the "analysis." When Perkins interpreted his texts, he did so by setting them always within the broader context of the chapter or the book itself.

While the chart provided the broadest outlines of his exposition, Perkins' discussion of each verse was much more detailed. For example, on Revelation 1:6 which read: "and made vs kings and priests to God euen his father: to him bee glorie and dominion for euremore, Amen," Perkins' chart showed this in its appropriate place as one of four divisions of the execution of the office of God the Son in His works.[25] But when Perkins came to handle the text, his discussion was divided into four points "for the better vnderstanding whereof." These four points were based on the words of the text rather than on only the key words "kings and priests." Perkins discussed

> First, the dignitie and excellencie of all true members of Christ, *They are Kings and Priests*. Secondly, when they be made kings and priests in this life, noted by the phrase of speech, *hath made*. Wherein he speaketh of the church on earth, and vseth a word that signifieth the time past. Thirdly, the manner how they become Kings and Priests; they are not so borne, but Christ hath made them such. Fourthly, to whom they be made such, *to God euen the Father*.[26]

When Perkins was finished with these points he wrote: "Thus much for the meaning of the words: Now follow sundry vses, from the consideration of these two dignities of beleeuers. And first their kingly dignitie affordeth matter both of instruction and consolation."[27] After listing six points of "instruction," Perkins spoke of the "consolations" that were given to true believers. He turned next to the duties taught by the "second dignitie," being "Priests vnto God." These were five points. Then Perkins finished with three points about the final phrase "to him bee glorie and dominion, for euermore, Amen."

Thus Perkins' chart represented just the barest outline of the structure of his exposition. A chart could have been prepared to exhibit all Perkins' divisions. But it would have been quite large indeed. The major reason for the bulk of the *Commentary* itself (over 160 pages) was that Perkins spent so much time in making applications of the meaning of the text to the conduct of his readers' (hearers') lives. This was the "use" section which in Ramist thought ought to follow the "doctrine" part methodologically. In the section of the commentary just cited, the "uses" would follow the "meaning of the words" part of the exposition. This was a major characteristic of Perkins' writings -- the theological ones as well as those of Biblical exposition. He lost no opportunity to press home for his audience the concrete ways that Christian doctrine or a verse of Scripture should in his opinion be related to their everyday lives.[28] To Perkins effective preaching and Biblical exposition demanded this ethical application. He wrote in commenting on Hebrews 12:1 that "the word not applyed to our selues, doth vs no good: it is like Physicke not taken, or food not eaten."[29]

These same characteristics just noted appear also in Perkins' *Commentary on the eleventh chapter of the Book of Hebrews* entitled *A Cloud of Faithfull Witnesses Leading to the heauenly Canaan*.[30] This work was originally preached as a series of Cambridge sermons evidently around the year 1595. The work began with the familiar Ramist division: "Concerning Faith, two points are necessarie to be knowne of euery Christian; the *doctrine*, and the *practise* of it." Perkins said that the whole doctrine of faith ("beeing grounded and gathered out of the word of God") is found in the Apostles' Creed, "which beeing alreadie by vs expounded.[31] It followeth in order (next after the doctrine) to lay downe also the practise of faith: for which purpose we haue chosen this 11 chap. to the Hebrewes, as beeing a portion of Scripture, wherein the said practise of faith is most excellently and at large set downe."[32] Again, Perkins clearly used the "doctrine/practice" pattern. This time, he said, it is the pattern to be followed not only with each text or passage from the Bible but in the whole enterprise of Christian faith itself. Perkins would expound both the Apostle's Creed and Hebrews 11 to give the full balance of the faith. "Faith" and "works" must both be represented. These both are "necessarie to be knowne by euery Christian," according to Perkins.³³

The commentary on Hebrews 11 differed from the Revelation commentary in that this work contained no chart or "general analysis" prefixed to it. But though the Ramist map was absent, Perkins' commentary can be outlined in the Ramist fashion. Perkins dichotomized this chapter:

> The partes of this whole chapter are two;
> 1. A generall *description of Faith*, 1. v. to the 4.
> 2. An *illustration* or declaration of that description, by a large rehearsall of manifold *examples* of aunctient and worthy men in the olde Testament, from the 4. v. to the end.³⁴

Then Perkins proceeded to divide the "description of faith" into three "actions or effects" (in the first three verses of the chapter). The first two of these were dichotomized into "meanings/instructions"; "meanings/uses" -- thus maintaining again the "doctrine/practice" paradigm. These were further divided as was the third "action or effect."

Perkins also divided his second major part into two.³⁵ These were of examples of faith in the Old Testament and his divisions were of those "such as are set downe seuerally one by one" (ch. 11:4-32); then "such as are set downe ioyntly many together" (ch. 11:32-40). The names Perkins listed as examples of faith in the Old Testament "severally" were divided into "natural Israelites" and these either "living near or after the flood" or "after the flood"; or "strangers from the church of God." The first to be dealt with in Perkins' exposition was Abel (11:4). The three sections of the verse describing Abel formed the basis for Perkins' discussion of him: His sacrifice was greater than Cain's; he obtained testimony with God; and though Abel is dead he "yet speaketh." Each of these divisions were dichotomized by Perkins and then further divided several times. A few of these when dichotomized further fell into the "doctrine/use" rubric. Perkins introduce this pattern by saying something such as "here we learne a worthy lesson of Christianitie." In the next paragraph he moved in a natural way to say: "for the use of this doctrine."³⁶ The "word/deed" pattern was made graphically clear when Perkins wrote of Abel being dead and yet "still speaking." There a bracket was drawn in the text to show the two ways in which the example of Abel's faith was a "neuer-dying Preacher to all ages of the Church":

> For there is a double teaching, namely, in ⎧ word, or deede.³⁷ ⎫

The order for Perkins was invariably the same. First would be the doctrine, or lesson, or "theory"; then followed the use, or instruction or "practice." Transferred to the realm of logic, Perkins like Ramus marshalled the "arguments" (invention) which to both men were self-evidencing axioms or "propositions." Then they were arranged for "disposition" (judgment) or "exercise" (use) according to the laws of method.³⁸

The divisions that make up the headings for a chart of Perkins' work were not merely arbitrarily selected. Perkins' main divisions and the different sections of the chart are set off by paragraphs in his works. That is, when Perkins partitioned a subject, he named his divisions and the parts of them in such a way that each point most always had a paragraph devoted to it. Perkins began with a topic sentence which served in a chart to name or define a division. The heading of a division when it was not a single word could most always be captured in a short phrase which came right from the text of Perkins itself. It is true that someone writing without Ramist method in mind could do this as well. A scholastic logician or theologian could also list points in a one, two, three fashion with a topic sentence to identify them. But there are important differences between the Scholastics and Ramists at this juncture.

The scholastic would move toward a conclusion by deriving his points from his proposition and from the point derived immediately prior to it. The Ramist would not do this. Each of the points Perkins listed for either "doctrine" or "use" are points that he apparently perceived to spring directly and immediately from his major proposition itself. He did not deduce them through a number of intervening propositions. He did not constantly use syllogisms to prove the truth of one point before moving on to the next. He did not construct a logical platform from which to display a final conclusion. Perkins did not so much seek to prove the points he made as simply to "unfold" them or draw them out directly from his text.

Perkins did use the reasoning process to secure his points on occasion when he was expounding the Bible. He found examples of the Holy Spirit's use of reasoning which to Perkins was perfectly valid. For example, on the verse on Enoch that read in part "neither was he found, for God had taken his away," speaking of the Holy Spirit Perkins wrote:

> And for his proofe, he first laieth downe his ground: then hee thereupon frameth his argument, consisting of diuerse degrees of demonstration....the holy Ghost frames his argument, to prooue that Henoch was taken away by faith: and it consisteth of many degrees of euidence. For before he was taken away, he was reported of that he had pleased God.
> But without faith it is impossible to please God. The degrees of the argument are these:
> 1. God himselfe tooke Henoch away.
> 2. Before he was taken away, he pleased God.
> 3. But without faith no man can please God. Therefore Enoch by faith was taken away.[39]

Perkins them expounded on each of the elements of this "argument" and missed no chance to apply a practical exhortation for each point.

Perkins was concerned throughout that his audience learn "not in iudgement and knowledge onely, to be able to talke of it (which is soone learned:) but in conscience and practise...."[40] Yet even though he used a syllogistic form and spoke of the "proof" of the argument, Perkins was still only seeking to "unfold" how the Holy Spirit showed that Enoch was "by faith taken away." The three points from which he deduced his opinion were taken directly from the Biblical text itself. They were not propositions of Perkins' own. He set them forth as he did to show how he perceived the Holy Spirit had "framed" his argument to prove that Enoch was taken by faith. These propositions of Scripture themselves did not need to be proved. They were self-evident, "axiomatic." But by using the syllogistic form, Perkins could portray the interior "logic" of Scripture and make it plain how in this case, Enoch was taken away "by faith." The first part of the verse Perkins was expounding clearly said: "by faith, Henoch was translated...." What came immediately following was the Holy Spirit's "proof" that "Henoch beeing taken into heauen, must needes be taken away by faith."[41] Perkins "unfolded" the logic of the Spirit's statement.

Here too Perkins again displayed a Ramistic understanding of the place and function of syllogistic reasoning. The syllogism served only to clear doubtful propositions by deriving them from self-evident axioms. Generally Perkins treated the statements of Scripture as axioms or true propositions. By expounding the Scriptures as he did (using Ramist method) he displayed graphically (whether the charts were prefixed to the work or could be drawn from them), how these axioms fit together in a pattern. If any part of the Scriptural record needed further elucidation, the tools of logic were at hand. Perkins shared Ramus' conception of logic. He saw the Holy Spirit as using the logical forms in Scripture to demonstrate how logic as an "art" was to be done. The Spirit demonstrated this by "arguing" through the proper forms. so the syllogism for both Ramus and Perkins was not an argument in itself. It was merely a way for the logician (and the exegete) to arrange an argument. This was all Perkins was doing when he used the syllogism to display the Scriptural argument concerning Enoch.

Perkins' exposition of Hebrews 11 went on for many pages. He devoted considerable space to explaining what lessons were to be learned and practiced from the examples of the "faithful" mentioned in the chapter. Perkins' exegesis proceded phrase by phrase. Yet one is conscious that Perkins saw all these phrases as fitting together as parts of a larger whole, the "general analysis" of the chapter itself. This meant that at many points Perkins took the words of the Scriptural text, the phrases, and grouped them or "translated" them into other words or phrases that served as the main heads for his divisions. For example, Hebrews 11:13 read: "All these died in faith, and receiued not the promises, but sawe them afarre off, and beleeued them: and receiued them thankefully, and confessed that they were strangers and pilgrimes on the earth." Perkins' treatment of this verse was phrase by phrase. But before he embarked on this exegesis, he grouped the phrases under headings. He wrote:

> Hitherto the Holy Ghost hath particularly commended the faith of diuers holy beleeuers. Now from this verse to the 17. he doth generally commend the faith of Abraham, Sarah, Isaac, and Iakob together; yet not so much their faith, as the durance and constancie of their faith. Particularly the points are two.
> 1. Is laid downe their constancie and continuance;
> All these died in faith.
> 2. That constancie is set forth by foure effects.
>   1. They receiued not the promises, but sawe them affare off.
>   2. They beleeued them.
>   3. Receiued them thankefully.
>   4. Professed themselues strangers and pilgrimes on the earth.[42]

Thus the phrases of this verse could be charted as "constancy of faith" and "effects" of this constancy. In this sense Perkins systematized or categorized the Biblical texts in this expositions. He gave attention to the Biblical phrases themselves and always drew "uses" from the "doctrines" they taught.

But the "order" he brought to the handling of the texts by grouping them and providing headings for them must have been done to facilitate "method." If one would look at the chart that could be constructed from Perkins' handling of the 11th chapter of Hebrews, one would not see merely a grouping of the Biblical phrases alone. One would see that Perkins had filtered the text and set the phrases as parts of larger groupings. The reader is in reality for Perkins observing the logical method used by God (through the Holy Spirit, Perkins would say) in framing this discourse of Scripture. In this sense the implications of the apparently innocuous Ramist philosophy become startling. The system was more than just classificatory logic when applied to Biblical interpretation. It was an attempt to perceive the logical plan in the mind of God that expressed itself through the flow of the Scriptural material. If this plan was uncovered it could therefore in addition reveal the true hermeneutics for Scriptural interpretation. The exact meaning of a text would be ascertained with certainty if the procedure used was able to uncover the mind of God behind the text. All other methods of interpreting that text would thus be false.

The Bible was the Word of God for William Perkins.[43] The Holy Spirit stood behind the writing of Scripture as well as with the interpreter who exegeted it.[44] The Ramist logic applied to Scripture by proponents like Perkins identified the very thought processes of the Divine mind that caused Scripture to be written.[45] When Scripture was "methodized" and "analyzed" after the Ramist fashion, the reader of the Ramist chart had instant access to the whole drift of God's thought as it expressed itself in this portion of Scripture. Thus when applied to Biblical exegesis, the Ramist philosophy had metaphysical implications.

The identity in Perkins' mind between his interpretation of the Biblical texts and the work of the Holy Spirit in framing them is apparent when Perkins wrote such things as: "the holy Ghost diuideth this reason into two parts, and handleth the same seuerally"; "here the holy Ghost prooueth the seond part of the former argument"; "but our Translation in this place is true and right, according to the words of the Text, and the meaning of the holy Ghost."[46] Perkins at times mentioned rules for proper hermeneutics.[47] But at the most basic level, Perkins apparently did not doubt that he was able to peer into the Holy Spirit's mind because he was "properly dividing" the Scriptural texts that the Spirit caused to be written. Perkins gave a proper place to the use of logic and to human reasoning rightly applied.[48] But the goal of it all was to see clearly how the Spirit had constructed this pericope of Scripture. By laying out his "analysis" in Biblical exposition (after the Ramist method) Perkins was making plain how the specific parts of Scripture -- parts of verses, verse, chapters, were related to a broader whole. By giving each of these small pieces a heading or "keyword," Perkins could diagram the Scripture section or book. Thereby he laid out clearly for all to see what the Holy Spirit actually had in mind as the Spirit caused the Scripture to be written.

The most detailed of the Ramist analyses attached to Perkins' works was the chart prefixed to Perkins' *A Godly and Learned Exposition Upon the Whole Epistle of Iude*.[49] This work was over 100 pages long and was made up of some 66 sermons Perkins preached on the book. The sermons were probably preached in the latter part of the 1590's since Perkins' commentary was not published until after his death by Thomas Taylor.[50] Taylor had heard these sermons preached and said that Perkins "had in his heart" to publish this commentary "if God had giuen him longer time."[51] While the sermons were preached in the last period of Perkins' life, this commentary is perhaps the clearest example from his *Works* of how Perkins applied the Ramist philosophy to his Biblical exegesis. For the detailed chart attached to this work is a fold-out chart covering in detail the main heads of Perkins' expositions. From it the elements discovered about Perkins' Ramist method in his commentaries on Revelation 1-3 and Hebrews 11 stand out.[52]

Perkins divided the whole letter of Jude into three parts: Salutation, Exhortation, and Epilogue. There was a further division of these and still more divisions, sometimes to ten or eleven divisions. Perkins used both the phrases from the text and his own terms to serve as headings. He used logical terms to display how the Holy Spirit has "argued." This argument, however (which began in verse 5), took the form of the answering of an "objection" raised against the Apostle's exhortation to "contend and fight for the faith, v. 3 with the reason thereof, v. 4."[53] As the initial chart lined out this "argument," Perkins said " a prolepsis answered in a perfect forme of syllogisme," consisting of a 1. Proposition. 2. Assumption. and 3. Conclusion was involved.[54] Perkins summarized the answer of the Holy Spirit to the objection (in verses 5-20) by framing a proposition: "the summe of which disputation is contained in this reason." Then he proceeded to prove this proposition: "The former proposition is not plainely set downe in so many words, but the proofe of it onely by an induction and enumeration of all examples of sinners...."[55] From there Perkins moved through a discussion of the three kinds of sinners who faced destruction. These were Israelites (v. 5), Angels (v. 6). and Sodom and Gomorrah (v. 7). He then turned to the "proofe of the second part of the former reason," the "assumption" (v. 8). Once more Perkins moved through this point after an initial dichotomy (the ground of sins; the kinds of sins) by induction. He listed 18 points of sin committed by deceivers. Verse 11 marked "the conclusion of the principall argument of the Epistle."[56]

Again, the significance of this use of logical language by Perkins was not in the fact that he structured his exposition by it. He did not use the syllogistic forms to prove his point time and time again. Syllogisms were not the controlling factor or the major tool Perkins used when interpreting the Bible. When he did use logical jargon, it was to elucidate how he saw that the Holy Spirit had already used logic within the structure of the passages of

Scripture. The controlling factor for Perkins was the Ramist method of division. He divided Scriptural statements and classified them into what be believed were valid headings that could then be charted. A clear skeletal structure of the Biblical work would then become apparent.

Perkins' *Commentary on Jude* also displayed the "doctrine/use" pattern. In many cases Perkins clearly identified what was "doctrine" by devoting a paragraph to it and labeling it "Doct."[57] He did the same with "use."[58] Also interspersed were sections labeled "Obiect." or "Quest." or "Answ." in which various objections and questions raised were answered.[59]

On the title page of Perkins' *Commentary* was the statement: "Where-vnto is prefixed a large Analysis, containing the summe and order of the whole Booke, according to the Authors owne methode."[60] The heading of this chart titles it: "A briefe viewe of the whole Epistle, drawne according to the Authors owne method." Since this work was not published until after Perkins' death, it would seem unlikely that he constructed the chart with that heading. The qualifying phrase "after the Authors owne method" would seem to indicate that the chart was added posthumously. Thomas Taylor, chosen by Perkins executors to publish this work and one whose own works bear the Ramist stamp, was in all probability the composer of this Ramist map.[61] Taylor found that this could be done by following the flow of Perkins' text. And surely the open highlighting of the fact that his chart was drawn according to the "authors owne method," indicated Taylor recognized that Perkins knew he was following a certain "methodical" or Ramistic approach through his exegetical pattern. There are some dichotomies in the chart and many multiple listings of points -- up to 18 in one head. The phrases of the Scripture verses were used in many places and along with them the "key-word" used by Perkins to identify the "place" that this had in the overall scheme of things. The pervasive use of brackets, the order in which the topics are considered in the text as related to the chart, and the whole movement throughout from most general to most specific offer the strongest conclusive proof that Perkins had wholeheartedly adopted Ramus' views on the nature of logic and logical method. In his commentaries, Perkins adapted Ramist teaching for the purposes of Biblical exegesis.

There were, however, several variations of this exact method among Perkins' commentaries on Scripture. Perkins' *Exposition of the Lords Prayer* was subtitled "in the way of Catechizing, serving for Ignorant People."[62] Prominent in this piece was a chart near the beginning entitled "A briefe Exposition vpon the Lords praier."[63] It was not the typical Ramist chart with branches extending to show the interrelatedness of the whole. Instead it displayed how Perkins handled this subject in catechetical form.[64]

Perkins divided the work into three parts: Preface, Petitions (including "A reason of praise of God") and Testification of faith. These were listed vertically next to the words of the prayer corresponding to them. In adjoining columns, Perkins ran a synopsis of "the meaning of the words"; "wants to be bewailed"; and "graces to bee desired." He divided his discussion of each phrase into numbered sections dealing in more or less all of them with the same pattern: the coherence, the meaning, the uses of the words; wants to be bewailed, graces to be desired. These parts were not included in all the phrases. But all of them embraced most of the parts.

This piece of Biblical exposition was constructed along slightly different lines from the other Biblical works of Perkins that used the Ramist method clearly. But it would be possible to construct a chart along Ramist lines from the Table given in the front of this piece. Yet for several reasons it does not seem that Perkins intended this to be done. One reason is the form of the Table as it now appears. Had Perkins consciously constructed his discourse in the usual way, the usual Ramist chart would have likely appeared. Also, some of the sections of the Table as it presently appeared, have only one member. A Ramist division always meant two or more members. Thus it would not be possible to carry the Ramist chart through consistently if it were drawn.

Why Perkins' *Exposition of the Lord's Prayer* was not handled in his usual Ramist fashion cannot be known with complete certainty. The best reason appears to be that Perkins conceived this as a catechism. Thus while the work was exegetical in nature, it was cast in a catechetical form. Throughout his treatments of the Biblical phrases of the Lord's Prayer, Perkins occasionally inserted a paragraph titled "Quest." But this was not done in all sections. More likely Perkins considered the numbered divisions made for each phrase to serve as the "questions." These headings: coherence, meaning, uses, wants, and graces thus functioned as "commoplaces" to focus attention on the same questions throughout each petition. The form of this catechism was not the same as Perkins' *Foundation of the Christian Religion* where the question/answer format was used. His Scriptural exposition here was longer and more detailed. But still, Perkins' main points could be reduced to phrases, compact enough to be included in his opening Table. The Table summarized the work. It was not a complete summary since it did not include a section on the "uses" or "coherence" of the phrases which were included in some of Perkins' expositions. But the Table gave a quick visual overview of the parts, the words, the meaning of the words, wants to be bewailed, and graces to be desired. These heads could serve as the permanent questions to be asked of each part of the Prayer.

Though this exposition of the Lord's Prayer was not a discourse arranged in a thoroughly Ramistic manner, it could be used in the way just described as a catechism. In its barest form it did follow Perkins' usual practice. The essence of the Table is the meaning of the words and then the dichotomy to be followed throughout: "wantes to be bewailed"; "Graces to be desired." In this sense, Perkins was being true to his Ramistic self. He first said what the words meant (definition) and then divided their meaning throughout under two heads (division).

Another variation on Perkins' usual Ramist style of Biblical exposition was his *A Faithfvll and Plaine Exposition Upon the two first verses of the 2. Chapter of Zephaniah.*[65] This piece was actually a 1593 sermon published after Perkins' death (1605) as "An Exhortation to Repentance." In this work Perkins took the two verses of his text, made five points of them using the words of the text (which were the "doctrines" derived) and organized these points under the theme of "searching" by which Perkins meant repenting. The five points were: duty; who must be searched; who must doe it; time limiting them, when to repent; and a reason urging them to do it. The majority of the treatise was devoted to the duty to "search" and this was expanded in five further points.

William Crashawe who provided the "Epistle Dedicatorie" to this sermon connected this work with Perkins' *Treatise of Repentance* "published 1593 wherein briefly (as his manner was) but soundly, pithily, and feelingly, he layeth downe the doctrine; and the very nature of Repentance."[66] But according to Crashawe, Perkins had later thought "he had not seriously and forcibly enough, vrged so great and necessary a lesson as Repentance is." Thus,

> shortly after, beeing desired and called to the duty of Preaching,
> in that great and generall assembly at Sturbridge Faire, he
> thought it a fit time, for this necessary and generall exhortation
> to repentance: to the intent, that as we were taught the doctrine
> of repentance in the former Treatise; so in these Sermons we
> night be stirred vp to the practise of it.[67]

This explanation accounts for the fact that this work is not as fully developed along Ramist lines as are others of Perkins' treatises. Rather than making every paragraph one that could be charted, this work was filled with exhortations to Perkins' audience who were buyers and sellers gathered at a Fair. These hearers came from all over the country. Perkins was very exact in telling them that they were still "ignorant" after "fiue and thirty yeares" of the Gospel being preached in England (1558-1593.)[68] This condition the people lamentably counted as "no sinne" according to Perkins. He continually urged his congregation to repent, to "search and trie our waies, and turne againe to the Lord."[69] He spent most the sermon developing the point of their duty to repent. In the most elaborate of these points he tells the crowd that their searching of themselves is to be made by the Law of God. This must be marked by three rules: that all have come from Adam and sinned in Adam; that "in euery man are all sinnes"; and that all are by nature God's enemies. Perkins then went on to summarize these points before moving into a more specific application of how these rules applied to the people themselves and the realm of England.[70] Perkins listed five of the most common sinnes of England, seeking to "rip vp the sores of our Nation, so that they may be healed to the bottome."[71] The urgency Perkins felt for this task came through when he said.

> God hath long spared, and he hath been long in trauelling, therefore (though nothing can be said in way of prophesy) I am in my conscience perswaded to feare, and that out of infallible grounds of the word of God, that a plague, and a iudgement, and that most feareful, hangs ouer England: and that it is alreadie pronounced vpon this Nation, and shall be as certainly executed, without a visible reformation.[72]

Perkins' sermon is a prime example of how Perkins the Puritan preacher exhorted a general audience to a course of action. Crawshawe claimed to have received this sermon of Perkins' "not deliuered to me from hand to hand, but taken with this hand of mine from his owne mouth." Perkins extended illustrations in this sermon. He spoke of a man passing over dangerous mountains at midnight and then in the morning seeing what he had been saved from. This was analogous, said Perkins, to the corrupt sinner being awakened to God's grace and seeing what he has passed through. These type of illustrations were certainly designed to catch the attention of the audience for a specific point. This was the same plan that Ramus in his prudential method had advocated. Other illustrations drawn from common life such as toothaches and wheat and chaff were for the same purpose.[73]

This work was not so carefully drawn according to Ramist method most probably because Perkins' audience was a general audience. There was a much wider cross-section of England represented there than Perkins usually preached to at Cambridge University. Thus a sermon more in the tradition of Ramus' prudential method was appropriate. Perkins was trying to urge the people to action in this address. This was an opportunity for the Puritan preacher to try to evoke the spiritual reformation he so frequently called to see. His primary purpose in this Biblical exposition was not to provide a balanced and "logicall" analysis of the verses from Zephaniah. Perkins drew the main heads of doctrine for his discourse from the text. But he developed these in a more clearly hortatory style than his other works demonstrate.

In 1598 Perkins published a Latin work dealing with the Bible entitled *Specimen digesti, siue, harmoniae bibiorum Veteris et Nove Testamenti*. This was later translated into English as *A Digest or Harmonie of the bookes of the old and new Testament*.[74] This work was designed to serve five functions according to Perkins. It was

1. An harmony or Chronicle of the times.
2. An harmony of the aunceint History, and of the Prophets.
3. An harmony of the Gospell.
4. An abridgement of the whole sacred Historie.
5. The notable hysteroses of euery chapter.[75]

This work was not so much a Biblical commentary as a Biblical chronology. The main body of the work was a listing of the principal events in the Bible with Biblical references on one side (and the equivalent passages where there was duplication) and along with some other figures, a running total of the "age of the world" when the Biblical event occured on the other. According to Perkins, the birth of Christ took place 3967 years after the world was created.[76] 5322 years after creation the final sequence predicted by the Book of Revelation will begin: the two Prophets are slain, the first resurrection occurs, the last judgment is rendered, and the saints are received into full glory.[77]

Perkins' "Introduction" to this work is arranged in the Ramist format.[78] Perkins said: "A Digest doth afford two things: the order of deedes done, and the order of the times."[79] From these initial divisions, Perkins moved through each and defined and explained it. He saw the time periods of the "old world" being divided into those times "without the Law" and those "with the Law." These together lasted from the Creation to the death of Christ.[80]

Perkins' early interest and mathematics was perhaps what impelled him to work out this detailed Biblical chronology. But even as he set the stage for its demonstration, he revealed how be perceived the divine time table to proceed. To present that thought to his readers, Perkins reverted to his customary Ramist method of delineating and dividing. Thus his presentation can be charted in the Ramist fashion.

After 1598 there are not works of Perkins dated until 1601. Indications are, however, that some of his posthumously published pieces were written in this period. For example, his *A Commentarie or, Exposition Vpon the First Five Chapters of the Epistle to the Galatians* which had to be supplemented with a commentary on Galatians 6 by Cudworth after Perkins' death, was the result of Perkins' "three years Lectures upon the Lords day" and so this must have been started around 1599. Given Perkins' normal output of one to three published works per year, it is not unlikely that many of the posthumously published works had their origins in this late period of his life.

All of these last works of Perkins began with a Biblical text or a longer portion of Scripture. Two of them, typical of his usual method of exegesis, had Ramist charts included at the beginning of the treatise. These were Perkins' *The Combat Betweene Christ and the Devill Displayed: or, A Commentarie upon the Temptations of Christ* (1604) and *The True Gaine: More in Worth Then All the Goods in the World* (1601), an exposition of Philippians 3:7.[81] These provide the basic structure of Perkins' exegetical procedures in handling these portions of Scripture.

In the *Commentarie of the Temptations of Christ* the title page announced that an "Analysis or generall view of this Combate" was prefixed to the work. This chart showed how Perkins related the 11 verses in Matthew 4 to each other. A feature of this work was that it was clearly divided into a discussion of each "point" or "circumstance" of Perkins' divisions and then the "use" for which each doctrinal point was to be put was mentioned. The inclusion of "uses" was normal for Perkins. But all of his works did not feature them as prominently as did this one. The "general analysis" did not include the "uses" in its format. It highlighted only Perkins' handling of the main heads. Even these, however, could be amplified if the analysis had given his further divisions. For example, Perkins divided Satan's "preparation to this conflict" into "both the time and the parts thereof."[82]

Perkins' *The True Gaine* divided his text, Philippians 3:7 into two main parts. They were named "protasis" or "proposition" and the "apodosis" or assumption.[83] Perkins then expounded these points according to the chart showing the Ramist order. Again, the chart at the beginning did not fully detail Perkins' exposition. Rather it laid out the basic framework for it. For example, in his early discussion of the "meaning" that Paul counted as "dung," the priviledgees, virtues, and works done before his conversion, Perkins expanded on five things that "may bee learned" from this.[84] He did similar amplifications with other parts of his main outline. Yet Perkins always returned to his main points and moved to his next division by noting what point he had just been expounding and what head he was beginning to discuss next. Thus the movement through the chart can be clearly and accurately followed. When Perkins finished discussing the main heads in order, he posed three final questions with various divisions of them. His movement here was from the most general to the most particular: "What shall cease in this estate? What we shall haue? What we shall doe?"[85]

Perkins' Biblical expositions often used the verses of a Scripture passage themselves for the main heads. Sometimes these would be summarized in a word or phrase that made it easier to get a general view of the passage. Thus the Ramist charts could give the quick summary or overview of the whole passage and the relations of the verses to each other. Perkins' works on the Sermon on the Mount and his commentary on Galatians can be seen this way in their broadest outlines. Both of these are long and detailed. They have numerous divisions and digressions to answer proposed "objections" and "questions." In the main, however, even these can be diagrammed in the Ramist way when the broadest and most general divisions of the works are noted.⁸⁶ Perkins' audience surely could not keep an overall "picture" of how Perkins was proceeding on his "mental roadmap" in their minds. But this method did provide a means of outlining even these larger portions of Scripture. As Perkins moved to his exposition of the particular verses, these often took on the characteristics of the whole itself in that these were further divided, dichotomized, and "unfolded" in the "general/particular" scheme. The sermonic injunctions that Perkins considered so important since right doctrine was to lead to "right living" in his view, could be styled in this written pieces as "uses."

In his commentary on Galatians, Perkins highlighted three things he believed constituted the "effectuall and powerfull preaching of the word." There were

> true and proper interpretation of the scripture, and that by it selfe: for Scripture is both the glosse, and the text. The second is, sauory and wholesome doctrine, gathered out of the Scriptures truely expounded. the third is, the Application of the said doctrine, either to the information of the iudgement, or to the reformation of the life.⁸⁷

These three features, meaning, doctrine, and application, were the essential ingredients to Perkins for a proper preaching and teaching of Scripture. They were the elements that he stressed in his sermons and Biblical commentaries. There were elements well-suited to be highlighted by the Ramist method.

The same pattern is seen particularly in Perkins' *How to Live and that Well: in All Estates and Times*.⁸² His text was Habakkuk 2:4 -- "The iust man shall liue by his faith." Perkins first discussed the "understanding of the words" by asking five questions. These were answered by dichotomous divisions and the last one through two further dichotomies and even further divisions.⁸⁹ A discussion of the "meaning" of the text followed (though strangely for Perkins, he did not identify at the outset of this section that he was dealing with the "meaning." This came at the end of his point). Perkins here dichotomized the life of the just man into "spiritual life" and "temporal life." Each of these were further divided. Finally, Perkins wrote: "Thus much for the meaning of the text, now followes the use."⁹⁰ Here too the dichotomy was used and then further dichotomy and divisions. Besides the Ramist ordering of this piece methodologically, its very title: "how to live, and that well," was reminiscent of Ramus' concerns for the arts themselves. He wished that they not just be "the arts," but that they be done "well." In Perkins' piece here, the "uses" of the doctrine were highlighted in a developed section of their own. To derive the meaning of a text alone was never enough for Perkins. He always went on urge his audience to make an appropriate change of attitude or life.

B. The Arte of Prophesying

One of Perkins' most important and influential works was his *The Arte of Prophesying Or, a Treatise Concerning the Sacred and Onely Trve Manner and Methode of Preaching*. This has been called the "first substantial treatment" of the subject of preaching by an Englishman since the Reformation and "an important contribution to the development of a method of preaching which broke with traditional rhetorical categories and methods."⁹¹ It became "the basic textbook for Puritan students"⁹² and was of significant value in the the formation of what is known as Puritan "plain style preaching."⁹³

The Arte of Prophesying was where Perkins spelled out most clearly his views of homiletics and hermeneutics. He provided the groundwork here for the practices he regularly followed in exegesis and Biblical interpretation. His primary goal was to provide a concentrated discussion that would be useful for those charged with interpreting Scripture and preaching its message. An examination of this work reveals that Perkins approached this task by reflecting on the question of the content and form of sermons in light of Ramus' logic and rhetoric.[94] In light of the emphases noted thus far in terms of the teachings, methods, and controversies of both Ramus and Perkins, *The Arte of Prophesying* is the theoretical foundation in which these emphases and methods are grounded. This work more than any other by Perkins gave his rationale for the way he approached and framed his treatments of matters theological, Biblical, practical, and polemical. It gave the framework in which his thought was cast. It is Perkins' clearest work to speak explicitly in the tones of Ramus. In short, Perkins' *Arte* fused the concerns of both Ramists and Puritans.

The 1592 Latin version of this work, *Prophetica*, was translated into English by Thomas Tuke, a Christ's College man several years after Perkins' death.[95] At the start, the subhead of the work: "A Treatise Concerning the sacred and onely trve manner and methode of preaching" was reminiscent of Ramus' teachings on method.[96] Perkins was clearly dealing with an "art" here. Like Ramus who sought a reform of all arts under his own method, Perkins wished to persuade his readers of "this order of Preaching, which here I handle."[97]

Ramus defined theology as "the doctrine of living well" and grammar as "the art of speaking well." Perkins defined "prophecie" in his *A Golden Chaine* as "the doctrine of preaching well."[98] The first sentence here in the *Arte* expanded this definition. Perkins wrote: "The Art or facultie of *Prophecying* is a sacred doctrine of exercising *Prophesie* rightly. Prophecie (or Prophecying) is a publike and solemne speech of the Prophet, pertaining to the worship of God, & to the saluation of our neighbour."[99]

Perkins' treatise was written according to Ramist method in an essentially dichotomous structure. A look at the broadest outlines of the chart that can be constructed from this work bears this out.[100] After his initial definition of "prophecy," Perkins divided his subject into two parts: "Preaching of the Word and Conceiuing of Prayers."[101] Perkins then spent ten chapters on issues relating to preaching and one chapter on prayer. With the exception of the ninth chapter on "memorie," the whole of the treatise was made up of divisions (usually dichotomies) that break down Perkins' definitions into both general and particular elements. Perkins as did Ramus, moved from the former of these to the latter.

Perkins spoke of the "perfect and equall obiect of Preaching" to be the "word of God." Then in a series of dichotomies he spoke of the nature and operation of the Word of God. Its nature consisted of its perfection and eternity with perfection being further divided into sufficiency and purity.[102] This word of God is "in the holy Scripture." "The Scripture," Perkins wrote, "is the word of God written in a language fit for the Church by men immediately called to be the *Clerkes*, of *Secretaries* of the holy Ghost."[103] Then followed a "syllogisme" (or forme of reasoning) that Perkins said captured "the summe of the Scripture:

> (a) The true Messias shall bee both God and man of the seede of Dauid; he shall be borne of a Virgin; he shall bring the Gospell forth of his Fathers bosome; he shall satisfie the Law; he shall offer up himselfe a sacrifice for the sinnes of the faithfull; he shall conquer death by dying and rising againe, he shall ascend into heauen; and in his due times hee shall returne unto iudgement. But (b) Iesus of Nazareth the Sonne of Mary is such a one: Hee (c) therefore is the true Messias.[104]

Perkins contined to explain: "In this syllogisme the Maior is the scope or principall drift in all the writings of the Prophets: and the Minor in the writings of the Euagelists and Apostles." Perkins did not go on to make deductions or draw further conclusions from this "forme of reasoning." It served rather to focus on the central theme of Scripture, or as he put it, on "the summe of the Scripture." From this point Perkins went on to discuss the Scriptures as "either the New Testament, or the Old." Again the Ramistic "either/or" appeared. Theologically, by linking the writings of the prophets with those of the evangelists and apostles as the "proposition" and "assumption" of his syllogism, Perkins gave silent testimony to the unity of the Old and New Testaments.

Perkins not only listed the books of the canonical Old and New Testament. He also gave a sentence to capsulize them and, of course, to classify them. The Old Testament has three categories of books: Historical (15), Dogmatic (4), and Prophetical which are preditions either of judgement or deliverance. These are the "greater prophets" (5) or "lesser prophets" (12). The New Testament canon is "partly histories and partly Epistles." The four Gospels, Acts, and Revelation are histories; the thirteen epistles of Paul and the rest of the letters are the "epistles."[105]

When Perkins finished his explication of the object of preaching, he turned to the parts of it. There were two: preparation and promulgation. Preparation was also dichotomized into private study and the parts of preparation. When Perkins discussed private study, he spoke in terms unmistakably Ramist:

> Concerning the study of Diuinity, take this aduice. First,
> diligently imprint both in thy minde and memor the substance of
> Diuinity described, with definitions, diuision, and explications of
> the properties. Secondly, proceed to the reading of the Scrip-
> tures in this order: Vsing a grammaticall, rhetoricall, and logicall
> analysis, and the helpe of the rest of the arts....[106]

The major dichotomy here, of the parts of preaching being prepartion and promulgation, reflected the sharp division Ramus made between the studies of logic and rhetoric. To Perkins the "substance" of Divinity consisted of definitions, divisions, and explications. Already in his early works it has been noted how his overall framework reflected these Ramist concerns and how his "analyses" of a subject all proceeded in the way Ramus advocated. In contrast to the scholastic logicians, Ramus established his system of logic as independent of Aristotelian categories, induction, or syllogistic reasoning. Now Perkins had applied Ramus' philosophy to the study of theology in all its various branches. He framed his theological work along the Ramist lines, adapting Ramist methods to suit the nature of the task at hand. Unlike medieval scholastic theologians or the emerging scholasticism of European Protestant theologians, Perkins did not look to Aristotle, or Aquinas for the theological method. He looked to Ramus.[107] Here in his *Arte of Prophecying* Perkins specifically recommended the Ramist procedure as the way in which the "substance of Diuinity" shall be studied and communicated. His perspectives on the nature of logic and how its tools were to be used were molded by the thought of Ramus. Perkins urged ministers to study the Scriptures by using "a grammaticall, rhetoricall, and logicall analysis and the helpe of the rest of the arts." This was the language of the Ramists who applied the Frenchman's methods to Biblical exposition.[108] Perkins himself used the tools of which he approved. When it came to advising his Puritan students on how to approach theological study and the understanding of the Word of God, Perkins relied on what he learned from Chaderton and what he read for himself. He relied on Ramus.

Perkins gave those studying the Bible privately another piece of advice. He wrote that "those things, which in studying thou meetest with, that are necessary and worthy to be obserued: thou must put in they tables or common place bookes, that thou maiest alwaies haue ina readinesse both old and new."[109] The reference here to "common place books" linked Perkins with the Renaissance tradition running back through the humanists -- Ramus and Agricola, to the ancient Greek rhetoricians.[110] The *loci* or "places" were actually "headings or key notions to which one turns to find out what is available in one's store of knowledge for discourse on any given subject."[111] The "arguments" found in Ramus' *Dialectic* in the bracketed tables grew out of the "topical tradition" rather than the "categorical tradition" of scholastic logicians' uses of Aristotle's *Categories*. Ramus' arguments stemmed from Agricola's *Dialectical Invention*. As Ramus himself made clear, these headings, or key phrases embraced by his brackets were actually Agricola's own topics or *loci*. As such they functioned as "commonplaces" in that they became the sources for arguments on all subjects. While these places were called "arguments" themselves, it was actually "arguments" that were stored in the *loci*.[112]

With the growth of the printing industry in the Renaissance, it was possible to assemble "commonplace books" in which rhetorical sayings or quotations could be collected. A precise idea, a particular expression or useful example could be rapidly found.[113] Such collections could be vitally important for both written endeavors and spoken speeches.[114] Such men as John Milton and John Locke used their "commonplace books" as indices to their libraries.[115]

Theological commonplace books were of valuable service to theologians and preachers. In the 1582 translation of Calvin's *The Institution of Christian Religion* by Thomas Norton, brief heads such as "Adam's fall," "Angels," "Ascending of Christ into heaven" etc. served as a type of index.[116] These could be readily expanded into commonplaces or summaries. Norton also provided "A Table....of Common Places, Wherein Is Briefly Rehearsed the Summe of the Doctrine concerning Every Point Taught in the Books Before at Large, Collected by the Author."[117]

A second type of theological commonplace, also found in various editions of Calvin's *Institutes*, was one in which an author's usage of Scriptural quotations was recorded. In his "To the Christian and Studious Readers" of *The Institution*, Anthony Marlorate explained this type of commonplace. He compiled such a "Table" of the Scriptural commonplaces that Calvin cited as well as a "Table" of the theological heads.[118] Marlorate extended his tables on Scripture places and commonplaces from books of New Testament commentaries into books in themselves. These books of Marlorate's commonplaces were recommended by Perkins in his *Arte of Prophecying*.[119]

Thomas Tuke, translator of Perkins' *Arte*, spoke of this work as a commonplace book in itself. In his "Dedication" to Sir William Armin, Tuke presented the *Arte* because "it is a Thesaurus and store-house of excellent precepts."[120] In Perkins' own "Dedication" to "the faithfvll Ministers of the Gospell," he wrote that he had "perused the writings of Diuines," and "gathered some rules out of them," about "that common place of diuinitie, which concerneth the framing of Sermons." Perkins did this because he "saw this common place so handled of many, as that it would remaine naked and poore, if all other arts should call for those things, which are their owne."[121] In words highly suggestive of his Ramist bent, Perkins wrote that his commonplace book of precepts would serve as a useful aid for memory. For Perkins' rules have been "couched" in "that methode, which I haue deemed most commodious: that they might be better for use, and fitter for the memorie."[122]

After he advised his readers to commence their commonplace books, Perkins went on to advise them on how to "frame" their books:

> 1. Haue in readinesse common place heads of euery point of diuinity. 2. Distinguish the formost pages of thy paper booke, into columnes, or equall parts lengthwise. In euery one of those pages set in the top, the title of one head or thiefe point, the contrarie side remaining in the meane while empty, that fresh paper may bee put to. 3. All things, which thou readest, are not to bee written in thy booke but those things that are worthy to be remembered, and are seldome met with. Neither must thou put the words of the Author in thy common places, but briefly note downe the principall points of stories and of things, that thou maiest see from what author to fetch them when thou shalt haue use: & make a point in the author himselfe, that thou maist know that the thing is there handled, which thou wrotest in thy common place booke. 4. Because some things doe very often offer themselves with a doubtfull signification, so as that thou canst not tell, if write then in thy common places,

from whence to fetch them, therefore to thy commong places,
thou must ioyne an alphabeticall table. 5. Alwaies prouided that
thou trust not too much to thy places. For it is not sufficient to
haue a thing written in thy books, vnlesse it be alwaies diligently
laid and locked up in thy memory.[123]

If Perkins' *Arte* can be regarded as a commonplace book, there is a broader sense in which the collected *Works* of Perkins themselves could be thus conceived. The standard three-volume editions of Perkins' works published from 1608 on have at their ends "An Alphabeticall Table of the chiefe points and Questions" handled in that volume. There is a "subject index" with the particular topic given and then short phrases describing an aspect of the subject and the page on which the reference is to be found. The reader is further aided by the division of the two columns of Perkins' pages into four parts: A, B, C, and D. Thus a reference can be instantly tracked down as to page and column and section. If one wanted to know what Perkins had to say about commonplace books, one found the reference: "Commonplace bookes, 651, 1, d" in the index to the second volume of his *Works*. On "Communion" the entry read:

see Lords Supper. Communion vnder one kinde, 554, 2, c.
vnworthie Communicants of two sorts, 82, 1, c. Communion
table, how called an alter, 553, 1, b.[124]

This Table provided the key to the corpus of Perkins and surely made his *Works* in themselves much more readily valuable to those Puritan ministers who followed his advice about commonplace books. Readers could turn directly to Perkins' thoughts on virtually any theological topic immediately. As a further boon, Perkins' *Works* were equipped with "A Table of choice places of Scripture explained or vindicated in this volume." This Scriptural index provided what Perkins himself urged his readers to cultivate -- a commonplace book containing book references to where certain "places" of Scripture were explained. These Tables were advertised in the title pages to Perkins' collected *Works* along with the Table in the front of the volumes that set forth the "distinct chapters, and contents of euery book" in the volume.[125] Given the bulk of Perkins' writings, no owner of his *Works* would have to face a sermon on a Scripture text or a theological or ethical subject without being fairly sure that he could promptly turn to an appropriate discussion of the point by Perkins, thanks to the indices to his *Works*.[126]

When Perkins finished explaining how to construct commonplace books for private study, he turned to the preparation of the sermon. This had two parts: Interpretation and "right diuision or cutting."[127] Interpretation meant the "opening of the words and sentences of the Scripture." The "supreme and absolute meane of interpretation, is the Scripture itself," according to Perkins. The three subordinate means were "the analogie of faith, the circumstances of the place propounded, and the comparing of places together." Perkins explained them in turn: "The analogie of faith, is a certaine abridgement or summe of the Scriptures, collected out of most manifest & familiar places." It has two parts -- the Apostles' Creed and the Ten Commandments. The "circumstances of the place propounded" are: "who? to whom? upon what occasion? at what time? in what place? for what ende? what goeth before? what followeth?"[128]

Here it can be noted that the three means of Scriptural interpretations advocated there by Perkins all had connections with rhetorical commonplaces. The questions Perkins posed for ascertaining the "circumstances of the place propounded" were ones which stemmed from the procedures that logic and rhetoric used for invention. In his *Comprehensive Collection of Commonplaces* John Foxe wrote in the "Preface" that "what are the circumstances" is a question among the twelve commonplace questions which logic asked.[129] Thomas Wilson in *The Arte of Rhetorique* gathered seven questions about "the circumstances." These were "i. Who did the deede. ii. What was doen. iii. Where it was doen. iiii. What helpe had he to it. v. Wherefore he did it. vi. How he did it. vii. At what tyme he did it."[130] In *The Arte of*

Prophecying Perkins dealt with such questions in his discussion of "collection." But there he turned to Ramist logic for his list of nine "arguments," the one Ramus gave as the means of primary and derived artificial invention.[131] These were the *loci* to which a logician or rhetorician went to discover "what to say" about a subject. The questions asked by artificial invention were termed "analytic" commonplaces. These were distinguished from inartificial commonplaces that were those quotations used as a basis for teaching authority.[132] Ramus had restricted the analytic commonplaces to logic. But they were often used by rhetoricians as well as by logicians.[133]

The "comparing of places together" which was Perkins' third means of Scriptural interpretation, was connected with the "inartificial commonplaces." Perkins dichotomized "comparison" into "comparing of the place propounded with itselfe cited and repeated elsewhere in holy writ" and the collation of "the place propounded with their places" and those were "either like or vnlike."[134] Examples of this method of Scriptural interpretation followed: Perkins listed five reasons why there might be alterations of a text when it occurs a second time in Scripture. Then he made a distinction when discussing place where similar Scripture texts occur. He distinguished between those "geneall' places that are then illustrated by "speciall" examples "in the same kind." Perkins' examples of these were Proverbs 28:13 and Psalm 32:3,4; II Samuel 15:25 and I Peter 5:6. It was here, for the comparison of these general and special places, that Perkins recommended "the common places of Marlorate gathered together with diligence."[135] This interpretation by collocation that Perkins advocated was connected with the "inartificial commonplaces" of the Ramists in that it was basically argument from testimony. From the logical point of view, an inartificial argument was no stronger than the reliability of an artificial argument. As Alexander Richardson put it: "Inartificial arguments have no ground but as they are backt with artificials."[136] By comparing one place in Scripture with another, Perkins was not proving the logical validity of the Bible itself. Instead he was using one part of Scripture as "testimony" to clarify another part of Scripture. In the Ramean logic this was an "artificial argument."[137] In a theological sense, Perkins was applying a primary canon of Protestant hermeneutics -- that Scripture is the best interpreter of itself.[138] This was a rule he frequently repeated throughout his writings.[139] Perkins saw the human arts and "especially the Art of Logicke" to be valuable in discerning between "true and false collections."[140]

The "collections" Perkins cited as illustrations of how to compare Scripture with Scripture nearly all involved the comparison of an Old Testament verse with one from the New Testament. The question of how these two Testaments are related was connected for Perkins with the "waies of expounding" Scripture. He repeatedly stressed that "there is one onely sense, and the same is the literall" sense of Scripture.[141] Thus Perkins rejected the four-fold senses of Scripture taught by the Church of Rome (literal, allegorical, tropological, and anagogical) as a valid method of expounding and explaining Scripture texts, particularly "difficult" passages.[142]

Perkins divided Scripture "places" into "Analogicall and plaine, or Crypticall and darke."[143] His basic rule was that when the natural sense of the words coincided with the circumstances of the same place and there was no conflict with the analogy of faith or other parts of Scripture, then the literal sense was to be adopted. Yet if this natural meaning of the words disagreed with the context, the analogy of faith or other places in Scripture where the meaning was perfectly clear were to be consulted. The sense of a passage should be seen as agreeing with the rest of Scripture, "if it agree with contrary and like places, with the circumstances and words of the place, and with the nature of that thing which is intreated of." In other words, the sense of the whole Bible had to be considered when interpreting Scripture. The example Perkins used to illustrate this was the saying of Jesus in I Corinthians 1:24: "This is my body which is broken for you." Perkins rejected a strictly literal interpretation here. He said that this violated an article of faith, the phrase in the Apostles' Creed "he ascended into heaven" and also went against "the nature of a Sacrament, which ought to be a Memoriall of the body of Christ absent." So Perkins interpreted this verse in another sense. He said: "In this place the bread is a signe of my body: by a Metonymy of the subiect for the adiunct." Perkins then went on to justify this interpretation.¹⁴⁴ Further, Perkins wrote of other helps for interpreting Scripture: adding additional words to clarify; distinguishing (in great detail) the various kinds of rhetorical figures of speech used in the Bible, how to reconcile contrary places, and how to determine meanings that are vague.¹⁴⁵

Perkins did not believe his methods would lead to anarchy in interpretation or "private interpretations." On the contrary, he claimed that they will be "sure, certaine, and publike: for it is the interpretation of God."¹⁴⁶ In this sense he drew no distinction between the text of Scripture and its interpretation by him. Perkins believed it was entirely possible to find "the genuine and proper meaning of the Scripture."¹⁴⁷ If this were not so, he argued, "wee shall draw any doctrine from any place."¹⁴⁸ At this point hermeneutics, like preaching (prophecying) itself, was more art than science.

Having discussed the first member of his dichotomy of the parts of preparation, Perkins turned to the second member: "the right cutting," or the "right deuiding of it."¹⁵⁰ This was further divided into two parts: "Resolution or partition, and Application." Resolution, as noted for Ramus, meant analysis. In Western logic and rhetoric the analytic commonplaces were used to carry this analysis out.¹⁵¹ Perkins explained resolution as consisting of dichotomous ingredients: "Notation" and "Collection."

Perkins defined "resolution" using Ramist images, as "the place propounded is, as a weauers web, resolued (or vntwisted and vnloosed) into sundry doctrines." Perkins saw this as the process in which Apollos of Alexandria was involved when the Scripture said of him: "Mightly he confuted with Iewes, with great vehemency publikely shewing by Scriptures, that Iesus was that Christ" (Acts 18:28). This type of resolution played a central role in Perkins' theological methodology. In the "notation" part of resolution, one simply noted the Scripture place where "the doctrine is expressed."¹⁵² In "collection," one deduced doctrines from texts where "the doctrine is not expressed."¹⁵³ Help in this task came from "the nine arguments" that Perkins took from the analytic commonplaces in Ramus' *Dialecticae libri duo* (1572).¹⁵⁴ These were: "causes, effects, subiects, adiuncts, dissentanies [differences], comparatiues, names, distribution, and definition."¹⁵⁵ While Perkins did not follow Ramus here in detail, he did use the order Ramus advocated. To illustrate how one gathered doctrines from "collected" places in Scripture, Perkins applied the commonplaces of "the lesser"; "the contrary"; "the Adiunct"; and "the Species" to seven pairs of Scriptural places.¹⁵⁶ This was where he warned that "collections ought to bee right and sound."

It has been noted already and frequently in the examination of Perkins' Biblical commentaries that the drawing of "doctrines" from texts was a standard procedure for Perkins. In light of Perkins' belief that there was only one real sense to Scripture, the literal, and his care not to take some texts too literally, Perkins had to be sure that the doctrines gathered from Scripture were "sound ones" in his opinion. Therefore he needed the help of Ramus' analytic commonplaces or "arguments" to be able to classify Scripture texts in the "proper" doctrinal slots. Perkins' commentaries with their origins in his sermons exemplified the method he urged his students to follow for their own "prophecying." Doctrines were to be collected from the Scripture text at hand. By "resolution" or "analysis" one broke the text down into its constitutive elements; by the opposite process ("genesis" in the Ramist system) one recombined the elements into a doctrinal proposition.

In this way a sermon or exposition of Scripture constructed after the manner of Ramus and Perkins, revealed the true logical, inner structure of the Bible in their eyes. The whole range of the arts, including the arts of logic and rhetoric were proper to use for analyzing texts according to Perkins.¹⁵⁷ When Scriptural places were "analogicall," that is, places "such as haue an apparent meaning agreeable to the analogy of faith, and that at the first view," the ordinary rules of invention applied. Here the meaning could be directly perceived since the text functioned as a self-evident axiom. With "crypticall" or "hidden places," one must invoke further procedures to come to Scripture's true meaning. For Perkins this meant testing the "natural sense" of the Scripture text with the analogy of faith, other perspicuous places of Scripture, the circumstances and the words of the place etc.[158] If it did not agree with these, then "the other meaning, which is giuen of the place propounded" (if it fulfills these requirements) is the one to be adopted. Basically, Perkins was suggesting that the further procedure needed to establish the true meaning of a "hidden place" was to subject such places to the rules of the syllogism.

Scripture places that were of doubtful meaning were to be tested syllogistically to see if they conformed to the rule Perkins established that Scripture must agree with itself and with "the analogie of faith, the circumstances of the place propounded, and the comparing of places together."[159] The example Perkins gave of interpreting "this is my body" was tested in precisely this syllogistic way. One of Perkins' tests for interpretation was: Does this test agree with the laws of logic? Syllogisms were useful for Ramus and now for Perkins not particularly to enable the logician (or exegete) to devise arguments but rather to discover or unveil arguments already in the text but hitherto concealed. Thus Perkins spoke of some places in Scripture as being "crypticall or hidden places...which are difficult and darke."[160] Once these "dark places" were properly analyzed or resolved and laid out "methodically" and considered in relation to the commonplaces of dialectic, Perkins claimed they would inevitably compose themselves into doctrinal axioms. This was the meaning of the imagery (used also by Ramus) in Perkins' definition of "resolution" (Gr. *dialusis*) as "a weauers web, resolued (or vntwisted and vnloosed) into sundry doctrines."[161]

The major difference between Perkins and Ramus in terms of their use of the "nine arguments" was Perkins' theological proviso that "Scripture alone" was to be the supreme authority. Perkins' approval of the use of logic did not mean he gave logic an elevated status over Scripture itself. Reason was useful but it must be reason which was subjected to and submissive to God. Human reason itself, Perkins said, "is no principle of religion. For it is imperfect and erronious and serues onely to make men without excuse."[162] Whereas Ramus could subject his treatment of the arts to his commonplaces and proceed logically, Perkins used the arts to illuminate Scripture. But as he did so, he subordinated the deductions and testimonies of non-Scriptural sources to his principle that Scripture alone had final authority.[163]

Perkins permitted "allegories" to be used. He cited the Apostle Paul on this and said they could have use since "they are arguments taken from things that are like."[164] But Perkins issued several caveats since he wished to stress that the true sense of Scripture was the literal sense: Perkins said: "Let them be used sparingly and soberly. 2. Let them not bee farre fetcht, but fitting to the matter in hand. 3. They must be quickly dispatcht. 4. They are to be vsed for instruction of the life, and not to prooue any point of faith." Doctrines must be drawn from the Scriptures themselves as Perkins outlined. He said, "any point of doctrine collected by iust consequence is simply of itselfe to bee beleeued, and doth demonstrate." There was no need for "humane testimonies, whether of the Philosophers, or of the Fathers." The only exception to this, Perkins wrote, was "unlesse they conuince the conscience of the hearer." But then they must be used "sparingly, and with leauing out the name of the prophane writer." In sermons there was need for only a "few testimonies of Scripture" and "sometimes there is neede of none."[165]

Perkins' next chapter dealt with the use and application of doctrines. But significantly here, Perkins did not urge his students to parade the "reasons" for their doctrines to their hearers. He did not instruct them to exhibit a string of quotations from illustrious authors or to reason with their congregation through a long string of syllogisms. Instead Perkins taught what be believed to be the proper method for resolving or analyzing Scripture so that the preacher might draw doctrines from it and apply them in practical ways. Perkins did not ask preachers to share with their people all the authorities or even all the logical processes that supported the doctrine preached. Instead he believed that when the doctrines were collected correctly, each was "simply or itselfe to bee beleeued, and doth demonstrate."[166]

The second part of "rightly dividing" a text in preparation for preaching was "application." Perkins defined application as "that, whereby the doctrine rightly collected, is diuersly fitted according as place, time, and person doe require."¹⁶⁷ The "foundation of application is, to know whether the place propounded be a sentence of the Law, or of the Gospell." The Law declares the "disease of sinne"; the Gospel "teacheth what is to be done." Perkins then went on to describe how one could decide on application. He based his decision on seven conditions of people.¹⁶⁸

The kinds of application were two: "mentall" or "practicall." Mental was related to the mind and was either "doctrine" or "redargution" (improving, confuting).¹⁶⁹ Doctrine informed one's mind on what is correct to believe. Redargution was that "whereby teaching is vsed for the reformation of the mind from error." Practical application was that which "respecteth the life and behauiour." It too was dichotomized by Perkins into "instruction" (Gr. *paideia*) and "correction" (Gr. *epanorthōsis*). Instruction was that "whereby doctrine is applied to frame a man to liue well in the family, common-wealth, and Church." Correction was that "whereby the doctrine is applied to reforme the life from vngodlinesse and vnrighteous dealing."¹⁷⁰ This last was done both generally and specifically. Perkins went on to show (by using Matthew 10:28ff.) how four kinds of application "doe offer themselues in euery sentence of the Scripture." These four kinds were doctrine, redargution, instruction, and correction. Perkins' final advice on application was:

> Thus any place of Scripture ought to bee handled: yet so as that
> all the doctrines bee not propounded to the people, but those
> onely, which may bee fitly applied to our times and to the pre-
> sent condition of the Church. And they must not onely be
> choice ones, but also few, lest the hearers bee ouercharged with
> their multitude.¹⁷¹

By holding to both the "resolution" for the forming of doctrine and to the "application" for the use of this doctrine, Perkins supported the bipolar thrust of the Ramist philosophy. The "theory/practice," "word/deed," "theology/ethics" pattern was held together and always in that sequence. For Perkins the goal of hermeneutics with all its rules and divisions was to come to a Scripture text's meaning so that "the word is made fitte to edifie the people of God."¹⁷² This goal was consistent with Perkns' description of the body of Scripture as a "doctrine sufficient to liue well" and theology as "the science of liuing blessedly for euer."¹⁷³ Perkins' concern for edification as the goal of theology came to fruition in his *Cases of Conscience*, his manual of pastoral care in which Scripture was applied to concrete, everyday manners.¹⁷⁴ The theoretical foundations for this approach were laid in Perkins' *Arte* where he urged the Scriptures to be "rightly diuided," then "applied" in "practical" ways for "correction" by using "admonition" for "specific" circumstances. This was the agenda for preaching as well as for Christian ethics. Thus the characteristics both of Perkins' works in theology and in Biblical exegesis reappear in his prescriptions for hermeneutics and homiletics: doctrines drawn from Scripture must be applied to ethical behavior.

To this point it has been possible to follow Perkins' *Arte* along the lines of the Ramist method by which it was constructed. In chapter IX, however, Perkins devoted a short space to "Of Memorie in Preaching" before he took up his Ramist pattern again in chapter X. Perkins' section on memory capsulized Ramist thought on this topic and highlights especially the issues raised by Perkins in his 1584 controversy with Dickson over the memory system of Bruno. Now, in instructing ministers on how to construct and deliver sermons, Perkins offered reasons why artificial memory systems were to be rejected and why his own method should be adopted.

Perkins rejected all artificial memory schemes because they aroused carnal affections and required an involved intellectual process. He urged instead that the preacher

> doe diligently imprint in his minde by the helpe of dispositions
> either axiomaticall, or syllogisticall, or methodicall, the seuerall

> proofes and applications of the doctrines, the illustrations of the
> applications, and the order of them all: in the meane time
> nothing carefull for the words, Which (as Horace speaketh) will
> not unvillingly follow the matter that is premeditated.[175]

As discussed above, Perkins' theory (following Ramus) was that if the discourse had been constructed according to proper method, the points to be made by the preacher would follow naturally in this mind once he visualized the Ramist chart with its divisions and branches. In light of Perkins' discussions of how to interpret and "rightly divide" the texts and then how to apply them, his references to disposition by axioms, syllogisms, and method (the same three divisions in the second half of Ramus' *Dialectic*) makes sense. To Perkins these were the keys to unlock the proper meaning of Scripture and the tools for constructing a sermon that was both dictrinally sound and practically relevant. Ramus had insisted in his last commentary on method that method was the "only way of understanding and memory."[176] Now in *The Arte of Prophecying*, Perkins suggested the same things. According to Perkins, Scripture interpreted as he outlined (following Ramus) would lead both to true understanding and could be almost automatically memorized. In short, Perkins could wholeheartedly agree with Ramus who said: "Order is the father of memory."[177]

Perkins returned to his Ramist pattern when he moved to the second part of preaching, promulgation of the sermon. He required two things here: "the hiding of humane wisedome, and the demonstration (or shewing) of the spirit."[178] Perkins urged the preacher to conceal his wisdom because "the preaching of the word is the testimony of God, and the profession of the knowledge of Christ, and not of humane skill: and againe, because the hearers ought not to ascribe their faith to the gifts of men, but to the power of Gods work." This did not mean, however, that ministers should preach unprepared. For according to Perkins

> if any man thinke that by this means barbarisme should be
> brought into pulpets; he must vnderstand that the Minister may,
> yea must priuately vse at his libertie the arts, Philosophy, and
> variety of reading, whilest he is in framing his sermon: but he
> ought in publike to conceale all these from the people, and not
> to make the least ostentation. *Artis etiam est celare artem*; it is
> also a point of Art to conceale Art.[179]

Related to this too was the "demonstration of the Spirit" in which the quality of the minister's life exemplified the Spirit of God dwelling within. Perkins dichotomized this demonstration into "speech" and "gesture" with speech being "spiritual" and "gracious." Spiritual speech, he said, is both "simple and perspicuous, fit both for the peoples vnderstanding, and to expresse the Maiestie of the Spirit." This being so, Perkins said that "neither the worde of arts, nor Greeke and Latine phrases and quirkes must be intermingled in the sermon."[180] From the viewpoint of the Ramist logic, this perhaps reflected a desire to avoid the inartificial arguments or arguments from testimony as a source of "proof" in a sermon. From a pastoral standpoint, Perkins' advising against a "show of learning" from the pulpit indicated his desire to see the Word of God preached without undue attention being diverted toward the messenger of that Word.[181] Perkins ended his *Arte of Prophecying* by devoting one chapter to the second part of Prophecying which was prayer.

As an Epilogue, Perkins closed with four points displaying "The Order and Svmme of the sacred and onely methode of Preaching":

> 1. To reade the Text distinctly out of the Canonicall Scriptures.
> 2. To giue the sense and understanding of it being read, by the Scripture it selfe.
> 3. To collect a fewe and profitable points of doctrine out of the naturall sense.

4. To apply (if hee haue the gift) the doctrines rightly collected,
to the life and manners of men in a simple and plaine
speech.[182]

The last thing Perkins wrote in this *Arte* was a list of "the writers which lent their helpe to the framing of this Arte of Prophecying." There were: Augustine, Hemingius, Hyperius, Erasmus, Illyricus, Wigandus, Iacobus Matthias, Theodore Beza, Franciscus Iunius." Surprsingly, the name of Peter Ramus is not mentioned. It has been suggested that this list means that "Perkins derives his doctrine from sources closer to Ciceronian rhetoric and scholastic logic than to the logic and rhetoric of Ramus."[183] It is true that Perkins did not follow Ramus in that under Ramus' law of justice, Ramus "did not permit preaching to be a separate art but assigned its precepts to logic or to rhetoric -- a position which Perkins refuses to defend."[184] Yet while it may be that Perkins did not expressly learn anything about the doctrine of preaching from Ramus, it is undeniable that he framed his discourses -- including *The Arte of Prophecying* -- in the Ramist pattern and under the influence of his teachings. The specifically theological influences on Perkins' understanding of the nature and function of Christian preaching undoubtedly came from the names Perkins mentioned. At this point Ramus was not included. But with other Protestants Perkins saw the work of preaching to be the minister's main duty. He believed that preaching the doctrine of the Prophets and Apostles joined with faith and obedience was "an infallible marke of a true Church."[185] But when it came to giving advice on the preparation and promulgation of sermons, Perkins by prescription and example showed the effects of Ramist teaching.

It needs to be noted also that there were other sources available which advocated emphases similar to those of Perkins' *Art of Prophecying*. There were available translations of N. Hemmingsen's *The Preacher* and A. Hyperius' *The Practis of Preaching*.[186] Hyperius had urged that rhetoric be learned by the preacher. But he saw that the preacher differed from the orator chiefly in the process of invention which Hyperius claimed must be linked to Biblical exegesis.[187] In this sense Hyperius subordinated traditional rhetoric to Biblical standards.[188] He produced a theology of homiletics that helped his students with practical advice and criticisms of their sermons before they were given.[189] Hyperius stressed an order to sermons where after the text was read, the preacher should use: invocation, *exordium*, proposition, confirmation, confutation and conclusion.[190] Perkins' four points in summary of his method, streamlined these even more. Perkins' emphases on "doctrine" and "use" were to be found among earlier preachers in the Puritan movement. Richard Greenham for one used these divisions.[191] Ursinus, the German theologian, had urged his readers to find the passage's proper sense, declare the order and coherence of doctrine, and then apply it.[192] Hyperius stressed the need for practical application and Martyr placed emphasis on plainness and simplicity.[193] So when Perkins listed the sources from which he drew, he could perhaps have included many more.[194]

So while these sources were surely present and it seems reasonble to assume that they did influence Perkins' thoughts on preaching, the influence of Ramus as outlined above was certainly strong. The detailed similarities between Perkins and Ramus on memory, method, the commonplaces and "arguments" are too striking to ignore. These things added to all the rest of the Ramist emphases make the Frenchman's influence sure. Certainly Perkins combined thoughts from many sources. But the amalgam he made of them was couched within the overall framework and teaching of the Ramist philosophy itself. *The Arte of Prophecying* and the other works examined this far show not only the internal characteristics of Ramist works, but also are definitely arranged structurally according to Ramist method. All of these factors combined make the Ramist influence marked and decisive. Perkins' training at Cambridge under Chaderton, his controversies over memory, the printed charts at the beginning of his works, and the overall casting of his pieces on all subjects into the Ramist pattern are the most telling evidence that Perkins viewed Ramust as the most suitable guide for theological method. In short, perhaps Perkins did not mention Ramus in his list of sources because Ramus' method "was so identified with the true method of logic that it was not thought of as a peculiar theory of Ramus. Ramus' logic simply was good logic.[195]

Chapter VI. RAMISM IN PERKINS' LATER WORKS

A. Theological Works

Perkins' *An Exposition of the Symbole or Creed of the Apostles* (1595) was as close as Perkins came to producing a complete systematic theology.[1] In this work Perkins dealt with the doctrine of the Church. In his *A Golden Chaine* he did not touch on it. It was during his discussion of the Church that Perkins dealt again with predestination.

Perkins explained why he did not base this work on a set text of Scripture. He argued that this was not always the practice of the early church as it often catechized "without handling any set text of Scripture." Perkins claimed that ministers of his time might do the same if "they doe confirme the doctrine which they teach with places of scripture afterward."[2] Perkins knew that the Apostles themselves did not pen the Creed. But he saw it as containing "the chiefe and principall points of religion, handled and propounded in the doctrine of the Apostles." The points of the Creed were thus "conformable and agreeable to their doctrine and writings."[3] This "summarie collection" of Apostolic doctrine was "gathered briefly out of the word of GOD for helping of the memory and vnderstanding of men."[4]

Before he began his actual exposition of the Creed, Perkins went through several "either/or" distinctions. The first was the "two kinds of writings in which the doctrine of the Church is handled": Divine or Ecclesiastical. The former of these is the Bible, the Word of God. The ecclesiastical writings, written by the Church were either "generall, particular, or proper."[5] Perkins also gave a discussion of faith which he defined as "a gift of God, whereby wee giue assent or credence to Gods word." It too was of "two sorts: either common faith, or the faith of the elect." The common faith was threefold: historical faith, temporary faith, and the faith of miracles. But these were all to be distinguished from the faith of the elect which has its principal object -- Jesus Christ.[6] After several more such distinctions, Perkins launched into his exposition of the particular parts of the Apostles' Creed.

Prefixed to this work was a Ramist chart. It was headed: "The resolution of the Creede."[7] Perkins claimed that the Creed "consists not of two heads, but of one, namely of faith onely, and not of loue also."[8] In making his divisions, Perkins said the Creed set down "two things concerning faith, namely, the action of faith, and its obiect, which also are the parts of the Creede."[9] Perkins dichotomized the "actions of faith" into believing "in a thing" and believing "a thing." These he further discussed as three and two parts respectively.

The "object of general faith" in the Creed, said Perkins, was "either God or the Church" as the chart indicated. For the rest of the treatise, Perkins followed this chart only in much more detail. He began by saying how he would handle each article of the Creed: "I. I will speake of the meaning of euery article. II. Of the duties which we ought to learne thereby. III. And lastly, of the consoltations which may be gathered thence."[10] With this framework in place, Perkins proceeded throught the Creed. He went from article to article within the overarching scheme of his chart or "resolution." Within this context, Perkins dealt with the heads: meaning, duties, and consoltations. Thus he moved in each article from its "doctrine," to its "ethical application," and finally to its most personal application the "uses" of each article for the Christian. Perkins therefore bound doctrine, ethics, and piety firmly together. Here was the Ramist philosophy wedded to Puritan "spirituality."[11]

Perkins' union of "faith" and "works" in the Creed was reminiscent of Ramus' own treatment. This was in his posthumously published *Commentariorum De Religione Christiana Libri IV* (*Commentary on the Christian Religion in Four Books*).[12] Ramus divided theology which he defined as "the art of living well" into two major divisions: doctrine and discipline. Doctrine was dichotomized into "faith" and the "actions of faith." In the "actions of faith," Ramus planned to deal with law, prayer, and the sacraments.[13] There were then to be followed by the second part of theology, church discipline which was to analyze doctrinal practice and church polity. But this part on discipline has not survived.[14]

The "faith/observance" scheme was thus thoroughly in the mind of Ramus as he set his treatment of the Apostle's Creed in the large framework of his understanding of the art of theology itself. With his precise method, Ramus thus highlighted what was part of Christian theology from its beginnings. This is the belief that faith must express itself in actions (works). Ramus distinguished theology from human philosophy in that "theology is comprised in faith in God and the actions of faith, but human philosophy embraces happiness by the contemplation of wisdom and the action of courage, temperance, and justice."[15] The right teaching of Christian theology was to lead to a life of practical obedience to God, Ramus said: "For the end of doctrine is not knowledge of things relating to itself, but practice and exercise" (*usus et exercitatio*).[16] To Ramus, "this is the effect of faith: just as fire cannot possibly exist without heat, nor sun without light, so too true faith cannot exist without honest and acceptable action to God."[17]

Ramus linked "teaching" in theology with its practical expression just as he had in his logic generally. He said, "the end of doctrine is not knowledge," so theology was prevented from becoming a purely speculative art. It was more a practical enterprise. Theology had to be usable in life and for life.

Perkins echoed these concerns. Now in the treatment of the Creed he was saying again that doctrine led to duty. He went even beyond this to ply the articles with this question: what "comforts" (consolations) or "benefits" are to be derived from doctrine?[18] Perkins' concern to see the Church of England "purified" and its members brought to a more zealous commitment to God in both thought and action was certainly the major impetus for keeping the concerns of ethics and piety alive in the midst of his theological writings.

For this, Perkins' Ramist methods and structures were ideally suited. The Ramist philosophy with its inherent stress on the unity of thought and action followed Perkins to further the aims of ethics and piety in the Church while he engaged in theological exposition. His treatment of the Apostles' Creed displayed these interconnections of doctrine, ethics, and piety. Perkins structured the work according to Ramist method and throughout was able to highlight the teaching of the Creed itself, what duties it implied, and what benefits were to be gained from its proper understanding.

Perkins dealt theologically with the doctrine of predestination in his exposition of the Creed. But in 1598 he produced *De praedestinationis modo et ordine* (*A Christian and Plaine Treatise of the Manner and Order of Predestination, and of the Largeness of Gods Grace* -- 1606 English translation) to deal with this subject more fully.[19] This piece was occasioned in large part to disputes in Cambridge University over predestination in the 1590's.

The main figures in the theological discussions were Peter Baro (1534-1599) and his pupil William Barrett.[20] Baro, Lady Margaret Professor of Divinity, had come to England in 1574 and had been ordained in Geneva by John Calvin. In Baro's lectures on Jonah in 1579, however, Puritan leaders William Whitaker, William Fulke, and Perkins' tutor Chaderton detected some divergences from the doctrines of Calvin. In particular these men believed Baro was leaning toward universalism in salvation and toward Roman Catholicism.[21]

Heated public controversy broke out in 1595. Baro's student William Barrett preached a sermon in St. Mary's church in April of that year in which he launched an attack on the strict Calvinist doctrine of predestination. A swift complaint to Archbishop Whitgift by the older Calvinists charged that this young man (not yet thirty-five)

> laboured to prove that justifying faith may finally decay and be lost, and consequently did maintain and teach the popish doctrine of doubtfulness of our salvation, against the comfortable certainty of true faith taught and preached in this our Church ever since the first planting of the Gospel amongst us; with most bitter railing upon those worthy men Calvin, Peter Martyr, Beza, Zanchius, and others, to the great offence of the godly.[22]

Within two weeks of the offending sermon, Barrett was forced to read a recantation that he later renounced when Whifgift urged toleration of Barrett's opinions since these were highly disputed matters.[23]

Further debate followed through the summer of 1595. In November, the Lambeth Articles were drawn up as a corrective to Barrett's "deficient" theology. These articles taught predestination and reprobation as stringently as possible. Though they were approved by Whitgift, the Queen was unwilling that such highly controversial doctrines be aired at all. So Elizabeth would not formally authorize them.[24]

Peter Baro next entered the fray. He preached a sermon on January 12, 1596 in which he bitterly attacked Perkins, Whitake, and the Calvinist position. He claimed that God created all humans in his image, to eternal life; Christ died "sufficiently" for all: and God's promises must be seen as being extended universally to all.[25] Baro thus put himself in the camp of those labeled "new Pelagians" by Perkins in his *Golden Chaine*.[26] Baro, in turn, had dismissed Perkins' charges in a manuscript entitled *Summa trium de praedestinatione sententiarum* (not published until 1613) as "illiberal calumny." Finally, Baro was forced to leave Cambridge since he could not muster the necessary political support to be re-elected to his professorship. He died in London in 1599.[27]

Perkins' part in the political ploys connected with these controversies is obscure. His 1598, *De praedestinationis* was written to sharpen his own theological position. It was this piece which Jacobus Arminius (1560-1609), a Dutchman, seized upon and produced a lengthy refutation to entitled *Examination of Perkins' Pamphlet on the Order and Mode of Predestination*. It was this work by Arminius that was to become "the basic document of Arminianism."[28] Perkins died before Arminius finished his work and Arminius' manuscript lay dormant until after Arminius' death. It was published in Leiden in 1612 and then along with Perkins' pamphlet was published again in 1617, just before the struggles at the Synod of Dort.[29]

In *The Manner and Order of Predestination* Perkins sought to anchor his doctrine securely in "the written Word of God." He also wished to show clearly the points at which his doctrine of predestination agreed with what he called "the grounds of common reason" and "the light of nature."[30] In his "Epistle to the Reader," Perkins delineated ten such axioms that he said any right-thinking natural man should be able to recognize.[31] This procedure by Perkins showed how he responded when his views were challenged. In this instance he wished to refute those who disagreed with his view of predestination (which he called "the Caluinists doctrine") on the basis of common sense or philosophy. According to Perkins, once an opponent could be intellectually convinced that the doctrine was reasonable, he would have no choice but to accept it as true. Perkins said his purpose was to "mitigate and appease the mindes of some of our Brethren, which haue bin more offended at it then was fit." He continued: "For I doe willingly acknowledge and teach uniuersall redemption and grace, so farre as it is possibly by the word. My minde is to pursue after peace, which is departing from us: and I would haue all men so interpret my fact."[32] By seeking as much ground in common with his opponents as he could, Perkins sought to mediate the dispute. But he still put forth his own views of predestination so clearly and forcefully as he could. He invoked not only the testimony of the Scripture, but also of "the Fathers themselues."

The title of this work, *Of the Manner and Order of Predestination* leads to the expectation that Perkins will be treating this doctrine in his usual Ramist fashion. This is so since the title highlights both the nature and "method" of the topic. A further hint that Perkins would proceed this way was when he wrote in his "Epistle to the Reader" that he will 'exhibite unto thee a view and picture of this doctrine." The visual imagery employed here accords perfectly with the visual imagery of Ramism and its skeletal charts. Perkins' recurring references to the "branches" of his topics further heightens the sense of the visual.[33] For Perkins as for Ramus, there was a sense in which if one could anatomize the subject, defining its "manner" and methodizing its "order," one could lay bare the inherent truth of the topic. The visual model or construct held the content of the truth. To make that truth "plain" and "evident" (terms Perkins frequently used),[34] one needed only to analyze the subject properly and order it according to the dictates of Ramism.[35]

Perkins began his work by defining predestination in his first sentence: "Predestination is the counsell of God touching the last end or estate of man out of this temporall or naturall life."[36] After his customary beginning, Perkins exhibitied his "view and picture" of the doctrine in a series of dichotomies touching the "end" of predestination (God's glory), the "means" of its accomplishment (creation and permission of the fall); and the "parts" of it (election and reprobation).[37] These parts were further dichotomized and other divisions made.

After his exposition of predestination in this way, Perkins moved on to deal with four direct objections to his doctrine.[38] To answer these "criminations." Perkins quoted extensively from the Church fathers. This section took the form of a running dialogue between Perkins and his opponents. Despite this basic format, however, Perkins' answers often "unfolded" into dichotomies and beyond that into mini-Ramist orderings which could be charted as such. These are prominent in Perkins' discussions of the will of God; sin; God's providence; necessity; events and grace.[39]

Perkins concluded by discussing in detail some 11 errors that the positions of his opponents entailed. These included his rejections of universal salvation, election based on foreseen faith, the believer's loss of saving faith, free will, etc. While Perkins did make some of his dichotomous distinctions in this section, he relied much more heavily on citations from Church fathers to prove his points.[40] Also, he occasionally turned to the syllogistic form. Once he used this to prove his point: twice he answereed the syllogism hurled at him by making an "either/or" distinction.[41]

A final "Corolarie, or addition" was added by Perkins. This consisted of what he termed "a most certaine theoreme, or undoubted truth." It was: "God hath not revealed Christ vnto all and euery man."[42] Perkins offered "proofes" for this theorem. They consisted of some Scripture passage first, and then references to the deaths of Socrates and Aristotle along with "Gentiles" who died without knowing Christ. From these he concluded with four "consectaries" or inferences. The "proofes," Perkins claimed were "euident by Scriptures and experience." In this treatise on predestination, therefore, Perkins presented his views according to the Ramist pattern. He dealt with errors and objections to his position on the basis of his reading of Scripture and Patristic authorities.

A final theological work from Perkins' later life to deal with predestination once more was his *A Treatise of Gods free Grace, and mans Freewill*.[43] This piece showed Perkins' penchant for the dichotomous division as it too was arranged in a Ramistic manner.[44] Perkins worked on the relationship between God's grace in the process of regeneration and the human will. He dealt most thoroughly with the "manner and form" of the divine and human wills while also lining out just what "strength" the human will had in the four estates Perkins perceived: innocency, corruption, regeneration, and glorification. Perkins' method as he expounded these divisions and the ones that unfolded from them was not to argue for their validity by deducing his conclusions from a long string of syllogisms. It was instead to arrange after the manner of Ramus. He used Ramist method to bolster his points and his "self-evident axioms" with appropriate citations from Scripture and the Chruch fathers.

B. Cases of Conscience

Perkins' concern for the application of his theology to the problems of human behavior expressed itself most vividly in his works on casuistry. *Cases of Conscience* were questions Perkins posed and answered in light of his theological presuppositions.

In 1592 Perkins published a work intended for "helping of the simple and vnlearned."[45] This was *A Case of Conscience, the Greatest that ever was: How a Man may know whether He be the Childe of God, or no*. This piece was cast in the form of a dialogue based on the first epistle of John. The conversation went back and forth between "the church" and "John." The answers of "John" were drawn directly from each verse of the First Epistle of John. Accompanying this short piece was "A Briefe Discourse Taken ovt of the Writings of H. Zanchius: Wherein the aforesaid case of Conscience is disputed and resolued."[46]

In this brief section from Zanchi, the contrast between Perkins' theological method and Zanchi's stands out. Zanchi was a Protestant scholastic theologian whose theological methodology was highly influenced by Aristotelianism.[47] The structure of the piece used by Perkins, its terminology, and the way it proceeded highlighted the differences between Perkins' Ramist approach and that of the post-Reformation Protestant scholastics.

The extract from Zanchi consisted of two "Assertions" that functioned as propositions which Zanchi sought to prove.[48] To do this for the first assertion, he made three major points called "testimonies." In these he established his points by means of the syllogistic form -- statement, statement, conclusion. It is on these that the weight of his arguments rested. For example, Zanchi concluded his first point this way:

> This testimony I will briefly comprise within this demonstration. Whosoeuer call vpon God, and in their hearts crie *Abba*, Father, they are the sonnes of God, and it is certain that thy thus crie by the spirit of God. And they which are the sonnes of God, are also heires of eternall life, and they haue bin predestinate to adoption: therefore it must needs be, that all they which are perswaded, that they are the sonnes of God by the holy Ghost, are predestinate to enterall life, and must be perswaded of it.[49]

Zanchi reasoned in the classical Aristotelian syllogistic form to prove his point. The use of this form was not, as seen in Perkins, to elucidate how the Bible itself was arguing. Zanchi used the syllogism to clinch his own argument.

The language of the scholastic logic was much more pronounced in Zanchi's second "testimony." He spoke of the "generall proposition" ("that all the faithful are elect to eternall life") and that "the assumption is concealed in the word of God." Zanchi reasoned:

> But when he giueth vs faith, he maketh euery one of vs to make an assumption by himselfe in his minde: *But I am of the faithful*: for I finde in my selfe that I truly beleeue in Christ. Therefore who is it that maketh this conclusion for thee, that *thou art predestinate to eternall life*? euen God himself: the proposition being taken forth of the Gospel, and the assumption proceedeth of the gift of faith. But that indeede by which we properly attaine to the knowledge of the matter contained in the conclusion, is the *middle tearme*, as they call it. Wherefore it is manifest, that God by the word of his Gospel, where he saith: *that all the faithfull are elect*: doth reueale to euery faithfull man his owne predestination. Onely this one things is to be required, that the faithfull man hearing the vniuersall propositions, in his minde should make an assumption. *But I am faithfull by the gift and grace of God*. And is not God said to haue reuealed to euery man his speciall malediction in this generall proposition, Deut. 27.26. *Cursed is euery one that doth not continue in all things that are written in this booke*, although he say to no many specially, thou art accursed? for euery one doth make this assumption, *that he is accursed*, because he knoweth most certainly that he doth not continue in all things that are written in the booke of the law.[50]

The structure of Zanchi's method was very plain. On the matter of the assurance of salvation, he called on his readers to reason their way to a satisfactory conclusion. They were to consider the "universal proposition," realize the "assumption" in the "middle term," see how their lives squared with what was required, and then come to the assurance of their predestination.[51]

The scholastic language reappeared in Zanchi's proof of his second assertion. There he spoke of the "effects of predestination." The first was the "causes efficient, or (if we wil so speake) the materiall causes of the latter."[52] Then Zanchi launched into a chain of theological terms that described the effects of predestination. Each one of these "necessarily" derived from the terms that went before according to Zanchi and the "laws of logic."

While this extract from Zanchi does not display the full range of the theological method of Protestant scholasticism, it does give an indication of how this method differed from the Ramism of Perkins and other Puritans. The method of the Ramists was to define and divide, moving from general to specific. The method of the scholastics was to assert the proposition and prove it logically, chiefly by using syllogisms.[53] The categories of Aristotelian philosophy were prominently used (as Zanchi identified the "efficient" and "material" causes). Inference proceeded from one step to the next based on the strict logical connections of the propositions. As has been said of Zanchi's method as a whole: "Throughout his works Zanchi usually stated a thesis, supplied a syllogism to prove the thesis, and then added an additional pair of syllogisms to prove the major and minor premises of the first syllogism."[54] While the work Perkins attached to his *A Case of Conscience* does not display this method in all its fullnes, it is a sample of how the scholastic method operated when doing theology.

Perkins' application of his theology to ethical issues took fullest form in his two major works on "conscience." His *A Discovrse of Conscience Wherein is Set Downe the nature, properties, and differences thereof* was published in 1596.[55] Perkins' reason for tackling such a subject was set forth in his "Dedication": "Conscience," he wrote, "is appointed of God to declare and put in execution his iust iudgements against sinners." Since humans do sin, however, against their consciences, Perkins penned this work so they "may see their follie and the great danger thereof, and come to amendement." This work served as a prelude to Perkins' most extensive work on conscience or practical theology -- *The Whole Treatise of the Cases of Conscience* published after his death.[56] As Perkins said, since "generall doctrine in points of religion is dark and obscure, and very hardly practised without the light of particular examples," he provided these examples or "cases" to help those whose consciences are stricken at some point. Perkins' skill at "resolving" such cases was such that he became known as one of the leading Protestant casuists of the sixteenth century.[57]

Both Perkins' *A Discourse of Conscience* and his *Cases of Conscience* (which he was working on at the time of his death) show the effects of his Ramist approach. They followed the typical Ramist pattern of structure. In *A Discourse*, Perkins divided the work into four chapters. These were: what conscience is; the actions or duties of conscience; kinds and differences of conscience; mans dutie touching conscience. Each of these individual chapters were drawn on the Ramist plan.[58] As Perkins moved through his discussions, he posed "arguments" and "objections" against his positions and answered each in turn.[59] He also raised "questions" and gave "examples" of what he meant.[60] But unfailingly Perkins returned and picked up the pattern. He moved through each of his divisions and on to the next in the way taught by Ramus. In three of his four chapters, his initial divisions were dichotomous. The next divisions (with the exception of one) were also dichotomous. Other divisions made included three, but in this work never more than four members.

A similar pattern was followed in Perkins' *Cases*. There were published in 1606 by Thomas Pickering who claimed to have kept as close as possible to "the Preachers owne words, without any materiall addition, detraction, or amplifications."[61] He did, however, divide the work into "bookes, according to the seuerall distrinct parts, the bookes into chapters, the chapters that were most capable of diuisions, into Sections." Pickering's purpose was "to help the memorie of the Reader, and to auoid tediousnesse the daughter of longsome discourses." Yet despite this boost for "memorie" -- of which Perkins himself would have doubtlessly approved -- Pickering maintained that Perkins' Methode remains the same in the bodie of the discourse, not admitting the least alteration." This was a sure indication that Pickering was aware of Perkins' awareness of "method" -- i.e. Ramist method.

According to Pickering, these lectures by Perkins were "deliuered with such perspicuitie, and disposed in such order and Methode, as fitteth best for the vnderstanding and memorie of any, whosoeuer shall peruse it."[62] With such obvious highlighting of these terms with Ramist overtones -- memorie, methode, order -- one would certainly be led to expect that Perkins had developed his *Cases of Conscience* according to Ramist principles.

Examination shows this to be the case. While the work is too expansive to chart in detail, it can be seen how Perkins set his structure Ramistically for dealing with the individual "cases" of conscience.[63]

Perkins divided this work into three books. The first book had 12 chapters; the second 16 chapters; and the third book had 6 chapters. The number of "cases" with which Perkins dealt was 148. But a mere perusal of the "Table of Contents" hides the fact that the underlying structure of the work was thoroughly Ramistic. Seeing only the 148 cases obscures the fact that these questions were related integrally to each other and to the structure of the work as a whole.

In his "preface" to the first chapter, Perkins declared "the Ground and Order of the Treatise following." He followed the same procedure here that he did for nearly all his works. He took a Scripture text, in this instance Isaiah 50:4: "The Lord God hath giuen me a tongue of the learned, That I should know to minister a word in due time, to him that is wearie." Perkins interpreted this to mean that "it was one speciall dutie of Christs propheticall office, to giue comfort to the consciences of those that were distressed, as the Prophet recordeth."[64] This power to execute such a duty was now passed on to Ministers of the Gospel according to Perkins. Pastors and teachers must carry this duty out. Perkins believed there was "a certaine and infallible doctrine, propounded and taught in the Scriptures, whereby the conscience of men distressed, may be quieted and releeued." This doctrine needed to be "drawne out of the written word of God."[65] This was what Perkins was attempting to do. He admitted, however, that "I will onely (as it were) walke by the bankes of it, and propound the heads of doctrine, that thereby I may, at least, occasion others, to consider and handle the same more at large."

But to do this, Perkins wished to proceed in a very specific "order": "First, I am to lay downe certaine Grounds or Preambles, which may giue light and direction to the things that follow: and in the next place, I will propound and answer the maine and principall questions of Conscience." The "grounds or Preambles" were "especially foure." These were concerning: confession, the degrees of goodness in things and actions; the degrees of sinne and the subjection and power of conscience. As the chart indicates, these were in turn further divided, very often again into dichotomies. Thus in fact, a whole theoretical or theological framework was constructed *before* Perkins delved into the "questions of conscience." Even before Perkins got to the numbered "cases," he had established a Ramistic framework in which to set them.

Basically, Perkins argued, questions of conscience can be "fifly diuided, according to the matters or subiect of them, which is man."[66] Yet man is to be considered "either apart by himself, or as he stands in relation to another, and is a member of a societie." As humans stand as members of society in relation, there is, according to Perkins a "twofold relation: to God, or to man." All in all, Perkins concluded:

> all Questions touching man, may be reduced to three generall
> heads. The first whereof is, concerning man simply considered as
> he is a man. The second, touching man as he stands in relation
> to God. The third, concerning man as hee is a member of one
> of the three societies; that is, either of the Family, or of the
> Church, or of the Common-wealth.[67]

These three questions became the subject-matter for each of Perkins' three books in the *Cases of Conscience*. Book I dealt with questions concerning "man simply considered in himselfe"; Book II with "Man as he stands in relation to God"; and Book III discussed

"Man as he stand in relation to man."⁶⁸

Given this background, it is apparent how these books are related to each other and to the over-all plan of the work. They stand as the further unfolding of the basic division of Perkins' basic dichotomy of the doctrine of conscience: the grounds and the questions of conscience. Collectively as three books they cover the whole web of relationships possible according to Perkins: man to himself; man to God; man to man. In Perkins' general Ramistic movement from general to particular, these "cases" stood as the *most* particular or specific applications of the doctrine of conscience, sanctioned according to Perkins from Isaiah 50:4.

As Perkins moved through his specific questions or cases, these too were related to the over-all Ramist plan and developed in that fashion. Perkins made it plain at the beginning of each book that "for orders sake" or "for the better and more orderly proceeding in this Discourse" all questions in this realm can be reduced to "some conuienient Subiect" or "heads."⁶⁹ These basic "heads" from the "places" into which specific cases or questions were then placed. There were three questions as the framework for Book I; four questions for Book II; and two main questions about "Vertue" (Perkins' designation for the relations of man to man) in Book III. Other of Perkins' 148 questions or cases fit into these schemes. But they were further elucidations on the basic structures that formed the Ramistic framework of the three Books.⁷⁰ Further Ramist charts could be constructed for the pattern of the rest of the questions.⁷¹

A typical example of how Perkins worked with a question is found in Book I, chapter VII, question 3. It asked: How a man beeing a distresse of minde, may be comforted and releeued?"⁷²

Perkins began with a short "answer" in which he said he would "onely set downe that which I take to bee most materiall to the doubt in hand." The following discussion was divided into five main sections.

The chart of this question indicates only the broadest divisions of Perkins' handling of this. On the question of the distress of the mind, Perkins found distresses to be both "general" and "special." General distresses were "fears" and "despairs." Special distresses or temptations were dichotomized into "of Trial" including "trial of the wrath of God" and "trial of the crosse"; and "of Seducement" which included seducements of "blasphemise," of one's "owne sinne" and of one's "imaginations." All of these were dealt with in Section 1 of Perkins' response.

Perkins then turned to the "general remedy of all difficulties." This, he claimed was the "applying of the promise of life euerlasting, in and by the blood of Christ." To do this, three things must be performed. One must "disclose the cause of his particular distresse, that the remedie may the better be applyed"; "trial must be made, whether the said partie, be fit for comfort yea or no?" (this to be determined by whether or not one was "humbled for his sinnes"). If one was not yet humbled, "friendly and Christian talke and conference" to bring one to "consider his owne sinnes" might help. Once the person considered the sins, he must "be sorrie for them." This sorrow, said Perkins, was not to be as "worldly sorrow." It must be "sorrow according to God." The sorrow must "bee not confused, but a distinct sorrow," that is sorrow for one's own sins directly. Thirdly, in applying the remedy for difficulties, there must be "the ministring and conuaying of comfort to the mind of him, that hath confessed his sinnes, & is truly humbled for them."

In section 3, Perkins considered some "false" ways of ministering comfort. He dealt here with the "doctrine of Vniuersall grace and redemption." Some, said Perkins, urge the verse that says "God would haue all men to be saued" (I Timothy 2:4). They seek to relieve distress of mind by "perswading a man that hee hath title in the Couenant of grace" simply because God desires all, universally, to be saved.

Perkins rejected this approach. He argued among other things that "all," "must not be vnderstood of all particulars, but of all kinds, sorts, conditions, and states of men, as may be gathered out of the former words: I would that prayers be made for all men, not for euery particular man." Perkins said that "the promise of saluation is not uniuersall, without exception, or restraint: and therefore application made by the vniuersalitie of the promise, admits some falsehood." Secondly, Perkins claimed that "this way of applying is also Vnfit." Here he attacked those who would misuse a syllogism like this: Christ died for all men: but thou art a man: therefore Christ died for thee." Perkins claimed:

> The partie distressed will grant all, and say, Christ indeede died
> for him, if hee would haue receiued Christ; but he by his sinnes
> hath cut himselfe off from his owne Saviour, and hath forsaken
> him, so as the benefit of his death will doe him no good.[73]

Perkins argued here that since "the promise of saluation is not uniuersall, without exception," it was wrong to draw a distressed person into assuming that the death of Christ was beneficial for him if that person "by his sinnes hath cut himselfe off from his owne Sauior, and hath forsaken him." Even if the syllogism was valid logically, it was not valid spiritually. The premise on which it was based (which Perkins called the "doctrine of Vniuersall grace and redemption") was not true. By this, Perkins was acknowledging at least tacitly, the dangers of syllogistic systems.

Section 4 of Perkins' discussion dealt with the proper grounds of comfort for those with distressed minds. Perkins listed here the ways in which one might be "brought within the Couenant." These were by "faith," "repentance," and the "love of God, which is the fruit of them both."

In section 5 Perkins spoke of the "way of bringing a man within the couenant." This was first "in making triall," i.e. asking if the person believes and repents, and whether he desires to believe and repent. Perkins had previously argued that God promised blessedness and life everlasting 'to the true and vnfained desire of grace." He cited the beatitude of Jesus that those who hunger and thirst after righteousness will be satisfied. Perkins claimed that "they are in Scripture pronounced blessed, which hunger and thirst after righteousness." The thirsty soul, feeling completely destitute of Christ, yet who "doth thirst after the blood of Christ, and desires to bee made partaker thereof," is blessed by God. For, Perkins claimed, "God is woont mercifully to accept of the desire of any good thing, when a man is in necessity, and stands in want thereof" (Psalm 10:17; 145:19). Perkins believed that in believers "God accepteth the will for the deede." After a person acknowledged even a desire to believe and repent, Perkins said "—some beginnings of faith and repentance will appeare, which at the first lay hid."

The second way to bring a person within the covenant was through the "applying of the promise of life euerlasting to the partie distressed." Here a syllogism with correct premises, according to Perkins could be profitably applied:

> Hee that hath an unfained desire to repent and beleeue, hath
> remission of sinnes, and life euerlasting: But thou hast an
> earnest desire to repent and beleeue in Christ. Therefore remis-
> sion of sinnes, and life euerlasting is thine.[74]

While at times of distress it is often as hard to make one accept a promise as it is to make fire and water mix, according to Perkins, one must nevertheless follow what "I take to be the onely generall and right way, of comforting a distressed conscience." In conclusion Perkins listed six rules to follow for good success in applying the promise of salvation.

This case study of how Perkins presented a typical case of conscience shows the detail into which he went. His answers to objections often turned on very fine distinctions. His lists of spiritual remedies, rules, and prescriptions (normally buttressed by Scriptural citations) often led into apparently minute detail. But this depth of detail should not obscure the central fact: in terms of general arrangement, Perkins structured the work along Ramist lines.

Perkins carefully fashioned this work according to his usual method. He set out his pattern clearly and related each branch of the "Ramist tree" to the trunk and to each other branch. Without a knowledge of the Ramist system, it would be possible to read this work (and Perkins' others) and be oblivious to the careful organizational procedure at work. What seem like endless enumerations and careful distinctions would not be perceived as following any over-all plan. The overarching significance of the method itself would be lost. Without seeing Ramus behind Perkins, one might even conclude that here was a scholastic, Aristotelian-oriented Protestant theologian at work. Due to the set-up of the *Cases of Conscience*, a look at the Table of Contents is totally deceiving in terms of what was at work for Perkins methodologically here. In the "Contents" one sees only "chapters" and "questions." It appears that Perkins has simply listed a group of topics, divided them into chapters and asked questions of each. Individual questions appear to follow from the one above without any special significance being attached to any.

But with the key to Perkins' method in mind, a different pattern emerges. To see Ramus behind it all is to see that some questions are more "general," some are more "specific." For example, in Book II, main question 3, Perkins distinguished betwen the "knowledge of God" and the "worship of God" that was either "inward" or "outward." In introducing the "outward worship" Perkins said: "To this belong many particulars, which I will reduce to eight seuerall heads." Then follow the eight heads. But Perkins discussed these eight over a period of 40 pages.[75] He then returned to main question 4 of Book II. The eight heads that Perkins discussed included questions in the Table of Contents numbered from 36 to 99. Yet from the Table itself or without a knowledge of Perkins' Ramist system, one would miss the relationship that these eight topics had to the larger body of the work. In the Table of Contents they appear to stand the same as the rest of the questions. Without seeing their relationship to the whole work they appear to be just so many more questions or even "scholastic distinctions." But by seeing the Ramist blueprint behind it all, one sees the definite order and "methode" at work here. That method, drawn from Ramus, carried with it other more far-reaching implications.[76]

Part of the need for a Protestant and Puritan "casuistry" in the sixteenth and seventeenth centuries was to answer the well-developed casuistry of the Roman Catholics.[77] The Roman Catholic Thomas Hill in 1600 wrote that this was one of the major benefits of being a Roman Catholic:

> And besides all this there are taught *Cases of conscience* in which is set down, what is sin, and what is not: the differences of sins, which great, which lesser, etc. which is a most fruitful and profitable kind of knowledge, and therefore is much studied and practised by Catholic priests, and divines, who teach the people thereby to rule, to order their lives and actions. Neither doth the Protestant meddle with these matters of conscience, but freighteth his ship only with faith, and never beateth his brain about sins, for he thinketh none to be imputed to such predestinated, as they all ween themselves to be, which causeth the people their followers to be utterly ignorant of the nature, differences, and quality of sins, and consequently nothing fearful, or stayed by any conscience to commit the same.[78]

Perkins' *Cases of Conscience* helped meet the need for a Protestant response to Roman Catholic casuistry. William Ames wrote in the "Preface" to his *Cases of Conscience* in 1639 that

> this part of prophecy hath hitherto been less practised in the school of the prophets, because our catpains were necessarily inforced to fight always in the front against the enemies to defend

> the faith, and to purge the floor of the church; so that they
> could not plant and water the fields and vineyards as they
> desired.[79]

Ames himself contributed to the literature on casuistry. His work furthered that which had been started by his teacher, William Perkins.

C. Polemical Works

Perkins' polemical attacks on astrology were mentioned above (see chapter IV). Similar to these were Perkins' polemical piece against witchcraft. It was entitled *A discovrse of the Damned Art of Witchcraft, so Farre forth as it is reuealed in the Scriptures, and manifest by true experience* and was constructed according to Ramist method.[80] It is not certain when this work was written. The title page says only that the subject was dealt with by Perkins "in his ordinarie covse of Preaching."[81] The prominence of concern about witches in England during the 1590's would make Perkins' topic a timely one.[82]

Though Perkins was skeptical about the benefits of astrology, he had no doubt that witches were real. He categorically rejected the opinion that witches existed only in the imagination. He believed that

> witchcraft is a rife and common sinne in these our daies, and
> very many are intangled with it, beeing either practitioners
> thereof in their owne persons, or at the least, yeelding to seeke
> for helpe and counsell of such as practise it.[83]

According to Perkins, Scripture taught the existence of witches. So Perkins took for the text of his *Discourse* Exodus 22:18 which read: "Thous shalt not suffer a Witch to liue." From the Bible Perkins claimed to derive his definition of a witch: "Witchcraft is a wicked Art, seruing for the working of wonders, by the assistance of the Deuill, so farre forth as God shall in iustice permit."[84] In *A Golden Chaine* Perkins had described the particular dangers he was as rising from this deceit practised by Satan so that

> beasts, but especially yong children, & men of riper yeares, are
> by Gods permission infected, poisoned, hurt, bounden, killed,
> and other molested; or contrarily, sometimes cured by Satan, by
> mumbling vp some few words, making certain characters and
> figures, framing circles, hanging amulets about the necke, or
> other parts, by herebes, medicines, and such like trumperie; that
> thereby the punishment of the faithles may be augmented, in
> reposing their strength vpon such rotten slaues, and the faithful
> may be tryed, whether they will commit the like abomination.[85]

Such statements led naturally for Perkins to the protection of society from witches. Perkins did not develop a full-scale demonology. But he agreed that death was a fitting penalty for a witch.[86] He permitted torture to be used, though "not in euery case, but only vpon strong and great presumptions going before, and when the party is obstinate."[87] Yet Perkins rejected trial by ordeal. He insisted that there by proper judicial safeguards. But the judge and jury already predisposed to believe the worst about "witches," these "safeguards" could have been flimsy at best.[88]

The adaptability of the Ramist system for a subject such as witchcraft is seen in the structure on which Perkins constructed his *Discourse*. He first explained why he chose to deal with this topic. Then he made an initial dichotomous division of his text: "What is a Witch"; "what is her due and deserued punishment."[89] The first member here dealt with definitions. Perkins devoted a chapter to each of the following: "What Witchcraft is"; "What is the ground of the whole practise thereof"; "How many kinds and differences there be of it." In his discussion of his definition, Perkins dealt with each phrase of the definition in turn under the heading of the "general nature of this Arte." His phrases of the definition were successively dichotomized. The second phrase of "What Witchcraft is" was the "ground of all the practises of Witchcraft," or the "particular" member of the dichotomous division. He defined his subject, divided his text, and moved from what he conceived to be a generall discussion to a more specific one.

The dichotomous structure was maintained in nearly every division of the work. As the chart indicates, the preponderence of the treatise was concerned with the nature of witchcraft both generally and particularly and what witches were, both "good and badde." The second major division, the punishment of a witch (death), received a treatment of less than one page.[90] The remainder of the piece was "the application of the doctrine of Witchcraft to our times." Perkins handled this by answering four particular questions that stemmed from his equation of witches in his time with those which Moses commanded to be put to death in Biblical times. Perkins wrote:

> The confessions of Witches recorded in the Chronicles of countries through all Europe, doe with common consent declare and manifest this point. So that howsoeuer our Witches may differ in some circumstances from those in the time of Moses, as either in the instruments, and means vsed, or in the manner & forme, or in some particular ends of their practises, yet in the substance and foundation of Witchcraft, they agree with them.[91]

Witches of all times according to Perkins, were guilty of making a covenant with the Devil.

Thus Perkins used the Ramist method to present his discourse on witchcraft. He moved from general to particular after his initial divisions and definitions. He also made "application" of his doctrine by pointing out the "uses" to which it could be put.

Perkins' polemics also had another target: the Roman Catholic Church. Perkins wrote two pieces toward the end of his life that attacked Roman Catholic theology and practise. These were *A Reformed Catholike* (1597) and his posthumously published *The forged Catholicisme, or vniuersalitie of the Romish Religion* (1604). In the former Perkins announced a three-fold purpose:

> The first is to confute all such Politickes as hold and maintaine, that our religion, and that of the Romane Church differ not in substance, and consequently that they may be reconciled: yet my meaning is not here to condemne any Pacification that tends to perswade the Romane Church to our Religion. The second is, that the Papists which thinke so basely of our religion, may be wonne to a better liking of it: when they shall see how neere we come unto them in sundry points. The third, that the common Protestant might in some part see and conceiue the points of difference betweene us and the church of Rome: and know in what manner and how fare forth, we condemne the opinions of the said Church.[92]

In this work, Perkins concentrated on 22 key issues that he described as "the places of doctrine." Perkins here followed another Fellow of Christ's College, Andrew Willet. Willet published his *Synopsis Papismi* in 1592 and he too attacked Rome through a topical approach. He presented the central issues in a summarized fashion rather than through a minutely detailed and scrupulously argued tone.[93] Perkins' method throughout was first to deal with the common ground between Protestants and Catholics before he went on to discuss the differences and reasons for the differences on each point. In this he followed Willet and also

William Whitaker.⁹⁴ This approach turned out to be successful for Perkins. 13 Continental editions of the work were produced. They were written in Latin, French, Spanish, German, and Dutch. The work was also frequently republished in English. An exiled English Catholic priest, William Bishop, wrote two large volumes to refute this work of Perkins'. He said, "I have not seen any book of like quantity, published by a protestant, to contain either more matter, or delivered in a better method."⁹⁵

Perkins' topical approach and format meant that he did not specifically develop his *Reformed Catholike* in the Ramist fashion. Here he dealt with the "heads of doctrine"; our consent, the difference, our reasons, objections of Papists, and answers to those objections. The specifically polemical nature of this work would appear to be the primary reason for this approach. Perkins was concerned with a number of theological doctrines. Each of these were developed in his piece in a separate discussion from the others. He covered them all under 22 "heads." To highlight the purposes he stated at the outset -- of showing the common ground with Rome and expressing the Protestant position to focus on the differences with Rome -- Perkin adopted his straightforward procedure. He himself was not trying to develop an argument. He was not interested in showing intrinsic interrelationships among parts of a Biblical text. If he was he would doubtlessly have used Ramist method.

But here Perkins was engaged in "theological warfare." He had to deal with doctrinal differences head on. He was in effect debating with the Roman Church. Therefore he set his piece in a combative format. At points he met the Catholics on the grounds of logical reasoning. He was not averse to using the logical tools, especially syllogisms, when they helped clarify his own position. Perkins used all the resources available to him to show the inadequacy of the Roman position. So in this polemical context a different framework was needed. Perkins varied from his usual style and method to meet the specific challenge of vindicating his own theological position against Roman Catholic theology.

Perkins extended his *A Reformed Catholike* with his *Problem of The forged Catholicisme*. In this work Perkins attempted to show that Roman Catholics were wrong in claiming that their dogmas were rooted in the early Church Fathers. Perkins claimed:

> It is unpossible for any popish Diuine in the world to shew out
> of the true monuments of the Councels and Fathers, and out of
> their naturall sense and meaning, that the faith of the present
> Church of Rome, it truly Catholike in those points wherein it
> dissenteth from the reformed Churches of the Gospell.⁹⁶

Perkins argued that the Reformed churches were the truly "catholic" churches and that the Church of Rome was guilty of all manner of theological "innovation" based on no legitimate justification from the writings of the Patristic fathers or of Scripture itself. At the very end, Perkins came to his conclusion or "consequent." He wrote:

> No Apostle, no holy Father, no sound Catholike, for 1200
> yeares after Christ, did euer holde or professe that doctrine of
> all the Principles and grounds of Relgion, that is now taught by
> the Church of Rome, and authorized by the Councell of Trent.⁹⁷

Perkins wrote this work for two reasons. One was to serve as a guide for students in their reading of the Church fathers. The second purpose was to act as a "counter-poyson against Iodocus Coccius." Coccius was a Belgian scholar who produced *Thesaurus catholicus* which he discussed doctrines that heretics misused and then gave the 'catholic' testimonies to "true doctrine." Perkins however, rejected many of the sources used in this work on historical grounds.⁹⁸

To accomplish his counter-purpose, Perkins divided his work into three sections. These were: a discussion of hermeneutical principles for interpreting the Fathers; a chronological and critical examination of Patristic and Scholastic literature in which Perkins attempted to establish which works were authentic; and finally an extensive section on the history of important doctrines. The first two of the sections were "Preparations to the Demonstration of the Probleme." The last section was "The Demonstration of the Probleme."

In the section on "The Demonstration of the Problem," Perkins did as he did in the *Reformed Catholike*. He reduced his project to "The places and heads of the controuersies." This time there were 60 such "places." Perkins did not follow any one set pattern for vindicating his position. He quoted extensively from the Fathers, however, to prove that the theology and practices of Protestant churches are more in accord with the historic catholic positions than are those of the Church of Rome. Thus his "Demonstration of the Probleme" became a veritable encyclopedia of Partristic literary quotations. It was, in short, the first Patrology in the English language.[99]

Again, Perkins' Ramism was not specifically useful for him here. He advanced his arguments to meet particular arguments of his opposition. He wished also to provide a resource for Partristic study as well as a powerful polemic weapon for Protestants to use against Roman Catholics. As he styled the piece on the title page, it was "An Introduction to young Students in the reading of the Fathers."[100] For this purpose Perkins turned to another type of format.

In 1597 Perkins published another work that did not exactly follow his normal methods of presentation. This was *A Graine of Musterd-seede: or, The Least Measure of Grace that is or can be effectual to saluation*.[101] Perkins wrote this small treatise to answer the question: "What is the least measure of grace that can befall the true childe of God, less then which, there is no grace effectuall to saluation."[102] The form of this work was six "conclusions." Each was followed by an "exposition." According to Perkins, these conclusions were set "in such order, as one shall confirme and explaine the other, and one depend vpon the other." This was an apparently more "scholastic" than Ramist way of proceeding. The statement/exposition pattern that each of the succeeding statements interlocked and was dependent upon the one proceeding it was more the method of Aristotle's syllogistic logic than Ramus' "descriptive logic." Perkins' first three conclusions were climaxed in this fourth conclusion: "therefore, is the grace itselfe."[103] His second conclusion spoke of "the first materiall beginnings...." -- a phrase again more reminiscent of Aristotle than Ramus. So clearly here was an instance where Perkins turned to scholasticism rather than Ramism for his methodology.

What is a possible explanation for this? Why would this work have been cast this way? *A Graine of Musterd-Seede* (1597) reflected some of the refinements Perkins was forced to make in his theology of the assurance of salvation. The debates of Cambridge University in the 1590's over the nature of God's grace and the question of whether or not one could have the assurance of one's salvation flared up into a burning theological issue for those involved.[104] Other disputes over predestination were closely connected to these.[105] Perkins' purpose in *A Graine of Musterd-seede* was to work out for the comfort of his readers, what the least measure of grace was that was needed to obtain salvation. If Perkins could do this, he believed he could provide a sure foundation of comfort for those with afflicated consciences over whether or not they were truly children of God.[106] Yet Perkins had to frame this in such a way as not to lose the crucial (for followers of Calvin) theological point that it was God who initiated salvation.

Perkins' *A Graine* dealt with this problem in its fourth and fifth conclusions. They were: "IV. To see and feele in our selues the want of any grace pertaining to saluation, and to be grieued therefore, is the grace itselfe;" "V. He that hath begun to subiect himselfe to Christ & his word, though as yet hee be ignorant in most points of religion, yet if he haue a care to increase in knowledge, and to practise that which hee knowed, he is accepted of God as a true beleeuer."[107] Perkins used Augustine to open the gate of salvation as widely as his theology would permit. One might be assured that God's grace was at work if one would "see and feele....the want of any grace pertaining to saluation, and to be grieued." This seemingly gave *human* initiative a wide latitude in which to work. The fifth conclusion gave hope to all the "ignorant" and "unlearned" for whom Perkins had written his Catechism years before. If these people were willing to *learn* and to *practice* what they knew -- they would be counted by God as "true beleeuers" (again the doctrine/life pattern appeared.)

But still, for Perkins that Reformed theologian there was the underlying assertion throughout that salvation was "the worke of God, and of God alone."[108] Perkins attempted here to ensure that those who sincerely desired to be saved were not turned away from this quest by a theology (which he propounded) that apparently stressed God's grace to the exclusion of the validity of any human initiatives. Perkins pushed the questions of the validity of human initiatives in seeking God's grace back one step. He considered a prior question of whether humans can do any act at all that will aid in their reconciliation with God. Perkins spoke of not the act, but the intention of the heart. He said: "a constant and earnest desire to be reconciled to God, to beleeue, and to repent, if it be in a touched heart is in acceptation with God, as reconciliation, faith, repentance itselfe."[109] Put slightly differently: "the desire of mercy, in the want of mercy, is the obtaining of mercy; & the desire to beleeue in the want of faith, is faith" according to Perkins.[110] This meant that Perkins was urging his hearers not to despair if they did not find ready evidence of their election by God in the works that their lives were producing (sanctification).[111] Perkins urged his hearers to labor to "grow in grace."[112] He wanted to assure those of troubled conscience that it was their faith and not any works they did that set them right with God. Yet at the same time, Perkins wanted them to strive for or seek after this faith. But above all, he wished them not to be discouraged if their labors seemed in vain. Perkins wanted his readers to come to the conclusion that: "God accepts the endeavour of the whole man to obey, for perfect obedience itselfe."[113] Perkins went on to clarify:

> if men endeauour to please God in all things, God will not iudge
> their doings by the rigour of his law: but will accept their little
> and weake endeauour, to doe that which they can do by his
> grace, as if they had perfectly fulfilled the law.[114]

Perkins would argue that this was not to permit semi-Pelagianism to slip into his system under the guise of Reformed theology. He wished to safeguard completely the fact that it was God's grace that initiated all acts and even all motivations. Only God could initially plant the "mustard-seede of faith" by His grace. But Perkins apparently sought to make sure that his readers were actively involving themselves in using the means of grace that God provided to come to their final assurance of salvation.[115]

With the need for such careful distinctions, Perkins evidently felt the need to present his argument in a more closely reasoned format than he usually did. This work did not have a Scripture text at its beginning. Perkins was thus not exegeting Scripture *per se*. The treatise was instead more of a syllogistic presentation (that was not completely shunned by Ramus) designed to clarify and fine-tune his theological position on faith and assurance. He wrote this at a time when theologians at Cambridge were vigorously arguing about such topics. Perkins added his prespective by casting his *A Graine of Musterd-Seede* in the form of theses to be proven and debated. Thus again it was apparently Perkins' polemical situation that turned him away from the Ramist format.

The year before he died, Perkins published another polemical work. This was his *A Warning against the Idolatry of the Last Times* (1601). This piece and the one bound with it "An Instrvction Tovching Religiovs or Divine Worship" were both constructed in Ramistic fashion.[116] These pieces criticized the Roman Church for what Perkins perceived to be its "idolatry" in worship with regard to the Virgin Mary, the Pope, the Saints, Crucifixes etc.[117] Perkins' attacks stemmed not only from his Protesant convictions in which he viewed these figures very differently than Rome did. But also Perkins argued against them because he claimed they were forms of "artificial memory."

Perkins' test for these works was I John 5:21 which read: "Babes, keep your selues from Idols." Basically Perkins saw the text as containing a command from God with both a negative and a positive pole. The first was what was forbidden -- idolatry; the second what was positively commanded -- worship. Thus Perkins divided his work into these two major parts. First was a warning against idolatry. Second was instruction on divine worship. Perkins argued that "it is the propertie of a diuine law, in forbidding any thing to command the contrarie."[118] Therefore he believed it was within the "scope of this place" to deal with the idols that are forbidden and the true worship that is commanded by God.[119]

In *The Idolatry of the last Times*, Perkins posed two questions: "What is an Idol?" and "How wee are to keepe our selues from them?"[120] After he dealt with these as the main divisions of the "meaning," the "forbidden part" of the text, he further divided them. Then he moved to his second division which was the reason why idols are forbidden. This Perkins explained by one work "babes" from the text. To expound this word, Perkins simply said that it meant "little children" and then that this was "applied in ten waies."[121]

This amounted to listing ten different ways the term "children" was used in Scripture and to whom it applied. After this, Perkins announced that he was earnestly exhorting all people to remember and heed this text. And, so that "they may the better be resolved," Perkins moved to a dichotomous division of his exhortation into the "greatness of the sinne" and the "attendants with idolatry." These attendants, Perkins said, included adulteries, fornications, severing from God, and punishments in body and soul. His final thrust in this piece was to show how "the Church of Rome is a worshiper of idols."

Perkins did this through the following syllogism:

>Babylon is a worshipper of idols.
>Rome is Babylon: *Ergo*
>Rome is a worshipper of idols.[122]

Perkins claimed that here "the maior is manifest" and the "minor is also manifest." He cited Revelation 17:18 -- "a city that rules ouer the kings of the earth" and that was, according to Perkins, "Rome which was the seat of the Empire in the daies of Iohn." Therefore, Rome and by Perkins' inference the Church of Rome was an idolater. To back up his polemical conclusion, Perkins finished this piece with some five reasons and five "particulars" where he quoted Roman Catholic writers and "showed" how they advocated idolatrous worship.[123] The syllogism was apparently a convenient form for Perkins to sharpen his conclusion and give the appearance that he had demonstrated this beyond question.

In his "Divine or Religious Worship," the positive prescriptions on worship were dichotomized by Perkins into the "meaning" and "kinds" of worship. The meaning he expounded through six points that served as commonplaces in his over-all system: foundation, rule, end, persons, place, and properties of worship. As to the kinds of worship, Perkins began a series of dichotomies: principal and less principal; of these properties/parts; generall and speciall etc. This part of his work was actually a treatise in itself. He made division after division without any attempt to tie his points with the text from I John. Instead, Perkins quoted extensively from the Church fathers and from other parts of Scripture as testimonies to the points he made.

D. Works on Christian Life, Ministry, and Vocation

Perkins' *Works* contained a number of pieces that dealt with issues relevant to the Christian lives of his readers. One such treatise was his *A Direction for the Government of the Tongve According to Gods Word*.[124]

This work was topical rather than being based on only one passage or verse of Scripture. It dealt with what Perkins perceived to be an important and abused aspect of living: how to "order thyselfe in speech and silence according to Gods word." Disregard of this question has led to "manifolde sinnes against God, innumerable scandals and grieuances to our brethren."[125]

Perkins' discourse was set up in Ramist fashion. He divided the subject of "the gouernment of the tongue" into three main aspects: requirements, parts, and exhortation. When diagrammed Ramistically, a certain symmetry appears.[126] The initial divisions of "requirements" and "parts" were dichotomized. So were the next divisions. The following divisions (reading from left to right and down on the chart) had three divisions with three members and two divisions with four members. The next divisions were dichotomized again.

Rather than seeing in this any hidden pattern or agenda on Perkins' part, it is better to consider this only accidental. Not all members of each division were divided again. Much of Perkins' discussion concerned the nine characteristics of gracious speech which were to him the evidences that God's grace was active. These included "questions and answers"/"objections and answers" interspersed and buttressed throughout by numerous Scripture verses. The only chapter that did not fit precisely into Perkins' pattern was a short chapter X: "On writting." This was inserted after his discussion of "holy speech" and before he began on his second major division: "holy silence." The chapter was added to say that "all this which is set downe concerning speech must as well bee practised in writing as in speaking."[127] The concluding chapter was "An exhortation to keepe the tongue." It gave five "Reasons" why Perkins hoped Christians would practise proper government of the tongue. The piece concluded with about half a dozen examples from church history (four from Foxe's *Book of Martyrs*) of those who faced God's judgment for abusing their tongues.[128]

Sometime in the early 1590's Perkins composed his *Christian Oeconomie: or, A Short Svrvey of the Right Manner of Errecting and ordering a Family, according to the Scriptures*.[129] This work was first written in Latin and then translated by Thomas Pickering in 1609.

Much has been written on the Puritan view of the family and domestic relations.[130] Dudley Fenner had published a small tract on *Household Duties* in 1592. Perkins' *Oeconomie*, however, went far beyond Fenner in scope and detail. But like Fenner's work, Perkins was organized in a thoroughly Ramistic fashion. The short initial chapter defined "Christian Oeconomie" as "the doctrine of the right ordring of a Family." It then defined a family as "a naturall and simple Society of certaine persons, hauing mutuall relation one to another, vnder the priuate gouernment of one." The second chapter spoke of two duties that belonged to a family: to God and to itself. The duty to God was to worship and serve Him. The service of God in a household according to Perkins had two parts: "a conference vpon the word of God, for the edification of all the members thereof, to eternal life" and "Invocation of the name of God, with giuing of thanks for his benefits." The families where this service to God was performed are "little Churches."[131] The duty of each family member to themselves as a household was to "employ themselues in some honest and profitable businesse, to maintaine the temporall estate and life of the whole."

After establishing these definitions, Perkins began the task of dividing his topic in the traditional Ramist way. His most basic distinction was the Family as divided into couples combined together as one; and "two persons of a miext or compounded nature and condition." These were divided into the Mast or Goodman of the family and the Goodwife of the House.[132] The bulk of Perkins' work concerned couples as one, dichotomized again into sorts as "principall" and "less principall." The principal sort was dichotomized into discussions of "marriage" and "married folks." The "doctrine/duty" division cropped up again in Perkins' discussion of marriage. Throughout this work there were paragraphs devoted to "cases" and their "answers." In the duties of marriage section, for example, Perkins wrote of cases where desertion by a married partner occured. In *Oeconomie*, Perkins followed the teachings of Martin Bucer who taught that whatever was not a true society was not a true marriage.[133] Since marriage was for mutual companionship and help, ill-treatment was as serious a breach as adultery. Remarriage was permitted by Bucer for each party. Perkins followed this line in permitting divorce for adultery and for remarriage by the innocent party after attempts at reconciliation had failed and there was no gift for continency.[134] He pointed out that in England then, it was impossible for the guilty party to remarry. But, like Bucer, Perkins approved of remarriage if the innocent party had remarried and the guilty party was showing signs of true receptance.[135] He also acknowledged several grouns for the dissolution and remarriage. One of these was for malicious and spiteful dealing "for this is as much as to betray one anothers estate and life to ther vtter enemies.[136]

But in his later years, Perkins adopted a stricter position. When he expounded the *Sermon on the Mount*, Perkins stuck with a literal reading of the Biblical text. Then he allowed divorce only for adultery. Then too be was able to strike a polemical not as he contrasted what he claimed was the "Biblical teaching" with the practice of the Papists.[137]

Thus, while the Ramist method guided Perkins through the divisions and subdivisions of governing a household "according to the Scriptures," it did not guarantee any one standard of Biblical interpretation. Perkins changed his position on divorce. Undoubtedly when he wrote his earlier work he believed he was being true to the Bible's teaching. Yet he would have felt the same way when he considered the topic later. In any one instance a Ramist theologian may believe that the mind of God could be uncovered. But this would not in itself guarantee any one consistent standard of Biblical interpretation as this instance about divorce shows. Ramist or not, the question of divorce and remarriage was one to be decided with theological and hermeneutical criteria in mind. In other words, the Ramist philosophy while providing Perkins and other Puritans with a useful tool for organizing and presenting their theological works, did not of itself significantly influence doctrinal considerations as this instance of Perkins' view of divorce shows. The appeal of Ramism to Puritans did not lie in the fact that it offered a congenial theological position per se. Certainly Ramus' status as a Protestant martyr, his commitment to Reformed theology and the philosophical implications of his thought combined to make Ramism attractive to the Puritans. But there were no explicit theological or doctrinal issues to which one necessarily had to be partisan towards in order to be a Ramist.

Perkins wrote two treatises in 1593 that dealt with other issues of the Christian life. These were *Of the Nature and Practise of Repentance* and *Of the Combat of the Flesh and Spirit*.[138] In his work on repentance Perkins commented that different theologians treat repentance in different ways. He mentioned Melanchthon's making it a fruit of faith and dividing it into two parts: mortification and vivification. Calvin, said Perkins, made faith a part of repentance and divided it into contrition, faith, and new obedience. Others "make it all one with regeneration."[139] Yet, Perkins claimed, "the difference is not in the substance of doctrine, but in the logicall manner of handling it. And the difference of handling ariseth of the diuers acception of repentance." Perkins then went on to explain how he purposed to handle the topic:

> It is taken two waise; generally, and particularly. Generally for the whole conversion of the sinner, and so it may containe contrition, faith, new obedience under it, and be confounded with regeneration. It is taken particularly for the renouation of the life and behauiour and so it is a fruit of faith. And this onely sense do I follow in this treatise.[140]

Perkins thus highlighted theological method or "logicall method" in dealing with the doctrine of repentance. By employing his Ramistic dichotomy, moving from the general to the particular, Perkins combined the insights of Melanchthon, Calvin, and others. In his treatment he self-consciously called attention to the method by which he would be dealing with this doctrine.

Perkins handled his theme by first defining repentance as "a worke of grace, arising of a godly sorrow; whereby a man turned from all his sins vnto God and bringeth forth fruities worthy unto amendment of life." After discussing parts of this definition, Perkins discussed the cause of repentance, how it was wrought and then turned to the parts of repentance: mortification and the rising to new life (Melanchthon's division.)[151] From that point on, most of Perkins' divisions were dichotomous or else division into three parts.[152]

When Perkins finished with the "nature" of repentance, he moved to a discussion of the "practice" of repentance. Here he followed Calvin's treatment as he considered "examination of the conscience by the commandments of God" by giving an elaborate list of the ways in which each of the Ten Commandments could be broken. The other duties of repentance were to confess one's sins, pray to God for pardon, and pray to God for grace and strength to walk in newness of life.[143] Perkins followed with discussion of the motives and time of repentance. He concluded with certain case studies to be resolved.[144] Methodologically, therefore, Perkins followed through the Ramist pattern: definition, divisions moving from general to particular, with the over-all "nature/practice" scheme. In conclusion he provided "cases" in a question/answer format. These were the most specific examples of repentance possible.

Perkins' treatise on *The Combat of the Flesh and Spirit* took Galatians 5:17 as it text: "For the flesh lusteth against the spirit, and the spirit against the flesha: and these are contrarie one to another, so that ye cannot doe the things which yee would."

To handle this verse, Perkins listed five points with which he dealt in turn: the combat of the flesh and spirit; manner; cause; persons involved; and the effects of this combat. These five were drawn from the words of the verse. In this sense, Perkins was doing his exegesis by dividing his "definition" (Scripture verse) into smaller parts and the expanding on each part in turn. He did this in line with his own instruction in *The Arte of Prophecying* to "collect a few and profitable points of doctrine out of the natural sense." As Perkins then moved through each point (except for the "cause" and "persons involved"). he divided them into two or three members with some of these being further divided (dichotomously) in the familiar fashion.[145]

In conclusion, Perkins added four points to see "what vse may be made" of the verse. He ended with a small chart that displayed in schematic form how the "voice of a man" -- carnal, regenerate, and glorified -- responds to the combat between flesh and spirit.[146] Perkins dealt with this issue of the Christian life in his usual Ramist manner. He took the main heads or loci of his discussion for the words of the text themselves. But he translated them into their relation to the theme at hand: the combat of the flesh and spirit. Thus the heads were oriented around the common theme and could be easily charted. Perkins thus "simplified" his text for the sake of his method. He then "expanded" on it again as he began to define and divide the particular heads. The picture of two major forces in "combat" here -- flesh and spirit --- was a "natural" for a treatise dichotomously arranged along Ramist lines.

In September, 1595 Perkins wrote a work designed especially to "serve for spirituall instruction." This was *A Salve for a Sicke Man*. It was addressed particularly to "Marriners when they goe to sea; souldiers when they goe to battell; and women when they trauell with childe."[147] This work was sub-titled "A Treatise containing the nature, differences, and kindes of death; as also the right manner of dying well." Perkins' text was Ecclesiastes 7:3: "The day of death is better then the day that one is borne."

Perkins divided this work into two sections as he divided the text into its meaning and uses. The bulk of the discourse was taken up with his elaborate discussion of how to die well and his comments on the fear of death.[148] He dealt with the meaning of the text in three questions: what death is meant; how can it be truly said that the day of death is better than the day of one's birth; and in what respect is it better? He devoted much space to the four "uses" of this text: there is a way to die well; do not fear death overmuch; how one may desire death; and death to the unbeliever as horrible.[149]

In Perkins' longest discussion on the way to die well, his major dichotomy was in the "preparation before death" and the "disposition in death." As the Ramist chart of this work shows, Perkins moved in his discussion of the first member of the dichotomy from the "general preparations" to the "particular." The second main "use," on not fearing death was also dichotomized into "fearing" and "not fearing." While the purpose of this "use" was to instruct Christians not to fear death, Perkins was enough of a realist to admit that there is a certain natural fear which for him was also dichotomized, into fear for the destruction of one's human nature and fear for the loss death brings to Church or commonwealth. The variety of the number of heads into which each division was divided was another testimony to the fact that Perkins was not addicted to the principle of dichotomy *per se*. Here, as in other words he tended to divide his most major points into two members.

But frequently also divided them into three and often five or six heads or more. Yet despite the length of the lists, Perkins always returned to the next major division and clearly indicated that he had done so. The symmetry in the charts of his works show that he always finished the divisions he began. In *A Salve for a Sicke Man* the "sense" or "meaning" of the text formed the "teaching" or "doctrine" element of the text's division; the "uses" followed quite naturally as the second element in good Ramean form.

A work that showed a stronger adherence to dichotomy as the major method of division was Perkins' *Epieikeia,* or *A Treatise of Christian Equity*. This was not published until after his death (1604), but was perhaps written while Perkins was still a Fellow of Christ's College since the substance was said to have been "deliuered publikely in Lectures" in Cambridge.[150]

Perkins' text here was Philippians 4:5: "Let your moderation of minde be knowne to all men: the Lord is at hand." He defined equity as "a rare and excellent vertue, whereby men use a true meane, and an equall moderation in all their affaires and dealings with men, for the maintaining of iustice, and perseruation of peace."[151] Private equity was "a moderate, euen, and equall carriage of a mans selfe, in all his priuate words and deedes, towards all other men, and all their words and deeds."[152] Equity was intimately related to love because it was "the propertie of true loue; to passe by many wants: and the more that a Christian is rooted in true loue, the more infirmities will he passe by...." Perkins saw the political ramifications of this. He wrote that this equity was

> the marrow and strength of a common weal, and where it is, there cannot be but peace and contentment in all estates; and so necessary, as without the practice of it, no house, family, societie, cittie, common wealth, kingdome, or Church can stand or continue.[153]

Perkins argued that God practiced this equity towards his creatures in that He withheld from them their just deserts. God moderated their terrors of conscience and counted their intentions more important than their actual achievements (or lack of them). Persons were spurred to the practice of equity in their social behavior, Perkins believed, because they did all their dealings in the presence of God, the Judge of judges. Therefore, Perkins warnted: "Vse equitie and moderation in your dealings, and remember who is at your elbow, stands by and lookes on, readie to iudge you for it."[154]

This tract by Perkins was constructed almost strictly in dichotomous fashion.[155] He divided the words of his text into two parts: an "exhortation" ("Let your equity be known before men") and an "excellent reason to enforce it" ("for the Lord is at hand"). Perkins gave a paragraph to discussing the importance of equity. Then he moved to examining two points: the nature of equity and the kinds of it. From there to the end of the work, Perkins' divisions were dichotomous. This is true except for one enumeration of the private kinds of equity in which Perkins listed four members of the division instead of two. Throughout, Perkins issued "cautions" that somewhat amplify the points he made. He also used common examples to illustrate his points. These functioned as "cases" that served as the most particular instances of what Perkins had described previously in more general terms.

On January 3, 1596 Perkins wrote a dedication for his work "A Declaration of the True Manner of Knowing Christ Crucified.[156] This was his exposition of Galatians 6:14: "God forbid that I should reioyce, but in the Crosse of our Lord Iesus Christ, &c." This work began with Perkins making his dichotomous division: "In the right way of knowing Christ crucified, two points must be considered: one, how Man for his part is to know Christ: the other, how he is to be knowne of man."

As the chart of this work shows, Perkins proceeded very "methodically" in his analysis of these two parts of his text.[157] For the first, Perkins discussed three parts: one must notice in one's mind; apply to one's heart; and know in the affections of the heart that Christ was crucified for one's personal redemption. These three points were further broken into dichotomies. Perkins' whole movement here was from the general to the particular. He began urging only the *consideration* of Christ as He is portrayed in the "history of the Gospell, as he is offered to thy particular person, in the ministery of the word and Sacraments." Perkins urged a person then to know his *need* of Christ and then to *want* Christ.

The second part of the knowledge of Christ was in the application whereby one knows and believes that his work of Christ was done personally: "that Christ on the crosse was *thy* pledge and surety in particular...."; and that this crucifixion of Christ "*is thine*, beeing really giuen thee of God the Father."

The third part of this knowledge was a response in a person's *affections* whereby one bestows his heart to Christ and then places "all our ioy, reioycing, comfort, and confidence in Him."[158]

Thus Perkins moved his readers from the broadest base -- contemplation of the man Jesus as presented in the Gospel; through a personal apprehension of one's need for Christ; to a commitment whereby one's life and comfort is entrusted *to* Jesus Christ. Perkins did not begin with a specific appeal to the spiritual condition of the reader and then move on to say how Christ could change that condition for the better. Instead he moved in the other direction. As Ramist method prescribed, Perkins began with the widest point of contact and progressively narrowed it to embrace the reader and that reader's response. In short, it was Ramus' and Perkins' natural progression from general to specific.

The major part of Perkins' discussion was his treatment of the first part of the second member of his initial dichotomy. This was on how Christ was to be known through his benefits. These benefits were three: Christ's Merit; Vertue; and Example. Each of these were dichotomized and again the general/specific pattern appeared. Perkins moved when talking of Christ's merit through reconciliation to the benefits of reconciliation. When talking of Christ's vertue he moved from "speculative" to "experimentall." When Perkins discussed Christ's example he spoke first of the "conformity" of one's life and then of the specific fact that Christ's example "hath something more in it then any other example hath or can haue: for it doth not onely show vs that wee ought to doe (as the examples of other men doe) but it is a *remedie* against many vices, and a *motiue* to many good duties."[159] Then Perkins spoke most specifically in the most personal of terms to describe how the knowledge of Christ informs one's attitudes and actions when one is wronged in word or deed, tempted, or was angry. In this way again, Perkins linked theological doctrine, here the doctrine of the atonement, with the most common occurrences of life that called for ethical behavior and benevolent piety.

Perkins' final discussions of the three-fold knowledge of God, neighbor, and self that "Christ crucified" produced, served as another springboard by which Perkins again personalized his appeal to his readers. He polemicized against Turkes, Jews, and Popish Churches that do not acknowledge Christ. He then went on to say how the "common Protestant likewise commeth short herein." Perkins cited Calvin (on Galatians 6:2) and listed three causes for this failure of Protestants to know and acknowledge Christ.[160] He concluded with the history of the passion of Christ, told in personal terms, and appealed directly to readers to apply this to themselves. Then he urged them to go further and "labour by faith to see Christ crucified in all the workes of God, either in thee or vpon thee."[161]

Perkins' works here was sermonic in style and evangelical in the sense of calling for a specific commitment of one's life to Jesus Christ. It displayed, though, the same Ramus-inspired concerns that Perkins' *The Arte of Prophecying* spelled out. Perkins "rightly divided" his text and then applied it. He moved from its "mental" application to its "practical" application.[162] He applied his doctrine practically for both "instruction" and "correction" as he urged in his *Arte*. For example, Perkins spoke of how Christ's example should lead to a conformity of one's life to Christ. He dichotomized this life into "spirituall life" where he spoke of its four parts (instruction) and "moral duties" both "general" and "speciall" (correction).[163] Clearly the influence of the *Arte* stood behind this piece and behind that, Ramus.

William Perkins preached to both general audiences and also to students studying for the Christian ministry. Several years after his death, two of his works directed towards these students were published. They were entitled *A Treatise of the Duties and Dignities of the Ministerie* and *The Second Treatise of the Duties and Dignities of the Ministerie*.[164] These two pieces were published as one with the title *Of the Calling of the Ministerie*. The sermons had been "deliuered publikely in the University of Cambridge" by Perkins according to the title plage. William Crashaw, who wrote "The Epistle Dedicatorie" asked rhetorically: "Who may more worthily describe the dignities of the Ministerie, then he, who neither by doctrine nor conuersation, was euer the least disgrace nvto his Ministry?" And, "who might better teach the duties of the Ministery, then he, who so discharged them, as Enuie itself cannot iustly reprooue, and the Enemies themselues cannot but commend?"

To this University audience, Perkins preached first from Job 33:23,24 and then from Isaiah 6:5-9. In handling these texts, he once more set them out in Ramist order.[165] The first treatise divided Job 33 into three parts: Preface (vs. 1-7), God's reproof of Job (vs. 8-12), and God's instruction of Job on how God deals with sinners (vs. 13-33). This last division was dichotomized by Perkins into God's preserving the sinner from falling (vs. 13-22) and God's restoring the sinner from being fallen (vs. 23-33). This last division was divided into the remedies and means of restoring (vs. 23-24) and the effects of restoring (vs. 25-33).

It was the first member of this last division (including the words of the text) that Perkins developed further. He did this by dividing this head into "repentance" -- which Perkins said was taught in Job 33:23, 24 by "implication" -- and "through a minister of God." Perkins said his point was that "God useth meanes in his mercie to preserue sinners from falling into sinne; but if they doe, then he in much greater mercy affordeth them meanes and helps to rise againe." One such means was "repentance," the second was "a minister of God."[166]

Perkins dealt with his subject by taking five phrases from his text and giving them a one word description. The text read:

> If there bee with him a Messenger, an Interpreter, one of a thousand to declare unto man his righteousnesse: Then will he haue mercy on him, and will say, Deliuer him, that he go not down into the pit: for I haue receiued a reconciliation.

Perkins' "heads" or "topics" for these ran:

1. By his titles, which are two, "An Angell, An Interpreter."
2. By his rarenesse, "One of a thousand."
3. By his office: which is, "to declare unto man his righteousnesse."
4. By the blessing that God giueth vpon the labours of this true Minister: which is, "then God will haue mercie upon the sinner."
5. By his Commission and authoritie in the last words; God will say, "Deliuer him, that hee goe not downe into the pit: for I haue receiued a reconciliation."[167]

By making such topical substitutions, Perkins' work can be more easily charted in the Ramist was as his further divisions show.

Perkins' procedure here and in other places showed his confidence in his ability to interpret a Scriptural phrase accurately and to capture its meaning in an equivalent word or phrase that would then fit more conveniently on to a Ramist chart. Perkins here followed Ramus and the "topical tradition" in logic where in line with humanists like Agricola and Valla, the essential task of the logician analyzing his text was to classify and arrange.

By using "topics" or "commonplaces," the key notions for the framing or "inventing" of a discourse were available. Now for Perkins (as for Ramus) the opposite procedure could also be used for explaining the meaning of a discourse (a Scripture text). The theologian (or logician) needed simply to assign each segment of that discourse to a "heading" or "topic." When all segments were collected they could be ordered into an explanatory discourse through the use of the laws of method. The headings fit neatly on to the Ramist charts that simplified the text's meaning and graphically represented how the various headings were interrelated. Perkins made further divisions for each of the five headings of his text as he elaborated what he believed the implications and constituent parts of each of the headings entailed. The same procedure was followed as he dealt with Isaiah 6:5-9 in his *Second Treatise.*

Perkins worked similarly in his *A Treatise of Mans Imaginations.*[168] His text was Genesis 8:21: "And the Lord said in his heart, I will henceforth curse the earth no more for mans cause: for the Imagination of mans heart is euill men from his youth." In this work, Perkins' first chapter was devoted to "the unfolding of the text whereon the Treatise is grounded." In this he set his text within the context of the eighth chapter of Genesis where God established laws with Noah "touching the restauration of nature perished by the flood."[169] Perkins then divided that text into three parts: the preface, the law, and the reason for the law. The law was split into: what God has done and what God will do hereafter. The reason for the law (or decree) was likewise dichotomized into "general" and "particular." The majority of this *Treatise* was devoted to the two members of the "particular" reason for God's decree. There were that: the heart and imagination of man are evil; and no good thoughts occur in every man naturally.

These were the two main points derived from Perkins' understanding of the verse at hand. He further divided these and at the same time moved farther and farther away from the actual words of the text itself. In this sense Perkins was not "unfolding" his text so much as constructing his theological points through the headings he chose to erect. When he described "what" the evil thoughts and imaginations of the human heart were he had three headings: against God, neighbor, and himself. These heads were not drawn from the Scripture text. They were instead Perkins' own constructs, though as he would hold they were derived from the general teaching of Scripture itself. In a work of this sort, the further one moved to the "right" on the Ramist chart, the further one moved away from the actual text of Scripture itself.

Perkins must have had some awareness of this. Some of his works were commentaries and sermons that took their main heads or topics directly from the words of the Biblical text. Other works, Perkins called "Treatises." In these, as in *A Treatise of Mans Imaginations*, Perkins may have begun with the text but went on to develop his subject much more in a specifically theological rather than exegetical way. He drew freely from standard theological terms and concepts. As Perkins continued through his divisions, he used texts from the Bible to bolster his points. In this sense he evidently believed the whole Scripture was relevant and should be brought to bear on the issue at hand. He thus erected his own theological structure as he went. So Perkins' "Treatises" tend to be oriented around theoligical topics rather than strict exegesis of a specific text. But for both types of works, Perkins used Ramist method.

Though Perkins' "treatises" were more theologically than exegetically oriented, he did not choose the points he wished to make in a completely arbitrary manner. In fact, it was the Ramist method that prevented this. According to Ramus, the division of the subject must rise from the subject itself and follow the general to particular pattern. Ramus said: "the method of teaching, therefore, is the arrangement of various things brought down from universal and general principles to the underlying singular parts, by which arrangement the whole matter can be more easily taught and apprehended.[170] Perkins applied this advice to his works by moving from division to division and supporting each point with biblical citations. Yet Perkins kept the overarching principle in mind. The Ramist law for right teaching was always there as the guiding goal. Methodologically whenever Perkins made a "division," he had to do so as part of his overall movement from general to specific. Therefore, even as he erected his theological points, he had to develop them in accordance with the prescribed "method." He could not be completely arbitrary. His prescriptions in the *Arte of Prophecying* were for the "notation" and "collection" of doctrines to lead to the "resolving" of the Scripture "place." But notation and collection were to be made with the nine arguments of Ramus there to follow.[171] These nine arguments constrained haphazard and capricious "proof-texting" and system building. By recommending the route to be followed: from definition to division to division, and always from general to particular with the help of the nine arguments, the Ramist had some safeguard from completely fanciful choices being made.

Perkins' works on the Christian life also included a piece on the callings of a Christian. His *Treatise of the Vocations* marked the first scholarly English theological treatment of this subject.[172] Perkins expounded "vocation" through four main headings. These were: causes, rules, parts and kinds, and good ending. Through the first two of these, Perkins did nothing but dichotomize in his divisions. As he moved through the "parts and kinds," his first heading was "general," his second "personal." These were divided into four parts and three parts respectively. Perkins particularly developed the "right use" of one's "personal" calling. To him there was a "personall calling" to some "particular office, arising of that distinction which God makes betweene man and man in euery society."[173] According to Perkins this had to be joined with the "generall calling" that all receive. This is the calling to lead godly lives and especially "a certaine kind of life, ordained and imposed on man by God, for the common good."[174] When these callings were rightly joined, Perkins said, all the actions done for others' good were good works. As Perkins laid out the obligations entailed for "holiness" and "constancie" in one's personal calling, he did so almost exclusively through divisions that had two members. Yet despite the strictness with which Perkins used "dichotomy," the chart of his work shows that there were divisions with more members as well.[175] Further, throughout the work there were "questions" inserted that served as "cases" to bring Perkins' essentially theological discussion to focus on practical instances.[176]

E. Summary

The above discussion of Perkins' *Works* has indicated the many ways that William Perkins used and adapted principles of Peter Ramus. Perkins approached his work as a theologian and preacher with the tools of Ramist logic and rhetoric firmly in hand. As he lectured and wrote he applied the Ramist system -- undoubtedly initially imbibed from his tutor Laurence Chaderton -- to the subjects with which he dealt. The above examination of Perkins' *Works* has shown that Perkins found the principles of Ramus suitable for "unfolding" all types of topics. Whether the work was specifically doctrinal in orientation, or dealt with a practical problem or "cases of conscience," Perkins approached it and expounded it after the method of Ramus. When he wished to "resolve" or give his exposition of a passage or verse of Scripture, Perkins used this method as his framework. The only exceptions appear to be when his work was directed specifically against a theological opponent or was geared particularly for a "common" (as Perkins called them "ignorant") set of people. Except for these, all Perkins' works can be charted in the Ramist fashion.[177]

The approach Perkins used in following Ramus' rules for method is the clearest sign of Ramism in Perkins' works. But as has been documented, Perkins' vocabulary and emphases also portray the Ramean influence. His *Arte of Prophecying* with its enumeration of Ramus' nine arguments from the *Dialecticae libri duo* (1572) is perhaps the clearest instance of Perkins' direct borrowing.[178] But other terms used by Perkins when seen in light of his overall "method." certainly have a Ramist ring as well. These include: the dichotomous members of a heading that are invariably spoken of as "either....or"; the "unfolding" of a topic into numerous "branches"; the constant stress on the "use" of a doctrine; the repeated pattern of "doctrine/use"; proper "order"; the approval of "grammatical, rhetoricall, and logical analysis" etc. All these contribute additionally to the conclusion that the Ramist influence on William Perkins was very strong.[179] The identification of Perkins as the author of *Antidicsonus* and his strong strictures against artificial memory in favor of Ramean natural dialectic enhances this conclusion.

The view of logic Perkins held was inherited from Ramus. Ramus reacted against the complexities of the scholastic logic with its heavy emphasis on the syllogism as the supreme instrument of demonstration. Ramus believed logic has a much simpler function. He favored the logical tradition associated with ancient rhetoricians -- Cicero and Quintilian, then revived by Renaissance humanists such as Valla and Agricola. Ramus saw logic or dialectic as "the art of discoursing well." There was only "one logic" for him. It could be used for discourses on the sciences as well as for the humanities and other liberal arts. This logic was more a method of argumentation with persuasion as its purpose rather than a strict demonstration based on certain formal linguistic patterns as the scholastics viewed logic. Thus as John Milton summarized the Ramist view: "logic uses reason, yet does not teach the nature of reason but the art of reasoning" (*ratiocinandi artem*).[180] As the "art of discourse" for the Ramists, logic therefore "treated neither of words nor of things, but it was the study of the framework of thinking and was the fitness or rule of argument."[181] For the Ramists, logical "proof" came primarily through examples rather than through syllogistic reasonings. To Ramus and his followers, syllogisms were helpful only to clear away the obscurity of doubtful propositions. When the logician had correctly done his job, a discourse would be laid out in propositions that were self-evidencing axioms and did not need the technical tools of logic applied to them. The truth of these statements, according to Ramus, will be intuitively perceived.

This view of the nature and function of logic was at work in William Perkins. He did not rely heavily on the syllogism to prove his theological points as did Protestant scholastics such as Zanchi. For Perkins as for Ramus, discourse (theological discourse) was not made up of a series of syllogisms. It was rather a series of axioms (that Perkins derived from the Bible) combined to form a meaningful exposition of a subject according to the principles of right method which were basically the movements from general to particular. Perkins the preacher and theologian constructed his works to be a "succession of sentences, not a display of deductions."[182] This was why "method" was so important to Perkins. Ramist that he was, he believed the way for proper teaching or instruction to take place (and like Ramus he saw this as the proper goal of all study of the arts) was to move in a way that enhanced the "order" of a topic so it might be better "unfolded": "for orders sake, and for the better unfolding of it," as he said.[183] Thus Perkins' works were judged to be "substantiall, concise, exact, methodicall."[184] He moved as Ramus taught from the most conspicuous idea to the least conspicuous. The was the "natural method."[185] The result was the branching charts found in Ramus and other Ramists. The terms that made up these charts served as the "places" or "commonplaces." They capsulized in the shortest way the topic of each paragraph or each major point. When a discourse was being delivered orally (as in a sermon), Perkins urged that these places which functioned as "proof" and "applications" of the doctrines "collected" from a text, be "imprinted" on the mind so that the speaker will quickly and accurately recall the point to be made.[186] Thus the topical tradition of logic was useful for Perkins as it had been for Ramus in enhancing the effectiveness of a speaker or writer who sought to persuade his audience.

The influence of Ramus on Perkins is clear. Along with many of his colleagues at Cambridge University who were likewise looking for the reformation and "purifying" of the spiritual condition of the Church of England, William Perkins found the Ramist philosophy to be excellent as an effective vehicle by which to convey his thought to other people.

PART V

SIGNIFICANCE OF RAMISM IN WILLIAM PERKINS

Chapter VII. IMPORTANCE OF PERKINS' USE OF RAMISM

A. Perkins' Legacy through his Students

The works of William Perkins were widely read in the seventeenth century. As such, they were a factor in shaping the theological viewpoints of those who came after Perkins. But Perkins' works had a personal impact as well. For examination of the writings of many of Perkins' students and associates at Cambridge University reveals that they not only imbibed a similar theology to Perkins'. But they also wrote and preached in a strikingly similar style to Perkins. Indeed it was a Ramist style.

It was through these students and associates that Perkins' Ramism was to have its enormous effect. It is possible to find evidences of the Ramist method in those connected with Perkins through to the time of John Milton (1608-1674) and his exposition of Ramus' logic published in 1672: *Joannis Miltoni Agnli, Artis Logicae Plenior Institutio, Ad Petri Rami Methodium concinnata*.[1] A survey of this line of Cambridge Ramists indicates how Perkins' legacy was appropriated.

Paul Baynes (d. 1617) was Perkins' successor at Great St. Andrews Church. Around 1621 William Ames contributed a "Preface" to Baynes' *The Diocesans Tryal* in which attested to his vew that Baynes was a worthy preaching successor to Perkins.[2] Baynes' sermons and commentaries on Scripture religiously followed the Doctrine, Reason, Use pattern that came to be characteristic of Puritan preaching.[3] But they were broadly arranged along Ramist lines with periodic brackets that displayed dichotomies given in the body of the texts of the commentary. The subtitle of Baynes' *An Entire Commentary Upon the Whole Epistle of the Apostle Paul to the Ephesians* (London, 1643) read: "Wherein the Text is learnedly and fruitfully opened, with a Logicall Analysis, spirituall and holy Observations, confutation of Arminianisme and Popery, And sound edification for the diligent Reader."[4] Other works such as *The Terrour of God Displayed against Carnall Securitie* (1634) and *A Caveat for Cold Christians* (1618) has similar characteristics.[5] Baynes had entered Christ's College in 1590 and served as Fellow from 1600-1604.

Daniel Rogers (1573-1652) entered Christ's College in 1592 and was elected Fellow with Baynes in 1600. He served until 1608. Rogers wrote a poem entitled "In Indignissimum Petri Rami fatum" on the death of Ramus in the St. Bartholomew's Day massacre. His exposition of II Samuel 24 (London, 1619) can be charted Ramistically. This work was called *David's Cost*.[6]

Thomas Taylor (1576-1633) was another student of Christ's College while Perkins taught there. He became a Fellow of the College from 1599-1604. Taylor translated Perkins' *Exposition on Jude* and described himself as one of Perkins' "ordinarie hearers in Cambridge."[7] It was perhaps Taylor who drew the large Ramist chart that accompanies that piece in Perkins' *Works*. Taylor's own works show clearly that he had learned the Ramist method well. His three volumes display Ramist charts throughout as well as large "analyses" of chapters and books of the Bible.[8]

The translator of Perkins' *Arte of Prophecying* was Thomas Tuke. Tuke was a "Royalist divine" who died in 1657. His own work *The High-Way to Heaven: or Doctrine of Election* was drawn according to Ramist method and can be charted in the Ramist manner.[9]

But the prime example of how powerfully the Ramist tradition was passed on by Perkins was Perkins' student William Ames (1576-1633). Ames was a student at Christ's College and was converted by Perkins' preaching. He went on to become a Fellow of Christ's College from 1601-1610. Ames, however, could not approve of some of the practices of the College and was subsequently suspended. Officially he was suspended for his statement in a sermon that card-playing was equivalent to the abuse of "Word and Sacrament."[10] Ames became a "radial Puritan of the rigidest sort" and would not conform to the established Church. He went to the Netherlands where his views of the church were forged through conversations with Robert Parker, Henry Jacob, and John Robinson.[11] Ames served for a time as a chaplain to Sir Horace Vere, commander of English forces. His friends secured his position as advisor to the presiding officer of the Synod of Dort. In 1622 Ames was invited to become a Professor of Theology at the University of Franeker. Ames was "a Calvinist of the most orthodox sort, a man of the Synod of Dort. His dogmatics was the Canons of Dort; He had no quarrels with any of the famous five points."[12]

William Ames, student of Perkins, had also been described as "the foremost seventeenth-century Puritan Ramist."[13] Ames "wrote, taught, and preached theological Ramism."[14] The interplay between Ames' Puritan views and his Ramism was especially strong. Ramus "provided Ames with method and organization, and the Puritan tradition did the rest. Puritanism infused Ames's theology with its intense piety and urgency; Ramism added precision to Puritanism's holy passion."[15] To Ames, "Ramist theology, better than any other approach, made revelation intelligible."[16]

The emphases of Perkins' Ramism were made even more explicit by Ames. He echoed Perkins in commending the use of logic for theology. Ames said: "Seeing, therefore, the powers of logic, let us train ourselves with the aim that we may be able to see distinctly into everything, to judge with certainty, and to remember consistently."[17] The "faith/observance" or "doctrine/life" emphasis of Perkins was followed through consistently and thoroughly by Ames. The clearest example of this was Ames' *The Marrow of Sacred Theology* (*Medulla SS. Theologiae*). This work was first published in 1623 and was a textbook of Calvinist theology that was republished quite frequently in the seventeenth century. It became the standard textbook for the instruction of clergy in New England.[18] This work was constructed in a thoroughly Ramistic fashion. It was equipped with Ramist charts to make its theology "visual."[19] This Ramist method made Ames' work thus scarcely distinguishable from the works of Perkins that were constructed in the same way.

Ames proceeded Ramistically in a way congenial to Perkins' Ramistic procedures. "Theology" according to Ames, was "the doctrine or teaching [*doctrina*] of living to God."[20] Here in a nutshell was Ames' whole treatise. Ames in line with Perkins and Ramus can be seen as saying essentially that "faith" and "works" are one.

After Ames' initial definition, he began the process of division. He divided "theology" into two parts: "faith" and "observance."[21] Ames said that these "two parts are always joined together in use and exercise." But "they are distinguished in their nature and in the rules which govern them."[22] Ames agreed with Perkins and Ramus that theology was not primarily a technical, philosophical subject. It was rather "a practical one." Ames wrote: "It is self-evident that theology is not a speculative discipline but a practical one."[23] Therefore, Ames said, "there is no precept of universal truth relevant to living well in domestic economy, morality, political life, or lawmaking which does not rightly pertain to theology."[24] Like Perkins, Ames saw theology to be "as wide as human experience and as long of life."[25]

Ames' "faith/observance" scheme was followed in his *Marrow* in terms of his dichotomous divisions. In that sense, theology was always a call for action or ethics for Ames as it had been for Perkins. The balanced symmetry of the Ramist Puritans' theology was not "art for art's sake" along or merely an exercise in theological method. Theology is instead "that good life whereby we live to God," according to Ames.[26] "Faith," said Ames, "is the resting of the heart on God."[27] This faith was to express itself in "observance" (*observantia*) which is "the submissive performance of the will of God for the glory of God."[28] Ames' concern for both parts of the *fides et observantia* dichotomy was stressed throughout his Marrow. But it also led him as it had Perkins before him to write on ethics more fully under the rubric of "cases of conscience." Ames' *Cases of Conscience* (*De Conscientia, et Eius Iure, vel Casibus*, 1622 and 1630) was an expansion of the second part of his *Marrow*. In the opening word to the readers of this work, Ames explained that his guide in this enterprise of casuistry was William Perkins. Ames said that Perkins who "amongst other things which he preached profitably, he began at length to teach, How with the tongue of the Learned one might speake a word in due season to him that is weary....by untying and explaining diligently, Cases of Conscience (as they are called).''[29]

Thus the Ramism of William Perkins was developed explicitly and fully by Perkins' student William Ames. Ames, often referred to as the "learned doctor" of Puritanism had a reputation equal to or surpassing that of his "master Perkins" among those of Puritan persuasion in England, the Netherlands, New England and elsewhere.[30] It is clear that Ames carried on the Ramism he learned from Perkins. In a real measure, then, the Ramist Puritan legacy of Perkins was significantly amplified by the prestige and influence of his student Ames. In this way Perkins' Ramism colored the theological method and understanding of a still wider group of Protestants. A great part of the significance and importance of Perkins' Ramism, therefore, can be attributed to the fact that he passed this Ramism on to his students and particularly to William Ames.

Ames was thus the key figure throught which Cambridge Ramism was disseminated in the seventeenth century. There were, however, other associates of Perkins and the Ramist George Downame whose works indicate that they too had learned Ramist method. One of these was John Downame (d. 1652), younger brother of George Downame. He entered Christ's College in 1589. Later he gained great popularity as an exponent of Puritan theology.[31] One of his major works was *The Summe of Sacred Divinitie First Briefly & Methodically Propounded: And Then More Largly & cleerly handled and explained* (London, 1630). As the title would lead one to guess, this work was constructed by Ramist method. John Downame's *The Christian Warfare* was done the same Ramist way and featured large Ramist charts at the beginning of each of its parts.[32] Downame referred to Ramus as "that great and Christian Logician."[33]

John Smith (or Smyth) entered Christ's College in 1586 and was a Fellow there from 1594-1598. He later broke with the Calvinism of his teachers, however, and separated from the Church of England. He fled to Holland in 1607 with his followers. In 1609 he rebaptized himself and 40 of his disciples. He thus became known as the "Se-baptist." He died in August, 1612. But significantly, the influence of Cambridge Ramism followed Smith despite his separatism. He used Ramist method in structuring his *A Paterne of True Prayer* (London, 1605). This his Ramism did not keep him from withdrawing from the established Church. It offered Smith instead a way to approach the Scriptures.[34]

Thus students of Christ's College while Perkins was in residence there helped perpetuate Perkins' Ramist approach to theology and exegesis. A direct line from Perkins to John Milton can be traced in that William Ames was a tutor to William Chappell who became a Fellow of Christ's from 1607-1634. Chappell wrote *The Preacher* published under his name in 1656. It was originally anonymously published in 1648 as *Methodus Concionandi* and was an adaptation of the Ramist principles for preaching.[35] This work was another link in the development of the fully-developed Puritan plain style sermon method. Chappell in turn was the tutor of John Milton. So the line of association of Perkins' Ramism ran through his students and associates at Christ's College, Cambridge. From these men and other not directly associated with Christ's, Ramist method was wedded to theology and adapted for various purposes, particularly for preaching. Other Cambridge men who were instrumental in this were William Gouge,[36] Thomas Granger,[37] and John Yates.[38] These men, their students and colleagues found Ramism an important tool for their various theological enterprises.[39] Insofar as they learned anything about Ramus from William Perkins, Perkins' own influence and the significance of his use of Ramism can only be considered to have been extended.

B. Theology and Ethics

Part of the impact of Perkins' use of Ramism was in the further spread of the Ramist philosophy through Perkins and his associates. But there were also further dimensions of importance. Ramism became a significant tool for Perkins and fellow Puritans. It did not specifically color their theology itself. Ramus' *Commentariorum* was his only specifically theological work.[40] But after he was converted to Protestantism, Ramus said: "my zeal for logic invaded the realm of religion."⁴¹ Ramus was so convinced of the usefulness of applying his method to religion that he promised: "the person who will have first applied this method to the organization of theology will bring an extraordinary light to illuminate all the parts of theology clearly and brightly."⁴² Yet Ramus' own work in this field has been described as "a rather commonplace statement of Reformed belief" rather than the shining light Ramus expected.⁴³ Ramus' own theology was more in line with Zwingli's than the Calvin's. This was particularly true in his view of the Sacraments. At one point, Perkins criticized Ramus' view of Christ's descent into hell.⁴⁴ So the content of Ramus' theology *per se* was not a significant factor in his influence of Perkins.

A strong similarity between Ramus and Perkins beside their common method was their definitions of theology. Ramus said that theology was "the art of living well" (*bene vivendi*).⁴⁵ Perkins wrote the "theologie, is the science of liuing bleesedly for euer."⁴⁶ Here the parallels are plain and they fit within the large context of Ramus' teachings. For Ramus the purpose of studying an art was to that one might learn to perform that art "well." Thus the study of grammar was to "speak well"; the purpose of geometry was to "measure well." In theology, according to Ramus, one learned to "live well" by its study. Ramus divided his theology into two parts: "doctrine" and "discipline."⁴⁷ Thus he wedded "doctrine" and "life"; "theory" and "practice." It is this two part division of theology that has been called the "Ramist gift of theology."⁴⁸ For "although the conception of theology as faith and observance was already implicit in Calvinism and Puritanism, Ramus and his followers in the name of scientific method made this organization and vocabulary an explicit characteristic of theology."⁴⁹ This pattern was noted throughout the works of Perkins as well. It was characteristic of Puritan Ramists in both England and New England.⁵⁰

The significance of Perkins' adaptation of Ramus at this point was that it permitted him and other Ramist Puritans to preserve the unity of theology and ethics. Perkins wrote long theological treatises. He also wrote long treatises dealing with specific practical or ehtical problems of Christian living. But in both types of works, the dual concern of "right belief" and "right living" were present. For Perkins, proper teaching led to proper action. Conversely; one could not "live well" or act "ethically" unless one's actions were suitably informed by right belief, Perkins always spelled out the ethical application or "uses" of his theological doctrines. Without these Perkins believed theology was of not real value. Perkins always undergirded his exhortations toward action or his resolution of a case of conscience with the theological reasoning that led to his position. This safeguarded his theology on the one hand from becoming purely a rationalistic enterprise with no practical value to the Church. On the other hand, it prevented his religion from becoming a religion for action's sake alone. One was prompted to act or to obey the ethical commands of Scripture, Perkins would say, on the basis of one's clear knowledge of what these commands were and what action should be taken according to the revelation of God. Thus again, "faith" and "works" were one. Both theology and ethics were crucial for Perkins. The interpenetrated each other throughout. Thus William Perkins would be both a master of "systematic theology" *A Golden Chaine; An Exposition of the Symbole* as well as a leading Puritan casuist. Perkins' use of Ramist method strengthened this unity of theology and ethics. Ramist teaching about the nature and goal of an "art" as well as the right ordering and "unfolding" of that art was used by Perkins to emphasize both "right teaching" and "right living."

C. Educational Tool

Ramus had sought educational reform by streamlining logic. His purposes were pedagogical. He wished to present a system whereby all arts could be easily and memorably mastered by students. For him, dialectic was the art of discerning well. The art of dialectic was the theory of discourse while rhetoric was the theory of communicating the results of dialectic to others.⁵¹

Besides producing Ramist theologians, Cambridge University also supplied men who presented Ramus as *the* authority on grammar, arithmetic, and geometry also. An edition of Ramus' *Rudimenta Graeca* (*Rudiments of Greek Grammar*) was published in London in 1581.[52] In London in 1585 *The Rudiments of P. Ramus his Latine Grammar. Englished and newly corrected* was printed and another edition produced by Cambridge.[53] Paul Greaves (fl. 1588-1616), a Cambridge graduate student at Christ's College, published a work entitled *Grammatica Anglicana* in Cambridge in 1594. This was subtitled *ad vnicam P. Rami methodum concinnata*.[54] Ramus' mathematical works made their first appearance in English with the translation published in London in 1590 by Thomas Hood (fl. 1582-1598), a Trinity College, Cambridge graduate, of Ramus' *The Elements of Geometry*.[55]

One of the most important works by a Cambridge Ramist was by William Kempe. Kempe was a Devon schoolmaster who translated Ramus' *Arithmetic* in 1592 but who wrote a work called *The Education of Children in Learning* in 1588.[56] This book was intended to inform parents and schoolmasters alike on a method of teaching logic and rhetoric to children on the basis of the methods of Ramus.[57] Kempe lined out a child's progress yearly until by age 12 the student had studied grammar thoroughly and was ready to tackle logic and rhetoric. Kempe wrote:

> Then shall followe the third degree for Logike and Rhetorike,
> and the more perfect understanding of the Grammar and
> knowledge of the tongues. First the scholler shal learne the
> precepts concerning the divers Sorts of argument sin the first
> part of Logike (for that without them Rhetorike cannot be well
> understood) then shall followe the tropes and figures in the first
> part of Rhetorike.[58]

Kempe approved of Ramus' use of "analysis" and "genesis" as eductional procedures. He also followed Ramus' other suggestions about the content of rhetorical study, logic, and grammar.[59] Kempe referred to Ramus himself only once in this work. He called Ramus "a most sufficient & approued author"; "that worthie ornament of arts & all good learning in our time."[60] Kempe's work along with others, notably Charles Butler's (of Magdalen College, Oxford) *Rhetoricae Libri Duo* (1598) based on Talon's *Rhetorica* became the leading textbooks of Ramism for the education of English youth until the last part of the seventeenth century.[61]

In a sense these developments are just what one should expect of the Ramist system. For it had at its base a quest for "classroom practicality."[62] The principal aim of all discourse was teaching (*doctrina*) for Ramus. As an educational method, Ramus brought simplicity to the heretofore complex subjects of logic and rhetoric. He brought clarity to obscure procedures. To Ramists, the art of logic (the art of discourse) should be within the grasp of every person.[63]

This emphasis of practicality, simplicity, and accessibility was surely part of Ramism's appeal as an educational method to the English Puritans and William Perkins. It has been suggested that one of the "most striking characteristics of the English Puritans was their belief in the value of education as a weapon against the three great evils of Ignorance, Prophaneness and Idleness."[64] Perkins believed that the study of the Arts was "good and lawfull" in the "schooles of learning." The Arts were "warrantable by the word of God, [and] so are they no lesse profitable and necessary in the Church."[65] Perkins encouraged the "joyning" of both religion and philosophy. He argued that

> Religion hinders not humane learning, as some fondly thinke;
> but is a furtherance and helpe, or rather the perfection of
> humane learning, perswading, and proouing, and conuincing
> that, which humane learning cannot. And thus we see how faith
> makes vs to vnderstand.[66]

On the other hand, Perkins claimed that while natural wisdom was a good gift from God, it was not better than "foolishnesse" unless it was united with "heauenly wisdome." The "miserie of this age" according to Perkins was that "men of excellent parts for naturall wisdome, haue no regard to season the same with spirituall wisdome." For Perkins claimed that "though a man had all the wisdome of the world, and by his wit could compasse vpon earth what his heart could wish, yet if he faile in prouiding for true happinesse, all his wisdome is but madnesse."67

In this attitude, Perkins was echoing the sentiments of Calvin. Calvin believed that those who have "tasted the liberal arts penetrate with their aid far more deeply into the secrets of the divine wisdom."68 Calvin believed that human sinfulness makes humans spiritually blind to the light of the divine wisdom and knowledge of God.69 But humanist that he was, Calvin urged and promoted the education process.70 The Academy of Geneva opened in 1559 and drew students from all over Europe.71 Calvin and his followers insisted on the necessity of an educated clergy for the Church.72 They established an educational system in Geneva so that "education was made cheap and compulsory, theoretically within the range of all. No one could escape at least a brush with learning in sixteenth-century Geneva."73 Instruction in the "languages and humanities" was necessary according to Calvin's *Ordinances*, if people are to be able to understand the lectures of those who teach theology. Therefore, "in order not to leave the Church deserted to our children, a college should be instituted for instructing children to prepare them for the ministry as well as for civil government," the *Ordinances* declared.74

The Puritan concern for an educated clergy is well-known. Part of the impetus behind the "prophecying" movements of the 1570's was to increase clergy knowledge of the "art of prophecying" (preaching). The Puritan program submitted to the 1584 Parliament supported a more learned ministry. Reform of the church was linked in the Puritan mind with the expansion of education.75

Further, Puritans favored a more general religious education for all society.76 While they did not have a distinctive program or theory of formal education for moving from grammar school to university, it is fair to say the Puritan leaders of the classical movement such as Chaderton, Perkins, and Greenham, linked the further success of reformation of the Church with the ability to educate the masses of people -- both adults and children.77 This was the important impetus behind the catechisms.78 Catechisms were to instruct their users on the essential facts of faith and to correct the errors into which people might fall. Perkins prefaced his Catechism by listing 32 such errors that "ignorant people" held as common opinions.79 These ranged from highly theological concerns: "That a man eates his Maker in the Sacrament" to warnings about how to spend one's leisure time: "That merrie ballads and bookes....are good to driue away the time, and to remooue heart qualmes." The emphasis throughout Perkins and his colleagues was that if right instruction was given and learned, "right living" according to godliness which was required by God should follow. As Perkins said regarding the purpose of educating children: "the next point of Education of children, is to prouide that they may liue well and lead a godly life."80 The unity of theology and ethics was inextricably bound up with the whole educative and faith-formation process for Perkins.

At its base, this drive for education in Perkins was rooted in his theology itself. This stemmed from his view of "edification." It was made clear in his commentary on Jude verse 20: "But yee beloued, edifie your selues in your most holy faith: praying in the holy Ghost." Perkins saw in this verse "the duty of euery beleeuer, which is to build himself up on his faith."81 Perkins listed six things required to do this: a deep sense of "miserie" about oneself; "knowledge of this doctrine of the Prophets and Apostles"; a "holy memorie, to lay vp the word of God in their heart as in a storehouse"; "faith" to believe the truth and apply it to oneself; a "deeper rooting" of the doctrine to bring comfort; and finally, an "unfained obedience vnto the whole word of God."

From these what is clear is the crucial place that "knowledge" or "understanding" had for Christian believers according to Perkins. He said people must build their faith on Jesus Christ as the foundation. Then they must have "knowledge of this doctrine of the

Prophets and Apostles; for vnlesse it be knowne, it can be no foundation." Perkins said, "Euery particular Christian is to be a practitioner of this duty in his owne person." Knowledge of the Bible and of theology was a duty strictly required of all Christians in Perkins' mind.

Therefore Perkins had to stress the educative duties of the Church and its ministers. They must see that people could understand the doctrine that was preached and taught. For only through understanding would come edification. So a method of teaching that would increase understanding and also help the "holy memorie" of people so they could "lay up the word of God in their heart as in a storehouse" would be important for Perkins. As he said, "He that remembreth not the doctrine of saluation can neuer build vpon it." Thus the Ramist method which could bring theology easily to the mind of everyone was an educational tool without parallel to Perkins. Ramism facilitated teaching and memory. These were two of the most crucial elements for the work of the Church and the ministry according to Perkins.

The Ramist method was a key tool for Perkins and other Ramist Puritans in carrying out their goals for education. Ramism focused on the purposes of pedagogy. It was designed so that any subject or art -- "secular" or "religious" could be communicated simply, clearly, and memorably. Its methodological process was to move from the most general to the most particular elements. This made the teaching clear as one illuminated general truths by concrete examples. Thus it was not surprising that the thoroughgoing Ramism of William Perkins led him to develop fully the "case-study" approach to education through his "cases of conscience."

The Ramist emphasis on practicality and utility struck a responsive chord with a Puritan who was eager to see people instructed in the rudiments of Christianity but also longed to see them translate theological doctrine into ethical behavior in daily living. The developed casuistry of Perkins was the outgrowth of his theological method. Perkins' plan was to apply Ramist principles of theology, Biblical studies, and the problems of Christian living. While Perkins and Richard Greenham had perhaps the widest reputations as "physicians of the soul," other Puritans followed their lead. Men such as William Gouge, Arthur Hildersham, Paul Baynes, and William Ames all practiced casuistry with their friends and others.[52] These particular men were also well-known Ramists.[53] While it may be too much to ascribe the origins of Puritan casuistry to an outgrowth of Ramism as a single source, Ramist method with its "doctrine/life" and "general/practicular" pattern surely was a powerful input into the development of systematized "cases of conscience" among Ramist Puritans such as Perkins and Ames.[54] While "the curing of afflicted consciences" was not new in itself -- ethical thinking and practical advice is also found in Luther, Melanchthon, Calvin, and Peter Martyr -- "what was new was Perkins' collection of these cases in a systematically arranged treatise."[55] Even more significat here is the Perkins' treatise was arranged Ramistically. When later Puritans such as John Owen (1616-1683) and Richard Baxter (1615-1691) dealt with casuistry, the Ramistic framework was gone.[56] Thus it was possible to do casuistry without Ramism. But cases of conscience fit quite naturally into a Ramist styem that wished to offer significant help for the edification of Christian believers by dealing with specific problems facing them.

Thus as an eductional tool, suited to communication, Ramism can be said to have had an important significance for Perkins. Perkins' main sphere of influence was in teaching men who would become parish clergy. Like others of the Puritan classical movement he held firmly to the idea that the Church of England should be one. He did not join the Separatists or identify himself outwardly with those favoring Presbyterian forms of Church government. He represented a moderate Puritansim interested primarily in the pastoral and spiritual renewal of the Church of England.[57] For this renewal to come, clergy must be educated Perkins believed. The laity needed instruction. To do this efficiently and effectively, Perkins turned to the Ramist method in which he himself had been schooled. It promised simplicity, clarity, and memorability. It made the Bible and theology accessible in an easy way to mind of everyone. It was thus the educational tool *par excellence*.

D. Plain Style Preaching

William Perkins has long been labeled the father of "plain style preaching." His *Art of Prophecying* was an extended treatment of homiletics and hermeneutics that was available to and well-used by generations of clergy in both England and New England.[88] In it Perkins spoke of resolving Scripture by collecting doctrines from the Biblical text and then applying these doctrines in various wasy for the purposes of informing, reforming, instructing, and correcting one's hearers.

The Puritan "plain style" as a form of sermon construction has been seen to arise from these views of Perkins, albeit in ";general outline."[89] Perkins lamented those who preached with elaborate rhetorical ornamentations and ostentations displays of human learning.[90] To him, the discourse of the sermon should be fit "both for the peoples understanding, and to express the Majesty of the Spirit."[91] Instead Perkins charged that for his contemporaries: "sermons are not in common reputation learned, neither doe they greatly please the most, vnlesse they be garnished with skill of arts, tongues, and varietie of reading."[92] Yet Scripture itself, argued Perkins, was written in a "style and speech" that is "plaine and simple without affectation, and yet full of grace and maiestie."[93] So the preacher, said Perkins, should preach the same way. Through the preacher the Spirit of God spoke with "plainenesse" and "powerfulnesse."[94] According to Perkins, the minister of the Word of God should speak so that what is said is "plaine, prespicuous, and euident, as if the doctrine were pictured, and painted out before the eyes of men."[95] Perkins said "It is a by-word among vs: *It was a very plaine Sermon.*" Then he added, "I say againe, *the plainer, the better.*"[96]

Three methods of sermon construction have been pointed out as prevalent in the Elilzabethan period. These were: the "ancient" form, using a topical exposition pattern;[97] "the new Reformed arrangement of Doctrine and Uses"; and the "modern style" modeled after the classical form of orations.[98] It was the second of these that Perkins' *Arte of Prophecying* fostered.[99] Basically, a "typical structure" known as the "plain style" sermon arose whereby the sermon proceeded "according to the order of the text, to give Doctrines, Uses, Objections and Answers, marked as such in the margin, with no attempt at the formal symmetry of the classical scheme."[100] Initially the text was "divided" and the doctrines collected. These were the most "general" statements of the Biblical material. "Reasons" explicated the doctrines and finally "uses" or "applications" were made to show the "specific" contemporary significance of the doctrines. Some sermons repeated this three-fold order for each "doctrine"; others put all "doctrines," "reasons," and "uses" together.[101]

The clearest ecclesiastical sanctioning of this method of sermon presentation came in the "Directory for the Publique Worship of God Throughout the Three Kingdoms of England, Scotland, and Ireland" adopted by the Westminster Assembly in 1644. The Westminster Divines said:

> In raising Doctrines from the Text, his care ought to bee, First, that the matter be the truth of God. Secondly, that it be a truth contained in, or grounded on that Text, that the hearers may discern how God teacheth it from thence. Thirdly, that he chiefly insist upon those Doctrines which are principally intended, and make most for the edification of the hearers. The Doctrine is to be expressed in plaine termes....The Arguments or Reasons are to be solid; and, as much as may bee, convincing. The illustrations of what kind soever, ought to bee full of light, and such as may convey the truth into the Hearers heart with spirituall delight....In the Use of Instruction or information in the knowledge of some truth, which is a consequence from his Doctrine, he may (when convenient) confirm it by a few firm Arguments from the Text in hand, and other places of Scripture,

or from the nature of that Common place in Divinity, whereof that truth is a branch.[102]

William Perkins' place in the evolution of the plain style sermon formula has been analyzed.[103] As noted above, MacIlamine's translation of Ramus' *Dialectic* published in 1574 was the first to advocate the use of Ramist method by clergy for the composing of sermons. MacIlamine had urged preachers in the final phase of their sermons to "make thy matter playne and mainfest with familiar examples & authorities out of the worde of God; to sett before the auditor (as euery heade shal geue the occasion) the horrible and sharpe punyshing of disobedience, and the ioyfull promises apparatyning to the obedient and godlie."[104] But Perkins went beyond MacIlmaine here. Perkins dichotomized this step. he divided the order into two types of Application: "Mentall" and "Practicall."[105] By so doing, Perkins played the way for further development of the "doctrine/use" system.

"Mentall" application for Perkins was equivalent to MacIlmaine's "examples & authorities out of the worde of God." It informed the mind. "Practicall" application for Perkins was equivalent to MacIlmaine's posing threats and rewards for his audience. It was for the "life and behavior" of the congregation, according to Perkins. He further dichotomized this into practical applications for "instruction" and "correction."

The "doctrine/use" pattern of Perkins has been noted throughout his works. His Biblical commentaries which had their origins in his sermons were drawn according to Ramist method in terms of their over-all plan. But as Perkins proceeded verse by verse, he most often noted a "doctrine" and then its "use."[106] A variation of this method was seen in Perkins' *How to Live, and That Well*. There Perkins took his text, Habakkuk 2:4 and treated it in three sections: words, meaning, and uses.[107] He defined his text under six initial heads (five questions) as the chart shows. Then he developed the "meaning" of it. This served as the "doctrine" part of his exposition. After that, Perkins spoke of the uses. The "uses" here corresponded with the "application" of the text that Perkins prescribed in his *Arte of Prophecying*. His treatment also displays his use of the dichotomizing of "applications" into "mentall" and "practicall" application. This is seen in his initial dichotomy of "uses" into "our judgment" (mental) and "right way of reformation of our lives" (practical). In the next dichotomy of the "right way of reformation of our lives" this practice was seen again. The branches of this member were "examination" (mental process) and "change" (practical obedience.)

The importance of Perkins' development of MacIlmaine's use of Ramist method here was that it provided clergy with the theoretical framework by which they could stress the need for changes in the lives and behavior of their people in their sermons. Doctrinal truths could be moved from their province as "general truth" derived from a Scripture text and made immediate with "specific" applications to the hearers' experience. To clergy like Perkins who were passionately concerned with the spiritual reformation of the Church of England, this practical application was a must. To Perkins, the ministers' natural duty was to oversee the people. He spoke to them both of the comforts of God in pardoning sin and admonished them to be warned of the future judgments of God on unforgiven sin.[108] Thus doctrinal truths must be much more than general statements. For spiritually-reformed minded Elizabethan clergy doctrines must be translated into the specifics of their hearers' situations because they dealt with matters on which literally depended one's life or death. Theology was bound up with ethics and the sermon was the primary vehicle through which people became aware of how the Word of God was to be applied to their immediate experience. Perkins' two-fold division of "mental" and "practical" application enabled the preacher both to inform his hearers' minds with doctrinal truth (as he perceived it) as well as to make specific the ways in which this doctrine should change a person's life ethically. Perkins' *Arte of Prophecying*, then, made Ramist method far more than merely a communication theory alone. Perkins' development of the method made it possible for him and other Puritan preachers to use the Ramist framework as a springboard for exhortation and action.

Perkins built on the Ramist foundation of MacIlmaine. The "method" had all the benefits Ramus believed were inherent in his system. Movement from general to particular was believed by Ramus and surely by his followers to be the "natural" method of all human minds and thus the most sound method for both teaching and learing. This was important to Perkins and preachers who wished to impart Biblical teaching to their hearers. In addition, this method made "memory" in preaching nearly automatic. Perkins' specific contribution to the art of communication for the preacher was to open up the avenue of appeal to people's wills as well as to their emotions. He provided a theoretical framework by which the preacher could validly impart information as well as instruct and correct the behaviour of his congregation. The goal was to move hearers to act in accordance with what they were instructed to believe.[109] The full development of the plain style formula came later than Perkins.[110] His method, as has been seen, is more Ramistic than invariably a "doctrine/reason/use" pattern though the "doctrine/use" scheme is prominent throughout his *Works*. But in the evolution of the plain style method of preaching, Perkins' adaptation of Ramus played a major role.

E. Art of Memory

The only chapter in Perkins' *Arte of Prophecying* that did not fit into the Ramist structure of the work itself was the chapter on "Memorie in Preaching." The thorough-going use of the Ramist structure as seen above indicates, however, that Perkins found in Ramism the most excellent and facile system for memory. His early *Antidicsonus* as well as his remarks in the *Arte* opposed Bruno's system of artificial memory based on the recall of images. Instead, Perkins urged the preacher to "imprint in his minde by the helpe of disposition either axiomaticall, or syllogisticall, or methodicall, the seuerall proofes and applications of the doctrines, the illustrations of the applications, and the order of them all."[111] If this was done, Perkins argued, one did not have to be careful about the words to use since they would follow naturally. Thus Perkins found in the Ramist system itself a "natural" memory system that enabled the preacher to preach after "the receiued custome for preachers to speake by *heart*."[112]

Perkins divided his advice about sermons into two parts: preparation and promulgation. This division reflected Ramus' distinction between logic and rhetoric. Ramus had rejected memory as a proper concern for rhetoric. By downplaying and dismissing the need for any specific memory system -- particularly any based on the images proposed by Bruno -- Perkins showed his agreement with Ramus. All adornments rhetorically were rejected by both. For Perkins, the preacher's speech was to be "both simple and perspicuous" and he was to show "grauitie in the gesture of the body."[113] The goal was not to construct elaborate discourses through the schema of the classical orators. The preacher did not need to move through the structures of *exordium, narratio, confirmatio and peroratio*. Instead, for Perkins, as Ramist method dictated the structure of a sermon by applying the principles of definition and distribution from general to specific (method), that structure which emerged became the key to organization and memory in the speaker's mind.[114] The "opening" of a Scriptural text and its "analysis" according to "method" furnished the structure for the sermon and that is a way which would be thoroughly impressed in memory for Perkins.[115] One memorized one's sermons by using the literary structure proposed by Ramist logic. As the Ramist William Ames taught: "Method is the art of memory."[116] To Perkins and the Ramists, Ramist method produced the most natural memory system.

The works of Perkins set out above according to their Ramistic structure show how completely adaptable Ramism as a memory system was for the Puritan preacher. These works had their origins for the most part in sermons. When they are charted according to their Ramist structure, the emergent outline shows how complete Perkins' commitment to the Ramist procedure really was. He agreed with Ramus who said that method was "the only way of understanding and memory."[117] This visual memory system permitted Perkins to deal with any theological topic or portion of Scripture.

F. Biblical Interpretation

William Perkins worked with Scripture as a Ramist. He legitimatized the use of Ramist tools of logic by sanctioning "grammatical, rhetorical and logical analysis." There terms have Ramist connotations and must be seen in their specifically Ramistic context. These tools of "analysis" pointed toward the "resolution" of a passage of Scripture. The method Perkins used throughout his writings was the method of Ramus. As the forgoing discussion has shown, he followed the invariable pattern of placing his test in the context of a Biblical book or chapter. Then he defined the words in his text. He began next the process of dividing or "distributing" the parts of his text.

Perkins perceived the task of the Scriptural interpreter to be the same as what Ramus declared the logician's task was: to discover and dispose of matter. The language Perkins used was that of a Ramist exegeting Scripture. As Perkins approached a passage or text he applied Ramist method: defining, dividing, classifying from general to specific.

The result was the Ramist chart. The terms Perkins used as the "branches" or divisions of this chart served as his "arguments" in the Ramist sense of being the "topics" or "commonplaces." These, arranged according to proper method, served as the one-word summaries of divisions so that at a glance one could detect the subject or topic of a division. When one preached, these commonplace heads were the key-words that triggered memory. For Perkins as for Ramus, "the principles of the arts are definitions and divisions; outside of these, nothing."[118]

Perkins' Ramist presuppositions here and his method of working with Scripture stood in marked contrast with the viewpoints and practice of Protestant scholastic theologians. Perkins did not use the Aristotelian categories and language that these writers did. His goal in Scriptural interpretation was to discover the "arguments" already present in his text. The exegete "uncovered" and classified these as Ramus taught. The scholastic method (and the view of logic that Ramus opposed) was based on deductions that could be made "logically" from the texts. The supreme weapon for arriving at truth for the scholastics was the syllogism. By arranging the terms of propositions in proper relationships according to the laws of logic, the scholastics moved from their text to a "logically sound" and proper inference based on the process of deduction. Perkins, Ramus and the humanist tradition in logic did not rely on the syllogism as the master instrument for compelling truth. Ramus taught that the first step in judgment was either "syllogism" *or* method. It was method that was used most. Ramists believed texts could be "unfolded" (as some of their charts literally had to be folded to fit into their books) by the proper method. When this was accomplished, the "interior logic" or thought pattern of the author could be plainly shown. The inner relationships of all parts of the discourse became immediately visible. Perkins never attempted to justify or "prove" the divisions he made. To him these divisions had yielded self-evident axioms, the validity of which was beyond questions. It was only when dealing with "crypticall" places where the "plain meaning" of Scripture was not readily apparent that Perkins resorted to the use of syllogisms.

Some of the implications of the differences between Ramist and scholastic approaches to the Bible have been spelled out elsewhere.[119] In general, however, suffice it to say here that the emphasis by Ramus on practicality and "use" kept Ramist theologians from seeing theology itself and the exegesis of Scripture as a purely theoretical discipline. This was one reason for the attraction of Ramism for English Puritans. A method of doing theology and approaching Scripture that maintained the unity of theology and ethics while providing a theoretical framework whereby the application of Scriptural principles to the lives of people could be part of every sermon was most valuable for those concerned with the spiritual reformation of the English Church. Scriptural interpretation and theological reflection were not ends in themselves for Ramist Puritans. Instead, Biblical exegesis and theological thought served a more vital and practical purpose. They were to function as ways for Perkins' definition of the purpose of theology to be realized: "to liue blessedly for euer."

It is beyond the scope of this study to say much about the political and social implications of Ramism for those who used it as a tool for Biblical interpretation. It is true that "Ramism was closely associated with the Presbyterian movement at Cambridge and the surrounding area during the 1570s and 1580s" and that "the list of Cambridge Ramists reads like a list of the most radical Cambridge Puritans."[120] But it is also true the "Ramism cannot easily be fitted into a left-right spectrum, except in so far as at Cambridge it was clearly associated with the Puritanism of Cartwright and his followers."[121] Ramism "certainly was not a radical force in, say, eighteenth-century Yale."[122] Ecclesiastically, those who used Ramism as a theological method for Biblical interpretation ranged from George Downame who became Bishop of Derry, Ireland, to Perkins who was loyal to the established Church, to John Udall who published a "trenchang presbyterian manifesto" using this method, to John Smith, the separatist "se-baptist."[123] Just as the content of Ramism per se did not color a person's theology proper (whether "Calvinist" or "Arminian"), it did not in and of itself inherently lead to a "radical" or "conservative" social stance.[124]

G. Philosophical Implications

There was a sense in which the Ramist logic was far more than a "method" of approaching a subject. In Perkins' writings the impression is clear that he believed expositions of Scripture could lay bare the very mind of God Himself. The Bible was the Word of God for Perkins. By employing the natural method of Ramus, Perkins and his fellow Puritans who were Ramists believed they could discover the mind of God as revealed in Scripture. The interior logic of the Holy Spirit, who stood behind the formation of Scripture, could be opened to view. The result was the Ramist chart that uncovered all the divisions of a discourse as they stood in relationship to each other.

Behind this view were metaphysical and philosophical implications. This is why Ramism is rightly called a "philosophy." Ramus himself stood in sharp reaction to the Aristotelians. But he nevertheless incorporated elements of both Aristotle and Plato into his logical system.[125]

The metaphysic on which Ramism rested was the "realist" as opposed to the "nominalist" view. This meant that Ramists believed that all concepts are objectively real. Alexander Richardson expressed this when he wrote: "When we define, do we not lay out the thing? *ergo*, if genus were onely mental, it could not give essence: so *causa*, *effectum*, and all other arguments are things real in nature, howsoever my Logick takes hold of them."[126] For the Ramists, logic could take hold of reality.

If this assumption were so, then every object as well as all relations or descriptions of these objects could be represented by an idea in the mind. This was the basis of Ramus' formulations of "invention" and "judgment." The task of the logician was "to lay open to view" the arguments that were present and objectively real. These arguments needed only to be "discovered," not constructed *de novo* by the mind. This was so because for the Ramists, the "arguments" were built into the very fabric of the universe itself.

William Ames, Alexander Richardson, and John Yates most fully developed the teachings of Ramus philosophically. They did this in a system called "technometria" (technology) or "encyclopedia."[127] This system viewed knowledge as a whole. It stood as a prologue or preface to the study of specific branches of knowledge. It provided a blueprint of the whole structure of human learning. The immediate purpose or end of technometria was to enable students to master the liberal arts curriculum quickly and efficiently by preconceiving the general nature and use of each art.[128]

Basically, the Ramists believed that all knowledge was one. God created all and governed all by His own unchangable laws. An "art" according to these men was "the rule of the making and governing of things to their end," said Richardson.[129] As Ames put it: "Art is the idea of *eupraxia* methodically delineated by universal rules."[130] For Ames, *eupraxia* was *bona actio* or "good action."[131] All disciplines of human learning, which to these men were: theology, logic, rhetoric, grammar, mathematics, and physics, proceed by certain right rules. These are established by God. An "art" simply lays out these rules. When grouped together, the arts form a great circular chain or *encyclopedia*. The links of this chain are the individual arts themselves.[132]

Ames and the Ramists taught that only God had true and perfect knowledge of these arts.[133] God's knowledge of the principles of the arts is *archetypal*.[134] Human understanding, however, are only derivative or refracted, i.e. *ectypal*.[135] God in Himself (*ens primum*) is unknowable to humans. But God has created the world and continues to govern it by His providence. He governs it, said Ames, according to the universal rules or precepts of art.[136] The things that God created are the "images" or "copies" of God's understandings ("types") that reflect the divine wisdom. Ames expressed this when he said that human understanding "expresses itself as if it were through a certain refraction in created and governed things that are our understanding's type, from which human understanding is gathered."[137] What Ames asserted here was that "God's own understanding is, though in a broken or refracted way, really 'impressed' or 'stamped' on the things created and governed by Him. It is from this 'type' or divine understanding impressed on things that man's own understanding of the principles of things is derived."[138] The "art" that is one in the mind of God is refracted in created things so that human perception is only able to see a *multiplicity* of rules or precepts.[139] Human understanding is different from God's understanding.[140] God Himself is the proper *subject* of all Art. Thus, "technologia as the theory of art is in some ways the Puritan equivalent of metaphysics, and it occupies the place of metaphysics in the Puritan curriculum."[141]

The "universal rules" that humans discovered as refractions of the mind of God were directed toward the purpose of art: *eupraxia*. Ames used the figure of an artist and an artifact. He argued that there could be no artistic activity performed (*eupraxia*) which did not produce an artifact or *eprattomenon* -- "that which has been made well or done well."[142] By this assertion, Ames laid the foundation for "rejection of the distinction between arts that are theoretical (not concerned with practise and thereby implicitly having no *euprattomenon*) and those which are practical (concerned with doing and making)."[143] For Ramus, Ames, *et. al.* theology was "the most special of all the arts."[144] It like all other arts involves practice (*praxis*), i.e. "good practice" (*eupraxia*) and it too produces an artifact. The artifact is the result (*euprattomenon*) of the art of theology which is expressed in the definitions of theology.[145] These have been pointed out above that for Ames "Theology is the doctrine or teaching of living to God." For Ramus, "Theology is the doctrine of living well." For Perkins, "Theologie is the science of liuing blessedly for euer."[146] Thus the "doctrine/life," "theory/practice" motif so strong throughout Perkins' works was here given its philosophical grounding. Theology was not merely a contemplative science. It was intensely practical for it resulted in action in the lives of those who learned its teachings (*doctrina*). The basic Ramist understanding of "art" undergirded the philosophical as well as theological presuppositions of how the Ramist Puritans viewed and did theology.

Ames went on to teach that through sense perception, observation, induction, and experience, humans could partially recover and reconstruccct the pattern of divine wisdom behind the arts. The principles and precepts can be laid bare because creation is God's ideas that humans must try to understand or interpret. Creation is the *euprattomenon* or "artifact" of God, the supreme artist.[147] By the use of logic, the most general art to Ames, one might be able to interpret nature, history, and particularly the Bible. Ames taught that "analysis of Holy Scripture is accomplished by the precepts of logic rightly applied."[148] This was logic's most important use -- to provide proper analysis of Scripture. For Ames and the Ramists, "by means of logic, the arguments that make up the precepts of faith and morals are to be invented or discovered, and then they are to be ordered by logical method."[149] As the logician (and theologian) worked to derive the self-evidencing axioms that were inherent in the statements of discourse (specifically in statements of Scripture), the task was next to present these in their proper relationships (method). When these were exhibited or "disposed" (*dispositio*) in correct order (from most general to most specific), demonstration (*iudicium*) of truth occurred.

In all this it was assumed that the mind will immediately give its assent to all true propositions which were actually axioms.[150] Thus Scripture quotations alone were sufficient to prove a point since these can function in discourse as self-evidencing axioms. In Perkins and the other Ramists, the Scripture citation is usually all that is needed to support a "division" made. This put Perkins in sharp contrast to the Protestant scholastic theologians such as Zanchi who used Scriptural citations as the first term in a chain of inference. By deductive reasoning, a logical conclusion was reached by these men.[151] For the Ramists, truth was directly, intuitively perceived. For, "the whole Ramist doctrine of judgment adds up to the assertion that proof by reasoning is less important that proof by immediate, direct perception."[152] To them, "syllogistic demonstration emphasized rather than proved the truth of a proposition, and this applied to the methods of immediate inference as well."[153]

Logic for the Ramists was the way reason worked in all art. God worked by synthesis in the creation and governing of the world. Humans worked by analysis in examining the Creator's handiwork. There was thus only "one logic" needed for all types of discourse or verbal communication from poetry, to oratory, to theology. Logic was not to be narrowly confined to certain places "where it was formally engaged in eliciting the points of agreement or disagreement among propositions."[154] It was instead, as Ramus said, "the art of discoursing well." It was the way in which humans could gain some access to the ideas of the divine Mind of God.[155]

William Perkins himself did not write a *technometic* treatise. He did not spell out the speculative underpinnings of the Ramist philosophy he used so extensively. It was left for his student Ames to labor at this task. The closest Perkins came was in his chart prefixed to *A Golden Chaine*. There he distinguished the divisions of "the bodie of holy Scripture." One branch was theology itself; the second the "attendents or handmaidens" of theology.[156] These "attendents" were defined in the typical Ramist way. This indicated Perkins saw them as not merely doing an activity, but as doing that activity "well" (*eupraxia*). Thus he said, Ecclesiasticall discipline was "a doctrine of well ordering the Church." Prophecy was "the doctrine of preaching well." Academie was "the doctrine of gouerning Schooles well" etc. So while Perkins did not spell out the principles that led to his stress on *eupraxia* as related to the whole field of human knowledge, there is no doubt that this Ramist understanding was the basis for his thought. Thus *technometry* was implicit in Perkins. It remained for Ames to spell out this "prologue to Puritan theology" in detail.[157]

Puritan *technometry* and the Ramist philosophy were based on the premise that a coherent and rational scheme of ideas exist in the mind of God. These are the ideas upon which God modeled the world and governs it. To know the structure and order of the universe is to know the mind of God and *vice versa*. The pattern of the world is intelligible and fixed in this view. When humans discern the pattern -- by methodically delineating the universal rules for the nature and use of the arts (*technometry*) -- they can lay hold of enduring truth.[158] *Ectypal* knowledge is at best an imperfect copy of *archetypal* knowledge (because of human limitation and sin). But it is knowledge all the same.[159]

The Ramist philosophy allowed no distinction (as Kant later did) between the *ding* and the *ding an sich*, the "thing" and the "thing in itself." Ramus was fully persuaded that his logic came from nature and the natural mind which had as their common and ultimate source, God Himself. The system of Ramus gave sure results for the Ramist to whom the subject/object problem was not an obstacle.[160] It gave access to truth that did not need to be proved in the scholastic, Aristotelian fashion. Instead, truth need only be asserted. For the Puritans who followed Ramus, Christian doctrine was a series of self-evincing axioms. These axioms were so self-evident as to remove all doubts of their truth.

The philosophy of Ramus provided definitions for and grounded theology's centering focus on God. This was where Puritans who followed Calvin believed the proper emphasis should be. Ramism as adapted by the Puritans did not give specific content to theology as such. The sources of theology for English Puritanism were more from Calvin's Geneva that Ramus' Paris. But Ramism did offer a secure philosophical base for men like Chaderton, Perkins, George Downame, and William Ames. In addition to its preserving the unity of theology and ethics, serving as an educational tool, providing a method for preaching and memory, as well as a method for Biblical interpretation, it gave Puritans a cosmology in which the very integrity of the Deity stood at the heart of the universe. Epistemologically, humans could know the Creator. They could study the orderly universe, and they could pursue "the principall end of our liuing here" which William Perkins said was "to performe seruice to men, and in this seruice to doe homage to God."[61] Ramist Puritans could do these things and come to this knowledge by means of the methods that God Himself had provided. This was the value of the Ramist philosophy for such a man as William Perkins.

APPENDICES

APPENDIX A

A SHORT HISTORY OF LOGIC

The immediate context of Ramus' reform emphases was the type of teaching and curriculum he had been subjected to as a student of the University of Paris. To see the significance of his proposed reforms it is helpful to understand the developments in the history of logic that led to the "scholasticism" which Ramus opposed.

When the universities of Paris and Oxford were formed near the beginning of the 13th century, the teaching of logic was given to the lower faculty of Arts. Since the philosophical works of Aristotle and his Arabic commentators were considered threatening to theological orthodoxy, their study was made by the higher faculty of Theology. The result was that within the Arts faculty, logic continued to develop along the formal and linguistic lines begun in the 12th century.[1] Throughout the late medieval period, the conception of logic given by Hugh of St. Victor (1096-1141) in the 12th century was still followed. He described logic as "the science of language" that arose to give rules and precepts to the habits which were in practice. "The skill of the logical arts," he said, "exhibits methods of argumentation and means of recognizing the arguments as such, so that it can be known which arguments are sometimes true and sometimes false, which are always true, and which always false."[2]

Along with grammar and rhetoric, logic was often described as one of the "linguistic" or "rational" disciplines in the medieval classifications of arts and sciences. Grammar taught how to speak correctly; rhetoric how to speak elegantly; and logic how to speak truly (*vere loqui*) or to make valid inferences.[3] As such, logic was a preamble to science proper. Its field was concepts, not things.[4] Logic formalized the usage of language so that exact distinctions could be made between inferences or "argumentations" that are formally valid and those that are formally invalid. So logic differed from other sciences of language such as grammar, rhetoric, etc. It differed because it had a prescriptive function and thus introduced non-arbitrary factors not found in these other sciences.[5]

This was the understanding inherited from Aristotle. His term for "logical" was "following from the premisses" (*ek tōn keimenōn or analutikos*).[6] In Aristotle's works the term "logical" (*logikos*) usually meant nearly the same as "dialectical," i.e. "probable."[7] Like Hugh of St. Victor was later to do, Aristotle treated logic as an "instrument" (*organon*) of study. It was preliminatry to the examination of each and every branch of knowledge.[8] Aristotle's extended work on the rules and principles of logic show, however, that he was not far from considering logic itself a theoretical discipline.

During the 14th and 15th centuries the standard textbook for the study of logic in the Arts faculties of European universities was the *Summulae Logicales* of Peter of Spain (1210/1220-1277; Pope at the time of his death as John XXI).[9] This work went through more than 150 printed editions. Logicians penned many commentaries on it in the 15th and 16th centuries.[10] Nearly one-third of the three and one-half year Philosophy course at Paris (and other European universities) was given to studying Peter of Spain according to Ramus.[11] Peter's work represented the successful systematization of logic.[12] Ramus as well as other humanists attacked it.[13]

As a commentator on Aristotle, Peter followed the organization of the *Organon*, Aristotle's collected logical works. The first and second books of the *Organon* were the *Categories* (*katēgoriai*) and *On Interpretation* (*peri ermeveias*). These served as preliminary treatises. The *Categories* or "predicaments" (*praedicamentai*) refer to the "terms" or to the way humans thinks about things.[14] In both the *Categories* and his work on the *Topics*. Aristotle listed ten "predicates" or "categories" usually given as: substance (*ousia*); quantity (*poson*); quality (*poion*); relation (*pros ti*); place (*pou*); time (*pote*); situation (*keisthai*); state (*echein*); action (*poiein*); and passion (*paschein*).[15] These classifications were the ways in which being was realized. *On Interpretation* dealt with "propositions" or declarative sentences (*apophantikos logos* or *apophansis*). The *Categories* gave the range of variabilities between a subject and predicate. *On Interpretation* concerned itself with the opposition of propositions (*anthithesis*) whereby some statements were true and some false depending on whether their subjects and predicates were universally or particularly affirmative or negative and how these were related.[16]

In the *Prior Analytics* (*Analutika Protera*), Aristotle dealt with inference and particularly the syllogism, the heart of his logical system. While Aristotle did not "invent" the syllogism, he did "prove" it in more detail than all the other ancients. To him it was the scientific instrument *par excellence*.[17] Aristotle defined "syllogism" as: "a propositional expression (*logos*) in which, certain things having been laid down, something other than what has been laid down follows of necessity from their being so."[18] At its simplest, the syllogism was in the form of an "if....then" proposition with three parts. These were a major premise, a minor premise, and a conclusion.[19] The mneumonic for the "moods of the syllogism" mentioned earlier, against which Ramus protested were ways of remembering the various "types" or "kinds" of syllogisms (*tropos*; *modus* -- mood) and whether they would produce a valid syllogistic inference.[20]

The initial division Aristotle made in his introductory chapter on syllogistic was between "perfect" and "imperfect" syllogisms. He wrote.

> I call that a perfect syllogism which needs nothing other than
> what has been stated to make the necessity evident; a syllogism
> is imperfect, if it needs either one or more components which
> are necessary by the terms set down, but have not been stated by
> the premises.[21]

A "perfect syllogism" then was one where the connection between premises (antecedent) and conclusion (consequent) was self-evident with no need of an additional proposition. Perfect syllogisms are indemonstrable (*anapodeiktoi*) and are now called "axioms" (*axiomata*). Imperfect syllogisms must be proved by use of one or more propositions resulting from the premises but different from then since imperfect syllogisms are not self-evident.[22] In the syllogistic procedure of advancing thought, the movement is from what is known (premises) to what is unknown (conclusion) by means of deduction. The movement is from general to particular.

In the *Posterior Analytics* (*Analutika ustera*) Aristotle wrote of the proof or conditions of knowledge and of what other principles (besides consistency) were needed to establish true logical inferences. In the midst of a complicated discussion of syllogistic demonstration, Aristotle spoke of "three laws" that all scientific propositions must demonstrate if they are to be true.[23]

The first law (*kata pantos*; *de omni*) can be called the law of universal application. This meant that according to Aristotle, the predicate of a proposition must be true for every case of its subject. The second law (*kata auto*; *per se*) referred to the requirement that a predicate of a strictly logical proposition must be harmonious within itself; must join things necessarily related -- cause and effect etc. The third law (*kath' holou*; *de universali*) meant that the predicate of a proposition which is strictly logical, must belong to the subject in a proximate and not a remote relation. These three laws referred to the middle terms of a syllogism so that the logician might demonstrate not only that a thing is so (*demonstratio quia* or *oti*), but also why it is so (*demonstratio propter quid* or *dioti*).[24]

For Aristotle, true scientific knowledge depended not only on knowing a phenomenon but also on knowing its cause. We must "know the cause on which the fact depends as the cause of that fact and of no other, and further, that the fact could not be other than it is."[25] People find themselves presented with facts or data which they know through their senses and for which initially there is no ready explanation. Thus they must proceed from the data at hand to develop principles to explain these data. As Aristotle wrote: "Thus it is clear that we must get to know the primary premises by induction; for the methods by which even sense-perception implants the universal is inductive."[26] Knowledge moves from the particular to the universal; from the particular or specific to the general by induction. Once general principles have been found, a person could work down to the data again by deduction.

Aristotle also made the distinction between what is prior logically in terms of being and what is known first by us. Humans usually know effects before they know causes, he argued, even though in the order of nature a cause would precede an effect.[27] But Aristotle believed too that by possessing the fact, the mind also possessed the principles to explain that fact, albeit in an obscure or implicit fashion.[28] Most of Aristotle's *Posterior Analytics* and much of his other works such as the *Physics* and *Nichomachean Ethics* were devoted to discovering the universal principle he was looking for, based on his sense impressions of the world around him. These principles were both "enunciations" (laws) and "definitions" (single terms divided into their individual elements).

Sometimes Aristotle spoke of one, sometimes of both.[29] But apparently he believed that these principles could be arrived at through the inductive process -- ascending from the experience of singulars to universal principles.[30] At the height of the inductive ascent stood the axioms or "dignities" (*dignitates*) that represented the highest, most unquestionable statements on which conclusions depend.[31]

The next works in the Organon were the *Topics* (*topika*) and *On Sophistical Refutations* (or *Fallacies*; *Peri sophistikōn elenchōn*). This latter work formed an appendix to the *Topics*. The *Topics* was divided into eight books on probable or dialectic truth. In it Aristole defined "dialectic" as the branch of logic which "reasons for opinions that are generally accepted."[32] He meant this to apply in matters where it was not possible to apply strict scientific demonstration to help in the quest for truth. "Dialectic," then, was a logic of "opinion," whereas rigid and formal demonstrations were the logic of "science." But despite these differentiations, the main difference between "dialectic" and "logic" for Aristotle was in the field of application rather than in terms of basic internal structure. This was because the method for determining what the best opinion was in a certain case still resembled the method used for ascertaining truth in science.[33]

In the *Topics*, Aristotle considered his "categories" as a classification of predicates. He enumerated the predicates that all propositions have in a scientific sense. Any statement to be truly scientific according to Aristotle can be classified as a statement of genus (*genos*), definition (*oros*), property (*idion*), or accident (*sumbebēkos*).[34] These Aristotle dealt with in separate books of the work: accident: Books II, III; genus: IV; property: V; and definitions: VI, VII.

The purpose of the *Topics* was "to discover a method by which we shall be able to reason from generally accepted opinions about any problem set before us and shall ourselves, when sustaining an argument, avoid saying anything self-contradictory."[35] Here Aristotle studied the "dialectical syllogism" as distinguished from the strictly "scientific syllogism." Aristotle said that the premises of a dialectical syllogism were not those things that are "true and primary which command belief through themselves and not through anything else" (scientific). Rather they were those "generally accepted opinions....which commend themselves to all or to the majority or to the wise."[36]

In Books II through VII, 3, after Aristotle discussed "the means by which reasonings are carried out," he turned to the "topics" (*topoi*) or "commonplaces." From these the arguments to be used in dialectical reasoning could be drawn.[37] The appendix to the *Topics*, the *Sophistic Elenchi* listed various types of fallacies that a "sophist" or false arguer will use to try to prove his own theses.

Peter of Spain's *Summulae logicales* followed the outlines of Aristotle's *Organon* with some additional tracts added.[38] Peter included a tract on the *loci* or *Topics*. But unlike Aristotle's *Topics*, Peter's treatment did not clearly distinguish his "places" or "sources for argument" from the strictly scientific demonstrations of the *Posterior Analytics*. Some of Peter's "places" corresponded to the scientific demonstrations outlined in Aristotle's *Posterior Analytics* which otherwise did not appear as a separate tract in the *Summulae*. What this meant was that Peter of Spain obscured Aristotle's distinction between "dialectic" that dealt with the logic of opinion or probabilities and the formal, valid scientific logic built around the syllogism. In dialectical (or rhetorical) argumentation, Aristotle said that the best to be hoped for in practical life was to be able to move from a question through a probable argument and on to a probable conclusion. The persuasion (*fides*) which resulted from this type of argument, however, Peter treated as though it produced precise, certain truth.[39]

Other late medieval logicians followed Peter of Spain. William of Ockham (c. 1285-1349) represented the maturity of medieval logic. Jean Buridan (c. 1295-after 1358), Walter Burley (or Burleigh; 1275-after 1349) and Albert of Saxony (c. 1316-c. 1390) also contributed. *The Logica Magna* of Paul of Venice (d. 1429) synthesized the whole tradition and represented late medieval logic in its most advanced form.[40] With the development of terminology and concepts such as the theory of supposition of terms, quantification, and the theory of consequences, medieval logic became increasingly formalistic in character.[41] An example of the heavy cumbersomeness and technicality of the language and thought of this kind of logic comes from Peter of Spain. At the age of 15 or less, a schoolboy was introduced to the *Summulae* and was expected to master:

> The second rule is that a proposition concerning the infinite, taken syncategorematically, is expounded by a copulative whose first part affirms the predicate of the subject taken according to some quantity, a continuous or discrete, and whose second part denies that the predicate is in such a subject according to a determined quantity: as 'Infinite men run,' which is expounded thus: 'Some men run and not so many as to exclude two or three more,' or thus: 'Some men run and as many as you please.'[42]

If the scholastic logic was to prevail, there was need for some symbolic system to rescue these tremendously complicated theorems from total obscurity. The advent of printing brought some relief to the situation. Men such as Jacques Lefevre d'Etaples (1455-1537; Iacobus Faber Stapulensis or Jacobus Faber), Thomas Murner, Pierre Tartaret, John Major, and Juan de Celaya all produced works that sought to simplify the linguistic quagmire by using diagrams.[43] These were chiefly geometrical representations that used variations of the circle. They sought to give visual projections of the relationships indicated in the printed text.[44] This diagrammatic approach was boosted by the ability of the printing press to reproduce multiple copies of even the most elaborate figures, a feat very difficult to accomplish through hand-copied manuscripts.[45] While the geometrical diagrms "simplified" logic to some degree, a more adequate system of "logical shorthand" would have to wait for the development of algebraic rather than geometrical symbols."[46] The outlines of logic prepared by d'Etaples and the others still had to deal, however, with all the complicated apparatus of the present scholastic logic. Any longer-lasting simplification of logic would have to come from a dramatic revolution within the science of logic itself.

A major reform of logic was initiated by the humanists. With its origins in Italy in the second half of the 14th century, the humanist movement spread to northern Europe. The man most acknowledged as having begun this revival of learning as Francesco Petrarca (1304-1374), known most commonly as Petrarch.[47] Petrarch was the first great representative of Renaissance humanism. He displayed an abiding hostility toward the scholasticism and university learning of the late Middle Ages. Though Petrarch was not in the strictest sense a philosopher, he launched broadside attacks against Aristotelian philosophy and logic.

The ancient whom Petrarch admired most was Cicero. From his Petrarch gained information on Greek philosophy.[48] Petrarch became convinced that Plato was the supreme philosopher. He wrote: "Plato is praised by the greater men, whereas Aristotle is praised by the greater number."[49] While Petrarch's Platonism was not a well-developed philosophical doctrine, it was an emphasis that helped pave a way for later humanist translations of Plato and neo-Platonism's prominence in the Florentine Academy.[50]

Yet Petrarch did not hold Aristotle in complete contempt. His knowledge of Aristotle's *Ethics* convinced him that medieval translators and commentators had misrepresented the original thinker. Thus Petrarch influenced a new attitude toward Aristotle. He spurred a study of Aristotle in the original Greek along with other writers and philosophers of the early Greek period. New translations by humanist scholars would replace the Latin translations of the Middle Ages. In this sense Petrarch gave impetus to Renaissance Aristotelianism as well as to Platonism.

But Petrarch made a further contribution. He gave later humanists a picture of ancient philosophic culture that stressed the place of rhetoric. For Petrarch as for Cicero the ideal of eloquence was highly esteemed.[51] Eloquence did not mean harmony and beauty of language. It meant persuasive power. To Petrarch, Cicero was the "prince" of Latin eloquence. Petrarch wrote of Cicero: "He held the hearts of men in his hands, he ruled his listeners as a king."[52] Like Cicero, Petrarch held the union of rhetoric and philosophy as his ideal.[53] The achievement for which all must strive was the effective use of knowledge and wisdom for the guidance of human affairs.[54]

The rhetoric of Cicero inherited by Petrarch and other humanists was made up of five arts. These five combined to produce a communication directed toward a popular audience. The five arts were: invention (*inventio*), arrangement (*dispositio*), style (*elocutio*), memory (*memoria*), and delivery (*pronuntiatio*). Cicero defined these five procedures this way:

> Invention is the discovery of valid or seemingly valid arguments
> to render one's cause plausible. Arrangement is the distribution
> of arguments thus discovered in the proper order. Expression
> [style] is the fitting of the proper language to the invented matter. Memory is the firm mental grasp of matter and words.
> Delivery is the control of voice and body in a manner suitable to
> the dignity of the subject matter and the style.[55]

In Roman times, Quintilian subjected the Ciceronian system to the most extensive analysis. He wrote in his *Institutio Oratoria* near the end of the first century A.D.: "The art of oratory, as taught by most authorities, and those the best, consists of five parts: invention, arrangement, expression, memory, and delivery or action."[56] In the 12 books of this treatise, Quintilian dealt with invention in books 3-6. This was the most troublesome of the speaker's tasks, he said. Quintilian's books summarized previous thinking on the matter. Arrangement was the subject of Book 7. Expression (which needed nearly as much space as invention) was examined in Books 8-10 and the first chapter of Book 11. Memory and delivery were the topics of the last two chapters of Book 11. Behind Quintilian's treatment was the authority of Cicero.

Classically, rhetoric was regarded as the theory of communication between a learned and the ordinary world; between expert and layperson. A common metaphor, with its origins in Zeno, Cicero, and Quintilian, was the picture of logic as a closed fist and rhetoric as an open hand. The "philosopher" dealt with the closely reasoned, scientific "logic" while the orator handled the more open, popular discourse.[57]

The tradition of rhetoric through the Middle Ages flowed in various streams during different time periods. One stream was the subordination of rhetoric to logic. This arose in the 12th century with the advent of the so-called "new Logic." Until then, the West had known Aristotle's works only through the Latin translations of Boethius (c. 480-524).[58] He had translated Aristotle's *Categories* and *On Interpretation* along with the *Introduction* (*Isagoge*) of Porphyry. These were supplemented by essays of his own on categorical and hypothetical syllogisms, dialectical and rhetorical arguments (or "topics") and a commentary on Cicero's *Topics*. This was called the "old logic." In the mid-twelfth century, the rest of the *Organon* became available: *Prior and Posterior Analytics, Sophistic Arguments* and the *Topics*. These came to be known as the "new logic." With the coming of the new logic, "logic" became distinguished from "dialectic" and rhetoric became the counterpart of dialectic.[59] Scientific or demonstrative proof was separated from probable proof. The devices Aristotle used in his *Rhetoric* to persuade began to be used in "dialectic" to form "probable proofs" in

Valla found in Cicero's works on oratory (and in Aristotle's *Topics* and Book II of his *Rhetoric*) the basic techniques for arguing "on both sides" (*in utramque partem*) of an issue "handled excellently." This rhetorical treatment, he argued, provided a viable alternative methodology to the "dogmatic" philosophy of the scholastic logicians.[74] Valla was particularly attracted to Cicero's methods of arguing as developed when he spoke for the Academic skeptics of the first century B.C.[75] Cicero believed there was a strategy or a distinctive *ratio argumentandi* of Academic skepticism that could determine which of two or more alternative beliefs was the more "probably" true. Cicero characterized this method of discourse when he said:

> The sole object of [Academic] discussions is by arguing on both
> sides to draw out and give shape to some result that may be
> either true or the nearest possible approximation to the truth.
> Nor is there any difference between ourselves and those who
> think they have positive knowledge except that they have no
> doubt that their tenets are true, whereas we hold many doctrines
> as probable which we can easily act upon but can scarcely advance as certain.[76]

Cicero saw this method as ideal for an orator since he always dealt with questions over which there was uncertainty. Since the orator and the Academic were aware of their uncertainty, according to Valla, they were closer to wisdom than were the philosophers.[77] Thus Cicero's skeptical dialogues were the supports on which Valla hung his alternative approach to dialectics.

The work Valla produced, *Disputationes dialecticae* (1439) castigated the Aristotelians and borrowed arguments from the Academic skeptics. On the whole its significance was in its movement away from the false certainty of deductive inference and questions of validity. Valla's focus was on other valid inference forms that did not (or would not easily) reduce to syllogisms.[78] Valla recognized the syllogism as any "valid deductive reasoning procedure." But he also dealt with "epicheiremes which were non-deductive strategies of obtaining verisimilitudes and persuasion." By stressing the paradoxical nature and undecidability of some deductive syllogisms such as "if someone dreams that he should not believe his dreams; and he believes his dream; then he should not believe his dreams," Valla (following Cicero) sought to devastate the argument of the rigid scholastics who wished to force assent to the fundamental principle that "every proposition is either true or false."[79]

By 1530 the new logic curriculum developed by humanists like Valla had almost completely triumphed over the programs of the high scholastics. In the years between the first publication of Peter of Spain's *Summulae* (written prior to 1246) and 1530, there were some 160 editions published. Between 1530 and 1639 only six editions were produced.[80] Humanist reforms of dialetic were built around Aristotle's *Topics* (not his other logical works), Cicero's *Topics* and the types of argumentation systematized in Boethius' *On Topical Differences* and *Commentary on the Topics of Cicero* (*In Topica Ciceronis*).[81] These types of argumentation were less formally structured than in traditional logic and were largely non-syllogistic. The humanist curriculum treated most of Aristotle's *Organon* but did not organize its material around the syllogism as medieval logicians did. For the humanists this "center" of logic (the syllogism) was only one way of argumentation among others. Sometimes the syllogism was considered such an "obvious" strategy that it was not thought to have much use in debate at all. The plan to begin the humanist curriculum with the treatment of dialectic via topics - theory and introducing the syllogism only later was a very important maneuver. It was more than just "rearrangement." It signalled a fundamental assumption that there were other forms of inference that held as much interest and validity as the syllogism.[82]

This program for the reform of logic had its fullest expression in the work of the "second way" humanist Rudolph Agricola. Like Valla, Agricola believed that a true reform of learning had to begin with a reform of dialectic. There was something intrinsically wrong with the current scholastic logic that betrayed a deeper erroneous attitude toward the gaining of knowledge as a whole according to Agricola. Both Valla and Agricola were most offended by the dogmatism of the prevailing systems.

Medieval logic was straining the syllogism beyond what the original texts intended. It was putting unbearable stress on the formal syllogistic approach in their view. Each term and proposition was minutely analyzed, valid syllogisms were constructed and checked, ill-formed or invalid syllogisms were detected. Yet the "dialectical arguments" (which were also part of Aristotle's program) and which where highly useful in the work of the orator who sought to persuade -- these were treated with very little consideration in the current logic manuals.[83] The sad result in the humanists' eyes was the weakening of this "disputational dialectic" in favor of very highly-technical skill with syllogistic.

Humanists believed that this perspective was too narrow. The scholastics did not account for the very successful argumentation used quite frequently by Cicero and particularly by Plato. According to the scholastics, Plato had no logical method at all.[84] Thus came the disillusionment of Valla and Agricola with high scholastic methods. But beyond this, the dogmatism of contemporary logic made the matter of distinguishing truth from falsehood a purely linguistic one. If the premises were checked, the syllogism properly formed, then "truth" was guaranteed. But the humanist heritage found the road to truth much more uncertain. Classical rhetoricians had developed methods through which both sides of a question could be presented plausibly before ultimate assent was given. To Valla and Agricola, the reigning logic was flawed because its dogmatic stance made the truth too simple. What was needed was an "undogmatic dialectic" built around topical rather than formalistic syllogisms.

German humanists as well as Erasmus, Melanchthon, and Ramus all acknowledged a debt to Agricola for his reforms of logic.[85] Agricola was born in the Low Countries. He studied law at Erfurt and Cologne. In 1468 Agricola went to Italy to continue his legal studies at Pavia and Ferrara.[86] There he imbibed the humanist tradition of linguistic and textual studies based on Cicero and Quintilian (though by this time Valla was dead). Before Agricola left Italy, he began work on his *Dialectical Invention in Three Books* (*De dialectica inventione libri tres*). He finished this work in Germany around 1479.

As the title indicated, Agricola's work was divided into three books. Dialectical *loci* or "places" were treated in Book I. The nature and use of dialectic was the subject of Book II. Book III treated creating the "effect" (*de effectibus*), expansion (*amplificatio*) and condensation of speech, facility (imaginative activity), arrangement of material, parts of oration, order of questions and arguments and the application and practice of dialectic (*de usu et exercitatione*).[87] As these subjects indicate, Agricola perceived "dialectic" in a wide and broad sense. To him it was practically equal to communication or "discourse" itself. The strong, practical bent of his handling of "invention" was evident too. For him and his humanist colleagues, dialectic must reflect real-life situations and must be able to be taught accordingly.

Agricola's initial definition of dialectic governed the way this art was perceived. He defined it as "the art of discoursing the probability of any subject, insofar as the nature of the subject is capable of creating conviction."[88] As with Peter of Spain, however, who approached logic through the scholastic mold, the distinctions between scientific demonstration and probable argumentation tended to blur in Agricola's writings. Earlier, St. Thomas Aquinas (c. 1225-1274) had sharply distinguished the various logics. In his commentaries on Aristotle's *Organon*, Aquinas had differentiated among scientific demonstration, a logic of probability (used for debate), a logic of the probably rhetoric (as a guide for practical decision or action), a logic of poetry, and a logic of false probability (sophistic).[89] Yet the technicalities of the scholastic philosophy as taught in universities made such carefully elaborated distinctions hard to maintain. The pattern upheld by Peter of Spain that there was but one logic called a "dialectic" that was "the art of arts and the science of sciences" was the pattern that prevailed.[90]

But whereas Peter's logic had given center stage to formal scientific demonstration, Agricola saw dialectic as ranging throughout all discourse. He did break with the luminaries with the current scholastic logic that betrayed a deeper erroneous attitude toward the gaining of knowledge as a whole according to Agricola. Both Valla and Agricola were most offended by the dogmatism of the prevailing systems.

Medieval logic was straining the syllogism beyond what the original texts intended. It was putting unbearable stress on the formal syllogistic approach in their view. Each term and proposition was minutely analyzed, valid syllogisms were constructed and checked, ill-formed or invalid syllogisms were detected. Yet the "dialectical arguments" (which were also part of Aristotle's program) and which where highly useful in the work of the orator who sought to persuade -- these were treated with very little consideration in the current logic manuals.[83] The sad result in the humanists' eyes was the weakening of this "disputational dialectic" in favor of very highly-technical skill with syllogistic.

Humanists believed that this perspective was too narrow. The scholastics did not account for the very successful argumentation used quite frequently by Cicero and particularly by Plato. According to the scholastics, Plato had no logical method at all.[84] Thus came the disillusionment of Valla and Agricola with high scholastic methods. But beyond this, the dogmatism of contemporary logic made the matter of distinguishing truth from falsehood a purely linguistic one. If the premises were checked, the syllogism properly formed, then "truth" was guaranteed. But the humanist heritage found the road to truth much more uncertain. Classical rhetoricians had developed methods through which both sides of a question could be presented plausibly before ultimate assent was given. To Valla and Agricola, the reigning logic was flawed because its dogmatic stance made the truth too simple. What was needed was an "undogmatic dialectic" built around topical rather than formalistic syllogisms.

German humanists as well as Erasmus, Melanchthon, and Ramus all acknowledged a debt to Agricola for his reforms of logic.[85] Agricola was born in the Low Countries. He studied law at Erfurt and Cologne. In 1468 Agricola went to Italy to continue his legal studies at Pavia and Ferrara.[86] There he imbibed the humanist tradition of linguistic and textual studies based on Cicero and Quintilian (though by this time Valla was dead). Before Agricola left Italy, he began work on his *Dialectical Invention in Three Books* (*De dialectica inventione libri tres*). He finished this work in Germany around 1479.

As the title indicated, Agricola's work was divided into three books. Dialectical *loci* or "places" were treated in Book I. The nature and use of dialectic was the subject of Book II. Book III treated creating the "effect" (*de effectibus*), expansion (*amplificatio*) and condensation of speech, facility (imaginative activity), arrangement of material, parts of oration, order of questions and arguments and the application and practice of dialectic (*de usu et exercitatione*).[87] As these subjects indicate, Agricola perceived "dialectic" in a wide and broad sense. To him it was practically equal to communication or "discourse" itself. The strong, practical bent of his handling of "invention" was evident too. For him and his humanist colleagues, dialectic must reflect real-life situations and must be able to be taught accordingly.

Agricola's initial definition of dialectic governed the way this art was perceived. He defined it as "the art of discoursing the probability of any subject, insofar as the nature of the subject is capable of creating conviction."[88] As with Peter of Spain, however, who approached logic through the scholastic mold, the distinctions between scientific demonstration and probable argumentation tended to blur in Agricola's writings. Earlier, St. Thomas Aquinas (c. 1225-1274) had sharply distinguished the various logics. In his commentaries on Aristotle's *Organon*. Aquinas had differentiated among scientific demonstration, a logic of probability (used for debate), a logic of the probably rhetoric (as a guide for practical decision or action), a logic of poetry, and a logic of false probability (sophistic).[89] Yet the technicalities of the scholastic philosophy as taught in universities made such carefully elaborated distinctions hard to maintain. The pattern upheld by Peter of Spain that there was but one logic called a "dialectic" that was "the art of arts and the science of sciences" was the pattern that prevailed.[90]

But whereas Peter's logic had given center stage to formal scientific demonstration, Agricola saw dialectic as ranging throughout all discourse. He did break with the luminaries of the past -- Cicero, Quintilian, and Boethius at one important point. Agricola affirmed that "there are no places of invention proper to rhetoric."[91] Cicero *et. al.* were wrong. They had treated "places" (topics) in rhetoric. For Agricola there was no proper difference between invention (*inventio*) and style (*elocutio*). Style was the orator's concern. But without defining what this style or "ornate speech" (*ornate dicere*) was, Agricola decreed that the *loci* belonged only to dialectic.[92]

The significance of Agricola's view here was to sever the relation between rhetoric and dialectic. In the traditional medieval scheme, the type of logic employed was (theoretcially) determined by the end toward which the discourse moved or its purpose. In scientific discourse, scientific demonstration was used. In discourse (such as debates) where a dialectical yes and no (*sic et non*) was called for, dialectical logic or the "logic of opinions" (Aristotle) was to be used. In speeches or orations where the final goal was persuading an audience, rhetorical logic and its devices were supposed to be employed. So while Aristotle had *loci* in both his dialectical work (*The Topics*) and his rhetorical work (*The Art of Rhetoric*), these *loci* took a dramatically different orientation in medieval logical theory. The dialectician would move through probabilities to truth while the rhetorician, also concerned with truth, would orient his speech primarily toward including action or reaction on the part of his listeners.[93]

With Agricola an important shift occurred. For him all discourse was to have the same purpose. That purpose was to teach. Agricola wished to eliminate the distinction between scientific demonstration and a logic of probabilities (dialectic). Rhetoric was to be concerned only with ornamentation for him. The *loci* of rhetoric were to be assimilated with dialectic into a general art of discourse. The objective of this art of discourse was to teach. Agricola wrote: "Sometimes we teach in order to make a person understand [science], but at other times just to persuade him [rhetoric].'"[94] Whenever a speaker moved a listener to action, teaching had occurred since by means of this discourse what had previously been unknown has now become known."[95] It was this end for which all discourse existed.

As a result of this view, Agricola naturally stressed *loci* more than he did the traditional Aristotelian "categories." These "commonplaces" were the headings or key notions from which one could find information to help in inventing or framing a discourse on a particular subject. The *loci* helped to answer questions or treat certain themes.[96] The *loci* were essential in Agricola's view of discourse. The goal of all discourse was teaching. Since teaching moved from the "known to the unknown" and since *loci* were things that were known, therefore teaching or instruction (and thus discourse) can occur by means of the *loci*. In this light, Agricola's view of language as essentially instructional in nature led him to stress the "topics" or *loci* in a very prominent manner.

For Agricola, *loci* were informally defined as "representations," "shared likenesses," and "middle terms." Formally he spoke of them as "nothing else but a certain shared characteristic of a thing [*communis quaedam rei nota*], by observing which all that is probable about a given thing can be discovered."[98] Traditional topics included such items as: definitions, genus, species, wholes, parts, comparisions, opposites, etc. When one needed something to say on a subject, to argue a case, or even to give an eulogy, these headings or loci gave invaluable help for deciding what to say and how to proceed. Agricola's goal was to rethink the ancient lists of topics, redefine, rename and rearrange them so they might be more easily taught and remembered. In later times some authors prided themselves on how many topics they could invent. Others gloried in how few they named. Agricola's contribution was not that he fundamentally altered the topics. But rather he streamlined their arrangement. From the nearly 340 now considered to be found in Aristotle, Agricola named 24.[99]

Agricola's views of the *loci* was connected to the understanding he had of the parts of dialectic. For him dialectic had two parts. First was invention (*par inveniendi*) which was "the part consisting in thinking out the middle term or argument." This mad a conclusion possible. Judgment (*pars iudicandi*), the second operation, was that "by which we judge similitudes.'"[100] The *loci* were important to Agricola in preparing and criticizing discourse through the following ways.

First, Agricola used *loci* as tools of analysis for the discourse of others. He wrote:

> What our order advises as of first and chief importance is that whoever desires to invent by means of the places must have them carefully and exactly learned. This knowledge of the places consists chiefly of two things: first, that one possess a clear and thorough knowledge of the number and nature of the places....The second essential for his knowledge of the places, and the more difficult task, is to refer arguments provided by the authors to their appropriate places.[101]

Secondly, Agricola used the *loci* in the process called "taking one's subject through the places" (*epiphrasis*). For example, with the word "man" Agricola said:

> Thus would we undertake to decribe man. First, we say from the place of definition that man is a rational animal. then, because the genus of man is animal, we say that man is an animal. For species we take everything into which we said in the previous book that man could be divided....And we say that a learned man is a man and an unlearned man is a man, and we could go in this way through all the differneces of the division....Next come the properties of man....[102]

Thirdly, Agricola argued that commonplaces could be used in the development of argument if the results of the *epiphrasis* process of the term in the subject was compared with the predicate term of the statement. As an example of this, Agricola dealt with the question: "Ought a philosopher to marry?" His process was as follows:

> First we will examine correspondences through all the places. Taking the definition of a philosopher as 'one who examines things human and divine with a concern for virtue,' let us compare it one by one with those things which were drawn fron the word 'wife.'...The definition of wife will not provide much, except for that part of the definition of philosopher ('concern for virtue') as it relates to part of the definition of wife ('for the sake of having children'). For interest in children seems to agree with concern for virtue, since it seems a duty of virtue to beget children.[103]

Agricola thus claimed that the places were crucial for meaningful communication. He formally defined the *loci*, classified them, and explained how to use them in the invention prong of his two-fold division of dialectic.

Agricola's division of logic into invention and judgment went back to Cicero and the rhetorical tradition rather than the strict logical tradition. In the second book of his *Topics*, Cicero divided dialectic this way with the first part (invention) decribed as being the *Topics* themselves. The second part taken alone Cicero called "dialectic" although others referred to it as "making judgment" or *critica* or disposition (*dispositio*).[104] Yet both Agricola and Cicero failed to produce extended treatments of their second part of logic. They did not expound on "judgment" or how the arguments developed in invention (through the *loci*) should be put together or arranged. Aristotle has used the first seven books of his *Topics* to treat the *loci* and only a section of the eighth and last book to show how to set up an argument. Ramus was to criticize Agricola for his neglect in filling out his second half of logic.[105] It was primarily with the *Topics* that both Agricola and Ramus dealt. In treatments of invention, though, Agricola fundamentally altered the usual scholastic tradition. Scholastic logic in the categorical tradition of the Aristotelians was built around simple terms, propositions and the argumentation process. The developed doctrine of the syllogism was at its very core. In place of this, Agricola proposed a dialectic of two parts -- invention and judgment, terms rooted in ancient rhetoric which had to do with persuasion. As such, humanist logical reforms were strongly oriented around the classical topical heritage.[106]

APPENDIX B

A SHORT HISTORY OF THE ART OF MEMORY

The art of memory has a long and complicated history.[1] It had its origins in the orators of classical antiquity who devised techniques of "artificial memory" to help improve their memories so they could deliver long speeches accurately. The general principle of these mnemonic practices was to learn first a series of *loci*. Most usually these were of the architectural type. Quintilian most clearly laid down this approach when he formed a series of *loci* in the memory by remembering a building with all its rooms and the statues and ornaments that decorated the rooms. Then images could be used as "anchors" or "weapons." One simply associated the images in one's speech with the various rooms and their decorative objects. When the speech was delivered, one move mentally through the rooms and the objects (literally the "places") and simply recalled what images from the speech were lodged there. This method assured the orator that his points would be remembered in the correct order since this order was fixed by the sequence of moving through the places of the building.[2] Various other rules were added to insure accuracy.

Once the *loci* had been formed and placed securely in the memory, they could be used over and over again to remember different material. The sequence of ideas thus would never be a problem. The images one used to connect the *loci* with the speech at hand were to be as strong as possible. The author of *Ad Herennium* urged this. The strongest images for memory were those that were active rather than vague. The author went on to say that the similitudes will be as striking as possible if

> we assign to them exceptional beauty or singular ugliness; if we ornament some of them, as with crowns or purple cloaks, so that the similitude may be more distinct to us; or if we somehow disfigure them, as by introducing one stained with blood or soaked with mud or smeared with red paint, so that its form is more striking, or by assigning certain comic effects to our images, for that, too, will ensure our remembering them more readily.[3]

Thus the author of *Ad Herennium* appealed to the arousal of emotional effects to insure a vital, accurate memory.

In the Middle Ages, scholastic philosophers and theologians such as Albert the Great and Thomas Aquinas used Aristotle's comments on memory to provide a psychological and philosophical basis for what they learned from the memory system of the *Ad Herennium*.[4] Aquinas' theory of memory touched base with Aristotle at the point of his theory of knowledge. Both assigned great importance to the imagination. Aristotle expounded his theory of knowledge in his *De anima*. In that work he argued that sense perceptions are first treated by the faculty of imagination; images are formed and these become the material for the intellectual faculty. Between perception and thought stood the imagination. Aristotle wrote: "the soul never thinks without a mental picture"; "no one could ever learn or understand anything, if he had not the faculty of perception; even when he thinks speculatively, he must have some mental picture with which to think."[5]

Aquinas treated artificial memory under the virtue of prudence in his *Summa Theologiae*.

There he adopted Aristotelian epistemology as his own in commenting on Aristotle and memory when he wrote that "man cannot understand without images (*phantasmata*); the image is a similitude of a corporeal thing, but understanding is of universals which are to be abstracted from particulars."[6] Memory for Aquinas took the images of sense impressions (it thus belonged to the same part of the soul as the imagination) and used them in the intellectual part of the soul for the thinking (and remembering) process. The *loci* used were a concession to human weakness in that it is easier to remember images from the senses than "subtle and spiritual things" without an image, according to Aquinas. He wrote:

> It is necessary for reminiscence to take some starting-point, whence one begins to proceed to reminisce. For this reason, some men may be seen to reminisce from the places in which something was said or done, or thought, using the place as it were as the starting-point for reminiscence; because access to the place is like starting-point for all those things which were raised in it. Whence Tullius [the perceived author of *Ad Herennium*] teaches in his Rhetoric that for easy remembering one should imagine a certain order of places upon which images (*phantasmata*) of all those things which we wish to remember are distributed in a certain order.[7]

Thus Aquinas grounded the *loci* of artificial memory in the Aristotelian theory of knowledge.[8]

In the Renaissance, the art of memory became especially prominent in the occult tradition. The memory rules of Aquinas were carefully Aristotelianized and rationalized. They sought the exclusion of magic at all costs. Aquinas stressed the devotional and ethical use to which memory might be put. He had dealt with it under the virtue of prudence. But along with the classical development of the art of memory through the centuries had also run another strand. This was the *Ars Notoria*, an art of memory associated with magic. It attributed its origins to Apollonius or sometimes Solomon.[9] The practitioner gazed at diagrams or figures obscurely marked (called *notae*) while magical prayers were recited. Through this the practitioner hoped to gain knowledge or memory of all arts and sciences. Different *notae* were for different disciplines. Aquinas had severely condemned this magic and carefully expounded his rules to avoid it.[10] In a sense this occult tradition and its connection with memory represented a profound change in attitude between the Middle Ages and the Renaissance towards the imagination. Aquinas viewed it (in the Aristotelian tradition) as a lower power that was used in memory. Use of the imagination to him was a concession to human weakness in that corporeal similitudes has to be used before proceeding to the higher level of intellectual thought. Imagination was thus crucial if humans were to maintain a spiritual outlook on the world since God communicated through nature as the human mind reflected on nature around it. The Renaissance occult tradition, however, elevated imagination into the human's highest power. Through it, one could grasp an intelligible world beyond mere appearances. Those who held this view believed that significant images could thus be appropriated.[11]

APPENDIX C

THE SPREAD OF RAMISM

For the most part until after his death, the works of Peter Ramus were published only in France. After 1572, however, Ramism penetrated other European countries, principally Germany, the British Isles, Switzerland, Alsace, and the Low Countries. Its presence in North America was chiefly in New England.[1]

Germany produced notable Ramists who applied the diagrammatic approach to knowledge to nearly all the arts and sciences. Johann Heinrich Alsted (1588-1638), the father of modern encyclopedism, constructed compends of all subjects according to the Ramistic dichotomous system.² Johannes Piscator (1546-1625) a German Protestant theologian sought to do a "logical analysis" in Ramist fashion on every book of the Bible. By doing this he wished to separate clearly the real "arguments" of the book as he called them, from all the rhetorical trappings with which the book was decorated.³ Amandus Polanus von Polansdorf (1561-1610) was a great systematizer of Calvinist theology. Bartholomew Keckermann (1571-1608) systematized theology along with other sciences and also history.⁴ Johannes Althusius (1557?-1638) methodized politics. While some of these men followed the Ramist method less closely than others, all still tried to lay out their material according to the basic Ramistic principle of: definition, division, division....⁵ Other prominent writers in this vein included Johann Thomas Freige (1543-1583), Andreas Libau (or Libavius; ca. 1550-1616), and Jan Amos Komensky (Comenius; 1592-1670).⁶

Holland was also a center for the diffusion of Ramism.⁷ Of particular strength there were the Puritan Ramists who settled there after fleeing England. The foremost theologian of these was William Ames (1576-1633). Ames was Professor of Theology at Franeker after having been a student of William Perkins' at Christ College, Cambridge as well as a Fellow there.⁸ Earlier, the Ramist works of Dudley Fenner (1558?-1587) were printed at Middleburg.⁹ The Dutchman Rudolph Snel van Roijen (Snellius) developed Ramism along mathematical rather than dialectical or rhetorical lines.¹⁰

APPENDIX D

CHRONOLOGY OF PERKINS' WORKS

The collected *Works* of William Perkins in the three-volume edition published between 1616-1618 total 2736 pages. Many of Perkins' treatises had long lives of separate publication before and after they were gathered into this collection. Between 1600 and 1635 there were at least 11 editions of the collected writings published with differing degrees of inclusiveness.¹

For the most part it is not difficult to date Perkins' writings. Many of the include a "Dedication" or "Epistle to the Christian Reader" signed by Perkins and dated. Other sources disclose the first printings of other works.² In yet others, internal evidence makes it possible to ascertain the time of the writing.³ Most of Perkins' posthumously published works were apparently written in the latter portion of Perkins' career.⁴

Given these means of dating, it is possible to construct a chronology of Perkins' works. The sequence in each instance may not be exact. But every indication is that the picture drawn is accurate. This chronology follows:

       1584 -- *Antidicsonus and Admonituncla ad Alexandrum Dicsonum*
       1585 -- *Resolution to the Countrey-Man*
               Four Great Lyers
       1586 -- *Treatise Tending Unto a Declaration*
       1587 -- *A Fruitful Dialogue*
       1588 -- *Foundation of the Christian Religion*
       1590 -- *Armilla Aurea* (1591 -- *A Golden Chaine*)
       1592 -- *A Case of Conscience*
               Exposition of Lord's Prayer
               Direction for the Government of the Tongue
               Prophetica (1606 -- *The Arte of Prophecying*)
       1593 -- *Two Treatises: Nature and Practice of Repentance*
                         Combat of Flesh and Spirit
       1595 -- *Exposition of the Symbole, or Creed of the Apostles*
               A Salve for a Sick Man
               Commentary on Revelation

1596 -- *A Discourse of Conscience*
True Manner of Knowing Christ Crucified
1597 -- *Reformed Catholike*
A Grain of Musterd-Seede
A Digest or Harmony
1598 -- *De Praedestinationis modo et ordine*
(1606 -- *Manner and Order of Predestination*)
1601 -- *The True Gaine*
A Warning against the Idolatrie of the Last Times
How to Live and That Well
1602 -- *A Treatise of God's Free Grace*

Posthumous Publications

1603 -- *A Treatise of Vocations*
Epieikeia
1604 -- *Exposition of Galatians*
Forged Catholic
Commentary on the Temptations of Christ
1605 -- *Of the Calling of the Ministerie*
1606 -- *Cases of Conscience*
Epistle of Jude
Treatise of Man's Imaginations
1607 -- *Commentary on Hebrews 11*
1608 -- *Commentary on the Sermon on the Mount*
Discourse on the Damned Art of Witchcraft
1609 -- *Oeconomie*

NOTES TO INTRODUCTION

¹ See Samuel Eliot Morison, *Harvard in the Seventeenth Century*, 2 vols. (Cambridge, Massachusetts: Harvard University Press, 1936); *The Founding of Harvard College* (Cambridge, Massachusetts: Harvard University Press, 1935); Perry Miller, *The New England Mind The Seventeenth Century* (1939; rpt. Boston: Beacon Press, 1594); hereafter cited as *NEM*. Cf. Hardin Craig, *The Enchanted Glass: The Elizabethan Mind in Literature* (New York: Oxford University Press, 1936).

² Miller writes of the Puritans: "We may say that they derived their ideas from the Bible, from Augustine and Calvin, Petrus Ramus and William Perkins," *NEM*, p. 7.
But a serious warning about Miller's work must be noted at the outset. In the "Foreward" to his *NEM* he wrote: "I have taken the liberty of treating the whole literature as though it were the product of a single intelligence, and I have appropriated illustrations from whichever authors happen to express a point most conveniently," vii. Yet this method is a form of what David Hackett Fischer has called the "idealist fallacy." This is when the thought of one person is made to stand for that of a varied group. Fischer wrote of Miller's method: "Many magnificient insights accompanied this impressionist method. But a serious flaw was embedded in it. New England Puritanism was an entity, but it was not an intellect. It was a cluster of many thousands of intellects. There were important normative patterns of behavior, but also a wide range of significant variations," *Historians' Fallacies Toward a Logic of Historical Thought* (New York: Harper & Row, 1970). p. 197. The same warning may be raised with regard to Miller's treatment of Ramism. It is detailed and presents a coherent picture. But, as has also been said, Miller's work "makes it possible to talk Ramism without reading Ramus himself," Walter J. Ong, *Ramus, Method, and the Decay of Dialogue* (1958; rpt. New York: Octagon Books, 1974), p. 4; hereafter cited as *Ramus*. For another criticism of Miller's handling of Puritanism see George M. Marsden, "Perry Miller's Rehabilitation of the Puritans: A Critique," *Church History*, XXXIX, No.1 (March 1970), 91-105.

³ Peter Sharratt, "The Present State of Studies on Ramus," *Studi Francesi*, XLVII-XLVIII (1972), 202. Ong has written more on Ramus than has anyone else. His major works are *Ramus* and the *Ramus and Talon Inventory* (Cambridge, Massachusetts: Harvard University Press, 1958); hereafter cited as *RTI*.

⁴ Ong, *Ramus*, p. 4.

⁵ Ong, *Ramus*, p. 5

⁶ See William Haller, *The Rise of Puritanism* (1938; rpt. Philadelphia: University of Pennsylvania Press, 1972); M.M. Knappen, *Tudor Puritanism* (1939; rpt. Chicago: University of Chicago Press, 1970); Louis B. Wright, *Middle-Class Culture in Elizabethan England* (1935: rpt. Ithaca, New York: Cornell University Press, 1958); and his "William Perkins: Elizabethan Apostle of Practical Divinity," *Huntington Library Quarterly*, III, 2 (1940), 171-196. Jan Jacobus van Baarsel published his dissertation as William Perkins. *Ene bi jdrage tot de kennis der religieuse ontwikkeling in Engeland, ten tijde van Koningin Elisabeth* (The Hague: H.P. De Swart & Zoon, 1912).

⁷ Haller, *Rise*, p. 64.

⁸ "Puritanism" may be defined simply as "a movement within the Church of England that sought to reform the Church to a more biblical pattern," Robert S. Paul, "The Accidence and The Essence of Puritan Piety," *Austin Seminary Bulletin*, XCIII, No.8 (May 1978), 37 note 8. Puritans were also known as "Precisians" or "the Precise" because "they were

those who wanted the worship, and later the order of the Church of England to be simplified and to conform more exactly to the pattern they found in the New Testament," Paul, p. 8. Paul continues: "It was primarily a movement that arose in the English Church during the reigns of Mary (1553-8) and Elizabeth I (1558-1603), which was suppressed under the first two Stuart kings (1603-42), which came to power during the Civil War, the Commonwealth and the Protectorate, and which was reduced again to Nonconformity and into disenfranchized and persecuted minority status by the restoration of the Stuart monarchy in 1660," p. 8. Cf. the definitions by Basil Hall, "Puritanism: the Problem of Definition," *Studies in Church History*, ed. G.J. Cuming (London: Nelson, 1965); Christopher Hill, "The Definition of a Puritan," *Society and Puritanism* (New York: Schoken Books, 1964), pp. 13-29; J.I. Packer, "Puritanism as a Movement of Revival," *The Evangelical Quarterly*, LII, No.1 (January-March 1980), 2; Patrick Collinson, *The Elizabethan Puritan Movement* (1967; rpt. London: Jonathan Cape, 1971), p. 27; hereafter cited as *EPM*. Haller, *Rise*, p. 3 etc.

[9] Keith L. Sprunger, *The Learned Doctor William Ames* (Urbana, Illinois: University of Illinois Press, 1972); "Ames, Ramus, and the Method of Puritan Theology," *Harvard Theological Review*, LIX (April 1966), 133-151; hereafter cited as "Method." Cf. the "Introduction" by John D. Eusden in William Ames, *The Marrow of Theology*, trans. and ed. John D. Eusden (Boston: Pilgrim Press, 1968) and Lee W. Gibbs, *William Ames Technometry* (Philadelphia: University of Pennsylvania Press, 1979); hereafter cited as *WAT*.

[10] Miller, *NEM*, p. 339.

[11] Miller, *NEM*, p. 339.

[12] Wilbur S. Howell, *Logic and Rhetoric in England, 1500-1700* (1956; New York: Russell & Russell, 1961), p. 207; hereafter cited as *L&R*.

[13] Howell, *L&R*, p. 207.

[14] H.C. Porter, *Reformation and Reaction in Tudor Cambridge* (1958; rpt. Hamden, Connecticut: Archon Books, 1972), p. 225 note 8.

[15] Ian Breward, "The Life and Theology of William Perkins 1558-1602," Diss. University of Manchester, 1963, pp. 19-20; hereafter cited as *L&T*. Cf. *The Work of William Perkins*, ed. Ian Breward, Courtenay Library of Reformation Classics (Appleford, England: The Sutton Courtenay Press, 1970), p. 172; hereafter cited as *Work*.

[16] Ong, *RTI*, p. 526.

[17] Sprunger, *Learned*, p. 147; cf. pp. 110, 14. Gibbs refers to Perkins' "one fully Ramistic work," *WAT*, p. 27.

[18] John G. Rechtien, "The Visual Memory of William Perkins and the End of Theological Dialogue," *Journal of the American Academy of Religion*, XLV/1 Supplement (March 1977), 80. Cf. Hugh Kearney, *Scholars and Gentlemen Universities and Society in Pre-Industrial Britain 1500-1700* (Ithaca, New York: Cornell University Press, 1970), pp. 51, 61. Christopher Hill, *Intellectual Origins of the English Revolution* (London: Panther Books, 1972), p. 292; hereafter cited as *IO*. Hill speaks of Perkins as a Ramist.

[19] Breward, ed. *Work*, p. 22; cf. pp. 10-12, 15ff.

[20] See Kearney, ch. 3: "The Ramist Challenge" for provocative suggestions along these lines.

NOTES TO CHAPTER I

¹ Ian Breward, "The Significance of William Perkins," *Journal of Religious History*, IV (December 1966), p. 116.

² A pensioner was a student who paid his own expenses at Cambridge University.

³ Collinson, *The Elizabethan Puritan Movement*, p. 125. On Chaderton see "Chaderton, Laurence," *Dictionary of National Biography*, eds. Leslie Stephen and Sydney Lee, 63 vols. (New York, 1885-1900); hereafter cited as *DNB*; Haller, Rise, pp. 54-55 and Porter, pp. 239ff.

⁴ Benjamin Brook, *The Lives of the Puritans*, 3 vols. (London, 1813), II, 129. Breward points out: "Just what happened is not clear, but the reference to the prodigal son receives some collaboration from an otherwise enigmatic clause in Perkins' will. He bequeathed his Bible to his son-in-law John Hinde. Although a child betrothal with Perkins' eldest daughter (baptised 10 July 1597) cannot be ruled out, an alternative explanation is that Perkins had an illegitimate daughter who had married by 1602," *Work*, p. 6.

⁵ Thomas Fuller, *Abel Redivivus* (London, 1651), p. 432.

⁶ All references to Perkins' writings in his published collected works are from *The Workes of that Famovs and Worthy Minister of Christ in the Vniuersitie of Cambridge, Mr. William Perkins*, 3 vols. (Cambridge: John Legatt, 1616-1618). Volume and page numbers without explanation are from this edition which is #19651 in *A Short-Title Catalogue of Books Printed in England, Scotland, and Ireland 1475-1640*, compiled by Alfred W. Pollard and G.R. Redgrave (London: The Bibliographical Society, 1926); hereafter cited as *STC*. In most cases, spellings and letter have not been modernized. Citations followed by an * are to the first 264 pages of Volume III which is a separate treatise not numbered with the rest of that volume. Textual variations in different editions of Perkins' *Workes* are not of major significance.

Perkins' comment on astrology is from III, 653. On Astrology cf. Don Cameron Allen, *The Star-Crossed Renaissance* (Durham, North Carolina, Duke University Press, 1941), p. 121 and Keith V. Thomas, *Religion and the Decline of Magic* (New York: Charles Scribner's Sons, 1971), pp. 298, 329n., 365-7, 370-371 as well as Paul H. Kocher, *Science and Religion in Elizabethan England* (San Marino, California: Huntington Library, 1953), *passim* for references to Perkins' views.

⁷ Thomas Fuller, *The Holy State and the Profane State*, a new edition with notes by James Nichols (London, 1841) p. 80.

⁸ Fuller, *Abel Redivivus*, pp. 432-433.

⁹ See Breward, *Work*, p. 7.

¹⁰ Samuel Clarke, *A Marrow of Ecclesiastical Historie* (London, 1654), pp. 416-417.

¹¹ Fuller, *Abel Redivivus*, p. 433.

¹² Charles Henry Cooper and Thompson Cooper, *Athenae Cantabrigienses*, 3 vols. (Cambridge, 1858-1913), II, 335.

¹³ Fuller, *State*, p. 81.

¹⁴ Samuel Clarke, *Lives of Thirty-Two English Divines*, 3rd ed. (London, 1677), p. 23.

between the "prayer book party" and the "Bible party" began to reappear when some wished to go beyond the Elizabethan settlement in religion and "to bring in a more drastic reformation movement." See Leonard J. Trinterud, "The Origins of Puritanism," Church History, XX (March 1951), 46-47 and H.G. Alexander, *Religion in England 1558-1602* (London: Hodder and Stoughton, 1977), pp. 57-64. This group wished to eliminate those liturgical practices in worship they considered "Romish" and "to model English church worship and government according to the Word of God." To them, the English Reformation had not gone far enough. See Horton Davies, *The Worship of the English Puritans* (London: Dacre Press, 1948), p. 1. See also his *Worship and Theology in England 1534-1603* (Princeton: Princeton University Press, 1970), pp. 41ff.

The term "Puritan" must be used flexibly. Puritanism was more than Presbyterianism. It also embraced Anglicans and Independents in the seventeenth-century. It is more than English Calvinism since Archbishop Whitgift, the arch-enemy of Puritanism was a Calvinist. The influences of Zwingli, Bucer and Luther also had their effects. Davies' distinction of "patient" and "impatient" Puritans is helpful. In the first group were those who "desired further reformation according to the Word of God and following the examples of the best Reformed churches, but who saw this as happening in the context of the nation; these were the Anglican and Presbyterian Puritans. In the second category we see those Puritans who, like Robert Browne, wanted a 'reformation without tarrying for anie' and who instead adopted the 'gathered chruch' concept of ecclesiology....This second group or series of groups organized themselves independently of the national church," *Worship and Theology*, p. 44.

[30] Fuller, *Church History*, III, 211.

[31] Peter Heylyn, *Aerius Redivivus or the History of the Presbyterians* (Oxford, 1670), p. 342. Neal, I, 464-465.

[32] See Cooper and Cooper, II, 335.

[33] Strype relates that in 1586 Capcot had charged the Fellows of the College with neglecting academic dress, public prayers, and holy communion; that they did not speak Latin in the court and in the hall; that their common places in chapel were so long as to cause the lectures to suffer, and that they preached "upon particular person (whose doctrines or person they liked not)"; and that "they ordinarily dined and supped out of the college." *Annals of the Reformation* rev. ed., 3 vols., (Oxford, 1824), III/1, 647. Strype reports that upon receipt of a letter from Lord Burghley, "upon complaint of his vice-chancellor concerning them," the fellows fired off a brisk letter to Burghley complaining that these injunctions infringed on their liberty. Some of those who signed the letter were Andrew Wilet, Cuthbert Bainbridge, Williams Perkins, Francis Johnson, and George Downame, "who were puritans," according to Strype, *Annals*, III/1, 649.

[34] Cooper and Cooper, II, 335.

[35] Breward, *Work*, pp. 4-5.

[36] Collinson give the names of other delegates whom he called "hardened, professional prebyterian leaders." They were Cartwright, Thomas Barber, and Laurence Chaderton; also Snape, Fludd, Stone, Gifford, Allen and moderator, John Harrison, *EPM*, p. 401. Cf. A.F. Scott Pearson, *Thomas Cartwright and Elizabethan Puritanism, 1535-1603*, (Cambridge: University Press, 1925), p. 332. The trial record reads: "Wm. Perkins saith, that Mr. Cartwright, and Mr. Snape, with others not named, met in conference in Cambridge, at St. John's two years past, about the disciplin in question," John Strype, *The Life and Acts of John Whitgift*, 3 vols. (Oxford, 1822), Bk. IV, Appendix IX, p. 275. Parts of the original are in Sisson.

³⁷ Cited in Breward, *Work*, p. 10 (from transcript). Breward doubts the truth of Perkins' first statement and explains his "taciturnity" by citing his Galatians commentary where Perkins distinguished between lying and feigning, and concealment (II, 183). Sisson argues that "what we have here is not the nonconformist discovered by the authorities and betraying his associates to save himself, but a conforming member of the Church of England whose Puritan sympathies have placed him in a position of some degree of danger, at least of deprivation, if not of imprisonment, and who refuses to take the easy course of "laying all open." The meticulous care with which he endeavours to answer all that he should (especially when it meant accusing himself) and the tenderness and self-questioning of his conscience appears painfully in the places where are most difficult to read as though we see on the untidy page the struggle of a man of conscience," pp. 501-502.

³⁸ Sisson, p. 502. [ ] is interlining; [ ] is deletion from the original transcript. In the original, Perkins' phrase was "sayeth he may not be compelled to expresse," Sisson, p. 501. When asked about the rooms in which this conference took place, Perkins had refused to say (in the final version): "for his conscyence sake forbeareth to set downe." Yet in the original transcript, the first rendering here was: that he "sayeth he may not be compelled to expresse," Sisson. p. 501. The rendering of Strype is: "but nameth him not, being not of the defendants."

³⁹ Sisson, p. 502.

⁴⁰ III, 65*.

⁴¹ III, 425. In 1592 Perkins had said nothing at all about the Prayer Book's value when he expounded the Lord's Prayer. But some ten years later in his *Exposition upon Christ's Sermon on the Mount* he wrote that using "a set forme of prayer, either publikely or priuately" was both "profitable and necessarie," III, 119*.

⁴² I, 229.

⁴³ III, 389.

⁴⁴ "To the Christian Reader" prior to *A Golden Chaine*, I, [9].

⁴⁵ III, 15*; I, 342.

⁴⁶ I, 193; III, 314, 260; I, 38.

⁴⁷ II, 225. Cf. I, 409 for his evangelical thrust.

⁴⁸ Breward, "Significance," p. 118.

⁴⁹ II, 605.

⁵⁰ See Louis B. Wright, "William Perkins: Elizabethan Apostle of Practical Divinity," p. 175 and Sprunger, *Learned*, p. 45 for these designations of Perkins. It was Perkins' student William Ames who was advisor to Johannes Bogerman, presiding officer of the Synod of Dort (1618-1619) where the controversy between "Calvinsim" and "Arminianism" came to a head. See Sprunger, ch. 3: "The Synod of Dort" in Learned. Jacobus Arminius had originally reacted strongly against Perkins' view of predestination. See Carl Bangs, *Arminius A Study in the Dutch Reformation* (Nashville: Abingdon Press, 1971), ch. 15: "Theology in Amsterdam: The Examination of Perkins' Pamphlet."

³⁷ Cited in Breward, *Work*, p. 10 (from transcript). Breward doubts the truth of Perkins' first statement and explains his "taciturnity" by citing his Galatians commentary where Perkins distinguished between lying and feigning, and concealment (II, 183). Sisson argues that "what we have here is not the nonconformist discovered by the authorities and betraying his associates to save himself, but a conforming member of the Church of England whose Puritan sympathies have placed him in a position of some degree of danger, at least of deprivation, if not of imprisonment, and who refuses to take the easy course of "laying all open." The meticulous care with which he endeavours to answer all that he should (especially when it meant accusing himself) and the tenderness and self-questioning of his conscience appears painfully in the places where are most difficult to read as though we see on the untidy page the struggle of a man of conscience," pp. 501-502.

³⁸ Sisson, p. 502. ⌐ ¬ is interlining; [ ] is deletion from the original transcript. In the original, Perkins' phrase was "sayeth he may not be compelled to expresse," Sisson, p. 501. When asked about the rooms in which this conference took place, Perkins had refused to say (in the final version): "for his conscyence sake forbeareth to set downe." Yet in the original transcript, the first rendering here was: that he "sayeth he may not be compelled to expresse," Sisson. p. 501. The rendering of Strype is: "but nameth him not, being not of the defendants."

³⁹ Sisson, p. 502.

⁴⁰ III, 65*.

⁴¹ III, 425. In 1592 Perkins had said nothing at all about the Prayer Book's value when he expounded the Lord's Prayer. But some ten years later in his *Exposition upon Christ's Sermon on the Mount* he wrote that using "a set forme of prayer, either publikely or priuately" was both "profitable and necessarie," III, 119*.

⁴² I, 229.

⁴³ III, 389.

⁴⁴ "To the Christian Reader" prior to *A Golden Chaine*, I, [9].

⁴⁵ III, 15*; I, 342.

⁴⁶ I, 193; III, 314, 260; I, 38.

⁴⁷ II, 225. Cf. I, 409 for his evangelical thrust.

⁴⁸ Breward, "Significance," p. 118.

⁴⁹ II, 605.

⁵⁰ See Louis B. Wright, "William Perkins: Elizabethan Apostle of Practical Divinity," p. 175 and Sprunger, *Learned*, p. 45 for these designations of Perkins. It was Perkins' student William Ames who was advisor to Johannes Bogerman, presiding officer of the Synod of Dort (1618-1619) where the controversy between "Calvinsim" and "Arminianism" came to a head. See Sprunger, ch. 3: "The Synod of Dort" in Learned. Jacobus Arminius had originally reacted strongly against Perkins' view of predestination. See Carl Bangs, *Arminius A Study in the Dutch Reformation* (Nashville: Abingdon Press, 1971), ch. 15: "Theology in Amsterdam: The Examination of Perkins' Pamphlet."

⁵¹ II, 616; III, 210*.

⁵² The *Institutes* are cited in I, 735; I [454]; the *Commentaries* in II, 614; I, 533; I, 631.

⁵³ See Breward, *L&T*, p. 8 and *Work*, p. 16.

⁵⁴ See Martyr (I, 533; II, 629, 640); Beza (I, 640; II, 614, 616, III, 696); Zanchius (I, 429ff.); Olevianus (I, 234); Tossanus (I, 640); Junius (II, 673; III, 411); and Marloratus (II, 654).

⁵⁵ L&T, p. 11, Cf. I, 640 and *Two Elizabethan Puritan Diaries*, ed. Knappen, p. 113. In 1613, Thomas Goodwin (age 12) was catechized on Saturday nights by Fellows of Christ College, Cambridge who used Ursinus' Catechism. See Haller, *Rise*, p. 75.

⁵⁶ See Luther (I, 640; III, 458); Melanchthon (I, 454, 533); Strigel (I, 644); Chemnitius (I, 640); Hemmingsen (II, 673); Illyricus (II, 489, 669); and Hyperius (II, 673).

⁵⁷ See for example, I, 306.

⁵⁸ I, 381-396 in drawn from Bradford and Tyndale.

⁵⁹ Breward, *L&T*, p. 7.

⁶⁰ Breward, *Work*, pp. 28-29.

⁶¹ I, 454.

⁶² Breward, *Work*, p. 29. In a later discussion, Breward sees the strong theological emphases of Perkins', gained from the continental sources as being the reason it is "an exaggeration" to call Perkins "the real father of pietism." A. Lang had listed five reasons to justify this claim: religious individualism, a central interest in the knowledge of election and conversion, the special role given to religious experience, zeal for individual souls and uncertainty about the place of the visible church. See *Puritanismus and Pietismus* (1941; rpt. Darmstadt: Wissenschaftliche Buchgesellschaft, 1972), pp. 126-131. But Breward claims Lang "has not always done justice to the theological concerns of Perkins and the more feeling-centred discussions of later pietists or puritans," Work, p. 108. See his discussion, pp. 107-110.

⁶³ Breward, *L&T*, p. 12. See also *Work*, p. 17.

⁶⁴ Breward, "Significance," p. 113.

⁶⁵ Breward, "Significance," p. 113. See also V.L. Priebe, "The Covenant Theology of William Perkins," Diss. Drew University 1967, p. 8. Before Perkins and Smith, Calvin and Beza were most often published among religious writers. See Charles D. Cremeans, *The Reception of Calvinistic Thought in England* (Urbana's University of Illinois Press, 1949), p. 65.

⁶⁶ Harris F. Fletcher, *The Intellectual Development of John Milton*. 2 vols. (Urbana, Illinois: University of Illinois Press, 1956-1961), II, 13.

⁶⁷ Lawrence Stone, "The Ninnyversity?", *The New York Review of Books* (January 28, 1971), p. 24.

⁶⁸ Fletcher, II, 13.

[69] John Peile, *Christ's College* (London: F.E. Robinson & Co., 1900), p. 14. See also Fletcher, II, 40-41. On Christ's College see too A.H. Lloyd, *Early History of Christ's College* (Cambridge: University Press, 1934); John Peile, *Biographical Register of Christ's College 1505-1905*, 2 vols. (Cambridge: University Press, 1910-1913); and John Venn, *Early Collegiate Life* (Cambridge: W. Heffer & Sons, 1913).

[70] Peile, *Christ's College*, p. 20.

[71] Mark Curtis, *Oxford and Cambridge in Transition 1558-1642* (1959; rpt. Oxford: University Press, 1965), p. 80.

[72] G.M. Trevelyan, *Trinity College An Historical Sketch* (Cambridge: University Press, 1946), p. 15. Trevelyan says that the tutors were "the ordinary Fellows taking two or three pupils each, by private arrangement with the pupisl or their parents, or by the order of the Master....A man depended on his Tutor for advice about studies and for teaching: there was no one else to perform the functions of a modern supervisor or director of studies. The tutorial system was indeed the very essence of the College life." Fellows had to take Holy Orders and were forbidden to marry. His marriage was why Perkins lost his Fellowship in 1595.

[73] Curtis, p. 79.

[74] See Gerald R. Cragg, *Freedom and Authority A Study of English Thought in the Early Seventeenth Century* (Philadelphia: Westminster Press, 1975), p. 138. The size of the Christ's College student population would be conducive to personal familiarities: "the round number of two-hundred students is probably as close as we can come to the number in residence in any given year before 1629," Fletcher, II, 41.
F.E. Stoeffler points out that "looking back over some decades the author of *The Life and Death of Mr. Bolton* notes: 'The precious name of Mr. Perkins shall like an ointment poured forth, fill all the quarters of this land with a fresh and fragrant sweetness, when nothing shall survive of his detractors, but their unsavory and unlearned spite against so holy a man,'" *The Rise of Evangelical Pietism* (Leiden: E.J. Brill, 1965), p. 51.
William Ames said of his teacher: "When being young I heard worthy Master Perkins, so preach in a great assembly of students, that he instructed them soundly in the truth, stirred them up effectually to speak after godliness, made the fit for the kingdom of God; and by his own example showed them, what things they should chiefly intend, that they might promote true religion in the power of it, unto God's glory and others' salvation," *Conscience, with the Power and Cases Thereof* (n.p., 1639), "To the reader." Clergy from far distances enlisted Perkins' advice. See Knappen, *Two Elizabethan Puritan Diaries*, p. 130.

[75] Chief among these have been Perry Miller, Louis B. Wright, and William Haller.

[76] John Eusden, *Puritans, Lawyers, and Politics* (New Haven: Yale University Press, 1958), p. 11.

[77] Knappen, Tudor Puritanism, p. 375. H.R. Trevor-Roper called Perkins "the most famous teacher whom Cambridge had produced since the Reformation." *Archbishop Laud, 1573-1645*, 2nd ed. (1940; rpt. New York: St. Martin's Press, 1962), p. 205.

[78] Haller, *Rise*, p. 91.

[79] Collinson, *EPM*, p. 125.

[80] Paul Seaver, *The Puritan Lectureships: The Politics of Religious Dissent, 1560-1662*

(Palo Alto, California: Stanford University Press, 1970), p. 114.

⁸¹ Christopher Hill, *God's Englishman: Oliver Cromwell and the English Revolution* (New York: Harper & Row, 1970). p. 38.

⁸² See Christopher Hill, *Society and Puritanism in Pre-Revolutionary England* (1964; rpt. London: Panther Books, 1969), p. 216. Hill says: "Calvin, Beza, Perkins, are often cited as the trinity of the orthodox." Perry Miller records that "the seventeenth century, Catholic as well as Protestant, ranked him with Calvin." See "The Marrow of Puritan Divinity," *Publications of the Colonial Society of Massachusetts*, XXXII (1936), 255.

⁸³ Trevor-Roper, *Archbishop Laud*, p. 17.

⁸⁴ Samuel Eliot Morison, *The Intellectual Life of Colonial New England*, 2nd ed. (New York: New York University Press, 1956), p. 134. Cf. Louis B. Wright, *The Cultural Life of the American Colonies 1607-1763* (New York: Harper & Brothers, 1957), *passim*. See also Thomas Goddard Wright, *Literary Culture in Early New England 1620-1730* (New Haven: Yale University Press, 1920), *passim*.

⁸⁵ Daniel Boorstin, *The Americans The Colonial Experience* (New York: Vintage Books, 1958), p. 11.

⁸⁶ Perry Miller, *Errand into the Wilderness* (1956; rpt. New York: Harper & Row, 1964), p. 57.

NOTES TO CHAPTER II

¹ The chief biographical sources of Ramus' life are Latin works produced by his colleagues: Johann Thomas Freige (Freigius), *Petri Rami vita* (Basileai, 1575); Theophile de Banos, *Petri Rami vita* (first appearing in Ramus, *Commentariorum de religione Christiana libri quatuor*, Frankfort, 1576; hereafter cited as *Commentariorum*); and Nicholas de Nancel, *Petri Rami Veromandui, eloquentiae et philosophiae apud Parisios professoris regii, vita, a Nic Nancelio Trachyeno Noviodunensi Rami discipula et populari descripta* (Parisiis, 1599). Some autobiographical references exist in Ramus' writings and some material comes from Ramus' opponent Jacques Charpentier. Nineteenth century biographies includes Charles Waddington, *Ramus: sa vie, ses écrits et ses opinions* (Paris, 1855). A discussion of this and other sources is in Ong, *Ramus*, pp. 17-18. See also *RTI*.

² Banos gives his age as eight. Pierre Bayle in *Dictionnaire historique et critique*, 5e edition revue....par M. des Maizeaux, 8 vols. (Amsterdam, 1740-56), III, 26 gives the age as twelve. Waddington also places him at twelve. See Ong, *Ramus*, p. 19.

³ This involved the legendary M.A. thesis of which more will be said below. See below, notes 60ff.

⁴ On these see *RTI*, pp. 46-66. Ramus' *Aristotelicae animadversiones* was a series of lectures which criticized "Aristotelians." It proposed a complete reconstruction of all philosophy. It became known as *Scholae Dialecticae* by its final 1581 edition. This is included in Ramus' *Scholae in liberales artes* (Basel, 1569; rpt. New York: Georg Olms Verlag, 1970). See also *RTI*, pp. 431-433.

⁵ Antonio de Gouveia charged that Ramus was out to "upset and muddle the whole curriculum" (*studiorum rationem tu praevertere et perturbare voluisti*) in *Pro Aristotele responsic adversus Petri Rami calumnias* (1543), fol. 4; see also I, 3 as cited by Ong, *Ramus*, p. 23.

Cf. *RTI*, pp. 493-495. There was no "pure" or "simple" dialectic extant for the instruction of young boys as Ramus asserted.

[6] The full text of the decree is in Waddington, pp. 49-52. See also Emile-Edmond Saisset, *Precurseurs et disciples de Descartes*, 2nd ed. (Paris, 1862), pp. 67-68 who cites a section of it.

[7] See Waddington, pp. 62ff; Nancel, pp. 15-19.

[8] See *RTI*, pp. 49-50.

[9] See *RTI*, pp. 68-69 on Euclides and pp. 82-87 for a discussion of Ramus' part in Talon's work.

[10] See Saisset, p. 70 who quotes several of Ramus' contemporaries.

[11] See *RTI*, pp. 79-81.

[12] Ramus and Talon then began to dedicate numerous works to the Cardinal.

[13] For a discussion of his title see Ong, *Ramus*, pp. 25-27.

[14] As a writer and speaker of Latin, Nancel called Ramus "by far the leader of his whole age," p. 31 as cited in Ong, *Ramus*, p. 21.

[15] According to Ramus himself, the change of heart occurred at the 1561 Colloquy of Poissy. But this comes from a recollection nine years later in a letter to Charles of Lorraine, with whom he had fallen out. Nancel, the closest source next to Talon, could give no specific reason for the change of Ramus' religious sympathies nor even its date. The suspicions of Ramus' earlier Protestantism come from the breaking of some of the Chapel rules at the Collège de Presles. See Nancel, pp. 70-71 cited on Ong, *Ramus*, p. 28.

[16] On the French Wars of Religion see *The Hugenot Wars*, trans. Julie Kernan, ed. Julien Coudy (Philadelphia: Chilton Book Company, 1969); James Westfall Thompson, *The Wars of Religion in France 1559-1576* (New York: Frederick Ungar Publishing Company, 1958); and William L. Langer, *An Encyclopedia of World History*, 5th ed. (Boston: Houghton Mifflin Co., 1972) for a brief outline. Also, the works of Robert M. Kingdon, *Geneva and the Coming of the Wars of Religion in France, 1555-1563* (Geneva: Droz, 1956) and *Geneva and the Consolidation of the French Protestant Movement 1564-1572* (Madison, Wisconsin: University of Wisconsin Press, 1967) are valuable.

[17] See the short account of Ramus' life in *The Logike of Peter Ramus*, trans. Roland MacIlmaine (1574), ed. Catherine M. Dunn (Northridge, California: San Fernando Valley State College, 1969), xii; hereafter cited as Dunn, ed.

[18] A contemporary life of Charpentier is Jean-Papire Masson, Vita Iacobi Carpentarii (Paris, 1575) cited by Ong, *Ramus*, p. 358.

[19] See the discussion of this controversy in Ong, *Ramus*, pp. 220-223 and the works mentioned in *RTI*, pp. 498-504. See also Waddington, pp. 168-180.

[20] See Dunn, ed., p. xii. Ramus had supposedly delivered an impassioned oration to the Hugenot army (and its German mercenaries) to persuade them to carry out the French military campaign. See Kingdon, *Geneva and the Consolidation of the French Protestant Movement* (hereafter cited as *GFPM*), p. 100 and Waddington, pp. 186-187.

[21] The designation is Ong's. See *Ramus*, p. 28.

[22] See Waddington, Pt. I, ch. VII for an account of these travels. Ramus was continually honored, often being called *Gallicus Plato*. See Dunn, ed., p. xiii.

[23] Erastus, Professor of Medicine at Heidelberg is best known for his view of the State's ascendancy over the Church in ecclesiastical matters. See "Erastianism," *Oxford Dictionary of the Christian Church*, 2nd ed., ed. F.L. Cross and E.A. Livingstone (London: Oxford University Press, 1974); hereafter cited as *ODC* and Ruth Wessel-Roth, *Thomas Erastus* (Lahr/Baden: Schauenburg, 1954).

[24] See Kingdon, *GFPM*, p. 101. Among the pastor who reprimanded Ramus was Theodore Beza, Calvin's successor. On Beza see Jack B. Rogers and Donald K. McKim, *The Authority and Interpretation of the Bible An Historical Approach* (San Francisco: Harper & Row, 1979), pp. 160ff.

On Strum see *ODC* and Ong, *Ramus, passim*. Sturm was a French humanist who lectured on the classics at the University of Paris from 1530-1536. He became a Protestant under the influence of Martin Bucer (1491-1551) and furthered the cause of the Reformation in Strasbourg.

[26] On Ramus' stay in Basel see Peter G. Bientenholz, *Basle and France in the Sixteenth Century* (Geneva: Librarie Droz, 1971), ch. 8 and Ong, *Ramus*, p. 28.

[27] Banos, *Vita in Ramus, Commentariorum*. On Ramus' theology see Paul Lobstein, *Petrus Ramus als Theologe: Ein Betrag zur Geschichte der protestantischen Theologie* (Strassburg, 1878).

[28] This was expressed in Ramus' *Commentariorum*. See also Lobstein, pp. 58-59.

[29] See Kingdon, *GFPM*, pp. 102ff. On the Synod see pp. 96ff.

[30] Kingdon, *GFPM*, p. 101.

[31] See Kingdon, pp. 103-104. Kingdon notes that Beza's criticism was more fully developed in a letter to Bullinger on January 14, 1572. Beza refused to hire Ramus to teach at Geneva's Academy because of Ramus' rejection of Aristotelianism. See John S. Bray, *Theodore Beza's Doctrine of Predestination* (Nieuwkoup: B. DeGraff, 1975), p. 28, n. 47. Cf. Rogers and McKim, pp. 161-162.

[32] The quote is from a letter by a synodical delegate De Lestre de Bearlieu to Beza (March 19, 1562) as given by Kingdon, *GFPM*, p. 106. Ramus' hope apparently was to follow the model of the secular government of his day where this type of weighted advice was part of city governments, provincial, and National Estates. Ramus never explained how the system of weighting would work.

[33] Quoted in Kingdon, GFPM, p. 109 from *Synodicon in Gallia Reformata*, 2 vols., ed. J. Quick (London, 1692), I, 112, art. IV.

[34] Quoted in Kingdon, GFPM, p. 110 from *Synodicon*, I, 113, art. XII. Only on the matter of the use of the term "substance" did the Synod make any concession. Use of the term for the French Reformed Church was not abandoned. But the Synod did recognize the right of "foreign churches" to do so. Further, modifications of the Church's position to bring it closer to the Zwinglian position on the Lord's Supper were also made. See Waddington, pp. 243ff.

³⁵ Cited by Kingdon, *GFPM*, pp. 110-111. He refers to a letter of May 18, 1572. Beza warned Ramus to stay away from Geneva. See Waddington, pp. 212-213.

³⁶ On the St. Bartholomew's Day massacre see *ODC* and the bibliography cited there. See also *The Massacre of St. Bartholomew*, International Archives of the History of Ideas, ed. Alfred Soman (The Hague: Martinus Nkjhoff, 1974).

³⁷ See Waddington, pp. 254-255 for a description of Ramus' assassination based on Banos and Nancel. See also Andre Bouvier, *Henri Bullinger, le successeur de Zwingli* (Paris: Droz, 1940), p. 412 for another account based on a contemporary source. On Carpentier's part see Ong, *Ramus*, p. 327, n. 68. See Kingdon, *GFPM*, pp. 112ff. on the published polemics after the Massacre.

³⁸ See Frank P. Graves, *Peter Ramus and the Educational Reformation of the Sixteenth Century* (New York: The MacMillan Co., 1912).

³⁹ See the complete listing in Ong, *RTI*. See also his article "Ramism," *Dictionary of the History of Ideas*, ed. Philip P. Wiener, 4 vols. (1968: rpt. New York: Charles Scribner's Sons, 1973), IV, 42. Ong divided Ramus' career into four phases; Rhetorical, Dialectical, Mathematical, and Religious.

⁴⁰ Among the numerous works on Renaissance humanism see the discussion by Paul Oskar Kristeller, *Renaissance Thought The Classic, Scholastic, and Humanist Strains* (1955; rpt. New York: Harper & Row, 1961), ch. I and Jerrold E. Seigel, *Rhetoric and Philosophy in Renaissance Humanism* (Princeton, New Jersey: Princeton University Press, 1968).

⁴¹ See Kristeller, p. 10. At the time of Cicero and Varro, *humanitas* meant the education of humans as such. This was what the Greeks referred to a *paideia*. The liberal arts were what distinguished humans from animals (Aulus Gellius, *Noctes Atticae*, XIII, 17). Through re-study of the works of classical history, Renaissance humanists held that a "rebirth" of the spirit of ancient times could occur. This rebirth of a spirit of freedom, which they saw as having been lost in the Middle Ages, could allow humans to see themselves as involved in nature and history and as capable of making these realms their own. The liberal arts were seen as the proper vehicles through which humanity could be thus educated and its true freedom exercised. See Nicola Abbagnano, "Humanism," trans. Nino Langiulli, *The Encyclopedia of Philosophy*, ed. Paul Edwards, 8 vols. (1967; rpt. New York: Macmillan Publishing Co., 1972), IV, 70; hereafter cited as *EP*.
The greatest percentage of Renaissance humanists were also Christians. Therefore, "Christian humanism" is a term to define those scholars "with a humanist classical and rhetorical training who explicitly discussed religious or theological problems in all or some of their writings," Kristeller, p. 86. For a discussion of "Christian Humanism and Christian Philosophy" see Charles B. Partee, *Calvin and Classical Philosophy* (Leiden: E. J. Brill, 1977), ch. I.

⁴² Kristeller, p. 10. See Walter J. Ong, "Introduction" to Petrus Ramus, *Sch. in lib. arts.*, p. VI*; hereafter cited as Ong, "Introduction."

⁴³ See William T. Costello, *The Scholastic Curriculum at Early Seventeenth-Century Cambridge* (Cambridge, Massachusetts: Harvard University Press, 1958), p. 45 and his discussion of "logic."

⁴⁴ Ong, "Introduction," p. VI*.

⁴⁵ Seigel writes: "Renaissance humanism was not a replacement for medieval scholasticism," p. 226. Cf. Kristeller, ch. 5: "Humanism and Scholasticism in the Italian

Renaissance."

⁴⁶ See Seigel's "Conclusion," especially p. 259. See also Richard McKeon, "Rhetoric in the Middle Ages," *Speculum*, XVII, No.1 (January 1942), 1-32.

⁴⁷ See Ong, *Ramus*, pp. 92-93. See also his "System, Space and Intellect in Renaissance Symbolism," *Bibliotheque d'Humanisme et Renaissance*, XVIII (1956), 224 where Ong writes: "In many ways, the greatest shift in the way of conceiving knowledge between the ancient and the modern world takes place in the movement from a pole where knowledge is conceived of in terms of discourse and hearing and persons to one where it is conceived of in terms of observation and sight and objects." He makes a similar point in his *The Presence of the Word* (New Haven, Connecticut: Yale University Press, 1967).

⁴⁸ See Waddington, p. 29 and Graves, p. 26. Ong in *Ramus*, pp. 37-41 discusses the authenticity of this thesis. He concludes that "it is quite possible that Ramus did not defend at his *inceptio* the anti-Aristotelian thesis commonly attributed to him," pp. 40-41.

⁴⁹ The translation is Ong's, *Ramus*, p. 41 from Ramus' "Scholae Dialecticae," *Sch. in lib. arts*, Bk. IV, 153. The phrase "to use" here (*usus*) refers to "practice in general, but particularly....to students' classroom exercise or drill," according to Ong, *Ramus*, p. 41.

⁵⁰ Perry Miller quotes Ramus as saying: "When I came to Paris, I fell into the subtleties of the sophists, and they taught me the liberal arts through questions and disputes, without ever showing me a single thing of profit or service," *NEM*, p. 123.

⁵¹ *Sch. Dialecticae* (hereafter cited as *Sch. dial.*) in *Sch. in lib. arts*, IV, 154. From Ong's translation in *Ramus*, p. 41.

⁵² Translated and digested in Ong, *Ramus*, p. 42 with numbers added for easier identification. The quote is from *Sch. dial.* in *Sch. in lib. arts.*, IV, 155. The "distribution" refers to two parts of dialectic: invention and judgment. The work of Agricola to which Ramus referred was *De inventione dialectica libri tres* in which Agricola dealt only with invention.

⁵³ These were invention (*inventio*) and judgment (*iudicium*).

⁵⁴ See *Sch. dial.* in *Sch. in lib. arts.*, IV, 155-156.

⁵⁵ See *Sch. dial.* in *Sch. in lib. arts.*, IV, 155-156.

⁵⁶ See Ong, *Ramus*, p. 44. Cicero was the verbatim source for this definition. See *De oratore*, ii. 138.

⁵⁷ See Howell, *L&R*, ch. 4; Neal W. Gilbert, *Renaissance Concepts of Method* (New York: Columbia University Press, 1960), ch. 4; Ong, *Ramus*, ch. XI; and his "Ramist Method and the Commercial Mind," *Studies in the Renaissance*, VIIII (1961), pp. 161ff.

⁵⁸ *Sch. dial.* in *Sch. in lib. arts.*, IV, 156 translated in Ong, *Ramus*, p. 44.

⁵⁹ *Sch. dial.* in *Sch. in lib. arts.*, IV, 156 translated in Ong, *Ramus*, p. 45.

⁶⁰ Graves, p. 26.

⁶¹ M.M. Dassonville, "La genèse et les principes de la dialectique de Pierre de la Ramée," *Revue de l'Université de Ottawa*, XXIII (1953), 329 (*mesonge*).

⁶² Miller, *NEM*, p. 123. Cf. Morison, *Harvard College*, I. 189. Ong traces the origins of these translations through Hegel's, *Alles, was Aristoteles gelehrt habe, sey nicht war*. See Georg Wilhelm Friedrich Hegel, *Vorlesungen uber die Geschichte der Philosophie*, III, in *Samtliche Werke* (Stuttgart: F. Frommann, 1927), XIX, 252 cited in Ong, *Ramus*, p. 45 (note 20).

⁶³ See *Aristotelicae animadversiones* (Paris, 1543: rpt. Stuttgart-Bad Cannstatt: Friedrich Verlag, 1964), fols. 74-75; hereafter cited as *Arist. anim.* Pierre Galland, a critic of Ramus, claimed that in Ramus' initial attacks: "You maintained that these works were the productions of some other upstart and crotchety sophist." translated in Ong, *Ramus*, p. 40 from *Contra novam academiam Petri Rami oratio*, 4th ed., (1551), fol. 8. See the account of this dispute in *RTI*, pp. 496-498.

⁶⁴ This is the interpretation advanced by P. Duhamel, "Milton's Alleged Ramism," *Publications of the Modern Language Association*, 67 (1953), p. 1036 and followed by Ong, in *Ramus*, p. 46 and his article in *EP*, VII, 66. Cf. "Comminiscor," in Charleton T. Lewis and Charles Short, *A Latin Dictionary* (1879; rpt. Oxford: University Press, 1969).

⁶⁵ See the examples cited by Ong, *Ramus*, p. 46. One of these is where Ramus speaks of "the *commentitia* of Aristotle" as opposed not to *true* arts or *true* precepts of arts, but rather as he says to "the precepts of arts ranged in a universally consistent and methodical order." Howell writes (accepting that Ramus was awarded his degree for defending his thesis) that to Ramus "all things affirmed on the authority of Aristotle are overelaborate, contrived, artificial," *L&R*, p. 146. He cites Waddington, pp. 28-29.

⁶⁶ On these, which begin: Barbara, Celarent, Darii, Ferioque...., see "Traditional Logic" and "Glossary of Logical Terms," *EP*, V.

⁶⁷ See Frances A. Yates, *The Art of Memory* (Chicago: University of Chicago Press, 1966), ch. X and below note 194ff. On Aristotle's mnemonics see Yates, pp. 31-35.

⁶⁸ Ong, *Ramus*, pp. 46-47.

⁶⁹ See *Sch. dial.* in *Sch. in lib. arts.*, IV, 157-158; Pierre Albert Duhamel, "The Logic and Rhetoric of Peter Ramus," *Modern Philology*, XLVI (1949), p. 163 and Craig, pp. 143-144; 150-151.

⁷⁰ These "Aristotelians" were Theophrastus, Eudemus, Chrysippus and other Academicians, Peripatetics and Stoics. See *Arist. anim.* (1543), fol. 3. They did not follow Aristotle's practice but only his written recommendations, that is the collection of Aristotle's works, the *Organon*.

⁷¹ See Ong, *Ramus*, p. 173. Cf. *Arist. anim.* (1543). fol. 3.

⁷² *Arist. anim.* (1543), fol. 3. Cf. fols. 67, 71-73 where Ramus charged Aristotle with failing to put dialectic into practical use and with barbarism and sophistry.

⁷³ *Arist. anim.* (1543), fol. 3.

⁷⁴ In his *Dial. inst.* (1543) Ramus wrote: *Denique dialecticae imaginem breviter & succinctè generum, formarumque perpetius quasi lineamentis adumbrare laboravi*, fols. 3-4. See *Dialecticae Institutiones* (Paris, 1543; rpt. Stuttgart-Bad Cannstatt: Friedrich Frommann Verlag, 1964); hereafter cited as *Dial. inst.*

⁷⁵ *Arist. anim.* (1543). fols. 2-3

⁷⁶ *le prince de ceste louange, Dialectique* (Paris, 1555), "Preface." Ramus also called Plato *l'Homère des philosophes*. See the critical edition of this work by M.M. Dassonville (Geneva: Droz, 1964), p. 51. On this work see *RTI*, pp. 178ff. In the "Preface" Ramus presented his views of the history of dialectic. He has been called "the first historian of logic." See I.M. Bochenski, *A History of Formal Logic*, trans. Ivo Thomas (Notre Dame, Indiana: University of Notre Dame Press, 1961), p. 4.

⁷⁷ For background on the developing history of logic prior to Ramus, see Appendix A. Ong, *Ramus*, ch. 6 and Graves have material on the eductional milieu of "arts scholasticism."

⁷⁸ Ramus used the image of the two arts as working together like head and heart. Their goal was to give expression to human thought. See *Arist. anim.* (1543), fol. 78 and Duhamel, "Ramus," p. 163.

⁷⁹ *Rhetoricae distincitiones in Quintilianum* (Paris, 1559), p. 18 as cited in Duhamel, "Ramus," p. 163. Ramus wrote in his *Dialectique* (1555): "....the art of knowing, that is to say, dialectic or logic, is one and the same doctrine in respect to perceiving all things," translated in Howell, *L&R*, p. 154. The reference is on p. 4 of the original edition; p. 62 of the Dassonville edition.

⁸⁰ *Dialectica virtus est disserendi, Dial. inst.* (1543), fol. 5.

⁸¹ *Dialegesthai (unde Dialectica nominatur) et disserere unum, idemque valent, idque est disputare, disceptare, atque omnino ratione ut.* See *Dial. inst.* (1543), fol. 5. Cf. Ong, *Ramus*, p. 176.

⁸² See *Dial. inst.* (1543), fols. 5, 6. All citations are from this edition.

⁸³ See Ong, *Ramus*, p. 177 and *Dial inst.*, fol. 6: *Naturalis autem dialectica, id est, ingenium, ratio, mens, imago, parentis omnium rerum Dei, lux denique beatae illius, & aeternae lucis aemula, hominis propria est....*

⁸⁴ *Arist. anim.* (1543), fol. 3.

⁸⁵ *Dialectica est ars bene disserendi.* See Ramus, *Dialecticae in libri duo A. Talaei pr. ill.* (1560), p. 9 and the different variants of this definition listed by Ong, *Ramus*, p. 350 (note 45). Ong also points out Cicero's use of this definition.

⁸⁶ *Didascalicon*, Lib. I, cap. xi, ed. Buttimer (1939), p. 21 as cited in Ong, *Ramus*, p. 179. Cf. pp. 347-348 (note 41) and *Ramus*, p. 180 where Ong discusses the various variations of the definition by Ramus during editions of his *Logic*. The chief difference is between editions using "dispute" and those using "reason."

⁸⁷ *Geometri*, Lib. I in *Arithmeticae libri duo, geometriae septem et viginti* (Basileae, 1569), p. 1 as cited by Ong, *Ramus*, p. 179.

⁸⁸ *Commentariorum*, fol. 6.

⁸⁹ See *Arist. anim.* (1543), fols. 3, 4. All citations are from this edition.

⁹⁰ *Arist. anim.*, fol. 4.

⁹¹ See *Dial. inst.*, fol. 57. This is reproduced in Figure 1.

⁹² *Arist. anim.*, fol. 4. See Ong, *Ramus*, p. 182.

⁹³ See Ong, *Ramus*, p. 183. Ramus wrote: "We shall use the terms of reasoning, that is, proof and argument, as being the most widely received and the most customary in this art," *Dialectique* (1555), p. 5 (Dassonville, ed., p. 64). The translation is in Howell, *L&R*, p. 155.

⁹⁴ These English terms come from a 1632 translation of Ramus' *Dialectic* by Robert Fage. In *Dial. inst.* these were in Latin: *caussae, effectus, subiecta, adiuncta, dissentanea; genus, species, nomen, notatio, coniugata, testimonia, comparata, divisio,* and *definitio*. These were rearranged in succeeding editions of Ramus' works. The 1555 *Dialectique* was reorganized and Ramus spoke of "artistic arguments" which created belief by themselves and their nature; and "non-artistic arguments" which needed more proof beyond themselves alone to be convincing. See pp. 5-6, 61 (pp. 63-64; 96, Dassonville, ed.) and Aristotle's *Rhetoric*, 1.1, 15. Ramus devoted fifty-five pages to artistic arguments (which he subdivided into "primary" and "derivative") but only five pages to non-artistic arguments. Primary artistic arguments were: causes, effects, subjects, adjuncts, opposites, and comparatives; derivative artistic arguments were: reasoning from name, from division, and from definition. Non-artistic arguments were particularized for each case. Howell argues that Ramus intended non-artistic arguments to be considered as a whole to be one item. Thus he would have ten "basic entitles" just as Aristotle had ten categories. See *L&R*, p. 156.

⁹⁵ See *Dial. inst.*, fols. 19-20.

⁹⁶ See *Dialecticae libri duo, Audomari Talaei praelectionibus illustrati* (1569), p. 273. Cf. *RTI*, p. 181.

⁹⁷ *Dialectique* (1555), p. 71 (p. 115, Dassonville, ed.). See also Howell, p. 158 who calls this "book" on "judgment" Ramus' "most influential" contribution to logic. The French reads: *Jugement est la deuziesme partie de Logique qui monstre les voyes et moyens de bien juger par certaines reigles de disposition.*...The 1574 English translation by Roland MacIlmaine renders this: "Disposition is a parte of Dialecticke, wich teachethe to dispose and place orderly the argumentes inuented, to the ende we maye iudge well and rightly: for we iudge of euery thing according to the disposition thereof," Dunn, ed., p. 41.

⁹⁸ See Ong, *Ramus*, p. 184.

⁹⁹ See *Dial. inst.*, fol. 20. These were different in his *Dialectique*.

¹⁰⁰ See *Arist. anim.*, fol. 73.

¹⁰¹ *Dial. inst.*, fol. 20 as cited in Ong, *Ramus*, p. 185.

¹⁰² See Ong's discussion in *Ramus*, pp. 185-186.

¹⁰³ This is Howell's rendering of the French: *Enonciation est disposition par laquelle quelque chose est énoncée de quelque chose* from *Dialectique*, p. 71 (p. 115, Dassonville, ed.), *L&R*, p. 158. MacIlmaine's English translation was: "Proposition is a disposition in the which one argumente is spoken for another," Dunn, ed., p. 41.

¹⁰⁴ On these see Howell, *L&R*, pp. 158-159.

[105] See *Dial. inst.*, fol. 27 as given in Ong, *Ramus*, p. 187.

[106] See *Dial. inst.*, fols. 27-28.

[107] See *Dial. inst.*, fol. 29.

[108] See Ong, *Ramus*, p. 188.

[109] *Arist. anim.*, fol. 58. See Ong, *Ramus*, p. 188.

[110] *Arist. anim.*, fol. 60: *Idem....demonstrare rem, et definire.*

[111] See Peter F. Fisher, "Milton's Logic," *Journal of the History of Ideas*, XXIII (1962), 53-54 and Ong, *Ramus*, p. 188.

[112] See Ong, *Ramus*, p. 189 citing *Dial. inst.*, fol. 35ff.

[113] See *Dial. inst.*, fol. 36 and Ong, *Ramus*, p. 189.

[114] *Dial. inst.*, fols. 38-39. Cf. *Hanc artium summam dialectica [facit]*, fol. 35.

[115] See above, notes 89 and 90. Cf. *Dial. inst.*, fols. 5, 7-8, 17.

[116] *Dial. inst.*, fol. 44. See Ong, *Ramus*, p. 190.

[117] *Dial. inst.*, fol. 44ff.

[118] *Dial. inst.*, fol. 36 cited by Ong, *Ramus*, p. 191.

[119] *Dial. inst.*, fol. 48.

[120] *Dial inst.*, fol. 48. See Ong, *Ramus*, p. 191. Ramus then went on to describe how interpretation took place through the three steps of judgment. See p. 192.

[121] *Dial. inst.*, fol. 52.

[122] See *Dial. inst.*, fols. 52-53 and Ong, *Ramus*, p. 193.

[123] For an account of the attacks on Ramus see Ong, *Ramus*, ch. X.

[124] *Dialectique* (1555), p. 4 (p. 63, Dassonville, ed.). See *RTI*, pp. 178ff. for a discussion of editions of Ramus' *Dialectic*. Cf. Dassonville's discussion, "Les Editions Francaises De La Dialectique," ch. 4.

[125] This edition at first included a commentary by Ramus' cohort Talon. The 1566 edition, published after Talon's death, saw *Talon's Praelectiones* rewritten by Ramus.

[126] See Ong, *Ramus*, p. 296 and *RTI*.

[127] *Inventio est pars dialecticae de inveniendis argumentis.* See Ong, *Ramus*, p. 223.

[128] See *Arist. anim.*, fol. 64.

[129] See the 1574 MacIlmaine translation, Dunn, ed., p. 10.

[130] See Howell's discussion of "judgment" in the 1555 *Dialectique*, *L&R*, pp. 158ff.

[131] *Dial. A. Talaei pr. ill.*, Lib. II, cap. i (1569), p. 273. This is translated in Ong, *Ramus*, p. 224.

[132] Howell, *L&R*, p. 160.

[133] As in Aristotle. See the opening of his *Nicomachean Ethics*, especially Book I, ch. 4 and his *Posterior Analytics*, I. Cf. J.M. Le Blond, *Logique et Methode chez Aristote* (1939; rpt. Paris: Librairie Philosophique: J. Vrin, 1970). Aristotle was concerned with what procedure to use in advancing toward knowledge with an unknown goal not yet in sight.

[134] See C.J.R. Armstrong, "The Dialectial Road to Truth: The Dialogue," *French Renaissance Studies* 1540-70, ed. Peter Sharratt (Edinburgh: Edinburgh University Press, 1976), pp. 36-51 for a study of the correlation between Renaissance "dialogue" and the philosophical and literary ethos of Agricola and other dialecticians. Cf. Gilbert, p. 124.

[135] See McKeon, pp. 11-12 who cites examples of the ancient crossing of lines between rhetoric and medicine as well as Ong, *Ramus*, p. 226.

[136] Ong sees it as having this signification in John of Salisbury, Lambert of Auxerre, and St. Albert the Great. See *Ramus*, p. 227.

[137] Ong, *Ramus*, p. 228.

[138] Ong notes that while Peter of Spain used the term at the opening of his *Summulae logicales* as a loose synonym for *ars* and *scientia*, and *doctrina*, he did not develop this. Later commentators on Peter explained the term as "a short and useful way of attaining something quickly," Ong, *Ramus*, p. 230. The Stoics also had equated *ars* (Gr. *technē*) with *methodus*.

[139] See Gilbert, pp. 121-122 who cites Melanchthon's statement in *Erotemata dialectices* (1547): "Thus the Dialecticians have adopted this word *methodus* for the most correct order of explication." The problem is that Melanchthon did not identify the dialecticians he had in mind.

[140] Ong, *Ramus*, p. 232. On Sturm see Gilbert, pp. 23, 72, 84 and 122ff. Gilbert cites the work of Carl von Prantl, *Geschichte der Logik in Abendlande*, 4 vols. (Leipzig, 1855-70) and his "Uber Petrus Ramus: Ein Vortrag," *Sitzungberichte der philosophisch-philologischen und historischen Classe der königlichen bayerischen Akademie der Dissenschaften zu München*, Band II, Heft II (1878), pp. 157-169 as suggesting Sturm as the one behind sixteenth century discussions of "method" in logic textbooks, Gilbert, p. 122.

[141] See *RTI*, p. 179.

[142] On Melanchthon see *ODC*; David C. Steinmetz, *Reformers in the Wings* (Philadelphia: Fortress Press, 1971), ch. 6; EP, III, 296, IV, 534ff.; V, 263 and Rogers and McKim, pp. 148-150.

[143] These were *Compendaria dialectices ratio* (*A Brief Notion of Dialectic* -- 1520); *Dialectices....libri quatuor* (*Dialectic in Four Books* -- 1528); and *In Ciceronis Topica scholia* (*Notes on Cicero's Topics*). See Ong, *Ramus*, p. 236 and Gilbert, pp. 125-128.

[144] See Gilbert, p. 125 who cites Melanchthon's praise of Aristotle in *Corpus Reformatorum*, eds. C.G. Bretschneider and H.E. Bindseil (Halle, 1834-1860), XI, 349; III, 362;

and XI, 654-655; hereafter cited as *C.R.*

[145] *Dialectica est ars seu via, recte, ordine, et perspicue docendi, quod sit recte definiendo, dividendo, argumenta vera conectendo, et male cohaerentia seu falsa retexendo et refutando, Erotemata Dialectica,* C.R., XIII, 513. This is given by Gilbert, p. 126. Cf. Ong, *Ramus*, p. 159.

[146] See C.R., XIII, 573 cited in Ong, *Ramus*, p. 158.

[147] ...*rectam viam seu ordinem investigationis et explicationis sive simplicium quaestionum sive propositionum,* C.R., XIII, 573.

[148] C.R., XIII, 573 as given in Gilbert, p. 126.

[149] On these see Howell, *L&R*, pp. 282-283 and Ong, *RTI*.

[150] *secundum iudicium credo vocas rationem artium tradendarum cuam Graeci methodon appellant....*"Pro Aristotele responsio adversus Petri Rami calumnias," *Opera iuridica, philologica, philosophica* (Rotterdam, 1766), pp. 810-811. In the original Paris edition of 1543 the remark is found in fol. 48. See Gilbert, pp. 132-133 and Ong, *Ramus*, p. 244.

[151] Ramus, *Dialectici commentarii tres authore Audomaro Talaeo editi* (Lutetiae, 1546), p. 83 as given in Ong, *Ramus*, p. 245.

[152] See *Dialectici comm. tres.*, pp. 87-90 and Ong, *Ramus*, p. 246.

[153] The translation is by Eugene J. Barber and Leonard A. Kennedy in *Renaissance Philosophy*, ed. Leonard A. Kennedy (The Hague: Mouton, 1973), pp. 115-155.

[154] Ramus wrote: "....in art and science what are prior and better known absolutely and by nature, namely the general and universal, lead the way and give rise to knowledge of the specific and particular, which are absolutely and by nature, subsequent and less well known," Kennedy, ed., p. 118 and p. iii.

[155] See Kennedy, ed., p. 121. Ramus also found the same thing in the difficulties raised by Aristotle's *Ethics* and *On the Parts of Animals*.

[156] Kennedy, ed., p. 125.

[157] Kennedy, ed., p. 129.

[158] See Kennedy, ed., pp. 128 and 112.

[159] Ong, *RTI*, p. 63. Ong describes this also as the work where "the quintessence of Ramist teaching on method is distilled," *Ramus*, p. 254.

[160] *Dialectica* (Basle, 1569), pp. 465-466 as given in Ong, *Ramus*, p. 249 who sees Ramus' movement here as being from "antecedents" to "consequents."

[161] *Dialectica* (1569), Bk. II, cap. xvii, pp. 542-543 as given in Ong, *Ramus*, p. 249.

[162] *Dialectica* (1569), Bk. II, cap. xvii, p. 563 as translated in Ong, *Ramus*, p. 250.

[163] *Dialecticae libri duo* (Lutetiae, 1574; same text as 1572), Bk. II, cap. xvii, pp. 72-73 as translated in Ong, *Ramus*, p. 251. Cf. R. Hooykaas, *Humanisme, Science et Réforme Pierre*

De La Ramée (1515-1572) (Leyde: E.J. Brill, 1958), ch. VIII: "L'Induction."

[164] See notes 96-98 above. On Schegk's attack see Gilbert, pp. 158-162 and Ong, *Ramus, passim.*

[165] See Ong, *Ramus*, p. 251 and Miller, *NEM*, pp. 125ff.

[166] *Dialecticae libri duo* (1574), Lib. II, cap. i. 51 cited in Ong, *Ramus*, p. 252. The final forms of Ramus' *Dialectic* as "methodized" in chart form are found in his *Sch. dial. in Sch. in lib. arts.*, fol. 608 and in Miller, NEM, p. 127. See Figures 2 and 3.

[167] See Graves, p. 155 and Elizabeth Flower and Murray G. Murphy, *A History of Philosophy in America*, 2 vols. (New York: G.P. Putman, 1977), I, 17. See note 131 above for judgment of enunciation.

[168] Dunn, ed., p. 41. Cf. Fisher, "Milton's Logic," p. 52.

[169] Quoted in Miller, *NEM*, p. 134.

[170] Quoted in Miller, *NEM*, p. 134.

[171] The definition is from the *Dialectique* (1555), p. 87 (Dassonville, ed., p. 125). Cf. p. 114 (Dassonville, ed., p. 152) as translated by Howell: "In brief the art of syllogism does not inform us of any other thing than that of resolving a stated question by the manifest truth of two well-arranged parts," *L&R*, p. 159.

[172] Quoted in Miller, *NEM*, p. 134. Miller wrote that for Ramus, "the stuff of judgment is not the syllogism but the axiom; the aim of an orator or preacher is a succession of sentences, not a display of deductions. When he has laid out the arguments and combined them into several axioms, he then ought to perceive from the axioms themselves what are their interconnections and what is their order; he should use the syllogism only when in doubt about formulating a particular proposition, or when incapable of recognizing the order of precedence among several statements." Alexander Richardson, a follower of Ramus wrote that "syllogisms serve but for the clearing of the truth of axioms," *The Logicians School-Master: or, A Comment upon Ramus Logick* (London, 1657), p. 335.

[173] See J. Maritain, *Formal Logic*, trans. Imelda Choquette (New York: Sheed & Ward, 1946), p. 190.

[174] See Costello, p. 48.

[175] On Ramus' divisions see MacIlmaine's translation, Dunn, ed., pp. 46ff.

[176] See Costello, p. 48.

[177] On this "downward" deductive movement of the syllogism see *The Puritans*, ed. Perry Miller and Thomas H. Johnson, 2 vols. (1938; rpt. New York: Harper & Row, 1963), I, 35-36: "The syllogism strikes downward vertically, so to speak, driving the mind before it, where disjunction extends horizontally for the contemplation of self-reflecting intelligence."

[178] See above notes 163 and 151.

[179] For Ramus' use of these laws see Ong, *Ramus*, pp. 258ff. and Howell, *L&R*, pp. 151ff.

¹⁸⁰ This is the phrase in the *Dialectique* (1555), pp. 120-121 (Dassonville, ed., p. 145). See Howell, *L&R,* pp. 160-161.

¹⁸¹ Dichotomies or divisions by twos might in a sense reflect other such bipolarities: thesis/antithesis, form/matter, act/potency etc. Yet Ramus did not always dichotomize in the same way. Patterns such as mental/extramental, similarity/dissimilarity are in his works. These divisions according to Ong are "sporadic and variable." He says "there is simply no ground on which we can account for Ramus' dichotomies," *Ramus,* p. 199. Kit Marlowe in *The Massacre of Paris* has the Duke of Guise denounce Ramus as a "flat dichotomist." Johann Piscator, on the other hand, called Ramus' dichotomies "most beautiful." Cf. Miller, *NEM,* p. 127.

¹⁸² Miller wrote: "The Ramean logic is the logic of a Humanist, the conclusions come from within, they are not reached by piling one brick upon another in a shaky and top-heavy sequence, but by the prompt and decisive arbitration of the natural reason between two possibilities," *The Puritans,* I, 35.

¹⁸³ *The Puritans,* I, 32.

¹⁸⁴ See Ong, *Ramus,* p. 264.

¹⁸⁵ Walter J. Ong, "Johannes Piscator: One Man or a Ramist Dichotomy?" *Harvard Library Bulletin,* VIII (1954), 153. Ong also says: "Writing 'logical analyses' had been at first an exclusively Ramist occupation and remains one of the most important points of connection between Ramism and subsequent milieux," "Peter Ramus and the Naming of Methodism," *Journal of the History of Ideas,* XIV (1953), 247.

¹⁸⁶ Ong points to Ramus' *Arist. anim.*, fol. 19 and comments: "Ramus objects to Aristotle's categories because they contain things only in potency, being supreme *genera* by means of which things can be classified....For the Ramist, things existed classified." *Ramus,* p. 355 (note 27).

¹⁸⁷ See *The Puritans,* I, 33. Miller and Johnson refer to Ramus' *Dialecticae Libri Duo* (London, 1669), pp. 10-14.

¹⁸⁸ See Howell, *L&R,* p. 163 who writes: "His followers tended to construe the natural method and the law of justice to mean the severest kind of dichotomizing, as if any given idea had only two members, one completely insulated from the other. But it is worth noticing that Ramus himself did not take the habit as seriously as that." See also Miller, *NEM,* p. 127 who does not see much other than dichotomies in Ramus.

¹⁸⁹ This was his comment in *Dialectique* (1555), p. 126 (Dassonville ed., p. 148). See Howell, L&R, pp. 161-162 who likens this whole process taking place to one drawing tickets from a jug at a lottery. As they are drawn, the logician performs his task and classifies them. Cf. Ong, *Ramus,* p. 246. See Ramus' *Rudimenta grammaticae graecae* (Paris, 1560) and other editions for charts and also the charts in *Grammaire* (Paris, 1572). See Graves, *Educational Reformation,* p. 130.

¹⁹⁰ See Howell, *L&R,* pp. 6-7.

¹⁹¹ *Dialectique* (1555), p. 4 (Dassonville, ed., p. 62). See Howell, *L&R,* pp. 154-155 for the translation. Cf. p. 16. Howell writes: "Nowhere is the issue between scholastic and Ramist indicated more sharply than it is in the words just quoted. Nowhere is the essential point in Ramus' reform of scholastic logic and traditional rhetoric stated more firmly that

it is right here," *L&R*, p. 155. Cf. Chaim Perelman and L. Olbrechts-Tyteca, *The New Rhetoric A Treatise on Argumentation*, trans. John Wilkinson and Purcell Weaver (Notre Dame, Indiana: University of Notre Dame Press, 1969), pp. 505-506.

[192] See Duhamel, "Ramus," p. 170; Ong, "Introduction," p. ix; Ong, "Ramism," p. 43; *Ramus*, ch. 12; Howell, L&R, p. 165 and his "Ramus and English Rhetoric: 1574-1681," *The Quarterly Journal of Speech*, XXXVII (1951) and Perelman and Olbrechts-Tyteca, p. 505.

[193] See Ong, "Introduction," p. ix. Olbrechts-Tyteca and Perelman observe that "when Agricola and Ramus try to make a sharp separation between dialectic and rhetoric by reducing the latter to the study of pleasing and ornate means of expression, they transfer to dialectic the problems of order, arrangement and method that were traditionally dealt with in works on rhetoric. It seems that this is where rhetoric merges with dialectic, despite the effort to separate them." pp. 505-506.

[194] See Ong, "Ramism," p. 43. For background history on the development of the Art of Memory prior to Ramus see Appendix B.

[195] On Bruno see EP, I, 405-408 and the bibliography listed there as well as Frances Yates, *Giordano Bruno and the Hermetic Tradition* (Chicago: University of Chicago Press, 1964).

[196] *EP*, I, 405. Cf. Yates, *Art*, p. 206.

[197] See *EP*, III, 489-490 and Yates, *Bruno*.

[198] *EP*, III, 490.

[199] *EP*, I, 407-408.

[200] See Yates, *Art*, p. 208.

[201] For pictures of these see Yates, *Art*, following pgs. 208 and 209. On Lullism see Yates, *Art*, ch. VIII.

[202] Yates, *Art*, p. 211. For a discussion of these see *Art*, pp. 212ff.

[203] See Yates, *Art*, ch. XIII. Bruno referred to Ramus as "that arch pendant of a Frenchman who has brought his scholasticism to the liberal arts." See Dorothea Waley Singer, *Giordano Bruno His Life and Thought* (New York: Schuman, 1950), p. 22. Cf. p. 76 (note 73). Bruno like Ramus had clashed with the ecclesiastical authorities in Geneva. See J. Lewis McIntyre, *Giordano Bruno* (London: Macmillan & Co., 1903), pp. 14-16.

[204] As Ong says of Ramus: "His whole scheme of arts, based on a topically conceived logic, is a system of local memory," *Ramus*, p. 280.

[205] This is the insight of Paolo Rossi, *Calvis universalis* (Milan, 1960), p. 140 cited in Yates, *Art*, p. 232.

[206] *Scholarum Rhetoricarum in Ciceronis Oratorem* in *Sch. in lib. arts*, Lib. XIX, col. 309 (1578 ed.). See Quintilian, *Institutio oratoria*, XI, ii. 36 as cited by Yates, *Art*, p. 233.

[207] *Dial. inst.*, fols. 57-58, cited in Ong, *Ramus*, p. 194. Cf. *Sch. in lib. arts.* (1569 ed.), col. 392 of Ramus' *Scholae rhetoricae*.

[208] See Yates, *Art*, p. 234. She cites Romberch's use of the ugly old woman *Grammatica* to stimulate memory by remembering her parts.

In a theological context, the Protestant Ramus reacted strongly against the use of images. In his *Commentariorum* when he explicated the second commandment, Ramus quoted Deuteronomy 4:15 which prohibits the erection of graven images. Ramus contrasted this with the idol worship of the Greeks and went on to point out that in Roman Catholic churches people bowed and burned incense before erected graven images. Yates suggests Ramus' sympathy with the iconoclastic movements of France, England, and the Low Countries is relevant to his attitudes toward images in the art of memory. See *Art*, pp. 236-237 citing *Commentariorum* (1577), pp. 114-115.

[209] See Yates, *Art*, pp. 241-242.

NOTES TO CHAPTER III

[1] For a short discussion of "The Spread of Ramism in Europe," see Appendix C.

[2] See the "Introduction" to the Dunn edition.

[3] James M. Anderson, *Early Records of the University of St. Andrews* (Edinburgh: Printed by T. and A. Constable Ltd., 1926), pp. 164, 165, 273 as cited by Howell, *L&R*, p. 179.

[4] See *RTI*, numbers 257, 265, 267, and 272.

[5] Dunn ed., p. 62 (note 31).

[6] See for example, the string of Scriptural quotes used to illustrate the similitude, Dunn, ed., p. 27 and Howell, *L&R*, p. 187.

[7] See Dunn, ed., pp. 6-7.

[8] Dunn, ed., p. 7. See the discussion of MacIlmaine by Eugenie Hershon Bernstein, *A Revaluation of the Plaine Genre of Homiletics in Its Evolution as a Theory of Persuasion from Ramus to John Wilkins*, Diss. University of California at Los Angeles, 1973, ch. IV.

[9] Dunn, ed., p. 6.

[10] See Bernstein's discussion, p. 73.

[11] See Bernstein, pp. 73-74.

[12] Dunn, ed., p. 58.

[13] Dunn, ed., p. 58.

[14] See Howell, *L&R*, p. 183 and Dunn, ed., p. 94. For the influence of the Ramist method on "plain-style preaching" see Bernstein, p. 76f.

[15] On Melville, see *DNB* and Kearney, pp. 53-60.

[16] For a discussion of Melville and these reforms see Kearney, pp. 53ff.

[17] See Thomas M'Crie, *Life of Andrew Melville*, 2nd ed., 2 vols. (Edinburgh, 1824), I, 24 and II, 419. See also Fletcher, I, 142.

[18] From *The Diary of Mr. James Melville 1556-1601* (Edinburgh, 1844), p. 38 as cited in Kearney, p. 57. John Durkan points out that "already some decades earlier a certain John Steward has defined him" (Ramus). See "The Cultural Background in Sixteenth-Century Scotland," *Essays on the Scottish Reformation 1513-1625*, ed. David McRoberts (Glasglow: Burns, 1962), p. 286.

[19] Alexander Morgan, *Scottish University Studies* (Oxford: University Press, 1933), pp. 65-73 and pp. 134-137.

[20] See G.D. Henderson, *Religious Life in Seventeenth-Century Scotland* (Cambridge: University Press, 1937), p. 275. See also Jack B. Rogers, *Scripture in the Westminster Confession* (Grand Rapids: Wm. B. Eerdmans Publishing Co., 1967), p. 89.

[21] See *Diary of Mr. James Melville*, p. 207 as cited in Kearney, p. 55.

[22] Kearney, p. 58.

[23] Kearney, p. 59.

[24] See *DNB*. On Ramus and the Scots see Ong, *Ramus*, p. 302 who points out that two natural sons of King James V were frequent dinner companions of Ramus.

[25] On Digby see *DNB* and Howell, *L&R*, pp. 194ff.

[26] This was also Francis Bacon's point in his *Advancement of Learning*. See Craig Walton, "Ramus and Bacon on Method," *Journal of the History of Philosophy*, IX (1971), pp. 289-302; Howell, *L&R,* pp. 369-370.

[27] On the controversy see *RTI*, pp. 506ff.

[28] Howell, *L&R*, p. 196.

[29] From Nash's "Preface" to Menaphon reprinted in G. Gregory Smith, *Elizabethan Critical Essays* (London: Oxford University Press, 1904), I, 316.

[30] This work was published in London in 1592. See the edition published in London by John Lane, 1922. An expanded treatment of the Harvey/Nash controversy is in Howell, *L&R*, pp. 196-199.

[31] From Richard Montagu, *Diatribae upon the First part of the late History of Tithes* (London, 1621), pp. 415-416 as cited in Howell, *L&R*, p. 201.

[32] Montagu, pp. 341-342 cited in Howell, *L&R*, pp. 201-202. Francis Bacon, while praising Ramus for reviving the three laws, also condemned him for introducing the "canker of Epitomes" and "uniform method and dichotomies." See *The Works of Francis Bacon*, ed. James Speeding, *et. al.* (Boston, 1860-1864), VI, 294; IX, 128. Cf. Walton.

[33] See *RTI* and the chart by Ong, *Ramus*, p. 296.

[34] See Robert D. Pepper, *Four Tudor Books on Education* (Gainesville, Florida: Scholars' Facsimiles & Reprints, 1966), pp. xxviii ff. and Kearney, ch. 3.

[36] The quote is from Hill, *IO*, p. 292. Cf. Kearney, p. 61 who says: "The list of Cambridge Ramists reads like a list of the most radical Cambridge Puritans...."; Sprunger,

Learned, p. 110.

³⁶ See Kearney, ch. 3 and Hill, *IO, passim*.

³⁷ See Howell, "Ramus and English Rhetoric," p. 303. The first English logician known was Alcuin who wrote his *De Dialectica* in Latin (while living in France) about 794. See *Patrologia Series Latina*, ed. J.P. Migne, 221 vols. (Paris, 1844-1904), CI, 951-976. This was a continuation of his *De Rhetorica*. See Wilbur S. Howell, *The Rhetoric of Alcuin and Charlemagne* (Princeton: Princeton University Press, 1941), pp. 5-8.

³⁸ See *STC #25809* and Howell, *L&R*, p. 29. Howell writes: "The chief reason why Wilson lost favor rapidly after 1567 is that Ramistic logic made its appearance in England in the fifteen-seventies and ended the reign of scholastic logic as we see it in Wilson and his predecessors," pp. 29-30.

³⁹ See Howell, *L&R*, pp. 98-110. See Wilson's *Arte of Rhetorique* 1560, ed. George Herbert Mair (Oxford: Clarendon Press, 1909). On the sources see R.H. Wagner, "Wilson and His Sources," *Quarterly Journal of Speech*, XV (1929), 525-537.

⁴⁰ *The Rule of Reason* (London, 1551). Sig. B2v. cited in Howell, *L&R*, p. 17 and "Ramus and English Rhetoric," p. 303.

⁴¹ See James R. McNally, "Prima pars dialecticae: The Influence of Agricolan Dialectic upon English Accounts of Invention," *Renaissance Quarterly*, XXI (1968), 171.

⁴² For a discussion of Wilson's system see Howell, *L&R*, pp. 12-31.

⁴³ See the section of Wilson in McNally, pp. 171-173.

⁴⁴ Agricola's term was *nota*. See McNally, p. 171 citing *Rule of Reason*, f. 37v.

⁴⁵ See McNally, p. 172.

⁴⁶ *Rule of Reason*, ff. 57-58 cited in McNally, p. 172.

⁴⁷ Howell did not fully recognize this. Wilson would have incurred the wrath of Ramus for following Cicero in permitting an overlap of dialectic and rhetoric. Wilson followed the traditional division of rhetoric into disposition (judgment), invention, style, memory, and delivery. See Howell, "Ramus and English Rhetoric," p. 303 and *L&R*, pp. 100ff.

⁴⁸ See *DNB* and Howell, *L&R*, p. 50 as well as Lisa Jardine, "The Place of Dialectic Teaching in Sixteenth-Century Cambridge," *Studies in the Renaissance*, XXI (1974), 54; hereafter cited as "Place."

⁴⁹ Howell, *L&R*, p. 50. See also Ivo Thomas, "Medieval Aftermath: Oxford Logic and Logicians of the Seventeenth Century," *Oxford Studies in Honor of David Callus* (Oxford: Clarendon Press, 1964), p. 301.

⁵⁰ McNally, p. 173. The fourth book on invention is "best described as an epitome of Agricola's *Dialectical Invention*," McNally, p. 174.

⁵¹ Howell, *L&R*, p. 51.

⁵² McNally, pp. 174, 175.

⁵³ See *DNB* and Howell, *L&R*, p. 50f. Carter was born around 1530 and died in 1590.

⁵⁴ See Ong's "Agricola Check List" in *RTI*, pp. 534-558.

⁵⁵ McNally, p. 157. See Ong, *Ramus*, p. 63. Ong also sees the tradition of placing judgment before invention as stemming more from Boethius than Aristotle, *Ramus*, p. 112.

⁵⁶ Howell, *L&R*, p. 55.

⁵⁷ See Fletcher, I, 141 who writes: "The method was to set down a definition to be memorized and follow it with an analysis and explanation of every word in it, torturing and twisting the material by illustration and example, using every possible device to make the material clear to the boy or young man learning it, and providing connections with everything else he knew or was learning about the subject."

⁵⁸ See McNally, pp. 176-177 for his conclusions.

⁵⁹ A "Dedicatory Poem" to Carter's work written by Thomas Drant included Ramus' name in a list of famous logicians of the past. See Howell's translation, *L&R*, pp. 55-56.

⁶⁰ On Lever see *DNB* and Howell, *L&R*, pp. 57-58.

⁶¹ *Witcraft*, sig. *3r. cited in Howell, *L&R*, p. 58.

⁶² On Bucer see Porter, pp. 51-55. Howell also points out that Lever said he was trying to prove that "the arte of Reasoning may be taught in englishe." Since Wilsons' *Rule of Reason* was published in 1551 it seems unlikely for Lever's remark to have been made after that time. See *L&R*, pp. 58-59.

⁶³ From *Witcraft*, p. 239 cited in Howell, *L&R*, p. 61.

⁶⁴ See Howell, *L&R*, p. 61.

⁶⁵ See Howell, *L&R*, p. 60.

⁶⁶ *Witcraft*, sig. **Ir-**IV cited by Howell, *L&R*, p. 62.

⁶⁷ See *Witcraft*, sig. **V-**2r cited by Howell, *L&R*, pp. 62-63.

⁶⁸ *Witcraft* (1573), p. 1 as cited in Joan Marie Lechner, *Renaissance Concepts of the Commonplaces* (New York: Pageant Press, 1962), p. 77.

⁶⁹ See Jardine, "Place," pp. 32-33.

⁷⁰ See Jardine, "Place," p. 35.

⁷¹ See the summary in Jardine, "Place," pp. 36-41.

⁷² This is the conclusion of those who have sifted through student notebooks, university curriculum statutes and the like for this period in the sixteenth century. See Kearney, p. 64. He writes: "On the evidence of a fair range of college material around 1600 we may conclude that Ramism had little direct influence at Oxford." James McConica writes: "The evidence from inventories is sufficient to indicate that these highly scholastic, logical treatises were current in the university [Oxford] throughout the Tudor period." See "Humanism

and Aristotle in Tudor Oxford," *English Historical Review,* XCIV, No. 371 (April 1979), 297. See also C. Schmitt, "Philosophy and Science in Sixteenth-Century Universities: Some Preliminary Comments," *The Cultural Context of Medieval Learning,* ed. John E. Murdoch and Edith Dudley Sylla (Dordrecht: D. Reidel Publishing Co., 1975), p. 498. Thomas concludes: "Ramism had widespread popular success, but did not by any means go unchallenged, and Oxford was conspicuous among the universities of northern Europe in preferring not indeed full-blown medievalism, but at any rate a line that was in intention more Aristotelian," Ivo Thomas, "Medieval Aftermath," p. 301.

[73] J. Bass Mullinger wrote that on the European continent, Cambridge had the reputation as the "leading school for the study of Ramistic logic," *The University of Cambridge,* 3 vols. (Cambridge: University Press, 1884-1911), II, 412. Cf. Miller, *NEM,* p. 117.

[74] See the list of Oxford men who owned copies of Ramus' works at their death as given in Curtis, p. 253. The most well-known Oxford Ramist was Dr. John Rainolds. See McConica, "Humanism and Aristotle," pp. 302ff. Charles Butler, "the most influential follower at that institution," prepared the books that carried the Ramist philosophy into English public schools in the seventeenth-century. See Howell, *L&R,* p. 193 and pp. 262ff.

[75] Howell concludes: "....the influence of Ramus at Cambridge was more fruitful and more presistent even though no more actual than at Oxford," *L&R,* p. 193.

[76] McConica, "Humanism and Aristotle," p. 301 (note 4). He also writes: "The evidence for a 'reception' of Ramus, if by that we mean the establishment of a group of scholars who single-mindedly advocated Ramus' critique of Aristotle, seems to me however to be tenous indeed."

[77] McConica, "Humanism and Aristotle," p. 301 (note 5). See also Meyrick H. Carré, *Phases of Thought in England* (Oxford: Clarendon Press, 1949), pp. 202-203; 212-213.

[78] On Case see Howell, *L&R,* pp. 190-191; McConica, "Humanism and Aristotle," pp. 298ff.; Schmitt, "Philosophy and Science," p. 500 and Carré, pp. 201-202. Case was a Roman Catholic, doctor of medicine, graduate and benefactor of St. John's College, Oxford.

[79] Leichester was the Oxford patron of Sir Philip Sidney whose secretary was the Cambridge Ramist William Temple. See below note 120.

[80] Cited in McConica, "Humanism and Aristotle," p. 300.

[81] McConica, "Humanism and Aristotle," pp. 300-301. For Case, Aristotle was *omnium philosophorum facile princeps.* See Carré, p. 201.

[82] Richard Hooker, *Of the Lawes of Ecclesiasticall Politie* (London, 1597), Book I, ch. 6, sec. 4.

[83] Howell, *L&R,* p. 193 citing Samuel Clark, *The Lives of sundy Eminent Persons in this Later Age* (London, 1683), pt. I, p. 128. See also Kenneth Charleton, *Education in Renaissance England* (London: Routledge and Kegan Paul, 1965), p. 153.

[84] From *Documents Relating to the University and Colleges of Cambridge* (London, 1852), I, 459 cited in Jardine, "Place," p. 43.

[85] *Documents,* I, 492 cited in Jardine, "Place," p. 44. See also the 1560 Statutes of

Trinity College which stipulated that every propective pensioner "should be examined and found fit for dialectical instruction," cited in Jardine, "Place," p. 44.

[86] Jardine, "Place," pp. 44-45.

[87] On the study of rhetoric in the elementary schools see T.W. Baldwin, *William Shakspere's Small Latine and Lesse Greeke*, 2 vols. (Urbana, Illinois: University of Illinois Press, 1944), I, ch. XXXI.

[88] Jardine, "Place," p. 59. See also Jardine's "Humanism and the Sixteenth Century Cambridge Arts Course," *History of Education*, IV (1975), 25; hereafter cited as "Humanism." Jardine writes: "....by the sixteenth century, all the dialectic manuals recommended in the university and college statutes at Cambridge and all those which occur regularly in contemporary book lists, belong to the "humanist" development initiated by Valla's dialectic," "Humanism," pp. 24-25. Fletcher notes that "by 1600 logic was a subject that was not and could not be reduced to a single textbook," I, 144.

[89] On Chaderton see *DNB* and William Dillingham, *Laurence Chaderton, D.D.* (First Master of Emmanuel), trans. E.S. Shuckburgh (Cambridge, 1884). The copy of this rare volume I have used is reproduced from the Newberry Library, Chicago. Cf. Peter Lake, *Moderate Puritans and the Elizabethan Church* (Cambridge: Cambridge University Press, 1982).

[90] It is not possible here to chronicle Chaderton's "Puritan" activities in depth. See references in Porter, Collinson, *EPM*, and Lake, esp. chs. 1, 3, and 10.

[91] Dillingham, p. 4.

[92] See Curtis, pp. 79-81. Curtis comments: "Formal lectures and academic exercises, however, comprised only a part of the instruction available within the colleges of Oxford and Cambridge. The work of the college tutors rather than the readings of the college lecturers was probably in the sixteenth and was definitely in the seventeenth century the most important influence on a scholar's education," p. 107. Cf. Fletcher, I, 144 and Collinson, *EPM*, p. 125.

[93] Dillingham, p. 5.

[94] Dillingham, p. 5.

[95] Howell, *L&R*, p. 222. See below note 128.

[96] Dillingham, p. 1.

[97] The phrase is Christopher Hill's in *IO*, p. 311. The founder was Sir Walter Mildmay, a Christ's College graduate. On Mildmay see Stanford E. Lehmberg, *Sir Walter Mildmay and Tudor Government* (Austin: University of Texas Press, 1964). Lehmberg recounts an incident when Queen Elizabeth said: "Sir Walter, I hear you have erected a Puritan foundation." Mildmay replied, "No, madam, far be it from me to countenance anything contrary to your established laws; but I have set an acorn which, when it becomes an oak, God alone knows what will be the fruit thereof." See Lehmberg, ch. 14: "Emmanuel College."

Mildmay said the aim of the College was "to render as many as possible fit for the administration of the Divine Word and Sacraments; and that from their seed ground the English Church might have those she can summon to instruct the people and undertake the office of pastors, which is a thing necessary above all others, " E.S. Schuckburg, *Emmanuel College* (London: F.E. Robinson and Co., 1904), p. 23 cited in Porter, p. 239. Cf. Kearney,

p. 61 and Collinson, *EPM, passim* as well as Dillingham, p. 7.

[98] See Haller, *Rise*, p. 54.

[99] See Dillingham, p. 6 who mentions a controversy with Peter Baro in 1580-81. See also Curtis, p. 213. Porter discusses Chaderton's debates on the doctrine of the assurance of salvation. See pp. 314ff. and pp. 398ff.

[100] Dillingham, p. 10. On the Hampton Court Conference see Collinson, EPM, *passim*; H.G. Alexander, pp. 135ff. and Mark H. Curtis, "The Hampton Court Conference and its Aftermath," *History*, XLVI (1961), 1-16.

[101] Again, this is Collinson's phrase, *EPM*, p. 125.

[102] Cited by Haller, *Rise*, p. 54.

[103] Dillingham, pp. 13-14.

[104] Walter Travers, *A Full and Plaine Declaration of Ecclesiasticall Discipline* (London, 1574), p. 144; cited by Collinson, *EPM*, p. 126. John G. Rechtien has pointed out the Ramistic structure of this work. See "Antithetical Literary Structures in the Reformation Theology of Walter Travers," *The Sixteenth Century Journal*, VIII, 1 (April 1977), 51-60.

[105] Cited in Collinson, *EPM*, p. 126.

[106] *The Second Parte of a Register*, ed. A. Peel, 2 vols. (Cambridge: University Press, 1915), II, 133-134.

[107] See "Life of Carter," in Samuel Clarke, *A General Martyrologie* (London, 1677), Pt. 2, p. 133. This "conference" approach to Scripture study was used especially in Zürich and was a smaller scale variety of the "prophesyings" begun in England in the 1560's. See Collinson, *EPM*, p. 127 and pp. 168ff.

[108] The microfilm of the sermon I used indicates it was published in London by Robert Walde-grave in 1586. The *STC* (#4925) and Collinson, *EPM*, p. 274 attribute it to Chaderton.

[109] See Chaderton, *A Fruitfull Sermon*.

[110] See Collinson, *EPM*, p. 274.

[111] On Harvey see *DNB*.

[112] See Harvey, *Pierce's Superogation* (London, 1593), reprinted in G. Gregory Smith, II, 281 as cited in Howell, *L&R*, p. 247. See also p. 263.

[113] See H.S. Wilson and C.A. Forbes, *Gabriel Harvey's 'Ciceronianus,'* University of Nebraska Studies in the Humanities No.4 (Lincoln, Nebraska: University of Nebraska Press, 1945). This work of Harvey's was the earliest interpretation of Ramist rhetoric printed in England. See Howell, *L&R*, p. 254.

[114] See H.S. Wilson, "Gabriel Harvey's Orations on Rhetoric," *English Literary History*, XXII, No.3 (September 1945), 173-174. Wilson writes: "...it is clear that as a teacher Harvey devoted his chief energies to popularizing the Ramist methods in the teaching of rhetoric especially, but apparently, insofar as his influence extended, in other branches of learning

as well," p. 180. When Wilson identifies Harvey as "Ramus's earliest influential advocate among English teachers," he has apparently not considered Chaderton.

[115] On Temple see *DNB* which calls him "the most active champion of the Ramists in England." His son Thomas Temple was a member of the Westminster Assembly. See Rogers, p. 90.

[116] See Howell, *L&R*, p. 204.

[117] See Howell, *L&R*, p. 204 who translates this quotation. It appears in Latin in Mullinger, II, 409 (note 5). On Sidney see *DNB* and F. Caspari, *Humanism and the Social Order in Tudor England* (Chicago: University of Chicago Press, 1954) as well as Joan Simon, *Education and Society in Tudor England* (Cambridge: University Press, 1967).

[118] Ong, *Ramus*, p. 302. Ong notes that the Wechels published some 172 or more editions of Ramus' own works as well as many involving both sides in later Ramist controversies. See also Simon, pp. 347ff. who describes Sidney's Continental tour as "a model of one planned to educational ends."

[119] See Ong, *Ramus*, p. 302.

[120] On this see J.P. Thorne, "A Ramistical Commentary on Sidney's *An Apologie for Poetrie*," *Modern Philology*, LIV, No.3 (February 1957), 158-164. Cf. Geroge W. Hallam, "Sidney's Supposed Ramism," *Renaissance Papers* 1963 (Durham, North Carolina: University of North Carolina Press, 1964), pp. 11-20.

[121] The Psalms Temple dealt with were: 1, 2, 16, 27, 34, 37, 39, 49, 50, 51, 73, 84, 90, 91, 94, 103, 104, 107, 116, 139.

[122] The quote is from Miller, *NEM*, p. 514 (note 8).

[123] All quotations are from "The Epistle Dedicatorie." Cf. Miller, *NEM*, p. 203.

[124] See Temple, *A Logicall Analysis of Twentie Select Psalmes*.

[125] On Wotton see *DNB* and Kearney, p. 65.

[126] See Hill, *IO*, p. 56. Kearney suggests that the initial appointments of Wotton and Henry Briggs (mathematics) who was also a Ramist were "part of a Ramist pattern" at that College. He says it was "a dominating influence behind the foundation of Gresham College," p. 65.

[127] See Howell, *L&R*, p. 233.

[128] See Howell, *L&R*, p. 222.

[129] Fraunce noted that his work had been redone three times while he was still a Fellow at St. John's College and three times while he was learning law at Gray's Inn. He also published a translation of Talon's *Rhetoric* in 1588 under the title *Arcadian Rhetorike*. See Howell, *L&R*, p. 257.

[130] Quoted in Howell, *L&R*, pp. 224-225.

[131] Howell, *L&R*, p. 228.

[132] On Downame see *DNB* and Howell, *L&R*, p. 208.

[133] Thomas Fuller, *The History of the Worthies of England* (London, 1662), p. 189.

[134] See Porter, p. 381.

[135] Hill, *IO*, p. 292. Downame went to Ireland as Bishop of Derry in 1593 according to Kearney, p. 62.

[136] See Howell, *L&R*, p. 211. Downame's Commentaries stand behind John Milton's *Art of Logic*. See Thomas S.K. Scott-Craig, "The Craftmanship and Theological Significance of Milton's Art of Logic," *The Huntington Library Quarterly*, XVII (November 1953), 1-16 for a comparison of Downame and Milton. See also Leon Howard, "'The Invention' of Milton's 'Great Argument': A Study of the Logic of 'God's Ways to Men,'" *The Huntington Library Quarterly*, IX (February 1946), 149-173; Fisher, "Milton's Logic"; and Christopher Hill, *Milton and the English Revolution* (New York: The Viking Press, 1977), pp. 240-241.

[137] Quoted in Miller, *NEM*, p. 129.

[138] See the Ramist chart at the beginning of George Downame, *The Covenant of Grace, or an Exposition upon Luke I, 73, 74, 75* (Dublin, 1631) and p. 5.

[139] See the chart at the beginning of *The Covenant of Grace*.

[140] See other charts in George Downame's works, for example in *Papa Antichristus, sive diatriba de Antichristo* (1620; STC--7119), pp. 192, 194, 195, 217, 219, and 220. The Ramist structure is apparent throughout Downame's works including "Of the Holie Invocation of God's Name" and "The Christian Exercise of Fasting" published together as *The Christians Sanctuarie* (London, 1604; STC--7113); *Lectures of the XV Psalme* (London, 1604; STC--7118). His *An Abstract of the Duties Commanded, and Sinnes Forbidden in the Law of God* (London, 1620) was "the summe and heads" of what was in "a very large Treatise upon the Decalogue" that was Downame's series of lectures some twenty years before. This work is composed of nothing but Ramist charts.

[141] *The Logicians School-Master* (1657), sig. A3v-A4r as cited in Howell, *L&R*, p. 209. On Richardson see Miller, *NEM, passim* and Sprunger, *Learned, passim*.

[142] Cited in Miller, *NEM*, p. 134. Fraunce said an axiom was "such a truth as is worthy credit without any discourse"; or, "what agrees to that which is *per se manifestum*."

[143] Miller, *NEM*, p. 135 quoting Richardson.

[144] Miller, *NEM*, p. 135 quoting Richardson.

[145] See Howell, *L&R*, p. 255.

[146] See Howell, *L&R*, p. 256.

[147] See Collinson, *EPM*, p. 266. On Fenner see *DNB*, and Keith L. Sprunger, *Dutch Puritanism A History of English and Scottish Churches of the Netherlands in the Sixteenth and Seventeenth Centuries* (London; E.J. Brill, 1982), pp. 23, 319-321. Fenner was jailed and suspended from the preaching office for not subscribing to the use of the Prayer Book as ordered by Archbishop Whitgift. Cf. Pepper, p. xxii.

[148] John Dover Wilson has argued that Schilders, who was an English-speaking Dutch printer, did not want to provoke English authorities by openly supporting English Puritans. See "Richard Schilders and the English Puritans," *Transactions of the Bibliographic Society*, XI (1910-1911), 65-134 cited in Pepper, p. xxiii. Cf. Sprunger, *Dutch Puritanism*, pp. 28, 308.

[149] Fenner's translation is found in Pepper. Reference to it will be from that volume, pp. 145-180. Cf. Thomas M. Walsh, "A Sixteenth Century Translation of Ramus and of Talaeus; Dudley Fenner's *The Artes of Logike and Rethorike*: An Edition and Study", Diss. St. Louis University, 1978.

[150] See Pepper, pp. 145, 146.

[151] Howell, L&R, p. 220. See Howell's brief discussion of some of these changes.

[152] See above p. 38 for MacIlmaine's disparaging remarks about the prudential method.

[153] Pepper, p. 167.

[154] Pepper, p. 167.

[155] The title page of the 1584 edition of Fenner's work reads: "The Artes of Logike and Rethorike, plainelie set foorth in the Englishe tounge, easie to be learned and practised: togeather with examples for the practise of the same, for Methode in the gouernment of the familie, prescribed in the word of God: And for the whole in the resolution or opening of certaine partes of Scripture, according to the same."
"The Order of Householde, described methodicallie out of the worde of God, with the contrarie abuses founde in the worlde" was the example of Ramist method applied to the question of how a household should be run. The two other treatises that were to show how Ramist method could be applied to Scripture interpretation were: "The resolution and interpretation of the Lordes prayer, out of Mat. 6.9 and Luke 11.2" and "The Epistle to Philemon." I have set out the Ramistic structure for Fenner's *Oeconomie* in Donald K. McKim, "Ramism in William Perkins," Diss. University of Pittsburgh, 1980, Figure 8. This work has various small diagrammatic charts throughout. See pp. 2, 5, 9. The chart of the "Epistle to Philemon" is set out in McKim, "Ramism," Figure 9. The interpretation of the Lord's Prayer by Fenner was also constructed along the Ramist lines.
No matter what the issue: a theological question, an interpretation of a Biblical book, or a short portion of Scripture, Fenner could apply the Ramist procedures. Pepper suggest that these last three treatises were written while Fenner was in prison. See p. xxv.

[156] Pepper, p. 167.

[157] On this see Knappen, *Tudor Puritanism*, pp. 372-374.

[158] See Fenner's *The Sacred Doctrine of Divinitie*.

[159] For the Ramist "analysis" of this work see McKim, "Ramism," Figure 10.

[160] From Pepper, p. 167.

NOTES TO CHAPTER IV

[1] See Appendix D for a discussion and chronology of Perkins' works.

² On this controversy see John Durkan, "Alexander Dickson and S.T.C. 6823," *The Bibliothek, Glasgow* University Library, III (1962), 183-190 and Yates, Art, ch. 12: "Conflict between Brunian and Ramist Memory."

³ According to modern dating, the work written "on the kolends of January" would have been published in early 1584. See Yates, *Art*, p. 267.

⁴ Durkan, "Dickson," p. 183.

⁵ This was suggested by Durkan, "Dickson," p. 183 and confirmed by Yates, *Art*, p. 267.

⁶ These are *S.T.C.* #19064.

⁷ *S.T.C.* #21089.

⁸ *S.T.C.* #19065 ("Admonitions to A. Dicson about the Vanity of his Artificial Memory").

⁹ See *Antidicsonus*, pp. 8-9.

¹⁰ Dickson, *De umbra*, pp. 54, 62 as cited in Yates, *Art*, p. 268.

¹¹ See Yates' discussion in *Art*, pp. 269-272.

¹² Yates, *Art*, p. 272.

¹³ As Yates says, *Art*, p. 267. See also p. 273.

¹⁴ Other practitioners of the art of memory--"Metrodorus, Rossellius, Nolanus, and Dicson himself are to be repelled. One must adhere as to a column, to the faith of Ramist men." See "Dedication" to *Antidicsonus* and Yates, *Art*, p. 273. Yates suggests that Perkins dedicated this work to Moufet, a member of Sir Philip Sidney's circle to try to counteract Hermetic influences there. See *Art*, pp. 318-319.

¹⁵ EP, I, 405. See also *Art*, ch. 11. Bruno dedicated this work to the Vice-chancellor and Doctors at Oxford. He described himself as "the waker of sleeping souls, tamer of presumptuous and recalcitrant ignorance, proclaimer of a general philanthropy."

¹⁶ For Dickson's connections with Bruno see Durkan, "Dickson," p. 185f.

¹⁷ *Antidicsonus*, p. 17. See Yates, *Art*, p. 273.

¹⁸ See *Antidicsonus*, pp. 18-19.

¹⁹ See *Antidicsonus*, p. 20.

²⁰ See *Antidicsonus*, p. 21.

²¹ *Antidicsonus*, p. 29 from Yates' translation, *Art*, p. 273.

²² The translation is Yates' from Ramus' *Scholae in lib. artes* (1578 ed.). She quotes from *Rhetoricae*, Book III, col. 214 of that work. The first passage Perkins quoted from Ramus' *Rhetoric* was Book I, col. 191. These differed in the 1569 edition. See the 1569 edition, Book I, col. 283 and *Sch. dial.*, Book XX, col. 773, *Art*, p. 274.

²³ This tract was called *Libellus in quo dilucide explicatur impia Dicsoni artificiosa memoria* (*A Pamphlet in which is Plainly Set Forth the Impiety of Dicson's Artificial Memory*).

²⁴ See *Antidicsonus*, pp. 36 and 44.

²⁵ *Antidicsonus*, p. 36: *Hic itaque peccatur in legem institiae & sapientiae.*

²⁶ See Yates, *Art*, p. 274.

²⁷ *Animatio tota & cum umbris ac locis corruit, & per se insigni impietatis macula inusta est.*

²⁸ See Yates, *Art*, p. 113 on Peter and *Antidicsonus*, p. 45 for Perkins' comments. Yates writes: "We may here be on the track of a reason why Ramism was so popular with the Puritans. The dialectical method was emotionally aseptic. Memorising lines of Ovid through logical disposition would help to sterilise the disturbing affects aroused by the Ovidian images," *Art*, p. 275.

²⁹ See Yates, *Art*, p. 275.

³⁰ *Libellus de memoria*, pp. 3-4.

³¹ See Yates, *Art*, p. 275.

³² Sig. C 8 *verso* of *Admonitiuncla* following Libellus. See Yates, *Art*, p. 275.

³³ *Libellus: Admonitiuncla*, Sig. E i. as given by Yates, *Art*, p. 276. Yates comments: "Using the terminology of the classical art, Perkins turns it against the classical art and applies it to the method." She sees this passage as "interesting evidence of how the method was developed out of the classical art yet was basically opposed to it on the fundamental point of images."

³⁴ II, 670. This work will be more fully discussed in Chapter V.

³⁵ II, 670.

³⁶ II, 670. See Howell, *L&R*, pp. 206-207.

³⁷ See John G. Rechtien, "The Visual Memory of William Perkins and the End of Theological Dialogue," *Journal of the American Academy of Religion*, XLV/1, Supplement (March 1977), 88.

³⁸ See above, ch. II, note 131.

³⁹ I, 686.

⁴⁰ I, 670.

⁴¹ I, 670.

⁴² I, 689.

⁴³ I, 622-623. See also I, 587ff.

⁴⁴ I, 686.

⁴⁵ I, 686.

⁴⁶ I, 695.

⁴⁷ Yates writes: "The 'Ramist man' must smash the images both within and without, must substitute for the old idolatrous art the new image-less way of remembering through abstract dialectical order," *Art*, p. 278. See also p. 279f. and her *Giordano Bruno and the Hermetic Tradition*, pp. 205ff. and 235ff. for a discussion of Bruno's dispute with the Aristotelians at Oxford.

⁴⁸ III, 476.

⁴⁹ This was proved in a 1939 article by Hugh G. Dick, "The Authorship of *Foure Great Lyers* (1585)," *Library*, 4th series, XIX (1939), 311-314. He cites an inscription in a Corpus Christi College, Oxford edition of this work in the writing of William Fulman a seventeenth-century antiquary, which attributes this work to Perkins. The companion piece, *A Resolution to the Countrey-man* is included in the editions of Perkins' *Works*. Chances are *Foure Great Lyers* was never included in the *Works* since the "ephemeral nature of the skit itself....would have been out of place in the collected writings of a prominent theologian," speculates Dick, p. 313. See also the revised *S.T.C.* #19721.7.

⁵⁰ See Don Cameron Allen, *The Star Crossed Renaissance* (Durham, North Carolina: Duke University Press, 1941), pp. 116ff. who suggests Perkins was following Nicholas Allen who in 1569 published "The Astronomers game for three Whetstones, played by two Masters of Art and a Doctor." This was a brief pamphlet holding up the predictions of Buckmaster, Securis, and Doctor Law to comparison and embarrassment, see p. 117. On Astrology and this whole topic see E.F. Bosanquet, *English Printed Almanacks and Prognostications* (London: The Bibliographical Society at the Chiswick Press, 1917); E.P. Wilson, "Some English Mock Prognostications," *Library* (1939).

⁵¹ III, 653 (misnumbered 963). In 1651 Thomas Fuller commented on Perkins' study of magic. See above, ch. I (note 8).

⁵² See Keith V. Thomas, *Religion and the Decline of Magic* (New York: Charles Scribner's Sons, 1971), chs. 10-12.

⁵³ Thomas, *Religion*, p. 285.

⁵⁴ Thomas, *Religion*, p. 287, 330.

⁵⁵ Calvin had written his *Avertissment contre l'astrologie judiciare* (C.R. VII, 509-544) in 1549. It was translated as *An Admonicion against Astrology Iudiciale* by G. Gilby in 1561.

⁵⁶ See III, 653. See also III, 654ff.

⁵⁷ III, 654. See also I, 43 where Perkins wrote that "this counterfeit arte withdraweth mens minds from the contemplation of Gods prouidence."

⁵⁸ III, 654, 667.

⁵⁹ John Calvin, *Institutes of the Christian Religion*, ed. John T. McNeill, trans. Ford Lewis Battles, Library of Christian Classics, 2 vols. (1960; rpt. Philadelphia: Westminster

Press, 1967), I. xvi. 3.

[60] See Yates, *Art*, p. 278. See also p. 235.

[61] III, 652. See McKim, "Ramism," Fig. 11.

[62] See III, 655, 656, 660, 661, 663, 666. Perkins spoke of the stars as "signes of generall things which happen ordinarily every yeare in nature among us." Instead of merely naming these ordinary things in regular prose style, they were diagrammed as follows:

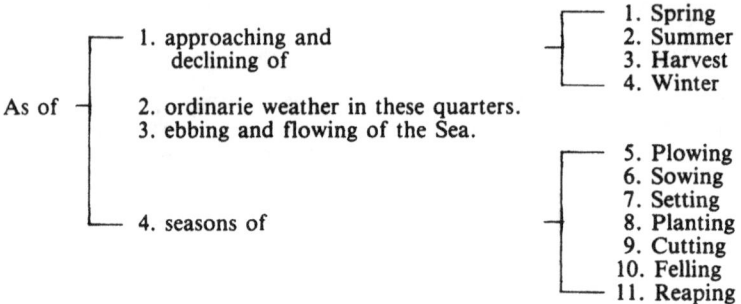

Bracketing in this way highlighted the points Perkins made. See III, 655.

[63] III, 651, 653.

[64] III, 653.

[65] See the "Dedication" to this work, III, at 464.

[66] III, 472, 473.

[67] This work was dated November 24, 1586 but was not published until 1588. It was revised and reissued in 1591, 1592, and 1595.

[68] I, 354.

[69] On the question of assurance of salvation see Gordon J. Keddie, "'Unfallible Certenty of the Pardon of Sinne and Life Everlasting,' The Doctrine of Assurance in the Theology of William Perkins (1558-1602)," *The Evangelical Quarterly*, XLVIII, No.4 (October-December 1976), 230-244 and Breward, "Introduction," to *Work*, pp. 80-99.

[70] I, 396.

[71] I, 396.

[72] I, 402.

[73] I, 398; I, 402.

[74] See Ong, *Ramus*, pp. 185 and 99.

[75] See *Dial. inst.*, fol. 57.

[76] See Miller, *NEM*, pp. 133-136.

[77] Ramus, *Dialectique* (1555), p. 114 as translated in Howell, *L&R*, p. 159 (see Dassonville, ed., p. 142).

[78] I, 402-404. See also Howell, *L&R*, pp. 159-160. See too Hooykaas, ch. 8: "L'Induction."

[79] I, 403. Perkins also referred to Aristotle as "the heathen philosopher," III, 691, 698.

[80] I, 356-362.

[81] I, 408-409.

[82] I, 381-396.

[83] I, 362-381.

[84] I, 362.

[85] See McKim, "Ramism," Figure 12. Perkins followed this pattern of the Ramist method until he came to the end and then listed six temptations of Christ and a discussion of why a Christian cannot fall from grace. See I, 374-381.

[86] I have dealt with this piece in my article "When God Seems Far Away," *Christianity Today*, XXIII, No. 27 (December 7, 1979), 24-26.

[87] See McKim, McKim, "Ramism," Fig. 13.

[88] See I, 368 and 417. This pattern occurs throughout Perkins' works.

[89] See Howell, *L&R*, pp. 162-163.

[90] *Dialectique* (1555), pp. 123-125 (Dassonville, ed., p. 147), cited by Howell, *L&R*, p. 163 from *Dialectique*, p. 123.

[91] See title page before I, 1. The work is found in I, 1-8.

[92] See Thomas F. Torrance's edition of collected catechisms, *The School of Faith The Catechisms of the Reformed Church*, ed. T.F. Torrance (London: Jas. Clarke & Co., 1959). Well-known are the catechisms of Calvin (1538; "Geneva Catechism," 1541) and Luther ("The Small Catechism" 1529; "The Large Catechism" 1529). See also *The Book of Concord*, ed. Theodore G. Tappert (Philadelphia: Fortress Press, 1959). pp. 327ff. and 357ff.

[93] See J.L. Wilson, "Catechisms and their Use Among the Puritans," *One Steadfast High Intent*. Proceedings of the Puritan and Reformed Studies Conference, 1966.

[94] I, 170.

[95] I, A2.

[96] See his Preface "To all Ignorant People that desire to be instructed," I, A2.

⁹⁷ As Perkins wrote in his *A Discourse on Conscience*: "...the understanding must first of all conceiue, or at the least haue meanes of conceiuing, before conscience can constraine....," I, 522.

⁹⁸ As Perkins wrote, "The least measure of knowledge without which a man cannot haue faith, is the knowledge of Elements, or the fundamentall doctrines of a Christian Religion," II, 363.

⁹⁹ See Calvin's 1541 Geneva Catechism which was made up of four main parts: Faith (including the Apostles' Creed), Law (Ten Commandments), Prayer (Lord's Prayer) and Word and Sacrament. These were all expounded as human worship of God. See Torrance, ed., pp. xii-xvi for an outline and analysis of some Reformed catechisms.

¹⁰⁰ See Breward, *Work*, p. 141.

¹⁰¹ See I, 9-116. The 1590 Latin edition had only 67 pages.

¹⁰² See A. Lang, *Puritanisms und Pietismus*, p. 115 who claimed Perkins demonstrated an "individualistic tendency" in his theology.

¹⁰³ See the modernized chart in Breward, *Work*.

¹⁰⁴ See Ford Lewis Battles, "Peter Lombard," Study Outline No.15 (Pittsburgh Theological Seminary, 1971) and Breward, *Work*, p. 171.

¹⁰⁵ This chart of the "Tabula Predestinationis" was essentially reprinted in 1582 in Beza's *De praedestinationis doctrina*. For Beza's chart see Richard A. Muller, "Perkins' *A Golden Chaine*: Predestinarian System or Schematized Ordo Salutis?" *Sixteenth-Century Journal*, IX, No. 1 (1978), 72-73. See McKim, "Ramism," Figures 15 and 16.

¹⁰⁶ On the characteristics of Protestant scholasticism see Rogers and McKim, pp. 185-187. Cf. R.T. Kendall, *Calvin and English Calvinism to 1649* (Oxford: Oxford University Press, 1979) who argues that Perkins followed Beza rather than Calvin on his doctrines of faith and assurance. See chs. 4 and 5. His essay "The Puritan Modification of Calvin's Theology" in *John Calvin His Influence in the Western World*, ed. W. Stanford Reid (Grand Rapids: Zonderman, 1982). pp. 199-214 makes the same point.

¹⁰⁷ Muller cites his "Predestination and Christology in Sixteenth Century Reformed Theology," Diss. Duke University 1976 for a full discussion of the theology of Beza's *Tabula*. See also Bray, pp. 71-72 and Philip C. Holtrop, "The Potter and the Clay--The Doctrine of Predestination," Part I, Unpublished Lecture, Calvin College, Grand Rapids, Michigan, 1977, pp. 132ff.

¹⁰⁸ Philip C. Holtrop, "Predestination in Calvin, Beza and the Later Reformed Orthodoxy," Calvin Seminary Lecture, Grand Rapids, Michigan, 10 February, 1977, p. 9.

¹⁰⁹ Holtrop, "Predestination....Orthodoxy," p. 9.

¹¹⁰ Holtrop, "The Potter and the Clay," I, 135.

¹¹¹ I, 11.

¹¹² Holtrop has translated this work. See *A Translation of Theodore Beza's Summa Totius Christianismi*....Unpublished translation, p. 2.

[113] I, 15.

[114] This has been a criticism of some supralapsarian systems of theology: that they subordinate Christ's role in predestination. The argument is that in these systems, Christ becomes only a "carrier" of salvation; that He plays no active role since the decree of predestination is made prior to grace. See J.K.S. Reid, "The Office of Christ in Predestination," *Scottish Journal of Theology*, I, (1948), 5-19; 166-183 and Karl Barth, *Church Dogmatics* II/2, trans. G.W. Bromiley *et. al.* (1957; rpt. Edinburgh: T. & T. Clark, 1967), 33. Cf. the critique of James Daane, *The Freedom of God* (Grand Rapids, Michigan: Wm. B. Eerdmans Publishing Co., 1973), ch. VII. Among numerous studies of predestination and the work of Christ in Calvin see Francois Wendel, *Calvin*, trans. Philip Mairet (1963; rpt. London: Collin, 1965), pp. 263ff.

[115] I, 24.

[116] I, 24.

[117] Muller, "Perkins' *Golden Chaine*," p. 76.

[118] Beza, *Totius*, trans. Holtrop, p. 7.

[119] See Muller, "Perkins' *Golden Chaine*," p. 76. The dotted line in Perkins' diagram showed the "order of the causes of salvation from the first to last." This line had its origin in the circle which Perkins called "God." But it is clear from his diagram of the Godhead that the Son (Jesus Christ) is fully included in this "God."

[120] I, prior to 11.

[121] As Muller puts it: "Causal theocentricity is paralleled by soteriological Christocentricity." He notes how this work of Christ is related to Christian believers in Perkins' chart in justification, sanctification, and vivification. Further, in relation to the reprobate, Perkins reversed the order of Beza's chart. In Perkins', reprobates with "no calling" are placed further from the center of the diagram than reprobates with "ineffectual callings." These latter have heard the Gospel, but rejected it. In that sense, they have at least been exposed to the message of the salvation. As Perkins indicates, they may display a "yielding of God's call" and even "temporary faith" before they ultimately "relapse" into "apostasy." But of course no lines can be drawn between this section of the diagram and work of Christ. Beza's chart had placed those with "ignorance of the Gospel" closer to the center than those who have shown "contempt of the Gospel offered." See Muller, "Perkins' *Golden Chaine*," pp. 77ff.

[122] See I, 79.

[123] I, 113.

[124] The *syllogismus* occurs in Beza's *Catechismus compendarius*, Part 5, q. 1 and Part 6, q. 6. Perkins mentions and uses it in I, 547 and I, 284.

[125] I, 113.

[126] See the nine effects listed by Perkins in I, 113.

[127] I, 112.

[128] Jakob Andreä was a Lutheran theologian who disputed with Beza at the Colloquy of Montbelliard in 1586. See John M'Clintock and James Strong, *Cyclopaedia of Biblical, Theological, and Ecclesiastical Literature*, 12 vols. (New York, 1895) and *The New International Dictionary of the Christian Church*, ed. James D. Douglas (Grand Rapids: Zondervan Publishing Co., 1974).

[129] These editions of Beza's *Tabula praedestinationis* were published in 1575, 1576, 1581, and 1595 under various titles. See S.T.C. #2001; 2002; 2049; and 2050 as cited by Muller, "Perkins' *Golden Chaine*," p. 71 (note 12.)

[130] I, 11.

[131] See McKim, "Ramism," Figure 17.

[132] I, 11.

[133] I, 15.

[134] I, 16.

[135] I, 24.

[136] I, 76, 83, 85, 91, 94.

[137] See Perkins' *A Golden Chaine, passim*.

[138] See between I, 94 and 95; 106 and 107.

[139] See McKim, "Ramism," Figures 18 and 19.

[140] See McKim, "Ramism," Figure 20.

[141] *A Golden Chaine* (London, 1591), ch. 32. In the third edition these basic descriptions were slightly expanded.

NOTES TO CHAPTER V

[1] Some of these sermons and the years they were preached or published are the Lord's Prayer (1592), Zephaniah (1593), Revelation (1595), and Hebrews (1596?).

[2] See III, 484 (sanctification); III, 521 (reprobates); III, 499 (justification).

[3] Perkins wrote: "Repetitions in Scripture are not idle, but of great use, and signifie unto us the necessitie of the thing repeated, and the infallible certentie of it," II, 226.

[4] II, 155. From the "Epistle Dedicatorie" to Perkins' commentary on Galatians.

[5] II, 156. See also *brevitas* and *perspicuity* as goals of exegesis for Calvin, Rogers and McKim, p. 115.

[6] See John Wilkins, *Ecclesiastes* (London, 1646), p. 43. See also Breward, *L&T*, p. 68.

[7] Luther's and Calvin's commentaries were set up this way as were Nicholas Ridley's. See Breward, *L&T*, p. 70.

⁸ Breward points to Peter Martyr's *Commentaries*, particularly pp. 41a-44b where Martyr discussed the Mass. Breward writes: "This was the Protestant counterpart of the medieval scholion, and occurs frequently in Luther's commentaries," *L&T*, p. 70. On Martyr see also Rogers and McKim, pp. 150-155.

⁹ On Piscator see Appendix C. Piscator also produced *Aphorisms of Christian Doctrine drawn for the most part from Calvin's Institutes, or Theological Commonplaces set out in brief maxims* in 1589 which went through twelve editions by 1630. Piscator appended charts to his *Exegesis or Explanation of the Aphorisms of Christian Doctrine* (*Exegesis sive Explicatio Aphorismorum Doctrinae Christianae*; Herborn, 1622) which diagram the *Aphorisms* in Ramist form. This "abridgement" of Calvin's *Institutes* had been done in a similar way by Guillaume Delaune in *Institutionis Christianae Religionis a Joanne Calvino Conscriptae, Epitome. In qua adversariorum obiectionibus breviter ac solidae responsiones annotantur* (London, 1583; second edition, 1584). The English translation was *Abridgement of the Institutes of Christian Religion composed by John Calvin. In which answers are set down to the objections of opponents* (Edinburgh, 1585; reprinted 1586 and 1587). Delaune's first edition had twelve pages of Ramist charts, his second had twenty-one. See John Platt, *Reformed Thought and Scholasticism The Arguments for the Existence of God in Dutch Theology, 1575-1650*, Studies in the History of Christian Thought, ed. Heiko A. Oberman (Leiden: E.J. Brill, 1982), ch. III who reproduces a chart from Delaune and Piscator, pp. 44-46.

¹⁰ F. Junius (1545-1602; DuJon) was Professor of Divinity at Leiden. He studied in Geneva from 1562-1565 and wroked with Tremellius on the Latin translation of the Old Testament. His *Opera Theologica* was published in two volumes at Geneva in 1607 and 1613. See Samuel Clarke, *A Marrow of Ecclesiastical Historie*, pp. 417-420; M'Clintock & Strong, IV, 1097; F.W. Cuno, *Franciscus Junius der Altere, Professor der Theologie und Pastor (1545-1602)* (Amsterdam, 1891); C. DeJonge, *De Irenische Ecclesiologie van Franciscus Junius (1545-1602)* (Nieuwkoop, 1980) and John Platt, *Reformed Thought and Scholasticism The Arguments for the Existence of God in Dutch Theology, 1575-1650, Studies in the History of Christian Thought*, ed. Heiko A. Oberman (Leiden: E.J. Brill, 1982), esp. pp. 122-127, 131-143 for the impact of Junius' *De Vera Theologia* (1594) in the development of arguments for God's existence in post-Reformation Dutch theology. For Junius' "logical analysis" see this *The Apocalyps* (Cambridge, 1596), p. 26 and the Table in the English translation of his *Apocalypsis* entitled *A Briefe and Learned Commentarie Upon the Revelation of Saint John....*(London, 1592). This is reproduced in McKim, "Ramism," Figure 21.

Lambert Daneau (1530-1595) was trained as a lawyer but gave up the legal profession to study theology in Geneva, arriving there in 1560. He became an associate of Beza and a well-known Calvinist theologian writing moral treatises, commentaries on Augustine, works on methodology, Biblical commentaries and ethical works as well as numerous polemical pieces. His life and work have been studied most fully by Oliver Fatio. See his *Nihil pulchrius ordine. Contribution a l'étude de l'établissement de la discipline ecclésiastique aux Pays-Bas ou Lambert Daneau aux Pays-Bas (1581-1583)*(Leiden: Brill, 1971) and *Méthode et Théologie Lambert Daneau et les debuts de la scolastique réformée* (Geneva: Droz, 1976) and his chapter, "Lambert Daneau," trans. Jill Raitt in *Shapers of Religious Traditions in Germany, Switzerland, and Poland, 1560-1600*, ed. Jill Raitt (New Haven: Yale University Press, 1981), pp. 105-119. Cf. the review of *Méthode et Théologie* by Richard A. Muller in the *Westminster Theological Journal* (Fall 1978), pp. 215-217.

Fatio sees Daneau as feeling both "aversion and fascination" for scholasticism. He resisted a theology which gave Aristotelian philosophy a priority over Scripture, yet also appreciated the "clear and rational constructions" of the scholastic method of Peter Lombard. Daneau was less inclined to use metaphysics than, for example Girolami Zanchi (1516-1590; see Rogers and McKim, pp. 155-160) and methodologically began with Scripture, proposing to "begin with the rhetorical, dialectical, and theological *loci* for each verse." In his method, Daneau "insists finally on practical application and moral exhortation which ought to follow the exposition of a theological *locus*." As Fatio points out, in this Daneau "foreshadows Puritanism" since for Daneau and the Puritans, "in practical terms the exposition of the theological locus does not suffice to teach that which is necessary for the instruction, edification, correction, and consolation of the Christian," *Shapers*, p. 113. Some of Daneau's Ramistically styled charts are reproduced in *Méthode et Théologie*, pp. 112*-117*. Cf. Daneau's *Twelve Small Prophets*, trans. J. Stockwood (Cambridge, 1594), pp. 228-241 and Platt, esp. pp. 119-122.

[11] See Daneau, *Twelve Small Prophets*, p. 270.

[12] See Breward, *L&T*, p. 70.

[13] See above, chapter III, note 155. Also noted was the sermon now attributed to Chaderton drawn Ramistically. See chapter III, note 109.

[14] Richard Turnbull, *An Exposition Upon the Canonicall Epistle of Saint James* (London, 1591), "To the Reader."

[15] Turnbull, "To the Reader." See Turnbull's "analysis" in McKim, "Ramism," Figure 22.

[16] Breward, *L&T*, p. 70. He writes that occasionally the exegesis of the writers earlier than Perkins "reflects sermon structure." Breward cites Edward Dering, *XXVII Lectures, or Readings, upon Parte of the Epistle written to the Hebrews* (London, 1583), pp. 46-47. He says, however, that Perkins' commentaries have a more "scholastic" structure than those of earlier Protestant scholars. It should be remembered, though, that a more detailed structure is not necessarily a more "scholastic" structure in the sense that "scholasticism" has been outlined as Ramus opposed it. Breward suggests that Perkins' more detailed structures might have been used more when his audiences were largely students who could follow his argument better.

[17] See the charts at the beginning of Perkins' *Exposition upon the whole Epistle of Jude* (III, 479) and *Commentarie upon the Three First Chapters of the Revelation* (III, 207).

[18] III, 259.

[19] III, 259. See also II, 650 and III, 95* where Perkins approves the study of logic so that "false collections" of doctrines would be avoided.

[20] See above, chapter II, note 79 from Ramus' *Rhetoricae distinctiones in Quintilianum* (Paris, 1559), p. 18. Ramus said, "The principles of the arts are definitions and divisions; outside of these, nothing," *Arist. anim.*, fol. 58. This meant that the logician's task was to classify by using proper "method." See Miller, *NEM*, p. 125 and Sprunger, *Learned*, p. 108.

[21] The first edition was published in 1604. The second, enlarged edition was published in 1606 and the third edition in 1607.

[22] Calvin would not expound the Book of Revelation. Later Puritans were not so reticent. See Christopher Hill, *Antichrist in the Seventeenth Century* (Oxford: University Press, 1970).

[23] See McKim, "Ramism," Figure 23 for the chart from III, 207.

[24] Title page at III, 207. On Thomas Pierson see Porter, p. 266 and Seaver, pp. 49-50.

[25] III, 225.

[26] III, 227.

[27] III, 227.

[28] Breward notes this in comparing some of Perkins' comments in his *Commentarie on Galatians* with the commentaries of Luther and Calvin on that book. See *L&T*, pp. 72-75.

[29] III, 200.

[30] III, 1-206. Perkins also exegeted Hebrews 12:1.

[31] III, 1. Breward gives the date of the Hebrews commentary as 1591. See *L&T*, p. 30. But Perkins referred to having already expounded the Apostles' Creed which would have been in his *Exposition of the Symbole, or Creed of the Apostles* (I, 117-322) which was published in 1595. So perhaps the Hebrews exposition is better dated around 1596.

[32] III, 1.

[33] III, 1.

[34] III, 1. See McKim, "Ramism," Figure 24.

[35] III, 14.

[36] See McKim, "Ramism," Figure 25 for a chart of this work.

[37] III, 22.

[38] See Ong, *Ramus*, pp. 190ff.; 283-284.

[39] III, 24.

[40] III, 26.

[41] III, 26.

[42] III, 26.

[42] III, 95.

[43] Perkins said this often: "The Scripture is the word of God written in a language fit for the Church by men immediately called to be Clerkes, or Seretaries of the holy Ghost," II, 647; "....the holy Scripture is no deuice of man, but the very word of the euerliuing God," II, 474.

[44] See I, 122; II, 649 etc. Perkins wrote: "....when any particular man comes to understand the Scripture this is by the working of Christ, hee opens his eyes. He gave the Disciples understanding as they went to Emmaus, to understand the Scriptures," III, 220. Perkins was confident that even when there are diverse understandings of a Scripture text, "we must still have recourse to Christ." Using the "tools" that God has given for understanding, Perkins claimed that "a man shall be able to find out the true sense: for Christ in Scripture expoundeth himself."

⁴⁵ This was "inspiration": "And these are not onely the pure word of God, but also the scripture of God: because not onely the matter of them; but the whole disposition thereof, with the style and the phrase was set downe by the immediate imspiration of the holy Ghost," I, 122.

⁴⁶ III, 103, 105, 129. In his more formal theological definitions, Perkins stressed the role of the Holy Spirit as the prime agent in the writing of Scripture. As he worked with the Scripture through exegesis and interpretation he did, however, pay attention to the human writers of Scripture and urged proper exegesis to ponder every sentence of Scripture "and euery circumstance of time, place, [and] person," II, 244. Perkins believed "the sense of Scripture is rather to be judged the word of God, then the words and letters thereof," III, 104*. As Breward comments, it is this emphasis "which kept the christological reference of the earlier reformers and did not fall with the conclusion of Illyricus that if the text was inspired, its inspiration must even extend to the Hebrew vowel points," *Work*, p. 48. See Rogers and McKim, chs. 2-4.

⁴⁷ See his *The Arte of Prophecying*, II, 650ff.; I, 583 etc.

⁴⁸ See III, 259; III, 95*; II, 650.

⁴⁹ III, 479-597.

⁵⁰ Taylor was a Fellow of Christ's College, Cambridge (1599-1604) and a reader in Hebrew there. He was a well-known Puritan preacher, once silenced for preaching against Bancroft. See *DNB*; Sprunger, *Learned*, p. 16; Hill, *IO*, p. 100; and Seaver, pp. 237 and 248.

⁵¹ "To the Christian Reader," prior to III, 479.

⁵² See McKim, "Ramism," Figure 26 for a reproduction of this chart.

⁵³ III, 521.

⁵⁴ In his text, Perkins did not use the phrase "a prolepsis answered in a perfect forme of syllogism." Nor did he name the second member of the syllogism, the assumption. This was solely the language of the chart.

⁵⁵ III, 521.

⁵⁶ III, 547.

⁵⁷ See III, 532, 534, 541, 549, 552, 559 etc.

⁵⁸ See III, 517, 520, 523, 531, 562, etc.

⁵⁹ See III, 537, 544, 571, 575, 579, etc.

⁶⁰ See III, 478.

⁶¹ On Taylor's Ramism see chapter VII below.

⁶² I, 323.

⁶³ I (following) 328. See Figure 27.

⁶⁴ Perkins published this work on the Lord's Prayer to counter a bogus work entitled "Perkins upon the Lords Praier" that had been published in London in 1592. He had not intended to deal with this topic since he believed "it is already sufficiently performed by others" (I, 327). But he did so and regarded the Lord's Prayer as "a samplar to teach us how and in what manner we ought to pray," I, 328.

⁶⁵ III, 411.

⁶⁶ This work was actually first published in 1593. See *Of the Nature and Practice of Repentance*, I, 453-469.

⁶⁷ "The Epistle Dedicatorie", III (prior to), 411.

⁶⁸ III, 413.

⁶⁹ III, 427.

⁷⁰ See III, 417, 418.

⁷¹ III, 420, 421. These were: ignorance of God's will and worship; contempt of the Christian religion; prophanation of the Sabbath; unjust dealing between man and man.

⁷² III, 423-424.

⁷³ See III, 412, 417, 418. See also Breward, *Work*, p. 291.

⁷⁴ II, 674-717.

⁷⁵ II, 677, "To the Reader."

⁷⁶ II, 720. Zacharias Ursinus (1534-1583) in his *The Summe of Christian Religion*, trans. H. Parrie (Oxford, 1587), p. 265 listed the calculations of others on this point: Melanchthon: 3963 years; Luther: 3960 years; Genevea Bible: 3943 years; Beroaldus: 3929 years.

⁷⁷ See II, 727.

⁷⁸ See McKim, "Ramism," Figure 28.

⁷⁹ II, 678.

⁸⁰ II, 157.

⁸¹ See III, 371-409 and I, 645-668. See McKim, "Ramism," Figures 29 and 30.

⁸² III, 387.

⁸³ I, 647. The terms "protasis" and "apodosis" were used only in the chart attached to the work.

⁸⁴ I, 648. Perkins divided the fellowship with Christ in virtue of his death into the sufferings of Christ in his person and those of his members and fellowship either within us or without us, I, 665. He listed eight effects of the doctrine of Christ's resurrection, I, 664.

⁸⁵ I, 667.

⁸⁶ See McKim, "Ramism," Figures 31 and 32. In his *A Godly and Learned Exposition upon Christ's Sermon on the Mount* (III, 1-264*), Perkins dealt with eight beatitudes that he treated as "points." These were each dichotomized into: "parties blessed" and "wherein that blessing consists."

Perkins' *A Commentarie or Exposition upon the five first chapters of the Epistle to the Galatians* is found in II, 153-432.

⁸⁷ II, 222.

⁸⁸ I, 475-486.

⁸⁹ See McKim, "Ramism," Figures 33a and 33b.

⁹⁰ I, 481. This corresponds to Ramus' use of *bene* ("well") and his emphasis on an art being used "in a practical fashion" or "effectively." See Ong, *Ramus*, p. 179 and above, chapter II, p. 74. For Ramus an art had both "nature" and "use." Once it had been taught, it was to bring good results--*eupraxia*. As William Ames asked: "What is the object and end of idea? It is *eupraxia*, that is, good action." See Sprunger, *Learned*, p. 115 and Gibbs, *WAT*, esp. pp. 93-98.

⁹¹ Breward, *Work*, p. 328. Howell writes that Perkins was the first Englishman to write of preaching in terms of the Ramistic dichotomous structure, *L&R*, p. 206.

⁹² Miller, *NEM*, p. 296.

⁹³ Bernstein, ch. IV.

⁹⁴ See Miller, *NEM*, p. 339.

⁹⁵ The English translation was published in 1606. On Tuke see *DNB* and Seaver, p. 139. The *Arte* is found in II, 643-673.

⁹⁶ See above, chapter II, p. 86 (note 153). Ong and Rechtien see in this title that "the claim of the two authors to purvey the only true method manifests the impossibility of dialogue inherent in Ramist method," "Visual Memory." p. 79; Ong, *Ramus*, p. 287.

⁹⁷ III, 645.

⁹⁸ See Ramus, *Commentariorum* (1569), p. 6 and Sprunger, *Learned*, p. 131. Perkins' definition is in I, 9.

⁹⁹ II, 646.

¹⁰⁰ In 1975 I wrote a paper entitled "Ramism in William Perkins' *The Arte of Prophecying*" in which I analyzed this work in light of its Ramistic structure. For convenience, however, I have included a chart similar to my own in McKim, "Ramism," Figure 34.

¹⁰¹ II, 646.

¹⁰² In the broader context of the development of the Reformed doctrine of Scripture, it is important to note that Perkins spoke of Scripture's "perfection" as being its sufficiency, which he related to its "proper end" or purpose (*scopus*). He wrote: "The scope of the whole Bible is Christ with his benefits," I, 484. For Perkins, Scripture's "purity" meant that it is "devoid of deceit and errour," II, 646. "Sufficiency" and "purity" were the two

members of the "perfection" of Scripture. In this understanding, by seeing "perfection" as meaning that "the word of God is so compleate, that nothing may bee either put to it, or taken from it, which appertaineth to the proper end therof" and then citing Psalm 19:7 which says "the Law of the Lord is perfect, converting the soule," Perkins was in line with Calvin and the early Reformed tradition on this point. By seeing Scripture's "purity" as related to deliberate "deceit"--a term with moral overtones, he is also in line with the Calvinian tradition. Protestant scholastic theologians later defined these terms as having to do with Scripture's scientific exactness in empirical matters. See Rogers and McKim, subject index: "error" and references throughout.

[103] II, 647.

[104] II, 647.

[105] II, 647-648. These divisions may also be charted.

[106] II, 650.

[107] On the theological method of post-Reformation scholastic theologians who appealed to Aquinas and Aristotle, see Rogers and McKim, ch. 3.

[108] See II, 650 and Ong, "Johannes Piscator," p. 153.

[109] II, 651.

[110] See Lechner, *Renaissance Concepts of the Commonplaces*.

[111] Ong, *Ramus*, p. 104.

[112] See Ong, *Ramus*, p. 105.

[113] See Rechtien, "Visual Memory." p. 75. Indices and Tables of Contents further enhance the ability to retrieve information and store knowledge.

[114] Originally rhetorical commonplaces were used by orators for speeches of praise or blame and frequently developed virtues and vices. See Rechtien, "Visual Memory," p. 76 and his "John Foxe's *Comprehensive Collection of Commonplaces*: A Renaissance Memory System for Students and Theologians," *Sixteenth Century Journal*, IX, No.1 (1978), 83.

[115] See Rechtien, "Visual Memory," pp. 76-77.

[116] See John Calvin, *The Institution of Christian Religion*, trans. Thomas Norton (London, 1582), Sig. Vvvi cited in Rechtien, "Visual Memory," p. 77.

[117] *The Institution* (1582), sig. Vvv2.

[118] See *The Institution* (1582), sigs. Aaaa2-Aaaa3v. for Marlorate's letter and Aaaa3v-Bbbb4v for his "Table of All the Thing Contained in This Booke or Volume." His "An Other Table in Which Are Contained the Places of the Bible according to the Course of the Olde and Newe Testament" is found on sigs. Bbbb4v-Kkkk4v. See Rechtien, "Visual Memory," notes 7 and 8.

[119] II, 654.

[120] II, 644.

[121] II, 645.

[122] II, 645.

[123] II, 651.

[124] II, Qqq3.

[125] Volume III of the *Works* began with the *Exposition of Christ's Sermon on the Mount* which has only the two Tables at its end. The rest of Volume III has no opening Table of Contents either but does have the subject and Scripture index at its end.

[126] The term "index" is an abridgment of *index locorum communium*. In printed works with indices, there was no need to memorize the commonplace headings since they could be instantly retrieved. Yet Perkins, advocate of Ramist memory that he was, counseled: "trust not too much to thy places," II, 651. John Foxe, who composed his *A Comprehensive Collection of Commonplaces...*, also warned about the dangers that indices posed to the traditional commonplaces. See Rechtien, "John Foxe," p. 86. Others who used commonplaces as models for content and organization were Robert Persons, Thomas Cartwright, John Jewel, and John Milton, p. 87.

[127] II, 651. The Greek term for the "cutting" was *orthotomia*.

[128] II, 652. See also Breward, *L&T*, p. 52 (note 3).

[129] John Foxe, *Comprehensive Commonplaces*, sig. B3 as translated by Rechtien, "Visual Memory." p. 83.

[130] Thomas Wilson, *The Arte of Rhetorique* (1553), fol. 10 as given in Rechtien, "Visual Memory," pp. 83-84. See also Howell, *L&R*, pp. 98-110.

[131] II, 663. See above, chapter II, p. 75 (note 94). Perkins often used the inquiry of circumstances as a rule for interpretation. See II, 244; I, 583 etc.

[132] See Rechtien, "Visual Memory." p. 84. "Artificial" arguments demonstrate themselves from facts at any time; "inartificial" arguments must be taken on trust or testimony. See Miller, *NEM*, p. 129.

[133] Rechtien, "Visual Memory," p. 84.

[134] See II, 652, 653.

[135] II, 653-654.

[136] Cited by Miller, *NEM*, p. 130. He notes a Harvard thesis: "Inartificial argument is the client of the artificial."

[137] See Miller's discussion of the Ramists' use of inartificial arguments and the authority of the Bible, NEM, p. 130.

[138] II, 651. This was what Perkins meant when he said that "Scripture it selfe is both *the glosse* and *the text*. Scripture is the best interpreter of it selfe," II, 334.

[139] See II, 334; I, 583; II, 651; II, 301.

[140] III, 95*. The context here was Perkins' refutation of faulty interpretation of Matthew 5:43. See above, note 19. For Perkins' approval of the use of Rhetoric for Biblical interpretation see II, 298.

[141] II, 651. See also II, 298.

[142] On the history of Biblical interpretation see among others Robert M. Grant, *A Short History of the Interpretation of the Bible*, rev. ed. (1948; rpt. New York: The MacMillan Company, 1966) and the sections on interpretation of Scripture in Rogers and McKim.

[143] II, 654.

[144] See II, 654, 655.

[145] See II, 655-662. Breward points out that L. Daneau in his *A Fruitfull Commentarie on the Twelve Small Prophets* lists some 25 tropes or figures, many with technical Greek titles. Perkins speaks of *anthopathia, metonimy,* and *synecdoche* (II, 656). See *L&T*, p. 53.

[146] II, 301.

[147] II, 663. Breward writes: "No contemporary of Perkins would have disagreed with the general validity of this principle, however much they might attack particular instances of 'gathering.'" He cites William Whitaker, *A Disputation on Holy Scripture*, ed. W. Fitzgerald (Cambridge, 1849), pp. 514-515. See *L&T*, p. 54.

[148] The translation is of the Latin: *quid libere quo libet*: "anything out of anything."

[149] Breward writes of *The Arte of Prophecying* that it "did not set the English theological scene on fire, but it deserves recognition as the first attempt in England to put the art of interpretation on a systematic basis, in which, as far as possible, individualism was overcome," *L&T*, p. 54.

[150] II, 662.

[151] Rechtien, "Visual Memory," p. 84.

[152] II, 662.

[153] II, 663.

[154] *Dial. libri duo* (1572), pp. 6-53. Howell writes that these nine arguments "are of course the nine places for the invention of arguments according to Ramus' dialectic, and Perkins was thinking of that very work when he penned this passage," *L&R*, p. 207.

[155] II, 663.

[156] These were in turn: lesser: John 10:34 and 10:35, I Corinthians 9:9 and 9:4; contrary: Galatians 3:13 and 3:9, 3:11a and 3:11b; adjunct: Hebrews 8:8 and 8:13; species: Romans 9:7 and 9:8, 4:18 and 4:23.

[157] See II, 650. William Ames wrote: "A doctrine must first be rightly found out, and then afterward hand[l]ed. The finding out is by Logick Analysis, unto which Rhetoricke

also and Grammar serveth," quoted in Miller, *NEM*, pp. 341-342.

[158] II, 654ff.

[159] II, 651.

[160] II, 654.

[161] II, 662. See also Ong, *Ramus*, p. 191, 233 and Miller, *NEM*, pp. 341-342.

[162] II, 334.

[163] See Rechtien, "Visual Memory," p. 85.

[164] II, 664.

[165] II, 664.

[166] II, 664. Since Perkins downplayed any display of human learning from the pulpit and did not urge a careful spelling out of the "reasons" for a doctrine, Bernstein argues that his *Arte* alone "could not have provided a theoretical framework sufficiently adequate to have supplied the full rationale which was obviously implemented in the Westminster definition of the Plain Style," p. 84. This was the doctrine, reason, use pattern. Miller, *NEM*, p. 339 and Howard Martin, "Ramus, Ames, Perkins and Colonial Rhetoric," *Western Speech*, 23 (1959), 76 have overemphasized Perkins' role in this development, says Bernstein.

[167] II, 664.

[168] See II, 665-668. These are: unbelievers who are both ignorant and unteachable; someone teachable yet ignorant; those who have knowledge but are not as yet humbled; those who are humbled; those who do believe; those who are fallen; and a mingled people.

[169] II, 668.

[170] II, 668-669.

[171] II, 669.

[172] II, 662.

[173] I, 11.

[174] See II, 152.

[175] II, 670. See above, chapter IV, p. 141 (note 35).

[176] See Rechtien, "Visual Memory," p. 89 citing *Dialectica A. Talaei prael. illus.* (1569), p. 501.

[177] Ramus, *Dialect. A. Talaei prael. illus.*, p. 483 cited in Rechtien, "Visual Memory," p. 74.

[178] II, 670.

[179] II, 670.

[180] II, 670-671.

[181] See Haller's description of plain-style preaching in *Rise, passim*.

[182] II, 673.

[183] Howell, *L&R*, p. 207. Ong, however, notes that on rhetoric, Cicero and Quintilian are "among Talon's and Ramus' real sources," *Ramus*, p. 274.

[184] Howell, *L&R*, p. 207. Perkins maintained that preaching if it too was not studied as an art with rules and definite method, would remain "naked" and "poor."

[185] See III, 445; I, 304.

[186] N. Hemmingsen, *The Preacher*, trans. John Horsfall (London, 1574); A.G. Hyperius, *The Practis of Preaching* (London, 1577). In this regard too, John Udall's *A Commentarie Upon the Lamentations of Jeremy* (London, 1593) should be mentioned. This was a homiletical treatise which sought to solve ministers' problems with doctrinal aspects of sermon design. It was equipped with Ramist charts that branched through five chapters of the book of Jeremiah. He proposed his method as "the best and most profitable" method of preaching. See Bernstein, pp. 91ff. and Everett Emerson, "John Udall and the Puritan Sermon," *Quarterly Journal of Speech*, XLIV (1958), 282-284.

[187] See Hyperius, *Practis*, p. 9.

[188] See P. Kawerau, "Die Homiletik des Andreas Hyperius," *Zeitschrift für Kirschengeschichte* (1960), 66-81.

[189] Fuller, *Abel Redivivus*, pp. 265, 517-518. See also Breward, *L&T*, p. 176.

[190] Hyperius, *Practis*, p. 22a. See also Hemmingsen, *The Preacher*, p. 15b and Breward, *L&T*, p. 184. The traditional arrangement in classical rhetoric was: exordium, narration, division, confirmation, confutation, and conclusion. See Aristotle, *Rhetoric*, 3.13.

[191] Richard Greenham (ca. 1535-1594) was a noted Puritan preacher. See Haller, *Rise, passim*. and Knappen, *Tudor Puritanism, passim*. See *The Workes of Richard Greenham*, ed. H. Holland (London, 1601), p. 160 and W.F. Mitchell, *English Pulpit Oratory from Andrewes to Tillotson* (London: S.P.C.K., 1932), p. 119 who points out the use of "use" in Musculus (1497-1563).

[192] Ursinus, *The Summe of Christian Religion*, p. 45.

[193] See Hyperius, *Practis*, p. 130a. and Peter Martyr, *The Commonplaces*, trans. A. Marten (London, 1583), 4.1.43. See also Breward, *L&T*, p. 185.

[194] Breward points out that T.H.L. Parker failed to take these types of influences into account when he suggests that Perkins' method is just a simplification of Calvin's homily form. See *L&T*, p. 185 citing *The Oracles of God* (London: Lutterworth Press, 1947), p. 125.

[195] Rogers, *Scripture in the Westminster Confession*, p. 92.

NOTES TO CHAPTER VI

[1] I, 117-322.

[2] I, 121.

[3] I, 121.

[4] I, 122.

[5] I, 122.

[6] I, 123, 124.

[7] See McKim, "Ramism," Figure 35.

[8] I, 121.

[9] I, 127.

[10] I, 128.

[11] In discussing Christ's descent into hell, Perkins notes a mistaken interpretation by Ramus. See I, 230.

[12] The four books were to deal with: faith (the Creed); law (the Decalogue); prayer (The Lord's Prayer); and the Sacraments.

[13] *Commentariorum* (1576). p. 3. Cf. Lobstein. Diagrammatically this would be:

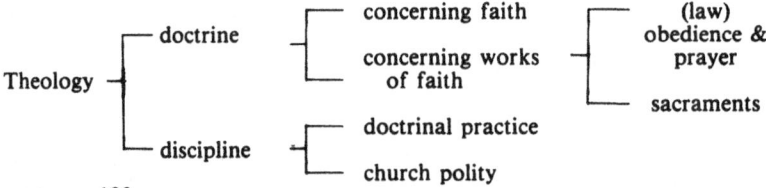

Cf. Greaves, p. 190.

[14] See Sprunger, *Learned*, p. 132 and his "Method," pp. 133-151.

[15] *Commentariorum*, p. 10 as translated in Sprunger, *Learned*, pp. 132-133.

[16] Cited in Sprunger, "Method," p. 137.

[17] Cited in Sprunger, *Learned*, p. 133 from *Commentariorum*, pp. 6, 96.

[18] See I, 47, 254, 267, 300, 309, 319 etc. on "benefits."

[19] II, 603-641.

[20] See Porter on Baro and Barrett and also Curtis, *Oxford and Cambridge in Transition*. Baro was an astrologer as well as a theologian, a fact not likely to endear him to Perkins.

See K.V. Thomas, *Religion*, p. 369.

²¹ See Dillingham, p. 6 for an account of Chaderton's public sermon.

²² Trinity College, MS, B (14) 9, p. 23 cited in Porter, p. 344.

²³ See Porter, pp. 354-356.

²⁴ For the text of the Articles see Porter, ch. 16 and especially pp. 365-366 and 371.

²⁵ See Porter, p. 380.

²⁶ See I, 10: "Epistle to the Reader."

²⁷ See Porter, pp. 386 and 389. In this work Baro outlined three views of predestination held in the Reformed Church.

²⁸ See Bangs, *Arminius*, p. 209 and his ch. 15: "Theology in Amsterdam: The Examination of Perkins' Pamphlet." See also Sprunger, *Learned*, pp. 45ff. Bangs points out the substantial influence of Ramus on Arminius. See chapter 4.

²⁹ The Synod of Dort affirmed the strict Calvinist position on predestination and related matters against the Remonstrants or Arminians. See Sprunger, *Learned*, ch. III: "The Synod of Dort." Perkins' work on predestination was translated into Dutch.

³⁰ On "Puritanism and Reason" and the "light of nature" see Rogers, pp. 82ff.; 106ff.; and 265ff. See also Robert S. Paul, *The Church in Search of Its Self* (Grand Rapids, Michigan: Wm. B. Eerdmans Publishing Co., 1972), pp. 52ff. and Christopher Hill, *Continuity and Change* (1974; rpt. Cambridge, Massachusetts: Harvard University Press, 1975), ch. 4.

³¹ II, 605.

³² II, 605.

³³ See I, 15; II, 11, 22, 321, 449, 479; III, 23*, 45*, 219*.

³⁴ See III, 424, 461; II, 18 etc. Notice also the titles of some of his works: *A Faithful and Plaine Exposition....; A Christian and Plaine Treatise....*

³⁵ See Ong, *Ramus*, pp. 314ff.: "The Spatial Model as Key to the Mental World."

³⁶ II, 606.

³⁷ See McKim, "Ramism," Figure 36.

³⁸ See II, 611-627.

³⁹ See McKim, "Ramism," Figure 37.

⁴⁰ See II, 630: "The power of God is either the power of creation, or of redemption"; II, 634: "Inherent grace, is either faith, or the gift which followeth faith." Cf. II, 636.

⁴¹ See II, 633 and II, 630, 636.

[42] II, 640, 641.

[43] I, 717-746.

[44] See McKim, "Ramism," Figure 38.

[45] I, 422.

[46] I, 423-438.

[47] On Zanchi see Rogers and McKim, pp. 155-160 and John Patrick Donnelly, "Calvinist Thomism," *Viator*, 7 (1976), 441-451.

[48] See I, 429 and 435.

[49] I, 430.

[50] I, 430.

[51] Perkins did not acquaint his readers so fully with the terms of syllogisms.

[52] I, 435.

[53] This was not all that was involved in the theological method of the Protestant scholastics. There was also a heavy dependence on metaphysics, reason, and philosophical speculation. See Rogers and McKim, p. 186.

[54] John Patrick Donnelly, "Italian Influences on the Development of Calvinist Scholasticism," *Sixteenth Century Journal*, 7, No.1 (April 1976), 90. On Zanchi's relationship to Aquinas' work, see Rogers and McKim, p. 156.

[55] I, 515-554.

[56] See II, 1-152.

[57] Among other works on "casuistry" see Ian Breward, "William Perkins and the Origins of Puritan Casuistry," *Faith and a Good Conscience* (n.p., 1963), pp. 5-17; "William Perkins and the Origins of Reformed Casuistry," *The Evangelical Quarterly*, XL, No.1 (January-March 1968), 3-20; Norman Keith Clifford, "Casuistical Divinity in English Puritanism during the Seventeenth Century: Its Origins, Development and Significance," Diss. University of London 1957; C.C. Markham, "William Perkins' Understanding of the Function of Conscience," Diss. Vanderbilt University 1967; and John T. McNeill, "Casuistry in the Puritan Age," *Religion in Life*, XII (1943), 76-89.

[58] See McKim, "Ramism," Figure 39.

[59] See for example, I, 525ff.; I, 541ff.

[60] See I, 533; I, 520.

[61] See "To the godly and wel-affected Reader whosoever," prior to II, 1.

[62] "Epistle Dedicatorie," prior to II, 1.

⁶³ See McKim, "Ramism," Figure 40.

⁶⁴ II, 1.

⁶⁵ II, 2.

⁶⁶ II, 12.

⁶⁷ II, 12.

⁶⁸ See II, 12, 48, 112.

⁶⁹ See II, 48, 112-113.

⁷⁰ See McKim, "Ramism," Figure 41.

⁷¹ See McKim, "Ramism," Figure 42.

⁷² II, 22.

⁷³ II, 24.

⁷⁴ II, 25.

⁷⁵ See II, 63-105.

⁷⁶ See below, chapter VII.

⁷⁷ H. Oki, "Ethics in 17th Century English Puritansim," Diss. Union Theological Seminary, New York, 1960, p. 180. See also Breward, "Origins of Puritan Casuistry," p. 9.

⁷⁸ Thomas Hill, *A Quatron of Reasons* (Antwerp, 1600), p. 79.

⁷⁹ William Ames, *Conscience*, "To the reader."

⁸⁰ III, 607-662. See McKim, "Ramism," Figure 43.

⁸¹ H.R. Trevor-Roper suggests that these lectures were given in Emmanuel College in the early 1590's. But he does not divulge the source of his information. See "Witches and the Witch Craze," in his *The European Witch-Craze of the Sixteenth and Seventeenth Centuries* (1956; rpt. New York: Harper & Row, 1967).

⁸² See A.J.J. Macfarlane, *Witchcraft in Tudor and Stuart England* (New York: Harper & Row, 1970), especially his diagrams and tables at pp. 26 and 81. See also K.V. Thomas, *Religion*. I have dealt more fully with Witchcraft in an unpublished paper, "The Social Functions of Witchcraft in Tudor-Stuart England," University of Pittsburgh, 1975.

⁸³ III, 607.

⁸⁴ III, 607.

⁸⁵ I, 40.

⁸⁶ III, 639, 650.

[87] III, 643.

[88] III, 652.

[89] III, 607.

[90] III, 639.

[91] III, 640.

[92] I, 555: "The Author to the Christian Reader." Cf. James C. Herbert, "William Perkins' 'A Reformed Catholic': A Psycho-Cultural Interpretation," *Church History*, Vol. 51, No. 1 (March 1982), 7-23.

[93] See Breward, *Work*, p. 515 and *L&T*, ch. 4 for background.

[94] See Whitaker, *A Disputation of Holy Scripture* and Breward, *L&T*, p. 118.

[95] W. Bishop, *Reformation of a Catholike Deformed* (n.p., 1604), "Preface." See also Breward, *L&T*, p. 152; *Work*, p. 516. Bishop was in turn answered by Anthony Wotton who was requested to do so by Archbishop Bancroft and Robert Abbot.

[96] II, 486.

[97] II, 602.

[98] J. Coccius, *Thesaurus catholicus*, 2 vols. (Cologne, 1601-1602). See Breward, *L&T*, p. 84 and his chapter "Not Lately Hatched at Rome."

[99] Breward, *L&T*, p. 80.

[100] II, 485: "Title Page."

[101] I, 535-644.

[102] I, 637.

[103] I, 641.

[104] See the account of these disputes in Porter, ch. 15 and Curtis, *Oxford and Cambridge in Transition*, pp. 219-223.

[105] See Porter, chs. 13, 14, 16, 17 and the material on Baro and Barrett.

[106] I, 637.

[107] I, 641, 642.

[108] I, 637.

[109] I, 638. This position has been criticized by Christopher Hill. See his "William Perkins and the Poor," *Puritanism and Revolution* (1958; rpt. London: Panther Books, 1969), pp. 212-233. Hill cliams that this puts salvation in the hands of the person himself. In the Reformed theological tradition in which Perkins stood, however, even the intention would be seen

as having been initiated by God. Thus God is the one responsible for a person's salvation.

[110] I, 639.

[111] Other theologians held a similar view. See Breward, *L&T*, p. 227 (note 1). He cites: Beza, *Pithie summe*, p. 76; Hyperius, *Practis of Preaching*, p. 109b; Greenham, *Works*, p. 238; and Zanchius, in Perkins' *Works*, I, 434.

[112] Cf. Zanchi's point in I, 434.

[113] I, 641.

[114] I, 641.

[115] See Breward, *L&T*, pp. 225ff.

[116] I, 669-716. See McKim, "Ramism," Figures 44 and 45.

[117] See I, 678, 679, and 685.

[118] I, 698.

[119] Perkins' concern not to go beyond what the Biblical texts truly implied is seen in his frequent use of this term "scope." Perkins often commented, for example about the parables, that "nothing may be gathered that is beside the scope thereof," I, 731. In focusing on the topics with which to deal in his works, he made references to the "scope of this text" (I, 485); the "scope and sense of words" (II, 172); the "intent and scope of the apostle" (I, 672) etc.

[120] I, 672.

[121] I, 694.

[122] I, 694.

[123] See I, 695, 696.

[124] I, 439.

[125] I, 439.

[126] See McKim, "Ramism," Figure 46.

[127] I, 450.

[128] I, 451-452.

[129] The date of this work is uncertain. See Breward, *Work*, p. 414.

[130] See Edmund S. Morgan, *The Puritan Family* (1944; rpt. new ed. New York: Harper & Row, 1966); Levin L. Schücking, *The Puritan Family*, trans. Brian Battershaw (1929; rpt. London: Routledge & Kegan Paul, 1969); Gordon S. Wakefield, *Puritan Devotion Its Place in the Development of Christian Piety* (London: Epworth Press, 1957), ch. 4; Lawrence Stone, *The Family, Sex and Marriage in England 1500-1800* (New York: Harper & Row, 1977). See

also Paul, "Accident and Essence," pp. 28ff. where he deals with the Puritan view of "The Church in the Home."

[131] III, 669, 670. The "private government of one" referred to the husband. As Perkins wrote of the married state: "of those two the one is alwaies higher, and beareth rule, the other is lower, and yieldeth subiection," III, 670.

[132] III, 670, 698ff. See McKim, "Ramism," Figure 47.

[133] On Bucer's views see Hastings Eells, *Martin Bucer and the Bigamy of Philip of Hesse* (New Haven, Connecticut: Yale University Press, 1924), pp. 20-43. A fuller treatment of Perkins' views is in Breward, *L&T*, pp. 299ff.

[134] See III, 687.

[135] See III, 690.

[136] III, 688.

[137] See III, 69ff.*

[138] I, 453-469; 469-474.

[139] I, 454 citing Melanchthon, *Loci communes* and Calvin, *Institutes*, III. iii. 9.

[140] I, 454.

[141] I, 455, 457.

[142] See McKim "Ramism," Figure 48.

[143] I, 462-463.

[144] Thus Perkins' use of "cases" was not limited to his works on casuistry.

[145] II, 673. See McKim, "Ramism," Figure 49.

[146] This chart is as follows:

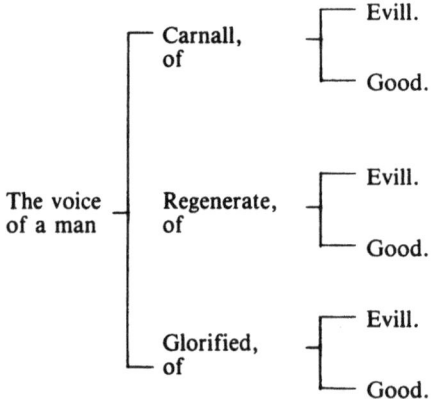

See I, 474.

¹⁴⁷ I, 489-514.

¹⁴⁸ See McKim, "Ramism," Figure 50.

¹⁴⁹ I have dealt with the contents of the treatise more fully in an unpublished paper: "Some Aspects of Death and Dying in Puritanism," Pittsburgh Theological Seminary, 1978.

¹⁵⁰ See II, 433-452. The title page indicates that these were public lectures. In his *Cases of Conscience* Perkins mentions "equity" but does not develop a discussion, II, 114.

¹⁵¹ II, 436.

¹⁵² II, 442.

¹⁵³ II, 436.

¹⁵⁴ II, 452 (misnumbered 425). For more on the sources of Perkins' views of equity see Breward, *L&T*, pp. 247ff. and *Work*, pp. 479-480.

¹⁵⁵ See McKim, "Ramism," Figure 51.

¹⁵⁶ See I, 625-634.

¹⁵⁷ See McKim, "Ramism," Figure 52.

¹⁵⁸ I, 626-627. The italics throughout are Perkins'.

¹⁵⁹ I, 629.

¹⁶⁰ I, 631.

¹⁶¹ I, 633.

¹⁶² I, 627, 628. An example of this is when Perkins spoke of "reconciliation," then the "benefits of reconciliation"; and the division of Christ's "vertue" into a "speculative" and "experimentall" knowledge.

¹⁶³ See II, 669 where Perkins defined "instruction." As Perkins divided "moral duties" into "general" and "special" here in *Christ Crucified*, so also in *Arte* he divided "correction" into "general" and "specific" corrections--an exact correspondence.

¹⁶⁴ III, 428-439; 440-463.

¹⁶⁵ See McKim, "Ramism," Figure 53.

¹⁶⁶ III, 429.

¹⁶⁷ III, 429.

¹⁶⁸ II, 453-483. See McKim, "Ramism," Figure 55.

¹⁶⁹ II, 456.

[170] *Dialecti. comm. tres.* (1546), p. 83 as cited in Ong, *Ramus,* p. 245.

[171] See II, 662, 663.

[172] Breward, *L&T,* p. 283.

[173] I, 754.

[174] I, 750.

[175] See McKim, "Ramism," Figure 56.

[176] See I, 762ff.

[177] The works not charted are *A Case of Conscience* where Perkins used a dialogue form and appended a selection from Zanchi; *A Grain of Musterd-Seede* where he argued his position on the assurance of salvation in light of the Cambridge University controversies; *A Fruitfull Dialogue concerning the End of the World* where he used the dialogue form to challenge astrologers; and his *A Reformed Catholike* and *The Problem of the forged Catholicism*, polemics against Roman Catholics.

Perkins' *The Foundation of the Christian Religion* was in the form of a catechism and his *Exposition on the Lord's Prayer* also was subtitled a "way of Catechizing." These were both directed at a more general audience labeled by Perkins in both pieces as "ignorant people." The sermon Perkins delivered at Stourbridge Fair on the first two verses of the second chapter of Zephaniah also was aimed at a more general audience when it was preached. It thus did not have Perkins' typical Ramean approach. Rather it was marked by more extended illustrations and examples from common life designed to move the hearers to repent of their sins.

[178] See II, 663.

[179] On these see:
"either...or" -- I, 126, 132, 531; II, 2, 6, 654; III, 681, 684, 695 etc.
"unfolding" -- II, 608, 458; II, 3 etc.
"branches" -- II, 436, 464, 479; I, 15; III, 23*, 45*, 219, 381 etc.
"doctrine/use" -- I, 741; II, 669; III, 684 etc.
"general/particular" -- I, 492, 743, 751; II, 1, 113, 329, 683; III, 444, 462, 640 etc.
"order" -- I, 540, 720, 750; II, 2, 608 etc.
"analysis" -- II, 650; III, 259 etc.

[180] John Milton, *Art of Logic* in *Works of John Milton*, Columbia edition (New York: Columbia University Press, 1931), I, ix, 75. See Fisher, "Milton's Logic," p. 42. Also useful is Craig Walton, "Ramus and the Art of Judgment," *Philosophy and Rhetoric*, III (Summer 1970), 152-164.

[181] Fisher, "Milton's Logic," pp. 42-43. See also Flower and Murphey, p. 14.

[182] The phrase is Perry Miller's. See *NEM*, p. 133. Charting the Works of Perkins is made easier in that most of his major divisions are listed first. As he moved from head to head Perkins began each new head with a new paragraph and usually a topic sentence to show clearly what point he was discussing.

[183] II, 608.

[184] By Cudworth in the "Epistle Dedicatorie" to the commentary on Galatians, II, 345.

[185] See Howell, *L&R*, pp. 160-161.

[186] See II, 670. Perkins' references to the "heads or places" of doctrines testify to his awareness of the "commonplace" tradition. See for example, III, 3.

NOTES TO CHAPTER VII

[1] On Milton see Fisher, "Milton's Logic"; Howard, "'The Invention....'"; Scott-Craig, "The Craftsmanship and Theological Significance of Milton's Art of Logic"; Fletcher, *The Intellectual Development of John Milton*; C. Hill, *Milton and the English Revolution*; J. Milton French, "Milton, Ramus, and Edward Phillips," *Modern Philology*, XLVII (1949), 82-87; Pierre Albert Duhamel, "Milton's Alleged Ramism," *PMLA*, LXVII (1953), 1035-1053 and Howell, *L&R, passim*.

[2] *The Diocesans Tryal* (1621), A1, A2.

[3] On this pattern see Bernstein and below here on "Plain Style Preaching."

[4] See the brackets in this work at pp. 217, 221, 244, 429, 635, 639, 682, 502 etc.

[5] See the brackets in *Terrour* at pp. 17, 23, 60 and Caveat, p. 3. On Baynes see Haller, *Rise, passim* and Sprunger, *Learned, passim*. It was said that Baynes was "very famous for answering Cases of Conscience, and therefore many doubting Christians repaired to him for satisfaction," cited in Sprunger, *Learned*, p. 162. He was known as "holy Baynes."

[6] On Rogers see Sprunger, *Learned*, pp. 16, 17 and Hill, *IO*, p. 134.

[7] III, 478.

[8] See for example Taylor's *A Commentary Upon the Epistle of St. Paul Written to Titus* (London, 1658). See Sprunger, *Learned*, p. 16; Hill, *IO*, p. 100 and Seaver, pp. 237, 248.

[9] See McKim, "Ramism," Figure 57. See Seaver, p. 139 on Tuke. He collaborated in the translation of Perkins' *De Praedestinationis* with Francis Cacot. Tuke echoed Perkins' language from *The Arte of Prophecying* when he wrote in his *The Picture of a True Protestant or, God's House and Husbandry* (also 1609): "Now before we weigh anchor, and launch forward with our vessels into the deepe, it will be first convenient for us to break the ice & by the explication of the words to prepare a way for the collection & application of the doctrines," pp. 142-143.

[10] See Sprunger, *Learned*, p. 24.

[11] See Sprunger, *Learned*, pp. 29ff. Sprunger comments: "Jacob, Parker, and Ames were Congregationalists of the non-separating kind; they refused to cut themselves off totally from the English church, but Robinson was a rigid Separatist who saw the English church as polluted throughtout," p. 29. Robinson, however, somewhat modified his position as a result of conversations and confrontations with Ames, p. 30. On Ames see further Mihály Hazagh, "Amesius és a Magyar puritánizmus," *Studies in English Philology*, IV (1942), 94-112; Hugo Visscher, *Guilielmus Amesius. Zijn leven en werken* (Haarlem, 1894); Karl Reuter, *Wilhelm Amesius: der fuhrende Theolge des erwachenden reformierten Pietismus in Beitrage zur Geschichte und Lehre der reformierten Kirche*, IV (Neukirchen, 1940). Visscher's and Reuter's works have been translated by Douglas Horton in *William Ames* by Matthew Nethenus, Hugo Visscher

and Karl Reuter (Cambridge, Massachusetts: Harvard Divinity School Library, 1965). Ames' relation to Pietism is studied by Reuter as well as in Heinrich Heppe, *Geschichte des Pietismus und der Mystik in der reformirten Kirche, namentlich der Niederlande* (Leiden: E.J. Brill, 1879), pp. 140-143 and F. Ernest Stoeffler, *The Rise of Evangelical Pietism*, pp. 134-141. Stoeffler calls Ames the "first theologian" of Reformed Pietism, p. 133. A. Ritschl, *Geschichte des Pietismus (1880-1886)* paid no attention to Ames while Wilhelm Goeters, *Die Vorbereitung des Pietismus in der reformierten Kirche der Niederlande bis zur Ankunft Labadies 1666* (Weimar, 1909) along with Reuter made Ames a significant influence in the Dutch and German pietism movements. Cf. Martin H. Prozesky, "The Emergency of Dutch Pietism," *Journal of Ecclesiastical History*, Vol. 28, No.1 (January 1977), 35.

[12] Sprunger, *Learned*, p. 128. Ames engaged in many polemics against Arminians.

[13] Sprunger, *Learned*, p. 15.

[14] Sprunger, *Learned*, p. 130.

[15] Sprunger, *Learned*, p. 142.

[16] Sprunger, *Learned*, p. 141.

[17] From Ames, "Demonstratio logicae verae," *Philosophemata*, p. 158 as cited in Sprunger, *Learned*, p. 141.

[18] See John Dykstra Eusden's "Introduction" to his translation of William Ames, *The Marrow of Theology*, trans. John D. Eusden (Boston: Pilgrim Press, 1968). Eusden writes: "For a century an a half William Ames's *Marrow of Theology* held sway as a clear, persuasive expression of Puritan belief and practice. In England, Holland, and New England nearly all those who aspired to the Puritan way read the book," p. 1.

[19] See McKim, "Ramism," Figure 58 for a chart of this work reproduced from Eusden's translation. The page numbers on the chart refer to this edition.

[20] *Marrow*, I. i. i.

[21] *Marrow*, I. ii. i.

[22] *Marrow*, I. ii. 4.

[23] *Marrow*, I. i. 10.

[24] *Marrow*, I. i. 12.

[25] This is Sprunger's phrase from *Learned*, p. 137.

[26] *Marrow* I. i. 8.

[27] *Marrow*, I. iii. 1.

[28] *Marrow*, II. i. 1.

[29] William Ames, *Conscience, with the Power and Cases Thereof* (n.p., 1639), "To the Reader." Cf. Sprunger, *Learned*, p. 154 for information about the printing history of this work.

³⁰ See Sprunger, *Learned*, ch. XI: "Doctor Ames of Famous Memory." Cf. Douglas Horton, "Let Us Not Forget the Mighty William Ames," *Religion in Life*, XIX, No. 3 (Summer 1960), 434-442.

³¹ See Haller, *Rise, passim*.

³² See *The Christian Warfare* (London, 1634), Hh3, Sss3 for charts.

³³ *The Summe of Sacred Divinitie*, p. 7.

³⁴ On Smith see Haller, *Rise, passim*; Porter, *Reformation and Reaction*, pp. 248-249 and Michael R. Watts, *The Dissenters From the Reformation to the French Revolution* (Oxford: University Press, 1978), *passim*, especially pp. 46, 72-73. Besides his method, Smith's language was very Ramistic as well. He wrote: "In handling whereof we will first propound some generall considerations: after descend to the particular exposition of the words thereof," *A Paterne of True Prayer* (1605), p. 13.

³⁵ On Chappell see Bernstein, ch. VIII and Howell, *L&R*, pp. 212-213.

³⁶ William Gouge was a Fellow of King's College (1602) having entered in 1595. His mother's sisters were married to William Whitaker, the Regius Professor of Divinity at Cambridge and to Laurence Chaderton. Gouge became known as an "arch-Puritan." Samuel Clarke related an incident in which Gouge stepped into a debate to defend Ramus. See *Lives of Thirty-two Divines* (London, 1677), p. 235 as cited in Howell, *L&R*, pp. 199-200. Gouge taught logic at his college and later became a member of the Westminster Assembly. His works are filled with Ramist charts. See for example: *An Exposition of Part of the Fift and Sixt Chapters of St. Paules Epistle to the Ephesians* (London, 1630); *Gods three arrowes: Plague, Famine, Sword, In three Treatises* (London, 1631); *A Learned and Very Useful Commentary on the Whole Epistle to the Hebrews* (London, 1655). See Haller, *Rise, passim*: Hill, *IO*, pp. 100, 292, 308; and Seaver, *passim*.

³⁷ Thomas Granger had been a student of Peterhouse College, Cambridge from 1598-1605. He wrote a Ramistic treatise on preaching called *Syntagma Logicum* (*The Logic Book*; He referred to it as *The Divine Logike*) in 1620. It has been described as "an English epitome of the standard commentaries on Ramistic logic, to which it adds dashes of scholastic doctrine for good measure; and it also emerges as an English commentary on the logical system epitomized in Ramus's *Dialecticae Libri Duo*," Howell, *L&R*, p. 231. Cf. Bernstein, ch. VIII who deals more fully with Granger and places him in the evolution of plain-style preaching. Granger's work *The Bread of Life, or Foode of the Regenerate* (London, 1616) was also constructed by the Ramist Method.

³⁸ John Yates (fl. 1612-1661) was a graduate of Emmanuel College where Laurence Chaderton was the Master. He was a student of Alexander Richardson who maintained an academy of sorts for Cambridge graduates at Barking, Essex. Yates' *Modell of Divinitie* (1622) was structured Ramistically. See Keith L. Sprunger, "John Yates of Norfolk: The Radical Puritan Preacher as Ramist Philosopher," *Journal of the History of Ideas*, XXXVII, No.4 (October-December 1976), 697-706. In 1615 Yates wrote an anti-Arminian book, *Gods Arraignement of Hypocrites* in which he defended John Calvin and William Perkins.

³⁹ For Ramist characteristics in the works of Thomas Hooker (1586-1647) an associate of Ames' and student of Richardson's see David L. Parker, "The Application of Humiliation: Ramist Logic and the Rise of Preparationism in New England," Diss. University of Pennsylvania 1972 and his "Petrus Ramus and the Puritans: The 'Logic' of Preparationist Conversion Doctrine," *Early American Literature*, 8 (1973), 140-162 as well as Alfred

Habegger, "Preparing the Soul for Christ: The Contrasting Sermon Forms of John Cotton and Thomas Hooker," *American Literature*, 41, 3 (March 1970), 342-354. Cf. Frank Shuffelton, *Thomas Hooker 1586-1647* (Princeton: Princeton University Press, 1977), references to Ramus and Perkins, *passim*.

[40] The four posthumous editions of this work were published in 1576, 1577, 1583, and 1594.

[41] Waddington, *Ramus*, p. 136 as given in Sprunger, *Learned*, p. 130.

[42] Ramus, *Commentariorum* (1577), p. 3 as given in Sprunger, *Learned*, p. 131.

[43] Sprunger, "Method," p. 135.

[44] See Lobstein, *Ramus*, pp. 40-41; Jurgen Moltmann, "Zur Bedeutung des Petrus Ramus fur Philosophie und Theologie im Calvinismus," *Zeitschrift fur Kirchengeschichte*, LXVIII (1957), 307ff.; and Sprunger, *Learned*, p. 132. Cf. I, 230.

[45] *Commentariorum* (1576), p. 6: *Theologia est doctrina bene vivendi*.

[46] I, 11.

[47] See Sprunger, *Learned*, p. 132. This was Ames' "faith/observance" scheme.

[48] Sprunger, *Learned*, p. 140.

[49] Sprunger, *Learned*, p. 133.

[50] See Sprunger, "Method," pp. 148-151 and Paul, "The Accidence and the Essence of Puritan Piety," pp. 23-26.

[51] See Howell, *L&R*, p. 165; Flower and Murphey, p. 19.

[52] See *RTI*, p. 346 (#581).

[53] See *RTI*, p. 328 (#555).

[54] See Howell, *L&R*, pp. 245-246. The subtitle read: "arranged according to the single method of P. Ramus."

[55] See *RTI*, p. 370 (#611); Howell, *L&R*, p. 246.

[56] A facsimilie of this work is found in Pepper, *Four Tudor Books on Education*. See Howell, *L&R*, pp. 258ff; T.W. Baldwin, *Small Latine and Lesse Greeke*, ch. XXXI; and Donald Lemen Clark, *John Milton at St. Paul's School* (1948; n.p.: Archon Books, 1964), *passim*.

[57] See Joan Simon, *Education*, p. 320.

[58] See Kempe (1588), G 2v. Cf. Clark, *Milton*, pp. 14-15 and Howell, *L&R*, p. 260.

[59] Howell, *L&R*, p. 260.

[60] Kempe, *Education* (1588), Aiijr. Cf. Pepper, p. xxviii.

⁶¹ See Howell, *L&R*, pp. 262ff. for a discussion of Butler and others who furthered the cause of Ramist rhetoric in England. Butler's text was published for schoolboys.

⁶² See Ong, *Ramus*, p. 260.

⁶³ See above, Ch. 3 (n. 130) for the comment in Fraunce's *The Lawiers Logike* about this as cited in Howell, L&R, p. 225.

⁶⁴ Lawrence Stone, "The Educational Revolution in England 1540-1640," *Past and Present* (1964), p. 71.

⁶⁵ III, 608.

⁶⁶ III, 9. Cf. III, 95*.

⁶⁷ III, 171*.

⁶⁸ Calvin, *Institutes* (1559), I. v. 2.

⁶⁹ See the opening chapters of Book I of the 1559 *Institutes*.

⁷⁰ See T.H.L. Parker, *John Calvin: A Biography* (Philadelphia: Westminster Press, 1975), pp. 126-129.

⁷¹ See W. Fred Graham, *The Constructive Revolutionary John Calvin & His Socio-Economic Impact* (Richmond, Virginia: John Knox Press, 1971), pp. 145-151.

⁷² See Robert W. Henderson, *The Teaching Office in the Reformed Tradition* (Philadelphia: Westminster Press, 1962), ch. 1: "The Genevan Reform in School and Church." Cf. Calvin, *Institutes* (1559), IV. iii. 2, 4, 5. In *Inst.* IV. iii. 4 Calvin names five offices in the church and says that pastors include the teaching function in their office.

⁷³ Graham, p. 151.

⁷⁴ "Draft Ecclesiastical Ordinances," in Calvin: *Theological Treatises*, ed. and trans. J.K.S. Reid, Library of Christian Classics (Philadelphia: Westminster Press, 1964), p. 63. Cf. John H. Leith, *Introduction to the Reformed Tradition* (1977; rpt. Atlanta: John Knox Press, 1978), pp. 77-79.

⁷⁵ On the prophecying movement and the 1584 Parliament see Simon, pp. 322, 327f. Cf. Hill, *IO*, p. 311.

⁷⁶ See Miller, *NEM*, ch. 3 and K.R.M. Short, "A Theory of Common Education in Elizabethan Puritanism," *Journal of Ecclesiastical History*, XXIII, No.1 (January 1972), 32.

⁷⁷ See Short, p. 32; Haller, *Rise*, p. 302; Knappen, *Tudor Puritanism*, ch. XXVI; Cf. Morison, *The Founding of Harvard College* and for the later period of English Puritanism, Richard Schlatter, "The Higher Learning in Puritan England," *Historical Magazine of the Protestant Episcopal Church*, XXIII (1954), 167-187.

⁷⁸ See Collinson, *EPM*, pp. 227, 349; Short, p. 40 (note 3). Greenham's Catechism discussed the Ten Commandments, the Creed, and the Lord's Prayer. See his *Works*, pp. 71-91.

⁷⁹ "The Epistle" prior to I, 1.

⁸⁰ III, 694.

⁸¹ II, 577.

⁸² See Clifford, "Casuistical Divinity," pp. 3-25 and Sprunger, *Learned*, p. 162.

⁸³ See Sprunger, *Learned*, p. 162.

⁸⁴ See Oki, p. 169 who points out that "the Puritans appear to have become more and more casuistric, and less and less political after their failure in a political reformation of the church and state. Numerous works on Christian directory or casuistry were produced in this particular span of time. This tendency was developed along with their preaching movement." See also Breward, "Origins" who makes no mention of Ramism in Perkins having anything to do with casuistry.

⁸⁵ Breward, "William Perkins and the Origins of Puritan Casuistry," p. 8.

⁸⁶ See Sprunger, *Learned*, p. 163. On the 17th century casuists see H.R. McAdoo, *The Structure of Caroline Moral Theology* (London: Longmans, 1949) and Thomas Wood, *English Casuistical Divinity in the Seventeenth Century* (London: S.P.C.K., 1952). Of special interest also is C.F. Allison, *The Rise of Moralism* (New York: Seabury Press, 1966).

⁸⁷ Breward, "Origins of Reformed Casuistry," p. 9 and Louis B. Wright, "William Perkins," p. 171.

⁸⁸ See Miller, *NEM*, pp. 335 and 339. Cf. Haller, *Rise*, pp. 130ff. Bernstein points to the importance of the definition and prescriptions for preaching found in Thomas Cartwright's *Directory of Church Government* found in his study after his death. One of Cartwright's instructions was that preaching was to be "in the style, phrase, and manner of speech,"..."spiritual, pure, proper, simple, and applied to the capacity of the people; nor of newfangledness, nor either so affected as it may serve for pomp and ostentation, or so careless and base as becometh not ministers of the Word of God," p. 22.

⁸⁹ John F. Wilson, *Pulpit in Parliament* (Princeton: Princeton University Press, 1970), p. 139.

⁹⁰ II, 670; III, 222.

⁹¹ II, 670.

⁹² II, 166. Perkins wrote: "...to take a text, and to make discourse vpon something in the said text, shewing much inuention of wit, & much reading, and humane learning, is not to preach Christ in a liuely manner," III, 222.

⁹³ II, 55.

⁹⁴ III, 430. Cf. II, 646: "The perfect and equall object of Preaching is the word of God, Luk. 16.29."

⁹⁵ II, 222. Hyperius had written: "Truth is delighted with plainness and simplicity," *Practis* (1577), 63b as cited in Breward, *L&T*, p. 183 (note 2).

⁹⁶ II, 222. Perkins advocated the concealing of "humane wisedome" because "the hearers ought not to ascribe their faith to the gifts of men, but to the power of Gods word," II, 670. Thus Perkins' own sermons were "quite undecorated in style." See J.W. Blench, *Preaching in England in the Late Fifteenth and Sixteenth Centuries* (Oxford: Basil Blackwell, 1964), p. 169. Alan F. Herr, *The Elizabethan Sermon A Survey and Bibliography* (1940; rpt. New York: Octagon Books, 1969), p. 91 says of Perkins that "rhetorical devices to tickle the ears of his auditors he spurns." Further on the Puritan plain style see Miller, *NEM*, ch. 12; Wilson, *Pulpit*, pp. 139ff.; Haller, *Rise*, ch. 4; Bernstein, ch. 1; and Robert A. Coughenour, "The Shape and Vehicle of Puritan Hermeneutics," *Reformed Review*, XXX, No.1 (Autumn 1976), 29ff.

⁹⁷ See Blench, pp. 100-101. Representatives of this form according to Blench were Bishop George Abbott, Bishop John King, Anthony Anderson, Edward Dering, John Rainolds, Roger Edgeworth, Richard Greenham, and Henry Smith. Cf. Horton Davies, *Worship and Theology in England 1534-1603* (Princeton: Princeton University Press, 1970), pp. 308ff. and his *Worship and Theology in England 1603-1690* (Princeton: Princeton University Press, 1975), ch. IV.

⁹⁸ Blench, pp. 102ff. This "modern style" form was used by Hyperius, John Jewel, Edmund Grindal, Richard Hooker, Thomas Playfere, and Lancelot Andrewes.

⁹⁹ The Latin commentaries of Musculus (Wolfgang Muesslin; 1497-1563) according to Thomas Fuller, "first brought in the plain (but effectual) manner of preaching by use and Doctrine," *Church History of Britain* (1655), Bk. IX, part 30, p. 222. Cf. Bernstein, p. 68 who concludes that "Musculus was, indeed, a figure of valued and lasting influence in the development of the Plain Style." He was cited often by Richard Bernard and John Wilkins. Cf. Breward, *L&T*, p. 182; *Work*, p. 50.

¹⁰⁰ Blench, p. 102. Wilson's study of sermons preached to the Long Parliament in the 1640's revealed that "whatever the exact arrangement, the implicit, if not explicit, structure of almost every exhortation to the Long Parliament exhibited this method of preaching. The 'plain style' was the universal mode of puritan sermons--at least in this pulpit," p. 141.

¹⁰¹ Wilson, *Pulpit*, p. 141.

¹⁰² See Bard Thompson, *Liturgies of the Western Church* (1961; rpt. New York: World Publishing Co., 1972), p. 364. Then followed instructions on confutation of false Doctrines, exhorting to duties, dehortation, reprehension, and publique admonition as well as comforting and applying.

¹⁰³ By Bernstein's dissertation "A Revaluation of the Plain Genre of Homiletics in its Evolution as a Theory of Persuasion from Ramus to John Wilkins."

¹⁰⁴ Dunn, ed., p. 7.

¹⁰⁵ II, 668.

¹⁰⁶ Nearly any page of Perkins' commentaries on Jude, or the Sermon on the Mount, or Galatians confirms this.

¹⁰⁷ I, 475-486. See the Ramist chart of this work in Figs. 28 and 29. This chart serves as an "outline" of the sermon.

¹⁰⁸ See Perkins' two-fold description of the ministers' work in III, 502. Cf. II, 337.

[109] Perkins believed that only the Holy Spirit could truly move people (the elect) to respond to the message of the Word of God. Since the Spirit was the ultimate persuader and not the preacher, Perkins did not stress the need for "proofs" or "reasons" in his homiletical theory. For him, "any point of doctrine collected by just consequence is simply of itselfe to bee beleeued, and doth demonstrate," II, 664. Bernstein sees later homileticians as introducing the "proof" element and emphasizing its importance. Thus, she says of Perkins, that "his homiletical treatise alone could not have provided a theoretical framework sufficiently adequate to have supplied the full rationale which was obviously implemented in the Westminster definition of the Plain Style," p. 84. The use of "reasons" in the sermons of John Cotton, Thomas Shepard, Thomas Hooker, Nehemiah Rogers and others leads Bernstein to conclude: "It would hardly appear then, that William Perkins' famous work, regardless of its immense popularity and historic prominence, could possibly have fathered the complete traditional Plain Style formula by offering only an implicit disavowal of the formula's central component. Unhappily, too large a number of scholars have overlooked Perkins' omission, and despite its inadequacy, identify *The Arte of Prophecying* as the sovereign hereditary model for the development of Plain preaching in England and America," pp. 88-89.

[110] In summary, Bernstein writes: "The results of this study reveal that a Doctrine and Use system of Plain preaching was officially established in England by the Elizabethan era. Roland MacIlmaine is identified as the earliest advocate of Ramus' Natural Method for the Plain clergy. William Perkins' homiletic is recognized as an extension of Ramus' Natural Method to accommodate the Plain pulpit's exhortational objectives. It is John Udall's homiletical interpretation of Ramistic Method, however, that is identified as the theory which brought the complete Doctrine, Reasons and Use formula into the Plain tradition. Examination of the innovations upon the Plain tradition offered by Richard Sibbes, Francis Bacon, Richard Bernard, Thomas Granger, and William Chappell reveal that their theories contributed importantly to the Plain Style's persuasive potential. After determining that the array of both classical and prophetically modern concepts these innovative theorists proposed greatly expanded the Plain Style's rational and emotional foundation, it is found that the Plain theory was given its most fruitful innovational treatment by John Wilkins. The conclusion is drawn that the Plain Genre reached its maturation in the seventeenth century through John Wilkins' reorientation of Ramistic Method. Wilkins universalized the Plain Method, and transformed the Plain Style into a pragmatically adaptive Rhetoric," p. viii.

[111] II, 670.

[112] II, 670.

[113] II, 670; II, 672.

[114] See Rechtien, "Visual Memory," p. 88.

[115] See Miller, *NEM*, ch. XI: "Rhetoric."

[116] Ames, "Theses logicae," p. 189 cited in Sprunger, *Learned*, p. 124. A Ramist had said: "What precepts soeuer the common Rehtoricians put downe for ordering of Exordiums and framing and disposing of the whole course of their speeche fitly and according to cause, auditors, time, place, and such like circumstances; all those I say, are altogether Logicall, not in any respect perteining to Rhetoricke, but as a Rhetor may bee directed by Logicall precepts of iudgement and disposition," cited in Miller, *NEM*, p. 316. Miller says: "Ramus' reform, in essence, amounted to abolishing the separate existence of any art of oratory, because he assumed that the precepts which led to a good address could not possibly

be others than those of logic, that arguments invented by dialectical laws and arrayed by the principles of method would wholly and efficiently furnish the materials and pattern of any discourse, in the fashion best suited to memorization," *NEM*, p. 317.

[117] Ramus, *Dialec. A. Talaei. prael. illus.* (1569), p. 501 as cited in Rechtien, "Visual Memory," p. 89.

[118] Ramus, *Arist. anim.*, fol. 58. See above Ch. 2, note 109.

[119] Rogers and McKim, chs. 3-6.

[120] Kearney, p. 61. Cf. Hill, *IO*, p. 292.

[121] Lawrence Stone, "The Ninnyversity?," *The New York Review of Books* (January 28, 1971), p. 23. Cf. Rechtien, "Literary Structures," who ties Ramism to Cartwright and Travers. Sprunger makes this comment: "Puritan exceptions there were, it is true, especially on the extreme edge of the movement where formal logic was seen as a possible barrier to the Spirit. Robert Browne [who was at Cambridge in 1570], the Separatist, not willing to tarry for any, not even for the logicians, decried 'vain logic' with its definitions and divisions." But, Sprunger notes, Browne "nevertheless, used the Ramist dichotomy in his *Booke Which Sheweth the Life and Manners of All True Christians* (1582) as a means of communicating with skeptical scholars." See Sprunger, "John Yates of Norfolk," p. 699. Cf. Kearney, ch. IV: "The Radicalism of the Sectaries" who underscores the rejection of logic by the sectaries.

[122] Stone, "The Ninnyversity?," p. 25.

[123] Udall's work was described this way by Collinson, *EPM*, p. 391. He referred to John Udall, *A demonstration of the truth of that discipline* (1593). Udall (c. 1560-1592) entered Christ's College in 1577-78 but graduated with his Bachelor of Arts degree from Trinity in 1580-81. He attempted to establish a presbyterian system of church government and was accused of authoring the Marprelate tracts. He perhaps imbibed the Ramism which both this work and his commentary on Lamentations show (with Ramist charts as parts of them) from Chaderton. Chaderton left Christ's College shortly after Udall entered. See Peile, *Biographical Register*, I, 145, 89. Udall was a Hebrew scholar. When James VI heard of his death he said, "By my soul the greatest scholar in Europe is dead," Peile, I, 146.

[124] Arminius constructed a Ramist chart on the doctrine of predestination in 1598 and his first edition of his *Dissertation on Romans Seven* (Leiden, 1613) also contained a chart on a large fold-out sheet. See Bangs, *Arminius*, p. 59 and his whole ch. 4: "The Influence of Petrus Ramus." Bangs writes: "Ramism is not the *differentia* between Arminius and Calvinism. Perkins, who Arminius charged with Calvinistic error on predestination, was no less a Ramist than Arminius," p. 63.

[125] Sprunger, "John Yates," p. 699. Cf. Craig Walton, "Ramus and Socrates," *Proceedings of the American Philosophical Society*, CXIV (1970), 119-139.

[126] *The Logicians School-Master*, cited in Miller, NEM, p. 147.

[127] From the Greek *technē*, "art," "skill," and *metron*, "measure" or "survey." This is defined as "the science of defining and delineating the arts according to their nature and use" by Sprunger, "Prologue," p. 115. Technometry has been much explored since Miller identified it with Puritanism (*NEM*, pp. 160-180). Cf. Ong, *Ramus*, p. 197; Sprunger, *Learned*, pp. 105-126; "John Yates." pp. 700-701; and Gibbs, *WAT* as well as his "William Ames's

Technometry," *Journal of the History of Ideas*, XXX, No.4 (October-December 1972), 615-624. Cf. his "The Technometry of William Ames," Diss. Harvard University 1968; Flower and Murphey, pp. 20ff.

[128] Gibbs, *WAT*, p. 32.

[129] Cited in Miller, *NEM*, p. 164.

[130] From the chart of William Ames, *Technometria* (London, 1633) reproduced in Gibbs, *WAT*, pp. 34, 35. See also Sprunger, "Prologue," p. 117. This chart is copied in McKim, "Ramism," Figure 59. Ames also defines *technometria* as "a precognition" *(praecognitio)* of the general nature of art and of the general use of art in the activities of human life," *Alia Technometriae Delineatio,* theses 1-2 cited in WAT.

[131] Ames, *Alia*, thesis 22 cited in Gibbs, *WAT*, p. 132.

[132] On *encyclopedia* see Sprunger, "John Yates," p. 702. He points out that "William Ames made a slight differentiation between *encyclopedia* and *technometria*. For him *encyclopedia* is the study of the entire circle of knowledge and *technometria* the study of the relationships of the individual arts included in the circle. Richardson and Yates combined both exercises into encyclopedia."

"Encyclopedia" has Greek and Roman origins out of which Ames' understandings developed. Ramus had picked up on Cicero's use of the Greek *technologia* as "a systematic treatment of grammar," *Letters to Atticus*, 4.16, trans. E.O. Winstedt, Loeb Classical Library (New York, 1912), 1: 314 cited in *WAT*, p. 21. Ramus developed the term further, however, to other subjects of the curriculum to understand technology as the art of arranging the contents of all curricular subjects properly. See Ong, *Ramus*, p.f 197. Johann Heinrich Alsted (see Appendix C) was the greatest of the European technometrists. Alsted organized, summarized, and diagrammed some 79 disciplines in his *Encyclopedia*, the first modern "encyclopedia." He attended the Synod of Dort and there likely met Ames. See Sprunger, *Learned*, p. 121.

Samuel Johnson of Connecticut (1696-1772) wrote a version of *An Encyclopaedia of Philosophy* in 1713 and 1714 which he entitled *Technologia ceu Technometria; Ars Encyclopaedia manualis ceu philosophia*. As Gibbs says, "This document is the best surviving American example of a student's application of Ramist method to the whole body of human knowledge," *WAT*, p. 45. This work was composed of 1271 theses and is translated from the Latin in *Samuel Johnson: His Career and Writings* (New York: Columbia University Press, 1929), 2:55-186. The translation is by H.W. Schneider.

The theses defended by students at Harvard in colonial times as well as Yale were commencement theses rightly called "technological theses." Many are obviously based on Richardson, Alsted, and Ames. See S.E. Morison's collection of these in *Harvard College*, 2:583-638 and *WAT*, pp. 41ff. Cf. Porter G. Perrin, "Possible Sources of *Technologia* at Early Harvard," *The New England Quarterly*, VII (December 1934), 718-724.

[133] Ames, *Technometry*, theses 45-48 in *WAT*, pp. 100-101 and Gibbs' commentary, pp. 146ff. This work is hereafter cited as Ames, Thesis.

[134] Ames, Thesis 45.

[135] Ames, Thesis 45.

[136] Gibbs, "William Ames's Technometry," p. 623.

[137] Ames, Thesis 45.

[138] *WAT*, p. 147. See also "William Ames's Technometry," p. 623.

[139] As Sprunger put it: "To God the truth of knowledge is obviously single and undivided; but, as it is reflected in creation like the refraction of a ray of light, it appears to man as multiple kinds of truth discernible as the arts," "Prologue," p. 117.

[140] Ames wrote: "Theology alone homogeneously transmits (1) the universal teaching about God, not as he is in himself (for he is not known in this manner by anyone except himself) but as he has revealed himself to us more clearly in the book of Scripture and more obscurely in the book of nature so that we might live well," Thesis 111 in *WAT*, p. 112.

[141] Flower and Murphey, p. 21. Cf. *NEM*, p. 161; Ames, Thesis 50 in *WAT*, p. 101 and *WAT*, p. 149. Richardson began his *Logicians School-Master* by discussing "being" (*ens*), pp. 1-2, 7. Ames criticized the Aristotelian and scholastic metaphysics when he, like Ramus, accused them of wrongly taking over the tasks of logic and theology. See Thesis 51 and 112 in *WAT*, pp. 101, 112 and *WAT*, p. 155.

[142] Ames, Thesis 32 in *WAT*, p. 98. Cf. *WAT*, p. 141.

[143] *WAT*, p. 141.

[144] Ramus, *Sch. metaphy.*, *Liber* I in *Sch. in lib. arts.*, col. 834; Richardson, *Logicians*, p. 69. Gibbs writes: "This is a profound new interpretation of the comprehensiveness and importance of theology as the most dignified of the arts and sciences. None of the other arts presuppose or need theology, and yet theology presupposes and uses all of the other arts. Nevertheless, in a very real sense all of the other arts are 'for the sake of' the art or teaching of theology," *WAT*, p. 140.

[145] Technically, Ames taught that theology is *doctrina* (doctrine or teaching) rather than art. This was because its truths are revealed by God. See *WAT*, p. 179 and Thesis 110. Cf. Sprunger, "Prologue," pp. 116-117.

[146] See Ames, *Marrow*, Bk. I, ch. 1; Ramus, *Commentariorum*, Lib. I, cap. 1 (1576), p. 6; Perkins, *Works*, I, 11. See Eusden's comments on these is his "Introduction" to Ames' *Marrow*, p. 47.

[147] See Flower and Murphey, pp. 22, 23 and Ames, Thesis 69 as well as *WAT*, pp. 157-158.

[148] Ames, Thesis 68. Ames defined "analysis" in his *Marrow* as meaning "observing the scope or purpose of the text and, by the art of logic, the means by which it is attained," I, xxxv, 24. Richardson had said: "The purpose of Logick is to direct man to see the wisdom of God." Cited in *NEM*, p. 160.

[149] *WAT*, p. 157. Cf. Ames, Theses 24, 67, 120. Flower and Murphey see in this "dual empiricism of Ramus--the empirical study of literature and of nature," a "path for the new science." Since "nature itself is God's discourse and science is the study of God's art....by thus focusing attention on the interpretation of natural phenomena, the Puritans opened a path for the new science. Detailed empirical observation of nature now became a duty; new discoveries were sought and prized as revelations of the divine wisdom. For the Puritans, science and religion were one: the early scientists of New England were chiefly ministers," p. 23. They cite Morison, *The Intellectual Life of Colonial New England*, ch. 10 and *NEM*, p. 217f.

Gibbs agrees with this assessment: "Ames strengthened the tendencies of Ramus toward empiricism, observation, and experiment, at least in the discovery of the principles of various disciplines. And if Ramus was a transitional figure between the old, authoritative, scholastic understanding of the arts and the new philosophy of Descartes and the new science of Bacon, Boyle, and Newton, Ames certainly progressed farther down the road of transition than did his master. Ames, with his influence in England, on the continent, and especially in early New England, not only helped clear the way for but actually helped introduce the new science," *WAT*, p. 159.

The relationship between Puritanism and the rise of science along with Ramus' place in it all is a debatable issue, however. See for example, Hugh Kearney, *Science and Change 1500-1700* (New York: McGraw-Hill, 1974) and the interchange between Kearney and Christopher Hill in *The Intellectual Revolution of the Seventeenth-Century*, ed. Charles Webster (London: Routledge & Kegan Paul, 1974). Cf. Hill, *IO, passim*; Hooykaas, *Humanisme, Science et Réforme and his Religion and the Rise of Modern Science* (Grand Rapids: Wm. B. Eerdmans, 1972). Major figures such as Bacon and Boyle are mentioned throughout these works as well as in Wilbur Samuel Howell, *Eighteenth-Century British Logic and Rhetoric* (Princeton: Princeton University Press, 1971). See also Craig Walton, "Ramus and Bacon on Method" for an assessment of their similarities and differences on method. Ames mentioned Bacon in Thesis 70. Despite Ames' belief that much can be learned from nature, this for him was always trivial in comparison to what is to be learned about God from Scripture. Scripture was always the true basis of knowledge of God and theology for Ames. See Flower and Murphey, p. 29; Gibbs, *WAT*, p. 181 and Eusden's "Introduction" p. 49.

[150] See Fisher, "Milton's Logic," p. 46.

[151] Bartholomew Keckerman (c. 1571-1609) of Danzig (along with Alsted) was known as a "Systematic" in that he sought to reform Ramus' logic and soften its implications. His goal was "to make Aristotle once more supreme in logic" with his *Systema Logicae* (1600). See Howell, *Eighteenth-Century*, p. 382; *L&R*, pp. 283, 302-303, 310, 312, 320, and 323; Ong, *Ramus*, pp. 298-300. When he did theology according to the Aristotelian method in *A Manuduction to Theologie, Done into English by T.V.* [Vicars] (London, 1622), he "stated a proposition and then proceeded to prove it by quoting authorities, but always logically. Thus, no matter what the claims made for the differences between theology and the so-called arts, their study was exactly the same, and thus theology became largely an extension of logical principles, ethical motives, physical principles, and metaphysical ideas." See Fletcher, II, 199-200; Cf. *WAT, passim* and Sprunger, *Learned, passim* on Keckerman.

[152] Flower and Murphey, p. 41. Fisher writes: "In all this Ramus assumed that reason and the senses gave an accurate report of the structure and extent of the universe for all practical purposes. Although Aristotle had asserted the possibility of knowing the world revealed by the senses according to reflection defined by logical method, Ramus apparently reduced the whole of epistemology to a simple intuition of the world by the act of reason," "Milton's Logic," p. 45.

[153] Fisher, "Milton's Logic," p. 46.

[154] Curtis, *Oxford and Cambridge in Transition*, p. 254. For the Puritan Ramists, "logic takes truth, existing in the mind of God and reflected in the thing, and organizes it into a systematized body of knowledge suitable for teaching, learning, and memorizing." This interplay between logic and religion was that "Puritan religion reached into every area of life, and by using *technometria*, the process was justified and vindicated by the soundest reasoning," Sprunger, *Learned*, pp. 123 and 120.

[155] Yet for the Puritans, the effects of sin were on the mind. Since the fall of Adam, they believed the mind has not worked as it should. "What was destroyed in the fall was not," they said, "any of the faculties themselves, but rather the due order and subordination

among them." Reason was confused and susceptible not to "judge rightly" since it is misled by human imagination. This was the thrust of Perkins' treatise *A Treatise of Mans Imaginations* (II, 453-483). Perkins defined the imagination as (primarily) "the frame, or framing of the heart" which was "the naturall disposition of the understanding after the fall of man" but even more "that which the minde & vnderstanding by thinking frameth plotteth, and deuiseth; that is for the effect thereof," II, 458. This imagination in humanity is unqualifiedly evil according to Perkins: "The minde and vnderstanding part of man is naturally so corrupt, that so soone as hee can use reason, he doth nothing but imagine that which is wicked, and against the Law of God," II, 458. See Flower and Murphey, p. 43.

The end result is that the will is now in rebellion against God. Both mind and will are gone awry. For Perkins: "The minde is naturally so corrupt that it cannot thinke a good thought, and therefore answerably the wil by nature is so corrupt, that it cannot will that which is truly good," II, 475.

Ames, of course, agreed. See *Marrow*, I. xiii. For both Ames and Richardson, the reason the arts are imperfect is that sin has made human powers needed for *eupraxia*, weak. See Ames, Thesis 61 and Richardson, *Logicians*, pp. 37, 39-40. Cf. *NEM*, pp. 250, 260, and *WAT*, p. 133.

[157] See above, chapter IV, notes 130 and 131. Though Perkins did not write on the whole arts, what he has here accords well with Ames. Ames said that "theology alone homogeneously delivers the whole revealed will of God for directing our morals, will, and life." See Thesis 113. He like Perkins, included ethics, household economy, or politics as "not really 'arts' or 'sciences' *per se* but rather faculties or uses of another 'art,' namely, the teaching of theology," *WAT*, p. 170 commenting on Thesis 92. Cf. Thesis 128. For Perkins, theology was the "principal science" comprehended in "the bodie of Scripture," I, 11.

[157] Sprunger, "Prologue," and *Learned*, ch. 6 are where he calls *technometry* the "Prologomena to Theology." As Gibbs points out, "Technometry is the final consequence of the Ramist dictum of method, which asserts that the most general by nature should precede the more specific. It is the result of the intellectual drive to construct a general and all-inclusive philosophy of unity, a metadiscipline that systematically integrates the whole body of knowledge," *WAT*, p. 36.

[157] As Ames put it theologically in his chapter on "The Decree and Counsel of God": "An idea in man, who attains knowledge by analysis, is brought in from things themselves. Things exist first in themselves and then come into the senses of men and finally to the understanding, where they can form an idea to direct a subsequent operation. But God knows all things by genesis and does not require knowledge through analysis of things; therefore all things are first in his mind before they are in themselves," *Marrow*, I, vii, 15.

[159] Flower and Murphey, p. 40. More broadly, Perry Miller summarized the importance of the technometric enterprise for Puritanism: "The most important point, speaking historically, is that through it Puritans secured everything their hearts desired in the realm of philosophy....It accounted for an intelligible universe without infringing the sovereignty of God; it showed how men could apprehend the intelligibles, even in a state nof sin, by an immediate and instantaneous recognition. It proved that intelligibles exist objectively, not in man's head but in the thing. It allowed men to glory in the possession of innate powers without giving them cause to conclude that grace was superfluous. It provided a philosophical account of the visible universe, or its nature and its origin, that was thoroughly compatible with the theology, which is supplemented and supported. It demonstrated that by an innate power or an inherent habit of methodical apprehension men could perceive that eternal and divine rules upon which the natural world is constructed, and that the sum total of this knowledge was a unified and coherent *organon*. It provided a framework in which the Puritan, while remaining a man of piety and a believer in original sin and irresistible grace, could

stabilize his intellectual heritage," *NEM*, pp. 175-176.

[160] As Miller put it: "The charm of the system in Puritan eyes was that it annihilated the distance from the object to the brain, or made possible an epistemological leap across the gap in the twinkling of an eye, with an assurance of footing beyond the possibility of a metaphysical slip," *NEM*, p. 149.

[161] II, 323; cf. II, 322.

NOTES TO APPENDIX A

[1] *EP*, IV, 529. On the transmission of Aristotle to the West see F. van Steenberghen, *Aristotle in the West: The Origins of Latin Aristotelianism*, trans. Leonard Johnston (Louvain: E. Nauwelaerts, 1955).

[2] Hugh of St. Victor, *Didascalion*, I, ch. 12 (P.L. 176, 749-750) as translated in Ernest A. Moody, *Truth and Consequence in Medieval Logic* (Amsterdam: North-Holland Publishing Company, 1953), pp. 13-14.

[3] Moody, p. 13 citing William of Sherwood's *Introductiones*, p. 30 and William of Ockham's *Expositio aurea*, I, fol. 1r. See Moody, p. 32 (note 2).

[4] Frederick Copleston, *A History of Philosophy*, 9 vols. (New York: Doubleday and Co., 1962), II/1, 188; hereafter cited as *HP*.

[5] Moody, p. 14. Moody points out that in this conception logic also serves to validate inferences made in other sciences. Boethius' statement that logic is both a science and an instrument of science was understood in this manner. "Formal" here indicates the criterion of logical truth was based on the way the constituents of the sentence or argument occur rather than on the meaning or context of the terms. See Moody, p. 15.
In the teaching of the arts, Cassiodorus (458?-?580) had instituted a plan whereby training was given in the *trivium* and *quadrivium*. The seven liberal arts were thought to encase all human knowledge. See Rogers and McKim, p. 37.

[6] I.M. Bocheński, *Ancient Formal Logic* (Amsterdam: North-Holland Publishing Company, 1951), p. 25; hereafter cited as *AFL*.

[7] Bocheński, *AFL*, p. 25.

[8] Aristotle wrote in his *Metaphysics* that "the attempts of some of those who discuss the terms on which truth should be accepted, are due to a want of training in logic; for they should know these things already when they come to a special study, and not be inquiring into them while they are listening to lectures on it," Bk. IV, ch. 3, 1005b, 1-5, *The Basic Works of Aristotle*, ed. Richard McKeon (New York: Random House, 1941), p. 736. Cf. Boechenski, *AFL*, p. 25 and *EP*, I, 155.

[9] An earlier and more original work was the *Introductiones in Logicam* by William of Sherwood (1200/1210-1266/1271). See *EP*, VIII, 317 and IV, 529. On Peter of Spain see *EP*, VI, 125-126; *HP*, III/1, 64ff. and Etienne Gilson, *History of Christian Philosophy in the Middle Ages* (1955; rpt. London: Sheed & Ward, 1978), pp. 319-323. Lambert of Auxerre's *Dialectics* written about 1250 was also widely known. See Gilson, p. 318.

[10] It has been said that it is not possible to count the number of Peter of Spain's commentators. See Maurice de Wulf, *Histoire de la philosophie médiévale*, 6th ed. (Louvain:

Institut supérieur de philosophie, 1934-1947), II, 85. John Major (1469-1550) the Scottish scholastic who taught at the University of Paris called Peter's work the "door to all logic" (*summularum liber, totius logices ianua*). See Ong, *Ramus*, p. 57. Cf. Gilson, p. 319.

[11] Ramus, *Pro Philosophica Parisiensis Academiae Disciplina in Sch. in lib. arts.* (1569), col. 1049; hereafter cited as *Pro. phil. disc.*

[12] See Philotheus Boehner, *Medieval Logic* (Chicago: University of Chicago Press, 1952), p. 77.

[13] *Pro. phil. disc.* in *Sch. in lib. arts.* (1569), col. 1049. See Ong, *Ramus*, pp. 58-59.

[14] See *EP*, I, 155; *HP*, I/2, 21-22; Bochenski, *AFL*, pp. 33-34 and William C. and Martha Kneale, *The Development of Logic* (Oxford: Clarendon Press, 1962), p. 23.

[15] In other references to these "categories" in Aristotle's works, neither the order nor the number were precisely fixed. See *EP*, I, 155; Kneale and Kneale, p. 23 and *HP*, I/2, 21 as well as Bochenski, *AFL*, p. 33.

[16] See *EP*, IV, 515 and Kneale and Kneale, p. 55 where this diagram is given:

Universal Affirmative (A)   Universal Negative (E)

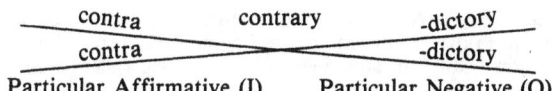

Particular Affirmative (I)   Particular Negative (O)

This is drawn from *De Interpretatione*, 7 (17b-30). See also *HP*, I/2, 16.

A universal affirmative and corresponding particular denial are opposed as contradictories (*antiphatikos*). This is also true of a particular affirmative and the corresponding universal denial. Of these, one state must be true, the other false.

A universal affirmative and a corresponding universal denial oppose each other as contraries. These cannot both be true. But their respective contradictories can both be true.

[17] See J.M. LeBlond, *Logique et Méthode chez Aristote* (Paris: Librairie Philosophique J. Vrin, 1939), pp. 59-60. See his whole discussion: "Li syllogisme en général," pp. 59-73.

[18] *Prior Analytics*, 24b 18. See *EP*, IV, 516.

[19] The subject of the conclusion is the "minor term" (*to elatton*); the predicate of the conclusion, the "major term" (*to meizon*) and the term occuring in both premises in the "middle term" (*to meson*).

[20] On the "moods" of the syllogism see *EP*, V, 69 and Jan Łukasiewicz, *Aristotle's Syllogistic from the Standpoint of Modern Formal Logic* (Oxford: Clarendon Press, 1951), ch. 2.

[21] *Analytica Posteriora*, i. I, 24b 22 as given in Łukasiewicz, p. 43.

[22] See Łukasiewicz, p. 43. See also his criticisms of Aristotle's syllogistic theory, p. 44f. and further Gunther Patzig, *Die Aristotelische Syllogistik* (Gottingen: Vandenhoeck & Ruprecht, 1959).

²³ On these "laws" see Howell, *L&R*, pp. 41-42; Ong, *Ramus*, p. 258. They are found in Aristotle's *Analytica Posteriora*, Book I, ch. 4. Howell presents these laws in the midst of a discussion of Vincent of Beauvais. Ong shows how Ramus adapted them.

²⁴ See Ong, *Ramus*, p. 259. As Howell comments: "His three laws are in other words three ways of being careful that statements yield no more than they should in they way of inferences and suggestions," *L&R*, p. 43. Cf. John Herman Randall, Jr., "The Development of Scientific Method in the School of Padua," *Journal of the History of Ideas*, I (1940), 186-187.

²⁵ *Anal. Post.*, I, 2, 71b as cited in HP, I/2, 24.

²⁶ *Anal. Post.*, II, 19, 100b. See LeBlond, p. 103.

²⁷ *HP*, I/2, 24. Cf. Ong, *Ramus*, p. 241.

²⁸ See Ong, *Ramus*, p. 243.

²⁹ See LeBlond, pp. 147ff. and his "La définition chez Aristote," *Gregorianum*, XX (1939), 351ff.

³⁰ See Ong, *Ramus*, p. 243. See also W.D. Ross, *Aristotle*, 6th ed. (1923; rpt. London: Methuen, 1955), pp. 38-39.

³¹ Ong, *Ramus*, p. 243. As Łukasiewicz writes: "Perfect syllogisms are self-evident statements which do not possess and do not need a demonstration; they are indemonstrable (*anapodeiktoi*). Indemonstrable true statements of a deductive system are now called axioms," p. 43.

³² *Topica*, 100a 30. See Howell, *L&R*, p. 16.

³³ See Howell, *L&R*, pp. 16-17. Later scholastic logic caused this distinction to disappear.

³⁴ A fifth predicable--species (*eidos*) was added by Porphyry. See Ross, p. 57 and Howell, *L&R*, p. 17.

³⁵ *Topica*, 100a 18.

³⁶ *Topica*, 100b 18-23.

³⁷ *Topica*, 108b 33. The Kneales write: "The name *Topics* is derived from the Greek word which originally meant 'place' but later came to signify a 'commonplace,' i.e. a recurrent theme or pattern in discourse," p. 34. This term had a use in classical rhetoric where "topics" are regions, places, or *loci* in a metaphorical sense, out of which a speaker hunts for arguments as a hunter hunts for game. See *The Rhetoric of Aristotle*, trans. Lane Cooper (1932; rpt. New York: Appleton-Century-Crofts, 1960), 2.22. Cicero's *Topics* condensed and systematized the use of the *loci* in Aristotle. See Howell, *L&R*, p. 24. In Aristotle, Ross calls the "topics" the "pigeon holes from which dialectical reasoning is to draw its arguments," p. 59.

³⁸ See the tabular listing of these in Boehner, p. 78.

³⁹ See a discussion of this by Ong, *Ramus*, pp. 60-63.

⁴⁰ *EP*, IV, 530.

⁴¹ *HP*, III/1, 64. Moody writes: "In this final stage of its development the *logica moderna* provided a framework within which the Aristotelian heritage was absorbed and reconstructed on new foundation." See *EP*, IV, 530.

⁴² From "Treatise on Exponibles" in *Summulae logicales* as cited in Ong, *Ramus*, p. 75.

⁴³ On d'Étaples see the works cited in Ong, *Ramus*, p. 335 (note 81). Like Erasmus, d'Étaples showed some sympathies for the Protestant Reformation but never accepted its central doctrines. See R.M. Cameron, "The Charges of Lutheranism brought against Jacques Lefevre d'Étaples," *Harvard Theological Review*, XIII (1970), 119-149; Eugene F. Rice, Jr., "The Humanist Idea of Christian Antiquity: Lefevre d'Étaples and his Circle," *Studies in the Renaissance*, IX (1962), 126-160. Cf. *ODC*.

⁴⁴ See the diagrams in Ong, *Ramus*, pp. 77, 78, 80, 81, 83, 84, 86, 87, 88, 90.

⁴⁵ Ong makes much of this in his theory that there was a major shift from the auditory to the visual culture with the growth of printing. See his works: *The Presence of the Word*; "System, Space, and Intellect in Renaissance Symbolism," *Bibliotheque d'Humanisme et Renaissance*, XVIII (1956), 222-239; "Ramist Method and the Commercial Mind," *Studies in the Renaissance*, VIII (1961), 155-172. Yates has questioned some of Ong's contentions with regard to the art of memory. See *Art*, p. 234.

⁴⁶ See for example the symbol systems of Gottlob Frege (1848-1925) and George Boole (1815-1864) as described in *EP*, IV, 225-237; 554-555; 552; and I, 346-347.

⁴⁷ See Herbert Weisinger, "Who Began the Revival of Learning? The Renaissance Point of View," *Papers of the Michigan Academy*, XXIX (1944), 561-567. On Petrarch see EP, VI, 126-128 and the works cited in Jerrold E. Seigel, *Rhetoric and Philosophy in Renaissance Humanism* (Princeton: Princeton University Press, 1968), ch. 2.

⁴⁸ Petrarch never advanced far enought in his own study of Greek to be able to read the philosophers in the original langauge. Petrarch called Cicero, "the man whom I had always loved beyond all others." See Seigel, p. 33 citing Petrarch's letters, *Le familiari*, XXIV, 2 and XXIV, 4.

⁴⁹ Cited in *EP*, VI, 127.

⁵⁰ See *HP*, III/2, 14. See too Paul O. Kristeller, *Studies in Renaissance Thought and Letters* (Rome: Edizioni di storia e letteratura, 1956), pp. 287-336 and his *Renaissance Thought*, pp. 59, 60, 69.

⁵¹ See Seigel, ch. 1: "Rhetoric and Philosophy: The Ciceronian Model."

⁵² *Rerum memorandarum libri*, II, 17, 6 as cited in Seigel, p. 34.

⁵³ Petrarch also recognized the problems inherent in this union. A basic principle of rhetoric was the adaptation or accommodation of one's speech to the audience. As the audience changed, so must the orator's message. Therefore the philosophic concern for consistency might be lost. On the use of "accommodation" in the history of the Christian Church with regard to understandings of the authority of the Bible see Rogers and McKim, *passim*.

A second rhetorical principle was imitation. A good humanist was urged to imitate worthy models from the past. The study of history provided encouragement for such imitation. But when one would find a new model to imitate and begin to do so, there would be no limits to the number of changes of models that one might make. So again, the ideal of consistency was lost. See Seigel, pp. 48ff. Cf. Myron Gilmore, "The Renaissance Conception of the Lessons of History," *Humanists and Jurists* (Cambridge, Massachusetts: Harvard University Press, 1963), pp. 14ff.

[54] *EP*, II, 113.

[55] Cicero, *De Inventione*, 1. 7. 9, trans. H.M. Hubbell, Loeb Classical Library (Cambridge, Massachusetts: Harvard University Press, 1949), pp. 19-21.

[56] Quintilian, *Institutio Oratoria*, 3. 3. 1. as translated by H.E. Butler, Loeb Classical Library.

[57] See Howell, *L&R*, p. 4. The title page of Howell's work illustrates the two views: *Eloquentia* and *Logica*.

[58] On Boethius see EP, I, 328; Gilson, pp. 97-106 and *passim*; ZHP, II/1, 116 and *passim*.

[59] Richard McKeon, "Rhetoric in the Middle Ages," *Speculum*, XVII, No.1 (January 1942), 10.

[60] The *topoi* belonged to both Aristotle's logic and his rhetoric. The terminology developed in Cicero's *Topics* (which condensed and systematized Aristotle) gave Boethius the Latin terminology that he and scholastic logicians used. As Howell writes of Cicero: "Cicero classifies the places of logic as intrinsic and extrinsic. Under the former head he evolves a final list of sixteen distinct places, whereas under the latter he speaks only of argument from authority, this entire head being devoted to what were called non-artistic proofs, or proofs not invented by recourse to the places," *L&R*, p. 25 citing Cicero, *Topics*, #8-24.

[61] McKeon, pp. 10-11.

[62] Even before Boethius had distinguished between rhetoric and dialectic in school curricula, Isidore of Seville (c. 560-636) had seen "logic" (Gr. *logos* meaning "rational") as composed of dialectic and rhetoric. See his *De Differentiis Rerum*, c. 39 (*PL* 83, 93-94) as cited in McKeon, p. 15.

[63] On the life and thought of Augustine see particularly Peter Brown, *Augustine of Hippo* (Berkeley and Los Angeles: University of California Press, 1969) and Rogers and McKim, pp. 22ff. Cf. McKeon, p. 5.

[64] See Augustine's *Confessions*, III. 3.6-5.9 (*PL* 32, 685-686) and Brown, pp. 40-41.

[65] Ambrose (c. 339-397) was Bishop of Milan and was instrumental in the conversion of Augustine to Christianity. See Augustine's *Confessions*, V. 13.23 and VI. 4, 5-6 (*PL* 32, 717 and 721-722). Cf. Augustine's account of the conversion of Victorinus the rhetorician in *Confessions*, VIII. 2.5 (*PL* 32, 751); Rogers and McKim, pp. 32-33.

[66] *Confessions*, X. 9.16-10.17 (*PL* 32, 786). See Cicero, *Orator*, 14. 45 as cited in McKeon, p. 6. Cf. Augustine's *De Doctrina Christiana*, I. 1-2 (*PL* 34, 19-20).

[67] See McKeon, p. 6 and Brown, ch. 23.

[68] See Cicero, *De Iventione* and Brown, ch. 4: "Wisdom." Augustine's comments are

in his *De Magistro* (*The Teacher*), 3. 5-6 and 11.36-12.46 (*PL* 32, 1197-1198 and 1215-1220)

[69] See Cicero, *Orator*, 14.45. The terminology also permitted adaptation for the contrasts between Augustine's "city of God" and the "terrestial city" in his *City of God*. On Augustine's allegorical Scriptural interpretation, see Rogers and McKim, pp. 32-33. Cf. McKeon, pp. 19-20.

[70] McKeon sees the culmination of the two streams of relationships between rhetoric and logic as reached in the 13th century. He points out that for Thomas Aquinas rhetoric was one of the parts of logic that was concerned with probable argumentation. For Bonaventura (1217?-1274), rhetoric was the culmination of the *trivium*. McKeon sees the tendencies "by which rhetoric was made part of logic and that by which rhetoric became an instrument of theology" as being "determined by the important methodological differences which separate the Aristotelians and the Augustinians," p. 23. Aquinas followed Aristotle; Bonaventura followed Augustine. See McKeon, pp. 23-25. On these issues as related to the authority and interpretation of Scripture, see Rogers and McKim, pp. 34ff. McKeon also traces a stream in which rhetoric developed independently of philosophy and dialectic. Among members of the group who promoted this, the *moderni*, was Anselm the Peripatetic and followers of the philosopher Drogo. See McKeon, p. 26f.

[71] On Valla see *EP*, VIII, 227-229; Seigel, ch. 5: "Lorenzo Valla and the Subordination of Philosophy to Rhetoric."

[72] On Bruni's efforts see Seigel, ch. 4: "Leonardo Bruni and the New Aristotle."

[73] See *EP*, VIII, 228.

[74] Lisa Jardine, "Lorenzo Valla and the Intellectual Origins of Humanist Dialectic," *Journal of the History of Philosophy*, XV, No.2 (April 1977), 153. While Valla rejected Aristotle's authority in logic, he was not averse to using him when his *Topics* and *Rhetoric* were helpful. This was because Cicero had commented these works.

[75] On the Platonic Academy dominated by the academic skeptics during Cicero's studies see *EP*, VII, 450. A thorough study of Cicero's work Academica is Charles B. Schmitt, *Cicero Scepticus: A Study of the Influence of the 'Academica' in the Renaissance* (The Hague: Martinus Nijhoff, 1972).

[76] Cicero, *Outlines of Pyrrhonism*, II. iii. 7-8 as given in Jardine, "Origins," p. 150. Cicero claimed Plato and Socrates were the original Academic skeptics.

[77] Jardine, "Origins," p. 151.

[78] See Jardine, "Origins," pp. 158ff. for a more detailed discussion of the *Dialecticae*.

[79] See Jardine, "Origins," p. 162. Cicero cited the famous "liar's pardadox": "Is it not a fundamental principle of dialectic that every statement....is either true or false? Is the following then true or false: 'If you say you are lying and you are telling the truth you are lying.'?" This classical paradox was attributed to Eubulides. See *EP*, V, 46.

[80] From Joseph P. Mullally, *The 'Summulae Logicales' of Peter of Spain* (Notre Dame, Indiana: University of Notre Dame Press, 1945). The same pattern is true with other works by Ockham, Burley, Burdian. Between 1639 and 1945 there was only one edition of Peter's *Logic* published. On the displacement in German universities, see Jardine, "Origins," p. 145 (note 11).

⁸¹ On Boethius' work on the *topoi* see O. Bird, "The Tradition of Logical Topics: Aristotle to Ockham," *Journal of the History of Ideas*, XXIII (1962), 307-323 and his "The Formalizing of Topics in Medieval Logic," *Notre Dame Journal of Formal Logic*, I (1960), 138-149.

⁸² See Jardine, "Origins," p. 145. Historians of logic such as W. Risse, *Die Logik der Neuzeit* (Stuttgart-Bad Cannstatt: F. Frommann, 1964), Band I do not perceive the significance of using the "topics" rather than the "syllogism" as the major focus of dialectic according to Jardine. Cf. Wilhelm Risse, "Die Entwicklung der Dialektik bei Petrus Ramus," *Archiv fur Geschichte der Philosophie*, XLII (1960), 36-72.

⁸³ Jardine comments: "This is evident in the cursory and derivative accounts of topics-theory (that portion of dialectic drawn from Aristotle's and Cicero's *Topica* and Boethius) in Peter of Spain's *Summulae logicales*, and particularly in its fifteenth-century *scholia*," "Origins," p. 148.

⁸⁴ This was what G. Trapezuntius, *Comparationes philosophorum Aristotelis et Platonis* (Venetiis, 1523) had said. See Jardine, "Origins," p. 148 (note 29).

⁸⁵ See Ong, *Ramus*, pp. 93-94 who cites William Harrison Woodward, *Studies in Education during the Age of the Renaissance* (Cambridge: University Press, 1906), pp. 79-80. Ramus learned Agricola's logic at the University of Paris from Sturm. See Ong, *Ramus*, p. 94 and Ramus' *Sch. in lib. art.* (1569), fol. a2 and a3.

⁸⁶ On Agricola see the sources cited in Ong, *Ramus*, p. 336 (note 14). He says the best study is H.E.J.M. van der Velden, *Rodolphus Agricola* (Leiden, 1911). In English, Woodward has a chapter devoted to Agricola. See pp. 79-103. Possibly one of Agricola's first teachers was Thomas à Kempis. See Ong, *Ramus*, p. 95 and Jardine, "Origins," p. 146.

⁸⁷ See Ong, *Ramus*, pp. 98-99.

⁸⁸ Agricola, *De inventione dialectica* (Paris, 1529), Lib. II, cap. ii, 156 as rendered in Ong, *Ramus*, p. 101.

⁸⁹ Ong cites Aquinas, In *I Post. anal.*, lect. 1. See *Ramus*, p. 101 and Ong's "The Province of Rhetoric and Poetic," *Modern Schoolman*, 19 (1942), 24-27.

⁹⁰ See Peter of Spain, *Summulae logicales*, ed. I.M. Bocheński (Turin, 1947), 1.01, p. 1. See also Hastings Rashdall, *The Universities of Europe in the Middle Ages*, ed. F.M. Powicke and E.B. Emden, 3 vols. (London: Oxford University Press, 1936), I, 247, 303 etc. and Ong, *Ramus*, p. 101.

⁹¹ Cited by Ong, *Ramus*, p. 101 from a 1518 edition of Agricola's *De inv. dial.*, Bk. II, ch. 24, p. 375. A similar position was taken in the 1529 edition at Bk. II, ch. 3, 215-220.

⁹² See Agricola, *De inv. dial.* (1518), Bk. II, ch. 24, 375 as cited by Ong, *Ramus*, p. 102.

⁹³ See Ong, *Ramus*, p. 102.

⁹⁴ Agricola, *De inv. dial* (1529), Bk. I, ch. 1, p. 2 as cited by Ong, *Ramus*, p. 103.

⁹⁵ See Agricola, *De inv. dial.* (1529), Bk. II, ch. 3, p. 163 as cited by Ong, *Ramus*, p. 103.

⁹⁶ Questions that have both a subject and predicate are called "complex themes" in

the humanist dialectical tradition. Other themes such as animal, body, humans etc. are called "simple themes." See Ong, *Ramus*, p. 104.

[97] James R. McNally, "'Prima pars dialecticae': The Influence of Agricolan Dialectic Upon English Accounts of Invention," *Renaissance Quarterly*, XXI (1968), 167 also mentions Agricola's views of reality and logic as fundamental constituents of his rationale for places: "Agricola, therefore, considers places indispensable to rational thought: language, reality, and logic all require a system of places or *loci* as the foundation stones of meaningful communication," p. 167.

[98] Agricola, *De inv. dial.* (1521), f. 4v as given in McNally, p. 168.

[99] See Ong, *Ramus*, p. 122 and McNally, p. 168. Ramus had ten places; Agricola twenty-four divided into sets of ten "internal" and fourteen "external" members. Internal places are subdivided into seven "intrinsic" and three "extrinsic" places. External places are split into four subgroups: four "cognates," three "circumstances," five "accidents" and two "repugnances." McNally provides a visual scheme of these—a form familiar in Ramist literature. Ong sees the psychological distinction between topical logic and categorical class logic to be in the fact that "the supreme genera or classes themselves are thought of not in a concept which echoes, however faintly, an auditory approach to knowledge, but rather in a concept formed on exclusively visualist, spatial analogies," *Ramus*, p. 112. See too William G. Crane, *Wit and Rhetoric in the Renaissance* (New York: Columbia University Press, 1937), pp. 53-54 for a list of Cicero's and Agricola's "topics." Crane diagrammed Agricola's according to their divisions.

[100] Agricola, *De inv. dial.* (1529), p. 7 as cited in Ong, *Ramus*, p. 112.

[101] Agricola, *De inv. dial.* (1521), ff. 95-96 as cited in McNally, p. 169. Agricola's innovation in topical theory was not so much in any dramatic alteration of Cicero and others. It was in his simplifying of the arrangement of the places. His concern was more for efficiency that for innovation. See A. Faust, "Die Dialektik R. Agricolas," *Archiv für Geschichte der Philosophie*, XXXIV (1922), 121.

[102] Agricola, *De inv. dial.* (1521), ff. 100-101 as cited in McNally, p. 170.

[103] Agricola, *De inv. dial.* (1521), f. 103 as cited in McNally, p. 170.

[104] An alternative tradition in later Renaissance writers such as Ralph Lever (*Witcraft*), John Seton, Thomas Wilson, and Thomas Blundeville reversed the two parts and made judgment the first operation and dialectic the second. See Ong, *Ramus*, p. 112 and Howell, *L&R*, pp. 50ff.

[105] See Ong's further discussion of his view that the Agricolan concept of the places reduced thought to spatial models and then reduced "mental activity to local motion," *Ramus*, p. 119. He sees the Agricolan tradition joining with mathematicism and Euclidean aims and ultimately asserting itself in Descartes' passion for having things "clear" and "distinct" as the *loci* each occupied a clear and distinct "pigeonhole" or "compartment" in the knowledge process. "Invention" or "finding" places Ong perceives as being essentially visionist in orientation. It displays the allied notion of Greek (and Latin) concepts of knowledge and understanding. "Judgment" is connected with the judicial procedure and categories or "accusations" according to Ong. He suggests that judgment implies "the Hebrew concept of knowledge (*yadha'*) which is analogous with hearing," *Ramus*, p. 114.

[106] Ong, *Ramus*, p. 125 comments that the Agricolan development of logic was "not

an anti-Aristotelian phenomenon in any sense except perhaps in spirit. It coincides with a return to Aristotle's text rather than to the text of Peter of Spain, Ockham, Buridian, Ralph Strode, Albert of Saxony, Dullaert, and other full-fledged logicians. The return is, in part, due to interest in the Greek tradition as interpreted by Cicero, who remains always the great determinant in so much Renaissance thought."

NOTES TO APPENDIX B

[1] The excellent source for this history is Frances Yates, *Art of Memory*.

[2] See Quintilian, *Institutio oratoria*, XI, ii, 17-22 and Yates, *Art*, pp. 2-3.

[3] *Ad Herennium*, III, xxii. Yates identifies Quintilian, Cicero, and the author of *Ad Herennium* as the three predoment Latin sources for the classical art of memory.

[4] See Yates, *Art*, pp. 32, 35, and 74ff.

[5] Aristotle, *De anima*, 432a 17; 432a 9 cited by Yates, *Art*, p. 32. See also Richard Sorabji, *Aristotle on Memory* (Providence, Rhode Island: Brown University Press, 1972).

[6] Thomas Aquinas, *In Aristotelis libros De sensu et sensato De memoria et reminiscenta commentarium*, ed. R.M. Spiazzi (Turin-Rome, 1949), p. 91 cited in Yates, Art, p. 70.

[7] *De mem. et. rem.*, ed., Spiazzi, p. 107 cited in Yates, *Art*, p. 72.

[8] In the same way Yates points out that the age of scholasticism with its stress on the abstract was also an age which saw an "extraordinary efflorescence of imagery, and of new imagery in religious art." Why? Aquinas explained when he considered why the Scriptures use imagery such as poetry and grammar--the lowest branches of knowledge to him. Aquinas answered his question by saying that Scripture speaks of spiritual things under the images of the corporeal "because it is natural to man to reach the *intelligibilia* through the *sensibilia* because all our knowledge has its beginning in sense." See *Summa theologiae*, I, I, *quaestio* I, *articulus* 9 as cited in Yates, *Art*, p. 78.

[9] See Yates, *Art*, p. 43 citing Lynn Thorndike, *History of Magic and Experimental Sciences*, II, ch. 49.

[10] See Aquinas, *Summa Theologiae*, II, II, *quaestio* 96, art. I, cited by Yates, *Art*, p. 204. Aquinas guarded against pitfalls into which Albert the Great may have been close to falling when he used the figure of a ram as one of his images. Aquinas suspected his teacher Albert of using one of the signs of the Zodiac (Aries) to unify the contents of memory. See Yates, *Art*. pp. 68-69.

[11] See Yates, *Art*, p. 230.

NOTES TO APPENDIX C

[1] See Ong, *Ramus*, ch. XIII and p. 296 where he gives a chart showing the distribution of editions of Ramus' *Dialectic* and *Rhetoric*. See also his "Ramism," p. 44 and Miller, *NEM*, Appendix A: "The Literature of Ramus' Logic in Europe."

[2] On Alsted see Ong, *Ramus*. pp. 163-165, 298 etc. and *The New International Dictionary of the Christian Church*. See also the Ramist-style charts for the subjects with which Alsted dealt at the beginning of his *Encyclopedia Septem Tomis Distincta (Herborn, 1630)*.

³ On Piscator see Ong, "Johannes Piscator" and Ramus, *passim*. Ong concludes that there was only one "Johannes Piscator" despite confusions in the entries of some Continental libraries. Ramist-style charts appear in Piscator's *Analysis logica Epistolarum Pauli* (1591).

⁴ In his *The Substance of Christian Religion,* 3rd ed. (London, 1600) Polanus divided his treatment of theology into "faith" and "good works." On both Polanus and Keckerman see Sprunger, *Learned, passim* and Howell, *L&R, passim*. See too P. Dibon, *La philosophie néerlandaise and siecle d'or* (Paris: Elsevier Publishing Co., 1954), pp. 103-104.

⁵ See Ong's evaluation of the Ramist tendencies in many writes in *RTI*, pp. 510ff. He decribes the "Mixt" and "Systematics" in *Ramus*, p. 299.

⁶ On these see Ong, *Ramus*, p. 298 and *RTI*.

⁷ See Dibon, *La philosophie* and his "L'influence de Ramus aux universités néerlandaises du 17e siècle," *Proceedings of the XIth International Congress of Philosophy*, Brussels, August 20-26, 1953, XIV (Amsterdam, 1953), pp. 307-311; Cf. Sprunger, *Dutch Puritanism*, pp. 320-321.

⁸ See Sprunger, *Learned*, ch. X: "Militant Puritanism in the Netherlands" and Sprunger, *Dutch Puritanism, passim* on Ames in The Netherlands.

⁹ On Fenner, see above, ch. III, notes 145 ff.

¹⁰ See Dibon, "L'influence," p. 308.

NOTES TO APPENDIX D

¹ On the editions of Perkins' works see Breward, *L&T*, Appendix II where he lists different editions and translations of Perkins' pieces. See also Breward, *Work*, Appendix I.

² *The Short-Title Catalogue* is helpful here.

³ As in Perkins' *A Fruitfull Dialogue Concerning the End of the World* where he speaks of "the yeare next ensuing" as "eighty-eight" (1588), III, 477.

⁴ Perkins' *Commentary on Galatians* is said to be his last work. Perkins expounded only the first five chapters. Cudworth contributed the exposition of the sixth chapter. See II, 154ff.

SELECTED BIBLIOGRAPHY

I. BACKGROUND SOURCES AND PURITANISM

Allen, Don Cameron. *The Star Crossed Renaissance*. Durham, North Carolina: Duke University Press, 1941.

Ames, William. *The Marrow of Theology*, trans. and "Introduction" by John E. Eusden. Boston: Pilgrim Press, 1968.

Blench, J.W. *Preaching in England in the late Fifteenth and Sixteenth Centuries A Study of English Sermons 1450-1600*. Oxford: Basil Blackwell, 1964.

Bray, John S. *Theodore Beza's Doctrine of Predestination*. Nieuwkoup: B. DeGraff, 1975.

Bretschneider, C.G. and H.E. Bindseil, eds. *Corpus Reformatorum*. Halle, 1834-1860.

Brook, Benjamin. *The Lives of the Puritans*. 3 vols. London, 1813.

Calvin, John. *Institutes of the Christian Religion*, ed. John T. McNeill, trans. Ford Lewis Battles. Library of Christian Classics. 2 vols. 1960; rpt. Philadelphia: Westminster Press, 1967.

Charleton, Kenneth. *Education in Renaissance England*. Studies in Social History, ed. Harold Perkin. London: Routledge and Kegan Paul, 1965.

Clifford, Norman Keith. "Casuistical Divinity in English Puritanism during the Seventeenth Century: Its Origins, Development and Significance." Diss. University of London, 1957.

Collinson, Patrick. *The Elizabethan Puritan Movement*. 1967; rpt. London: Jonathan Cape. 1971.

Cooper, Charles Henry and Thompson Cooper. *Athenae Cantabrigienses*. 3 vols. Cambridge, 1858-1913.

Costello, William T. *The Scholastic Curriculum at Early Seventeenth-Century Cambridge*. Cambridge, Massachusetts: Harvard University Press, 1958.

Cremeans, Charles D. *The Reception of Calvinistic Thought in England*. Urbana, Illinois: University of Illinois Press, 1949.

Cross, F.L. and E.A. Livingstone, eds. *The Oxford Dictionary of the Christian Church*. 2nd rev. ed. London: Oxford University Press, 1974.

Curtis, Mark H. *Oxford and Cambridge in Transition 1558-1642 An Essay on Changing Relations between the English Universities and English Society*. 1959; rpt. Oxford: University Press, 1965.

Dickens, A.G. *The English Reformation*. New York: Schocken Books, 1964.

Dillingham, William. *Laurence Chaderton, D.D.*, trans. E.S. Schuckburgh. Cambridge, 1884.

Donnelly, John Patrick. "Calvinist Thomism." *Viator*, 7 (1976), 441-451.

———. "Italian Influences on the Development of Calvinist Scholasticism." *Sixteenth Century Journal*. Vol 7, No.1 (April 1976), 81-101.

Emerson, Everett. "John Udall and the Puritan Sermon." *Quarterly Journal of Speech*, XLIV (1958), 282-284.

Fletcher, Harris Francis. *The Intellectual Development of John Milton*. 2 vols. Urbana, Illinois: University of Illinois Press, 1956-1961.

Fuller, Thomas. *Church History of Great Britain*. 3 vols. London, 1837.

Haller, William. *The Rise of Puritanism*. 1938; rpt. Philadelphia: University of Pennsylvania Press, 1972.

Herr, Alan F. *The Elizabethan Sermon A Survey and Bibliography*. 1940; rpt. New York: Octagon Books, 1969.

Hill, Christopher. *Society and Puritanism in Pre-Revolutionary England*. New York: Schocken Books, 1964.

Hooykaas, R. *Religion and the Rise of Modern Science*. Grand Rapids: Eerdmans, 1972.

Horton, Douglas. "Let Us Not Forget the Mighty William Ames." *Religion in Life*, XIX, No.3 (Summer 1960), 434-442.

Kawerau, P. "Die Homiletik des Andreas Hyperius." *Zeitschrift für Krichengeschichte*. (1960), pp. 66-81.

Kingdon, Robert M. *Geneva and the Coming of the Wars of Religion in France, 1555-1563*. Geneva: Droz, 1956.

———. *Geneva and the Consolidation of the French Protestant Movement, 1564-1572*. Madison, Wisconsin: University of Wisconsin Press, 1967.

Knappen, M.M. *Tudor Puritanism*. 1939; rpt. Chicago: University Press, 1970.

———, ed. *Two Elizabethan Puritan Diaries* by Richard Rogers and Samuel Ward. 1933; rpt. Glouchester, Massachusettes: Peter Smith, 1966.

Kocher, Paul H. *Science and Religion in Elizabethan England*. San Marino, California: Huntington Library, 1953.

Lang, Augustus. *Puritanismus and Pietismus*. 1941; rpt. Darmstadt: Wissenschaftliche Buchgesellschaft, 1972.

Lloyd, A.H. *Early History of Christ's College*. Cambridge: University Press, 1934.

Macfarlane, Alan. *Witchcraft in Tudor and Stuart England*. New York: Harper & Row, 1970.

Mair, George Herbert, ed. *Wilson's Arte of Rhetorique 1560*. Oxford: Clarendon Press, 1909.

Marsden, George M. "Perry Miller's Rehabilitation of the Puritans: A Critique." *Church History*, XXXIX, No.1 (March 1970), 91-105.

McAdoo, H.R. *The Structure of Caroline Moral Theology.* London: Longmans, 1949.

M'Crie, Thomas. *Life of Andrew Melville.* 2nd ed. 2 vols. Edinburgh, 1824.

McIntyre, J. Lewis. *Giordano Bruno.* London: Macmillan & Co., 1903.

McNeill, John T. "Casuistry in the Puritan Age," *Religion in Life*, XII (1943), 76-89.

Miller, Perry. *Errand into the Wilderness.* 1956; rpt. New York: Harper & Row, 1964.

_____. "The Marrow of Puritan Divinity." *Publications of the Colonial Society of Massachusetts,* XXXII (1936), 247-300.

_____ and Thomas H. Johnson. *The Puritans A Sourcebook of their Writings.* 2 vols. Rev. ed. 1938; rpt. New York: Harper & Row, 1963.

Mitchell, William F. *English Pulpit Oratory from Andrewes to Tillotson.* London: S.P.C.K., 1932.

Morgan, Edmund S. *The Puritan Family Religion and Domestic Relations in Seventeenth-Century New England.* 1944; new ed. New York: Harper & Row, 1966.

Morison, Samuel Eliot. *Harvard College in the Seventeenth Century.* 2 vols. Cambridge, Massachusetts: Harvard University Press, 1936.

_____. *The Founding of Harvard College.* Cambridge, Massachusetts: Harvard University Press, 1935.

_____. *The Intellectual Life of Colonial New England.* 2nd ed. New York: New York University Press, 1956.

Muller, Richard A. "Predestination and Christology in Sixteenth Century Reformed Theology." Diss. Duke University 1976.

Mullinger, J. Bass. *The University of Cambridge from the Earliest Times to the Decline of the Platonist Movement.* 3 vols. Cambridge, 1873-1911.

Murdoch, John E. and Edith Dudley Sylla, eds. *The Cultural Context of Medieval Learning.* First International Colloquium on Philosophy, Science, and Theology in the Middle Ages, Andover, Massachusetts, 1973. Dordrecht: D. Reidel Publishing Co., 1975.

Neal, Daniel. *History of the Puritans.* 5 vols. London, 1822.

Oki, H. "Ethics in 17th Century English Puritanism." Diss. Union Theological Seminary, New York 1960.

Partee, Charles B. *Calvin and Classical Philosophy.* Leiden: E.J. Brill, 1977.

Paul, Robert S. "The Accidence and the Essence of Puritan Piety." *Austin Seminary Bulletin,* XCIII, No.8 (May 1978).

Pearson, A.F. Scott. *Thomas Cartwright and Elizabethan Puritanism 1535-1603*. Cambridge: University Press, 1925.

Peel, Albert, ed. *The Second Parte of a Register*. 2 vols. Cambride: University Press, 1915.

Peile, John. *Biographical Register of Christ's College, 1505-1905*. 2 vols. Cambridge: University Press, 1910-1913.

_____. *Christ's College*. London: F.E. Robinson & Co., 1900.

Pollard, Alfred W. and G.R. Redgrave. *A Short-Title Catalogue of Books Printed in England, Scotland, and Ireland 1475-1640*. London: The Bibliographical Society, 1926.

Porter, H.C. *Reformation and Reaction in Tudor Cambridge*. 1958; rpt. Hamden, Connecticut: Archon, 1972.

Rechtien, John G. "John Foxe's 'Comprehensive Collection of Commonplaces': A Renaissance Memory System for Students and Theologians." *Sixteenth Century Journal*, IX, No.1 (April 1978), 82-89.

Rogers, Jack B. *Scripture in the Westminster Confession*. Grand Rapids: Eerdmans, 1967.

_____ and Donald K. McKim. *The Authority and Interpretation of the Bible An Historical Approach*. San Francisco: Harper & Row, 1979.

Schlatter, Richard. "The Higher Learning in Puritan England." *Historical Magazine of the Protestant Episcopal Church*. XXIII (1954), 167-187.

Seaver, Paul. *The Puritan Lectureships: The Politics of Religious Dissent, 1560-1662*. Palo Alto, California: Stanford University Press, 1970.

Short, K.R.M. "A Theory of Common Education in English Puritanism." *Journal of Ecclesiastical History*, XXIII, No.1 (1972), 31-48.

Simon, Joan. *Education and Society in Tudor England*. Cambridge: University Press, 1967.

Singer, Dorothea Waley. *Giordano Bruno His Life and Thought*. New York: Schuman, 1950.

Stephen, Leslie and Sydney Lee, eds. *Dictionary of National Biography*. 63 vols. New York, 1885-1900.

Stoeffler, F. Ernest. *The Rise of Evangelical Pietism*. Leiden: E.J. Brill, 1965.

Stone, Lawrence. "The Educational Revolution in England 1540-1640." *Past and Present* (July 1964), pp. 41-80.

_____. *The Family, Sex and Marriage in England 1500-1800*. New York: Harper & Row, 1977.

_____. "The Ninnyversity?" *New York Review of Books* (January 28, 1971), pp. 21-29.

Strype, John. *Annals of the Reformation*. 4 vols. Oxford, 1822-1824.

Thomas, Keith V. *Religion and the Decline of Magic.* New York: Charles Scribner's Sons, 1971.

Trevor-Roper, H.R. *The European Witch-Craze of the Sixteenth and Seventeenth Centuries and other Essays.* 1956; rpt. New York: Harper & Row, 1967.

Trinterud, Leonard J. "The Origins of Puritanism." *Church History,* XX (March 1951), 37-57.

Vander Molen, Ronald J. "Anglican against Puritan: Ideological Origins during the Marian Exile." *Church History,* XLII, No.1 (March 1973), 45-57.

Venn, John. *Early Collegiate Life.* Cambridge: W. Heffer & Sons, 1913.

Wendell, François. *Calvin: The Origins and Development of his Religious Thought,* trans. Philip Mairet. 1963; rpt. London: Collins, 1965.

Wilson, E.P. "Some English Mock Prognostications." *Library* (1939).

Wilson, H.S. "Gabriel Harvey's Orations on Rhetoric." *English Literary History,* XII, No.3 (September 1945), 167-182.

Wilson, H.S. and C.S. Forbes. *Gabriel Harvey's 'Ciceronianus.'* University of Nebraska Studies in the Humanities No.4 Lincoln, Nebraska: University of Nebraska Press, 1945.

Wilson, John F. *Pulpit in Parliament.* Princeton: University Press, 1970.

Wood, Thomas. *English Casuistical Divinity in the Seventeenth Century.* London: S.P.C.K., 1952.

Wright, Louis B. *Middle-Class Culture in Elizabethan England.* Ithaca, New York: Cornell University Press, 1935.

Yates, Frances. *Giordano Bruno and the Hermetic Tradition.* Chicago: University Press, 1964.

II. LOGIC, RHETORIC AND HUMANISM

Bird, O. "The Formalizing of Topics in Medieval Logic." *Notre Dame Journal of Formal Logic,* I, (1960), 138-149.

_____. "The Tradition of Logical Topics: Aristotle to Ockham." *Journal of the History of Ideas,* XXIII (1962), 307-323.

Bocheński, Innocentius M. *A History of Formal Logic.* Trans. Ivo Thomas. Notre Dame, Indiana: University of Notre Dame Press, 1961.

_____. *Ancient Formal Logic.* Amsterdam: North-Holland Publishing Co., 1951.

Boehner, Philotheus. *Medieval Logic.* Chicago: University Press, 1952.

Brown, Peter. *Augustine of Hippo.* Berkeley and Los Angeles: University of California Press, 1969.

Cameron, R.M. "The Charges of Lutheranism brought against Jacques Lefèvre d'Étaples." *Harvard Theological Review,* XIII (1970), 119-149.

Cooper, Lane, ed. *The Rhetoric of Aristotle.* 1932; rpt. New York: Appleton-Century Crofts, 1960.

Copleston, Frederick. *A History of Philosophy.* 9 vols. New York: Doubleday & Co., 1962-.

Crane, William G. *Wit and Rhetoric in the Renaissance.* New York: Columbia University Press, 1937.

Faust, A. "Die Dialektik Rudolf Agricola." *Archiv für Geschichte die Philosophie,* XXXIV (1922), 118-135.

Gilson, Etienne. *History of Christian Philosophy in the Middle Ages.* 1955; rpt. London: Sheed and Ward, 1978.

Howell, Wilbur Samuel. *Eighteenth-Century British Logic and Rhetoric.* Princeton: University Press, 1971.

———. *The Rhetoric of Alcuin and Charlemagne.* Princeton: University Press, 1941.

Humanists and Jurists. Cambridge: Harvard University Pres, 1963.

Jardine, Lisa. "Humanism and the Sixteenth-Century Arts Course." *History of Education,* IV (1975), 16-31.

———. "Lorenzo Valla and the Intellectual Origins of Humanist Dialectic." *Journal of the History of Philosophy,* XV, No.2 (April 1977), 143-164.

———. "The Place of Dialectic Teaching in Sixteenth-Century Cambridge," *Studies in the Renaissance,* XXI (1974), 31-62.

Kneale, William C. and Martha Kneale. *The Development of Logic.* 1962; rpt. Oxford: Clarendon Press, 1971.

Kristeller, Paul Oskar. *Renaissance Thought The Classic, Scholastic, and Humanist Strains.* 1955; rpt. New York: Harper & Row, 1961.

———. *Studies in Renaissance Thought and Letters.* Rome: Edizioni di storia e letteratura, 1956.

Le Blond, J.M. "La définition chez Aristote." *Gregorianum,* XX (1939), 351ff.

———. *Logique et Méthode chez Aristote.* 1939; rpt. Paris: Librairie Philosophique J. Vrin, 1970.

Lechner, Joan Marie. *Renaissance Concepts of the Commonplace.* New York: Pageant Press, 1962.

Łukasiewicz, Jan. *Aristotle's Syllogistic from the Standpoint of Modern Formal Logic.* Oxford: Clarendon Press, 1951.

Maritain, Jacques. *Formal Logic.* Trans. Imelda Choquette. New York: Sheed & Ward, 1946.

McConica, James. "Humanism and Aristotle in Tudor Oxford." *English Historical Review,* XCIV (April 1979), 1-32.

McKeon, Richard. "Rhetoric in the Middle Ages." *Speculum*, XVII, No.1 (January 1942), 1-32.

_____. ed. *The Basic Works of Aristotle*. New York: Random House, 1941.

McNally, James R. "Prima pars dialecticae: The Influence of Agricola Dialectic Upon English Accounts of Invention." *Renaissance Quarterly*, XXI (1968); 166-177.

Moody, Ernest A. *Truth and Consequence in Medieval Logic*. Amsterdam: North-Holland Publishing Company, 1953.

Mullally, Joseph P., ed. and trans. *The 'Summulae Logicales' of Peter of Spain*. Notre Dame Indiana: n.p., 1945.

Ong, Walter J. "The Province of Rhetoric and Poetic." *Modern Schoolman*, 19 (1942), 24-27.

Oxford Studies in Honour of Daniel Callus. Oxford: Clarendon Press, 1964.

Patzig, Gunther. *Die Aristotelische Syllogistik*. Gottingen: Vandenhoeck & Ruprecht, 1959.

von Prantl, Carl. *Geschichte der Logik in Abendlande*. 4 vols. Leipzig, 1855-1870.

Randall, John Herman. "The Development of Scientific Method in the School of Padua." *Journal of the History of Ideas*, I (1940), 177-206.

Rashdall, Hastings. *The Universities of Europe in the Middle Ages*, ed. F.M. Powicke and E.B. Emden. 3 vols. London: Oxford University Press, 1936.

Rice, Eugene F., Jr. "The Humanist Idea of Christian Antiquity: Lefèvre d'Étaples and his Circle." *Studies in the Renaissance*, IX (1962), 126-160.

Risse, Wilhelm. *Die Logik der Neuzeit*. Stuttgart-Bad Cannstatt: F. Frommann, 1964.

Ross, W.D. *Aristotle*. 6th ed. London: Methuen, 1955.

Schmitt, Charles B. *Cicero Scepticus: A Study of the Influence of the 'Academia' in the Renaissance*. The Hague: Martinus Nijhoff, 1972.

Seigel, Jerrold E. *Rhetoric and Philosophy in Renaissance Humanism The Union of Eloquence and Wisdom, Petrarch to Valla*. Princeton: University Press, 1968.

Sharratt, Peter, ed. *French Renaissance Studies 1540-70*. Edinburgh: University Press, 1976.

Sorabji, Richard. *Aristotle on Memory*. Providence, Rhode Island: Brown University Press, 1972.

van Steenberghen, F. *Aristotle in the West; The Origins of Latin Aristotelianism*. Trans. Leonard Johnston. Louvain: E. Nauwefaerts, 1955.

van der Velden, H.E.J.M. *Rodolphus Agricola*. Leiden: A.W. Sijthoff's, 1911.

Weisinger, Herbert. "Who Began the Revival of Learning? The Renaissance Point of View." *Papers of the Michigan Academy*, XXIX (1944), 561-567.

Woodward, William Harrison. *Studies in Education during the Age of the Renaissance.* 1906; rpt. New York: Russell & Russell, 1965.

de Wulf, Maurice. *Histoire de la philosophie médiévale.* 6th ed. Louvain: Instit supérieur de philosophie, 1934-1947.

III. RAMUS AND RAMISM

Bangs, Carl. *Arminius: A Study in the Dutch Reformation.* Nashville: Abingdon Press, 1971.

Bernstein, Eugenie H. "A Revaluation of the Plaine Genre of Homiletics in its Evolution as a Theory of Persuasion from Ramus to John Wilkins." Diss. UCLA 1973.

Carré, Meyrick H. *Phases of Thought in England.* Oxford: Clarendon Press, 1949.

Craig, Hardin. *The Enchanted Glass: The Elizabethan Mind in Literature.* New York: Oxford University Press, 1936.

Dassonville, M.M. "La genèse et les principes de la dialectique de Pierre de la Ramée." *Revue de l'université de Ottawa,* XXIII (1953), 322-355.

_____. ed. Pierre de la Ramée *Dialectique* (1555). Genève: Librairie Droz, 1964.

Dibon, P. "L'influence de Ramus aux universités du 17e siècle." *Proceedings of the XIth International Congress of Philosophy.* Brussels, August 20-26, 1953. XIV (Amsterdam, 1953), 307-311.

Dibon, P. *La philosophie néerlandaise au siècle d'or.* Paris: Elsevier Publishing Co., 1954.

Duhamel, Pierre Albert. "Milton's Alleged Ramism." *PMLA,* LXVII (1953), 1035-1053.

_____. "The Logic and Rhetoric of Peter Ramus." *Modern Philology,* XLVI (1949), 163-171.

Fisher, Peter F. "Milton's Logic." *Journal of the History of Ideas,* XXIII (1962), 37-60.

Flower, Elizabeth and Murray G. Murphy. *A History of Philosophy in America.* 2 vols. New York: G.P. Putman, 1977.

French, J. Milton. "Milton, Ramus, and Edward Phillips." *Modern Philology,* XLVII (1949), 82-87.

Gibbs, Lee Wayland. "The Technometry of William Ames." Diss. Harvard Univerity 1968.

Gibbs, Lee W. *William Ames Technometry.* Philadelphia: University of Pennsylvania Press, 1979.

_____. "William Ames's Technometry." *Journal of the History of Ideas,* XXX, No.4 (October-December 1972), 615-624.

Gilbert, Neal W. *Renaissance Concepts of Method.* New York: Columbia University Press, 1960.

Graves, Frank P. *Peter Ramus and the Educational Reformation of the Sixteenth Century.* New York: The MacMillan Co., 1912.

Hallam, George W. "Sidney's Supposed Ramism." *Renaissance Papers, 1963.* Durham, North Carolina: University of North Carolina Press, 1964.

Hill, Christopher. *Intellectual Origins of the English Revolution.* 1965; rpt. London: Panther Books, 1972.

———. *Milton and the English Revolution.* New York: Viking Press, 1977.

Hooykaas, R. *Humanisme, Science et Réforme Pierre de la Ramée (1515-1572).* Leyede: E.J. Brill, 1958.

Howard, Leon. "'The Invention' of Milton's 'Great Argument': A Study of the Logic of 'God's Ways to Men.'" *The Huntington Library Quarterly*, IX (February 1946), 149-173.

Howell, Wilbur Samuel. *Logic and Rhetoric in England 1500-1700.* 1956; rpt. New York: Russell & Russell, 1961.

———. "Ramus and English Rhetoric: 1574-1681." *Quarterly Journal of Speech.* XXXVII (1951), 299-310.

Kearney, Hugh F. *Scholars and Gentlemen: Universities and Society in Pre-Industrial Britain 1500-1700.* Ithaca, New York: Cornell University Press, 1970.

Kennedy, Leonard A., ed. *Renaissance Philosophy.* The Hague: Mouton, 1973.

Lobstein, P. *Petrus Ramus als Theologie: Ein Beitrag zur Geschichte der protestantischen Theologie.* Strassburg, 1878.

des Maizeaus, M., ed. *Dictionnarie historique et critique.* 5e édition. 8 vols. Amsterdam, 1740-1756.

Martin, Howard M. "Ramus, Ames, Perkins and Colonial Rhetoric." *Western Speech*, XXIII (Spring 1959), 74-82.

Miller, Perry. *The New England Mind The Seventeenth Century.* 1939; rpt. Boston: Beacon Press, 1964.

Moltmann, Jurgen. "Zur Bedeutung des Petrus Ramus fur Philosophie and Theologie in Calvinsimus." *Zeitschrift für Kirchengeschichte*, LXVIII (1957), 295-318.

Ong, Walter J. "Johannes Piscator: One Man or a Ramist Dichotomy?" *Harvard Library Bulletin*, VIII (1954), 151-162.

———. "Peter Ramus and the Naming of Methodism." *Journal of the History of Ideas*, XIV (1953), 235-248.

———. "Ramist Method and the Commercial Mind." *Studies in the Renaissance*, VIII (1961), 155-172.

———. *Ramus and Talon Inventory.* Cambridge, Massachusetts: Harvard University Press, 1958.

———. *Ramus, Method, and the Decay of Dialogue.* 1958; rpt. New York: Octagon Books, 1974.

_____. "System, Space and Intellect in Renaissance Symbolism." *Bibliotheque d'Humanisme et Renaissance*, XVIII (1966), 222-239.

_____. *The Presence of the Word*. New Haven: Yale University Press, 1967.

Parker, David L. "Petrus Ramus and the Puritans: The 'Logic' of Preparationist Conversion Doctrine." *Early American Literature*, VIII (1973), 140-162.

_____. "The Application of Humiliation: Ramist Logic and the Rise of Preparationism in New England." Diss. University of Pennsylvania 1972.

Pepper, Robert D. *Four Tudor Books on Education*. Scholars' Facsimiles & Reprints. Gainesville, Florida, 1966.

Perelman Chaim and L. Olbrechts-Tyteca. *The New Rhetoric: A Treatise on Argumentation*. Trans. John Wilkinson and Purcell Weaver. Notre Dame, Indiana: University of Notre Dame Press, 1969.

Perrin, Porter G. "Possible Sources of 'Technologia' at Early Harvard." *The New England Quarterly*, VII (December, 1934), 718-724.

Ramus, Peter. *Aristotelicae animadversiones*. Paris, 1543; rpt. Stuttgart-Bad Cannstatt: Friedrich Frommann Verlag, 1964.

_____. *Arithmeticae libri duo, geometriae septem et viginti*. Basileae, 1569.

_____. *Commentariorum de religione Christiana, libri quatuor*. Frankfurst, 1576: rpt. Frankfurt: Minerva Gmbh., 1969.

_____. *Dialecticae institutiones*. Paris, 1543; rpt. Stuttgart-Bad Cannstatt: Freidrich Frommann Verlag, 1964.

_____. *Dialecticae libri duo, Audomari Talaei praelectionibus illustrati*. Basle, 1569.

_____. *Dialectici commentarii tres authore Audomaro Taleo editi*. Lutetiae, 1546.

_____. *Grammaire*. Paris, 1572.

_____. *Rhetoricae distinctiones in Quintilianum*. Paris, 1559.

_____. *Rudimenta Grammaticae Graecae*. Paris, 1560.

_____. *Scholae in liberales artes*. Basel, 1569; rpt. New York: Georg Olms, 1970.

_____. *The Logike of Peter Ramus*. Trans. Roland MacIlmaine. Ed. Catherine M. Dunn. San Fernando Valley State College Renaissance Editions No.3 Northridge, California: San Fernando Valley State College, 1969.

Rechtien, John G. "Antithetical Literary Structures in the Reformation Theology of Walter Travers." *Sixteenth Century Journal*, VIII, No.1 (April 1977), 51-60.

Risse, Wilhelm. "Die Entwicklung der Dialektik bei Petrus Ramus." *Archiv für Geschichte der Philosophie*, XLII (1960), 36-72.

Saisset, Emile-Edmond. *Précurseurs et disciples de Descartes.* 2nd ed. Paris, 1862.

Scott-Craig, T.S.K. "The Craftmanship and Theological Significance of Milton's Art of Logic." *The Huntington Library Quarterly,* XVII, No.1 (1953), 1-16.

Sharratt, Peter. "The Present State of Studies on Ramus." *Studi Francesi.* XLVII-XLVIII (1972), 201-213.

Sprunger, Keith L. "Ames, Ramus, and the Method of Puritan Theology." *Harvard Theological Review,* LIX (April 1966), 133-151.

_____. "John Yates of Norfolk: The Radical Puritan Preacher as Ramist Philosopher." *Journal of the History of Ideas,* XXXVII, No.4 (October-December, 1976), 697-706.

_____. "Technometria: A Prologue to Puritan Theology." *Journal of the History of Ideas,* XXIX (1968), 115-122.

_____. *The Learned Doctor William Ames.* Urbana, Illinois: University of Illinois Press, 1972.

Thorne, J.P. "A Ramistical Commentary on Sidney's *An Apologie for Poetrie.*" *Modern Philology,* LIV, No.3 (February 1957), 158-164.

Waddington, Charles T. *Ramus, sa vie, ses écrits et ses opinions.* Paris, 1855.

Walton, Craig. "Ramus and Bacon on Method." *Journal of the History of Philosophy,* IX (1971), 289-302.

_____. "Ramus and Socrates." *Proceeding of the American Philosophical Society,* CXIV (1970), 119-139.

Walton, Craig. "Ramus and the Art of Judgment." *Philosophy and Rhetoric,* III (Summer, 1970), 152-164.

Yates, Frances A. *The Art of Memory.* Chicago: University Press, 1966.

IV. WILLIAM PERKINS

Baarsel, Jan Jacobus van. *William Perkins: Eene bijdrage tot de Kennis der religieuse ontwikkeling in Engeland ten tijde van Koningen Elisabeth.* The Hague: H.P. De Swart & Zoon, 1912.

Breward, Ian. "The Life and Theology of William Perkins." Diss. University of Manchester 1963.

_____. "The Significance of William Perkins." *Journal of Religious History,* IV (December 1966), 113-128.

_____. ed. *The Work of William Perkins.* The Courtenay Library of Reformation Classics. Appleford, England: The Sutton Courtney Press, 1970.

_____. "William Perkins and the Origins of Puritan Casuistry." *Faith and a Good Conscience* (1963), pp. 5-17.

_____. "William Perkins and the Origins of Reformed Casuistry." *The Evangelical Quarterly*, XL, No.1 (January-March, 1968), 3-20.

Dick, Hugh G. "The Authorship of *Foure Great Lyers* (1585)." *The Library*, Fourth Series, XIX (1939), 311-314.

Durkan, John. "Alexander Dickson and S.T.C. 6823." *The Bibliothek*. Glasgow University Library, III (1962), 183-190.

Hill, Christopher. *Puritanism and Revolution*. 1958; rpt. London: Panther Books, 1969.

Keddie, Gordon J. "'Unfallible Certenty of the Pardon of Sinne and Life Everlasting' The Doctrine of Assurance in the Theology of William Perkins (1558-1602)." *The Evangelical Quarterly*. XLVIII, No.4 (October-December 1976), 230-244.

Markham, C.C. "William Perkins' Understanding of the Function of Conscience." Diss. Vanderbilt University 1967.

McKim, Donald K. "Ramism in William Perkins," Diss. University of Pittsburgh 1980.

McKim, Donald K. "Ramism in William Perkins," *The Arte of Prophecying*. Pittsburgh Theological Seminary, 1975.

_____. "When God Seems Far Away." *Christianity Today*, XXIII, No. 27 (December 7, 1979), 24-26.

Muller, Richard A. "Perkins' *A Golden Chaine*: Predestinarian System or Schematized Ordo Salutis?" *Sixteenth Century Journal*, IX, No.1 (April 1978), 68-81.

Perkins, William. *The Workes of the Famovs and Worthy Minister of Christ in the Vniuersitie of Cambridge, Mr. William Perkins*. 3 vols. Cambridge, 1616-1618.

Priebe, V.L. "The Covenant Theology of William Perkins." Diss. Drew University 1967.

Rechtien, John G. "The Visual Memory of William Perkins and the End of Theological Dialogue. *Journal of the American Academy of Religion*, XLV/1 Supplement (March 1977), 69-99.

Sisson, Rosemary A. "William Perkins, Apologist for the Elizabethan Church of England." *Modern Language Review* (1952), 495-502.

Wright, Louis B. "William Perkins: Elizabethan Apostle of Practical Divinity." *The Huntington Library Quarterly*, III, No.2 (1940), 171-196.

SIXTEENTH AND SEVENTEENTH CENTURY SOURCES

Agricola, Rudolph. *De inventione dialectica*. Paris, 1592.

Alsted, Johann Heinrich. *Encyclopedia Septem Tomis Distincta*. Herborn, 1630.

Ames, William. *Conscience, with the Power and Cases Thereof*. n.p., 1639.

de Banos, Théophile. *Petri Rami vita libri quatuor*. Francofurti, 1576.

Baynes, Paul. *The Diocesans Tryal*. London, 1621.

———. *The Terrour of God Displayed against Carnall Securitie*. London, 1634.

Beza, Theodore. *De praedestinationis doctrina*. Geneva, 1582.

———. *Summa Totius Christianismi, sive Descriptio et Distributio Causarum Salutis Electorum et Exitii Reproborum, ex Sacris Literis Collecta*. Geneva, 1555.

Bishop, W. *Reformation of a Catholike Deformed*. n.p., 1604.

Browne, Robert. *Booke Which Sheweth the Life and Manners of All True Christians*. London, 1582.

Calvin, John. *The Institution of Christian Religion*. Trans. Thomas Norton. London, 1582.

Chappell, William. *The Preacher*. London, 1656.

Clarke, Samuel. *A General Martyrologie*. London, 1677.

———. *A Marrow of Ecclesiastical Historie*. London, 1654.

Clarke, Samuel. *The Lives of Sundry Eminent Persons in this Later Age*. London, 1683.

———. *Lives of Thirty-Two English Divines*. 3rd ed. London, 1677.

Coccius, J. *Thesaurus Catholicus*. 2 vols. Cologne, 1601-1602.

Daneau, Lambert. *Twelve Small Prophets*. Trans. J. Stockwood. Cambridge, 1594.

Dering, Edward. *XXVII Lectures, or Readings, upon parte of the Epistle written to the Hebrews*. London, 1583.

Downame, George. *An Abstract of the Duties Commanded, and Sinnes Forbidden in the Law of God*. London, 1583.

———. *Lectures on the XV Psalme*. London, 1604.

———. *Papa Antichristus, sive diatriba de Antichristo*. London, 1620.

———. *The Christians Sanctuarie*. London, 1604.

———. *The Covenant of Grace, or an Exposition upon Luke, I, 73, 74, 75*. Dublin, 1631.

Downame, John. *The Christian Warfare*. London, 1634.

———. *The Summe of Sacred Divinitie First Briefly & Methodically Propounded: And Then More Largly & cleerly handled and explained*. London, 1630.

Fenner, Dudley. *The Artes of Logike and Rethorike*. Middleburgh, 1584.

———. *The Sacred Doctrine of Divinitie Gathered out of the Word of God*. London, 1585.

Foxe, John. *Pandectae locorum communium* [*A Comprehensive Collection of Commonplaces*].

London, 1572.

Fraunce, Abraham. *The Lawiers Logike*. London, 1588.

Freige (Freigius), Johann Thomas. *Petri Rami Vita*. Basileae, 1575.

Fuller, Thomas. *Abel Redivivus*. London, 1651.

———. *Church History of Britain*. London, 1655.

———. *The History of the Worthies of England*. London, 1662.

———. *The Holy State and the Profane State*. New ed. with notes by James Nichols. London, 1841.

Galland, Pierre. *Contra novam academiam Petri Rami oratio*. 4th ed. Paris, 1551.

Gouge, William. *A Learned and Very Useful Commentary on the Whole Epistle to the Hebrewes*. London, 1655.

———. *An Exposition of Part of the Fift and Sixt Chapters of St. Paules Epistle to the Ephesians*. London, 1630.

———. *Gods Three arrowes: Plague, Famine, Sword, In three Treatises*. London, 1631.

de Gouveia, Antonio. *Pro Aristotele responsio adversus Petri Rami calumnias*. Paris, 1543.

Granger, Thomas. *The Bread of Life, or Foode of the Regenerate*. London, 1616.

———. *The Divine Logike*. London, 1620.

Greenham, Richard. *The Workes*. Ed. Henry Holland. London, 1601.

Harvey, Gabriel. *Foure Letters and certaine Sonnets*. London, 1592.

———. *Pierece's Superogation*. London, 1593.

Hemmingsen, Nicholas. *The Preacher*. Trans. John Horsfall. London, 1574.

Heylyn, Peter. *Aerius Redivivus or the History of the Presbyterians*. Oxford, 1670.

Hill, T. *A Quatron of Reasons*. Antwerp, 1600.

Hooker, Richard. *Of the Lawes of Ecclesiasticall Politie*. London, 1597.

Hyperius, Andreas Gerhard. *The Practis of Preaching*. London, 1577.

Junius, F. *The Apocalyps*. Cambridge, 1596.

Keckerman, Bartholomew. *A Manuduction to Theologie, Done in English by T.V.* London, 1622.

Lever, Ralph. *The Arte of Reason, rightly termed, Witcraft*. London, 1573.

Martyr, Peter. *The Commonplaces*. Trans. A Marten. London, 1583.

Masson, Jean-Papire. *Vita Iacobi Carpentarii*. Paris, 1574.

Montagu, Richard. *Diatribae upon the First part of the late History of Tithes*. London, 1621.

de Nancel, Nicholas. *Petri Rami Veromandui, eloquentiae et philosophiae apud Parisios professoris regii, vita, a Nic Nancelio Rachyeno Noviodunensi Rami discipula et populari descripta*. Paris, 1599.

Piscator, Johannes. *Analysis logica Epistolarum Pauli*. London, 1591.

Polanus, Andreas. *The Substance of Christian Religion*. 3rd ed. London, 1600.

Quick, J., ed. *Synodicon in Gallia Reformata*. 2 vols. London, 1692.

Richardson, Alexander. *The Logicians School-Master: Or, a Comment upon Ramus Logicke*. London, 1629.

Smith, John. *A Paterne of True Prayer*. London, 1605.

Taylor, Thomas. *A Commentary Upon the Epistle of St. Paul Written to Titus*. London, 1658.

The Prayer Book of Queen Elizabeth 1559. London, n.d.

The Second Prayer Book of King Edward VI. London, n.d.

Travers, Walter. *A Full and Plaine Declaration of Ecclesiasticall Discipline*. London, 1574.

Tuke, Thomas. *The High-Way to Heaven: or The Doctrine of Election*. London, 1609.

_____. *The Picture of a True Protestant or, God's House and Husbandry*. London, 1609.

Turnbull, Richard. *An Exposition Upon the Canonicall Epistle of Saint James*. London, 1591.

Udall, John. *A Commentarie Upon the Lamentations of Jeremy*. London, 1593.

_____. *A Demonstration of the Truth of that Discipline*. London, 1593.

Ursinus, Zacharias. *The Summe of Christian Religion*. Trans. H. Parrie. Oxford, 1587.

Whitaker, William. *A Disputation on the Holy Scripture against....Bellarmine and Stapleton*. Trans. W. Fitzgerald. Parker Society. Cambridge, 1849.

Wilkins, John. *Ecclesiastes*. London, 1646.

Wilson, Thomas. *The Arte of Rhetorique*. London, 1553.

_____. *The Rule of Reason*. London, 1551.

Yates, John. *A Modell of Divinitie, catechistically composed*. London, 1622.

_____. *Gods Arraignement of Hypocrites*. London, 1615.

www.ingramcontent.com/pod-product-compliance
Lightning Source LLC
Chambersburg PA
CBHW080429230426
43662CB00015B/2225